Complete Guide to Appraising Commercial and Industrial Properties

Complete Guide to Appraising Commercial and Industrial Properties

Peter C. Robinson, A.S.A.

PRENTICE-HALL, INC.

Englewood Cliffs, N.J.

Prentice-Hall International, Inc., *London*
Prentice-Hall of Australia, Pty. Ltd., *Sydney*
Prentice-Hall of Canada, Ltd., *Toronto*
Prentice-Hall of India Private Ltd., *New Delhi*
Prentice-Hall of Japan, Inc., *Tokyo*
Prentice-Hall of Southeast Asia Pte. Ltd., *Singapore*
Whitehall Books, Ltd., *Wellington, New Zealand*

©1977 by

Prentice-Hall, Inc.
Englewood Cliffs, N.J.

Fifth Printing . . . . . September, 1981

Library of Congress Cataloging in Publication Data

Robinson, Peter C
   Complete guide to appraising commercial and industrial
properties.

   Includes index.
   1. Real property--Valuation. I. Title.
HD1387.R579   333.3'36   76-46438
ISBN 0-13-160028-1

Printed in the United States of America

Dedicated in loving admiration to Margaret Strater Robinson, whom I lured as a beautiful and gifted young dancer from Martha Graham's tutelage; brought sweet, lively children into the world with her, and shared with her the raising of Chris, Sylvia, and Carole to the happy adults they are today. This book is also dedicated in memoriam to Guy, our youngest. I turn to William Butler Yeats for an expression of Peggy's thirty-five years of devotion to us all:

O chestnut tree, great rooted blossomer.
Are you the leaf, the blossom or the bole?
O body swayed to music, O brightening glance,
How can we know the dancer from the dance?

from "Among School Children" (1928)

About the Author

Peter C. Robinson's 32 years of expertise in the field of real estate appraising is evident in this new book. During that period, Mr. Robinson appraised an unusually broad range of properties of all types and sizes worldwide. A member of The American Society of Appraisers and of the American Right of Way Association, his first book, *How to Appraise Commercial Properties,* was published by Prentice-Hall, Inc. and was widely accepted.

What This Book Will Do for You

This is a detailed and comprehensive book on the appraisal of both commercial and industrial properties, supplying the methodologies involved in the evaluation of both categories and a broad range of model appraisals demonstrating the principles and techniques as they are used in actual practice.

Often, appraisers and assessors are perplexed when choosing a method of valuation for a given problem. They reach for simplicity and they stretch for accuracy, and all too frequently find that the two do conflict. Clearly, there is a point beyond which no process may be simplified and still retain logical and useful coherence; but, then too, there is a point beyond which further complications confuse the problem. The trick is to come up with simple yet accurate systems for getting the job done.

This book seeks to arm you, the appraiser, with such systems. It will enable you to coordinate the principles of appraising with the complexities of their application, to articulate problems and work out their solutions. In addition, this is the first book to emphasize the mortgage-equity method as an applied science in the determination of value. This method consists of making tests for the most likely profitable use; following accurate techniques and procedures for market analysis and income capitalization; and finally determining value through the combined gristmill actions of the Income Approach and a Comprehensive Market Study.

The methodologies for writing professional appraisals of commercial and industrial real property for all purposes, including insurance, taxation, mortgage financing, and condemnation, are all demonstrated in the model appraisals of Parts Two and Three of this book.

The function of an appraisal is to answer a simple, fundamental question: What is a property worth (under defined terms and conditions of value, of course)? For instance, an investor wants to sell his Topeka, Kansas shopping center and wants to know fair market value of the land and the building within 60 days. Or, a container manufacturer seeks market value of his 200,000-square foot plant in Memphis for intercorporate accounting purposes. He allows two weeks for the work. A frozen food concern needs to establish value for new mortgage financing of its small New Jersey plant. The appraisers are given a week to do the job. A variety store chain asks what effect local increased taxation has had on one of its warehouse properties. Should local and state property assessments be challenged accordingly? They want answers within a month.

How can you accomplish these tasks quickly and accurately? By specialization and centralization as demonstrated in the model appraisals of this book. These models show that such studies can be accomplished anywhere, anytime, on time, if systems of thought and tested techniques are marshalled in an orderly and precise fashion. This book shows you how to do that . . . with the inestimable help of strong legs.

This book is divided into three parts: Part One details the processes and principles to be applied to the evaluation of commercial and industrial property. Part Two illustrates the methodologies of appraising commercial (income) properties, with model appraisals showing all the elements of investment value. Part Three is devoted to a broad range of industrial properties—single purpose, special purpose, and general purpose.

Peter C. Robinson

ACKNOWLEDGMENTS

In the preparation of this book, I am indebted to a number of master-appraisers for their thoughtful advice and warmth and friendship in extending to me the benefits of their wisdom and experience.

These gentlemen are: Dexter MacBride, C.A.E., F.A.S.A; Matthew Leydens, A.S.A.; John F. Eshak, Jr., Appraisal Technologist, Evaluators Institute; Patrick A. Flynn, A.S.A., AR/WA; Edward M. Freda, M.A.I.; Morris Jacks, P.E., A.S.A.; the late Harry Kussner, A.S.A., AR/WA; Joseph Kitson, A.S.A.; William T. McCarthy, S.R.A.; John Moore, S.R.A.; John Purdon, A.S.A.; William D. Roy, Licensed Oregon Appraiser; John Rowlson, M.A.I., S.R.E.A.; Sylvia Haggerty, Sylvia Wade, and Barbara Kiley, executives of the American Society of Appraisers; George S. Sinclair; C.E.O. Walker, past president of the American Society of Appraisers; and my very dear friend, Francis L. Gorka, A.S.A., current President of the American Association of Appraisers.

As Members of the Appraisal Institute (M.A.I.), the American Society of Appraisers (A.S.A.), or the Society of Real Estate Appraisers (S.R.E.A.), these trained eyes and ears belong to a legion of property experts who have, in the past sixty years, raised their professional disciplines to accreditation in the highest courts of the nation and have been recognized abroad as well.

This book owes its content to the entire profession, since it conveys only that input invested in the writer by good teachers and industrious companions from each of the appraisal societies, and more than several enlightening seminars conducted by the American Right of Way Association (AR/WA).

I am also indebted to master-builder and author William Zeckendorf, Sr., of New York; Rocco De Palma, financial analyst, of Greenwich, Connecticut; Lorraine Boyle Allen of Sherman, Connecticut; A. C. Hauenstein, A.S.A.; Helen Zukowski, of Stratford, Connecticut; Mr. & Mrs. Ralph Gangi, of Greenwich, Connecticut; Nicholas Wood, specialist in warehouse distribution centers throughout the nation; and Dr. William L. Kinnard, who holds the chair of Real Estate at the University of Connecticut, for sage reflections, professional consultations, and enthusiastic support in the development of this effort. Also, Leslie A. Beveridge, Industrial Engineer, Greenwich, Connecticut; Luba Doyle, of East Paterson, New Jersey, and Mrs. Jean Dee of Greenwich, Connecticut, for typing, proofing, and correcting the manuscript; Timothy Piso, A.S.A., for editorial assistance; Victoria Peloquin, investor in commercial properties; and to the late Richard S. Nesser, Executive Director of the Evaluator's Institute, for suggestions and advice. Importantly, thanks to Greenwich attorneys Jonathan D. Carlisle in regard to contracts and leases and to William Burke Lewis in regard to court testimony and trial procedures.

I am indebted to Design Engineer Andrew J. Ryan for the excellent illustrations of construction layouts and area maps.

And last, but not least, I wish to express my deep appreciation for the educational and news information services of The National Association of Realtors; The American Society's periodical "Valuation"; the Appraisal Institute's "Appraisal Journal"; and the "Real Estate Appraiser," published by the Society of Real Estate Appraisers.

Contents

Chapter 3, cont.

Appendix (cont.)

PART ONE

The Process and Principles of Measuring Value in Commercial and Industrial Properties

A real estate appraisal is simply a value conclusion based on the examination of existing economic factors. Because these intrinsics are subject to an extraordinary array of variables, an appraisal is a kaleidoscope of research, documentation, and resolution.

1

The Making of a Commercial and Industrial Appraisal

The making of an appraisal is a problem-solving process, figuratively like "passing a camel through the eye of a needle." How are you going to reduce the massive beast into a refined but strong and unbroken thread, pass it through the narrow eye of reflection and valuation, and emerge with your problem clearly solved?

First, use the system, or "methodology," hereinafter described. This will avoid approaching each part of the problem as a new situation and will eliminate guesswork as to which aspects of value are dominant.

Second, define the situation in all of its parts, and link them in written form into a full statement of the problem, thus making the *purpose* and *function* of the appraisal clear at the outset.

Next, set *objectives* and define these clearly. Separate the objectives into priorities, such as (1) land value; (2) value of the improvements; (3) value of the leasehold interest. Then proceed carefully from one to another. You thus have set up your targets.

Now develop alternate courses of attack on the targets. For instance, does the purpose of the appraisal call for attack via the *Cost Approach,* the *Income Approach,* or the *Market Data Approach?* On two of these approaches? Or all three?

Weigh each of these alternatives against your objectives and be systematic about it. That is to say, assess the positive and negative sides of each approach as applied to the subject under appraisement.

Now follow the logical course of attack you have planned. Don't waiver by changing your objectives late in the game. Stick to the system.

Having all the facts at your fingertips is an essential first ingredient in the appraisal process. Getting the facts requires effective sources of information, such as brokers, bankers, builders, lawyers, newspapermen, and trade periodals. Thorough research of markets, labor pools, distribution patterns, transportation facilities, population trends, and civic ordinances have a heavy bearing on valuation of both commercial and industrial properties.

The system and its implementation is outlined in Figure 1, The Appraisal Process. Following this system, you will be able to articulate to the court, or to those attorneys, accountants, lenders, borrowers, investors, or assessors who may have commissioned your service, the *rationale* by which you developed this or that method, and how you arrived at your conclusions. The court for one, will insist on systematic development of the value premise, clarity of expression, and forthright testimony. Other clients, if they are professionals, will require the same articulation. So much for system and articulation. What kinds of value can the appraiser be seeking?

VALUE

Property may be defined as all the rights to future benefits arising from ownership. The value of a property is the present or discounted worth of these future benefits. Depending on the nature of the property, the conditions surrounding it, and the use to which it is put, there are three primary kinds of value into which this book will delve: *market value, investment value,* and *insurable value.* A fourth concept, *value in use,* will be discussed briefly but will not figure prominently in our applications.

Market Value: Those classes of property that are bought and sold in a competitive market are said to have a "market value." The legal definition of market value is "that price which a seller, willing but not compelled to sell, would accept from a buyer, willing but not compelled to buy." Market value is measured by comparison with market prices of comparable properties.

Investment Value: Those classes of property that produce or are intended to produce benefits in the form of net earnings are said to have an "investment value." Investment value is "the present worth of the earning expectancy." It is measured by estimating the earning percentage based in the risk involved.

Insurable Value: This is to measure the element of destructibility in buildings, not including land, by fire, storm, or vandalism, which can be protected by insurance.

Value in Use: Classes of property that have a value to their owners arising from the future benefits that such properties are expected to produce for their owners are said to have a "value in use." Value in use, in the case of improvements or chattels, is measured by estimating depreciated reproduction cost.

Value in Use vs. Value in Exchange

A property may have one value in use and a different value in exchange. For example: The State Highway Department asks for an appraisal showing *fair market value* (value in exchange for money) of an electrical equipment wholesaler's property in condemnation proceedings; location is at a main artery intersection in the heart of an urban industrial district; land area is about three acres.

The electrical wholesaler's buildings are aging, two-story, brick, containing hundreds of racks and bins for the assortment and storage of thousands of kinds of cable, connectors, fixtures, and tools. His showroom and sales offices are antiquated. His yard (land) is arranged so that large panels and transformers can be manufactured

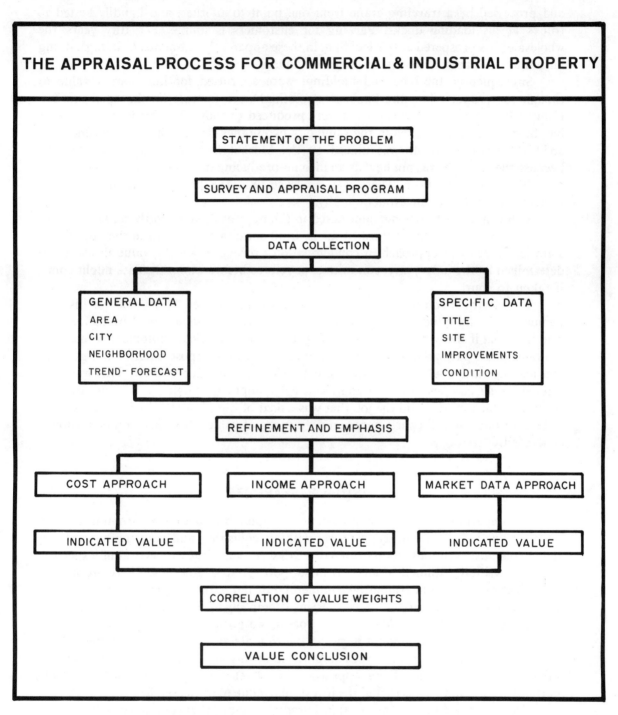

FIGURE 1

and processed by a traveling crane from one point to another, and handily hefted to trucks at his loading docks. Parking for customers is ample. For fifty years the wholesaler has prospered at this location, in these apparently outmoded buildings, doing an annual business of several millions of dollars.

Subsequently, the land and buildings were appraised for fair market value as though the property (not the business operation) were for sale on the open market. Comparable sales under market data were produced to show that this type of property had been recently purchased in the same city by another firm in the same business for $330,000. Greatest weight was placed on the Market Data Approach, at $300,000, because the property was not held as an income-producing investment, but was operated as a utility by the owner. There was no lease, and the property was not the type customarily traded as investment realty.

Value in use here was not considered in the appraisal, and rightly so, because the condemning authority had not asked for it. Eminent domain custom in the appraiser's state forestalled this approach in condemnation procedure, leaving value in use to be determined by the judge, jury, committee, or referee before whom the case might come, if taken to court.

The electrical equipment wholesaler in this case received $1,500,000 for his condemned land and buildings as value in use in a settlement determined by the referee, who held that if the wholesaler were selling to another electrical equipment wholesaler, the value of the particular design and layout of his special-purpose land, buildings, bins, and loading yard would be five times greater than in the open market. This was considered a *just compensation* for the electrical equipment wholesaler's dislocation in business. The appraiser did the job that was asked of him, but the court emphasized a different value. Not all courts agree on definitions of value where just compensation is concerned.

INITIAL RESEARCHES

In preparing to write your report, it is impossible to evaluate commercial (investment) or industrial (utility) property without collecting and researching pertinent data. You must eventually compose a written description of the property as of a specified date and written arithmetical analysis in support of initial findings. There are just too many factors involved in evaluating commercial or industrial property to try to process them all in your head or to rely on memory in attempting to articulate them.

Purpose: At the beginning of the process, we must examine the purpose of the appraisal. Purpose is paramount in preparing to write an appraisal of commercial and industrial property, for instance, "The purpose of this appraisal is to find fair market value," or "The purpose of this appraisal is to determine insurable value," or "The purpose of this appraisal is to find the investment value of the leased fee."

The Approaches: It is most often found that more than one approach must be weighed and correlated to establish a *value conclusion*. In addition to the *reproduction cost* or *depreciated cost*, the Income Approach (capitalized value) and the Market Data or Comparative Approaches to value are brought into play.

Market Value: This book will deal primarily with evaluation of commercial and industrial properties for the purpose of estimating fair market value. It assumes the reader is not a newcomer to real property appraisal terminology. Fair market has been acceptably defined in the courts as follows: "The price that a property will bring in a competitive market under all conditions requisite to a fair sale, which would result from negotiations between a buyer and a seller, each acting prudently, with knowledge and without undue pressure."

Function: Requests for market value appraisals of commercial or industrial property arise from everyday needs such as these: (1) toward conveyance, sale, or lease; (2) toward just compensation in condemnation; (3) toward a basis for taxation; (4) toward mortgage financing.

> **Note:** Purpose and function can most often be expressed together in one paragraph early in the written report, for example:
>
> "The appraisal was made for the purpose of estimating the market value of the subject property, including land and improvements, as of January 1, 1976; and its function is to serve as a guide to an equitable and fair assessment in an ad valorem appeal for the current year."

There are many other needs to be served in making an appraisal, with purposes other than market value to be estimated. The function of an appraisal is to serve a need. It is important to distinguish between the purpose of an appraisal (to estimate a specified kind of value) and the function that this evaluation will serve, i.e., why the appraisal is being made.

It is also proper to state the function, e.g.: "To estimate market value for mortgage financing," or "To estimate value as a fair basis for merger." However, the appraiser is sometimes given the purpose of estimating fair market value without being told the function, or the "why." This should not deter him from going ahead with his estimate of fair market value, the purpose.

STATEMENT OF THE PROBLEM

The appraisal process requires an orderly procedure for making a value estimate of commercial or industrial property. It consists of stating the problem; making a market, or labor and distribution, survey and property analysis; gathering all necessary basic data; applying the Cost Approach, the Income Approach, and the Market Data Approach, where possible; and, finally, forming a conclusion.

Begin the appraisal process by writing a clear statement *of the problem.* Any doubt about the purpose of the appraisal should be resolved at once. Here are five basic steps in defining the problem:

1. Identify the property to be evaluated.
2. Specify the rights inherent.
3. State the purpose of the appraisal and its functions (to estimate market value, for instance, for just compensation in condemnation proceedings).
4. Fix the date as of which the estimate is to be made.
5. Define the value to be estimated.

The Five Basic Steps Amplified in Outlining the Problem

1. *Identification of Property*—First, identify the property by a mailing address so that your reader can go to the property to inspect it also. For instance: "822 Bank Street, Park City, Connecticut, situated on the northwest corner of North and Green Streets. Land is 150 feet front by 200 feet deep, improved with a sixth story and basement, brick office building with stores on the ground level."

   The correct legal description of the property is also necessary for positive identification. This description can be obtained from the existing deed or from the public records.

2. *Property Rights Inherent*—The second step in stating the problem is to determine the rights inherent to the property. An appraisal is not only an evaluation of physical land and buildings; it also evaluates the rights that one or more individuals have to the ownership and use of the land and improvements. It may be that an appraisal of only a part interest in the property is wanted.

   The property rights or interests to be appraised may be, for example, the value of rents to be received plus a reversionary right at the end of a lease term. The air rights over a specified area or designated subsurface rights or the value of a tenant's interest in an existing lease or an easement or right of way may have to be evaluated. *You cannot define your problem precisely until you know exactly what property rights are involved.*

   Establish at the outset exactly which rights are to be evaluated. This makes it possible to estimate accurately the complexity of the assignment, the research required, the time necessary to write the appraisal, whether or not to call for specialized asssistance, and the likely cost.

3. *Purpose and Function of the Appraisal*—A clear statement of the reasons for making the appraisal is the third step in stating the problem. The purpose of the appraisal and the function it is to serve indicate the data to be gathered, the methods to be employed, the type of data and factors likely to wield the most influence, and the type of report required. While the purpose of an appraisal may be to estimate market value, the function for which it is needed will vary. For example:

   (a) If the purpose is to estimate market value for mortgage financing, the stability of the commercial district is significant because the lender is concerned not only with present worth but with the stability of that value during the period the mortgage will be in force.

   (b) If the purpose is to estimate market value for possible purchase of a property, current sales of comparable properties, the rate of return the property is producing, and the availability of comparable substitute properties are probably the most pertinent and influencing factors to consider.

   In each instance above, you would be reporting fair market value. But the data with most weight in formulating your final estimate of value and the arrangement of your report would reflect the function of the appraisal. Therefore, in defining the problem you try to develop an exact statement of the appraisal's purpose and function so that it is clearly understood by, and acceptable to, your client. There are instances when a client will be clear about the purpose but unwilling to divulge the function. This should not deter you from estimating fair market value if that is the purpose, but in this case you should explore *highest and best use* as an initial surrogate function.

4. *Date of Value Estimate*—The fourth step in stating the problem is the date of the value estimate. The specific date is important because the value of real property varies. The factors that create or destroy value are always in the process of change. An opinion of value is good only for that period in time for which it was formulated. Usually an appraisal assignment is for a value estimate as of the present, or near future. But there are occasions when you will be asked to appraise a property as of some date in the past. Such a value estimate may be required for tax purposes, to settle an estate, or to adjust an insurance claim.

It is costly and time consuming to research all conditions affecting a property in the distant past, and the client should be made aware of this at the outset.

5. *Definition of Value*—The fifth step in assaying the problem is to spell out the value to be estimated. A property has, of course, only one market value as of a given date. But there are times when value for a special purpose, such as value in use, is the question. If the value estimate is to be based upon special conditions, the definition of value must be stated accordingly.

SURVEY AND APPRAISAL PROGRAM

Once the problem is clearly defined, you are ready to make a tentative survey of the subject property in terms of its use, location, condition, and desirability. Gradually, the tentative approach will lead to concrete conclusions. Attack the problem first by estimating its highest and best, or most likely profitable, use. If it is a commercial property, a market study is initiated. If it is an industrial property, a labor-distribution pattern survey is indicated. At this point the survey starts to become concrete.

The highest and best use of a property is often its present use; that utilization usually conforms to the use permitted under zoning regulations. There are instances, however, where you will find that the existing use may not be its highest and best use. In this event, you must judge the other factors that influence highest and best use (see chapter 5).

In the survey and appraisal program, the data likely to be required in the appraisal should be established early. This will depend upon the type of property being appraised since a great deal more information would be required in the appraisal of a frozen food plant than of a frozen custard stand. Choice of an approach that will develop the most rational value indication will also indicate the type of data required. In appraising income properties, income data is most often paramount, but in some appraisals the application of all three approaches is important. Therefore, cost data and market data may also be necessary.

MACRO-MARKET VIS-A-VIS MICRO-MARKET SURVEY
FOR COMMERCIAL PROPERTIES

The demand for goods or services, housing, lodging, or offices at a site in a given *commercial* district most often rests on far-flung, external economic and social forces working in sympathy, or in conflict, with the marketing magnetisms of the site. The interface relationships of such data, the one *general* (macro-market) and the other *specific* (micro-market), will be referred to and demonstrated in this book under the double label in the interest of reminding the appraiser that in his market survey and property analysis he uses two instruments: first, a telescope applied to general data, then, a microscope to "zoom down" on the specific; or vice versa.

THE LABOR AND DISTRIBUTION SURVEY
FOR INDUSTRIAL PROPERTIES

Industrial managers relegate varying degrees of importance on *access to labor and raw materials,* and *distribution patterns* for delivery of their finished products. The technical demands of evaluating industrial properties require special data collections and a working knowledge of the several valuation techniques. Scrutinizing industrial zoning practices, construction costs, and land-use planning is essential. And these appreciations must be supported by a knowledge of the principles of taxation, local economic trends, and an eye for location factors.

How to Begin

Programming the appraisal helps to establish a working tempo for the appraiser and his assistants. A clear picture of the nature of the work to be done by the appraiser himself and by each person selected to assist him will smooth the handling of the assignment. It is the appraiser himself who must estimate the final value conclusion, sign the report, and be ready to testify in court that he personally inspected the subject property and made the valuation. His assistants can be of no help in the end product. They can aid in the collection of data, take photographs, make measurements, check calculations, draw maps, and do research, but the appraiser alone sums it all into coherence and value estimate.

Thus, the appraiser, having established highest and best use in his mind, now proceeds to collect data that will document and support his conviction about the subject property. (In the process, he may encounter surprise data that negates his first conviction, causing him to start again with highest and best use.) At this point the appraiser is ready to solidify his tentative survey into a concrete *market analysis* (if subject is commercial) or *labor-distribution study* (if industrial), which will be the foundation of his fully developed report. He and his assistants proceed with two categories of data, as follows.

Macro-Market Survey for an Appraisal of Commercial Property

General data relates to conditions in the nation, region, city, trade area, and neighborhood that affect its value. (a) Regional and city data pertains to factors such as population trends, price levels, levels of employment, and other external influences. (b) The trade area embraces the greater metropolitan spread of a city to include suburbs within thirty minutes' drive of the subject trade center. This area should be calculated in terms of number of households, median family income, and dollar volume of total retail sales per annum. (c) Commercial district (or micro-market) data is less broad in its scope than city, trade area, or regional data since it pertains to factors present in a smaller area. Commercial district data would point to typical land uses, zoning controls, public utilities, transportation facilities, shopping facilities, and the quality of the properties comprising the district. It would also include a record of the sales of comparable properties to be investigated and analyzed in the appraisal.

Micro-Market Survey for an Appraisal of Commercial Property

Specific data concerns the title, the site, the buildings and the economic influences. (a) Title history will be secured in the course of identifying the property. It is vital to know who owns the property; the type of ownership deed; what easements and encroachments, if any, exist; zoning regulations; assessed value and taxes; and deed or other restrictions. (b) Site data would include a description of the size, shape, and topographical nature of the land and the types of public improvements thereon, such as walks, curbs, water mains, sewers, gas, electricity, width and kind of street paving, and traffic controls nearby. (c) Building data would include a complete description of the physical improvements and its condition together with an analysis of its layout. (d) The economic influences in the neighborhood area and region as they affect the site and its improvements should be stated here. Is access easy and safe? Is there crime incidence nearby frightening customers or employees? Is the ambience one of decay and decline? Or is this an uptrend locale with pedestrian patronage and safe approaches? Is parking plentiful and street lighting adequate? Does the property attract customers or employees? Elaborate on the magnetisms or defects of the property and its environment.

Labor Pool Survey for an Appraisal of Industrial Property

General data relates to the availability in the nation, region, city, and industrial zone of the types of labor requisite to the particular plant under appraisement. (a) Regional and city data includes factors such as population trends, employment levels, union practices, indigenous labor skills, and attractions such as mobile home parks that would induce labor from other parts of the nation or region. (b) Comments are also necessary on the industrial zone and its accessibility to labor, types of unions established in the area, together with a breakdown of skilled labor versus unskilled labor.

Distribution Survey—Location Analysis for an Appraisal of Industrial Property

Specific data concerns the title, the site, the buildings, and the immediate industrial locale. (a) Cite the legal description of ownership; easements and encroachments, if any; zoning regulations; assessed value; and taxes. (b) Site data must include a description of the size, shape, and topography and subsoil conditions, with a definition of public improvements at hand or on site, such as paved walks, curbs, sewers, utilities, and a description of street paving, lighting, and traffic controls. (c) Building data must include a detailed breakdown of physical improvements with an analysis of layout, process flow, degrees of physical deterioration, functional and economic obsolescence with ages of the buildings stated and remaining economic life established. (d) The immediate industrial locale must be analyzed and related to distribution patterns in the region and to sources of supplies and raw materials.

THE THREE APPROACHES TO MARKET VALUE

Years of experience in evaluating commercial and industrial properties have crystallized three main methods for estimating fair market value:

1. The current cost of reproducing a property less depreciation from all sources, that is, deterioration and functional and economic obsolescence, or the Cost Approach.
2. The value the property's net earning power will support, based upon a capitalization of net income, or the Income Approach.
3. The value indicated by recent sales of comparable properties in the market, or the Market Data Approach.

In some assignments, the appraiser of commercial or industrial property utilizes all three approaches. The use of all three approaches when possible (and it isn't always possible) is standard appraisal technique.

CORRELATION AND VALUE CONCLUSION

The last step in the appraisal process is the correlation of the indications of value derived by the Cost, Income, and Market Data Approaches. In correlating these approaches into the value conclusion, weigh the purpose of the appraisal, the type of property, and the strength of the data processed in each of the three approaches.

For instance, in the case of a nearly new retail store, if the appraisal were being made for insurance purposes, the greatest weight might be assigned to the Cost Approach. In the case of an antiquated income-producing apartment house, greater weight would fall on the Market Data and Income Approaches. In the absence of conclusive market data in this case, your selection would be narrowed to the Income Approach.

You reach a final conclusion of value by weighing two or three preliminary value estimates and considering the spread between the minimum and maximum figures. You would place emphasis on the approach that appears to be the most logical solution to the stated appraisal problem.

The documented development of the data considered and analyzed, the methods used, the opinions and conclusions reached in formulating your conclusion value all comprise your *appraisal report*. Your report is the palpable product of your investigations and your service. It is the consummation of your contract with your client, for which you will receive your fee.

REMUNERATION

Usually the client will expect you to quote a firm fee in advance of his request for an appraisal. This means an appropriate estimate of the scope and complexity of the problem, the work hours involved, and the personnel and travel time needed. This estimate should not be given hastily. If the property is nearby and well known to you, it may be evaluated in a few days. With a more complex problem to resolve, it can take weeks or months to research and cull significant data and can require the services of professional assistants. In the latter case, for example, the fee should cover your time spent with lawyers, realtors, contractors, engineers, accountants, architects, bankers, and building managers. It must include consultation fees you pay for engineering, architectural, and other specialized services.

Relations with Client

Your proposal to your prospective client should be set forth in a letter acquainting him with the problem in this manner:

1. Identification of the property.
2. Statement of rights to be appraised.
3. Purpose of the appraisal.
4. Definition of the value to be estimated.
5. Date as of which the estimate is to be made.
6. Date on which the appraisal report will be delivered.
7. Quotation of the fee.

The client's agreement that he approves the terms can be his signature on a copy of the letter. This commitment from the client is important. It puts client and appraiser in agreement about the nature of the problem and will avoid misunderstanding when the report finally is presented.

THE WRITTEN REPORT

Information contained in the appraisal report is invaluable to those negotiating real estate transactions. It is the basis of just compensation when condemnation must be employed. It is supporting evidence for mortgage financing, in tax accounting, for investment analysis, and for insurability. The information may set the stage for a corporate merger, a long-term lease or sale of major properties, or for a new airport, a new seaport, a new church, a new university, a new hospital, indeed a new city. It should be a vehicle of opinion loaded with ideas as well as facts, because an appraisal conjures up the future by confronting the present on the tracks of the past.

The appraisal report must be a comprehensive account of the appraisal process employed. The premises and conditions under which the appraisal was made must be stated, and an adequate description of the physical property must be included. Reasonable discussions and analyses of the approaches employed in the appraisal process should be elucidated. These things, along with others, should give convincing evidence of the soundness and reasonableness of the appraisal process and of the appraiser's valuation conclusion.

The appraisal report should be sufficiently documented to enable a reader unfamiliar with the appraised property to obtain a good mental picture of it and to understand the appraisal process employed and the analyses to the conclusion of value. As a minimum standard of acceptability, each narrative appraisal report involving property of substantial value should contain adequate coverage of the following items:

1. Address of property appraised.
2. Owner's name and address.
3. Signed certificate of valuation substantially as follows:
    "This is to certify that I have personally inspected the property described herein, that the facts and data used herein are, to the best of my knowledge and belief, true and correct, and that the appraised value represents my best and unbiased judgment of the fair market value of the property. I have no present or intended future interest in the property. A statement of my qualifications as appraiser is included in this report."
4. Purpose of appraisal (and function, if given).
5. Date of valuation.
6. Estate appraised, i.e. fee simple or otherwise.
7. All assumptions and limitations (concluding valuation premise).
8. Adaptability, including highest and best use.
9. Market survey and property analysis:
    (a) Comparable transactions
    (b) Income
    (c) Trend of values
    (d) Adequate analysis, including physical characteristics and condition
    (e) History of the property and its surroundings
10. Summary of controlling factors of value.
11. Value conclusion.
12. Maps, photographs, etc.
13. Qualifications of appraiser.

THE IMPORTANCE OF YOUR APPRAISAL

The appraisal of real estate is a recognized profession controlled by strict ethics as represented in codes adopted by the American Society of Appraisers, the American Institute of Real Estate Appraisers, and the Society of Real Estate Appraisers.

The culmination of any real estate transaction is irrevocably concerned with the question of its fair market value. The marrow of the transaction is, therefore, the appraisal and fair market value estimate. This places the transfer of real estate on a more complicated plane than exchanges concerned with expendable commodities where the field of duplication is practically unlimited and supply or production is capable of seasonal control to meet demand. The importance of sound appraisals cannot be exaggerated.

In the Cost Approach, the fair market value of the land raw is added to the depreciated replacement cost new of the improvements to arrive at an indication of the value of the property. The value of the raw land is always estimated separately by a study of comparable sales. The estimate of reproduction cost new of the improvements is based on the current cost of labor and materials for construction of improvements of a like utility. From this cost new estimate is deducted the depreciation that can be observed in the buildings. The resulting value is known as the value indicated by the Cost Approach.

2

A Measure of Value:
How to Use the Cost Approach

While the courts sometimes accept the actual or original cost of a structure as proof of value in ad valorem tax appeals and eminent domain condemnation cases, and assessors often push this claim to value, it must be noted that a hard-headed investor would not consider this as true cost. The investor would be concentrating on his capitalized net income or the profitability of use.

Not only is cost testimony admitted in court, but it is sometimes given important, even dominant, weight. Unfortunately, it is often fallible evidence. Except in rare cases involving institutional properties, such as a courthouse, public library, public school, or church, where rental income or comparative sales in the marketplace are beside the question, the Cost Approach cannot, by itself, be construed to give "fair market value." It can give, however, *one measure of value,* usually "the upper limit of value," but not always.

For instance, it cost the promoters of the Empire State Building about $50,000,000 to put up that structure in 1934. In 1940 it was still 50% empty, showing a capitalized rental income value far below its original cost. An appraisal at that time would have showed depreciated cost as the upper limit of value. By 1956, when it was sold, the Empire State Building was fully rented at higher per-square-foot values than had been dreamed of by its original owners. Therefore, an appraisal of the property in 1956 would have showed value by the Income Approach at about $80,000,000—far above its original cost.

Replacement or reproduction cost is a measure of value in commercial and industrial buildings, but only that—*one measure.* In times of severe currency deflation or inflation, cost is only relative to what is taking place in the market.

It is not only tax assessors and the judiciary whose value judgments are influenced by the Cost Approach to a greater degree than an expert appraiser would deem prudent. Even investors are reluctant to accept the view that a property might be worth less than what they paid for it. The appraiser has to present unpleasant facts to an emotional investor or user when he says, "Your property today is worth less than what it cost to build." Nevertheless, he must show more than one measure of value to still the palpitations of his client. He must understand replacement or reproduction cost new (RCN), the acceptable methods of depreciation applied to cost new, and the weight that can be attributed to the Cost Approach *as supported by the Income and/or Market Data Approaches.*

Let us, therefore, set forth some definitions concerning the strengths and limitations of the Cost Approach.

COST AND VALUE

Replacement Cost—The replacement cost of a structure is the overall cost of construction necessary to replace the subject building with a substitute of like utility. This includes labor, materials, supervision, contractor's profit and overhead, architect's plans and specifications, sales taxes, and insurance. This term is largely associated with appraisals for insurable values.

Reproduction Cost—The reproduction cost of a building is the total cost of construction required to replace the subject building with an exact replica. This term is most generally applied to appraisals for ad valorem tax appeals, condemnation, and fair market values. For the purposes of this book, the term "reproduction cost" will appear most often.

Principle of Substitution—This economic principle states that the price of a commodity tends to be no higher than the price of a substitute having equal utility, available without undue delay. This is the basis of the Replacement Cost Approach to value.

VALUE FOR REPRODUCTION

To determine the cost of reproducing a property, the first impulse is to make a detailed quantity analysis of the numerous elements entering into the cost of building, just as the contractor does in making his bid. For quick estimating and appraising, however, it has been found quite satisfactory to find an average cost per square foot of floor space or cubic foot of contents, and to apply this average cost against buildings of like size and shape.

When furnishing a detailed quantity analysis, you are dealing with a subject that is definite in some ways and in others indefinite. The evaluator may count the bricks or he may use some other form of measurement to arrive at his conclusion of reproduction costs, but, unlike the contractor, no question of labor troubles or bad weather plays a part in his estimate. A good appraisal is based largely on the law of averages. You know from past experiences that it takes so much material and that it requires just about so much time in labor to perform a certain building operation. But, again unlike the contractor, you have an economic problem based on the law of averages known as *depreciation and obsolescence.* Here enters the indefinite phase of your work. You have scientific tables for depreciation and methods of charges for obsolescence, but their application depends largely on your own individual judgment.

In applying square-foot or cubical-contents methods for arriving at reproduction costs, you first find the area or cubical contents of the building; then determine the classification of the building, that is, determine its type of construction; and then select a cost factor that applies to that class of building, such as "Commercial Class A," or "Industrial Class B."

Cost factors are usually found by averaging the costs for a large number of buildings. Frequently they neglect to make allowances for differences that occur in practically all construction, such as variations in size of building, differences in length of walls or the expanse of walls around a given ground area or given cubical volume, and especially the constant changes taking place in the prices of materials and labor, and in the value of the dollar.

The square-foot or cubic-foot method is obviously the quickest and most convenient method for finding reproduction costs. It is accurate for any one particular type of construction, for a building of a given size, for one particular time, and one particular place. Furthermore, it is possible, by calculating such cost factors for all types of buildings in all sizes and kinds of construction and by providing methods for modifying these costs according to changes in prices, for you to make use of this quick, convenient, and time-saving method with results equivalent in accuracy to the detailed analysis method of arriving at reproduction costs.

THEORIES OF DEPRECIATION

Why is depreciation such a controversial topic in law and accounting and in commercial and industrial appraisals? Because of the inherent difficulties of *measurement.* It is no simple matter to determine the influence of wear and tear and the onslaught of time (physical depreciation) plus the phenomena of obsolescences and inadequacy (functional and economic inutility) on a given facility. In fact, half a century ago the late Harold Hotelling, economist, declared that certain situations demand the development of formulae that await the further progress of pure mathematics,[1] and his prognosis remains unchallenged to this day.

However, in spite of the inherent difficulties of estimating depreciation in quantitative terms, most of the disputes that arrive in court, and even make their way into the textbooks on appraisal and accounting, are of a more rudimentary type. They are due either to failure to compromise or foggy understanding of the meaning of "value" as it is

[1]Harold Hotelling, "A General Mathematical Theory of Depreciation," 20 Jour. AM. Stat. Assn. 340-353 (1925).

affected by depreciation. So serious is this confusion of opinion that not even simple evidentiary problems are clearly drawn in cases of litigation. The disputants, the assessors, and the judges do not get far enough in their analyses to fairly recognize and articulate their meanings.

The following various meanings of "depreciation" may help to clarify the appraiser's approach to logic: In appraisal practice, the word "functional" applies only to the physical aspects of a building. "Functional inutility" refers to a loss of usefulness because of an inherent physical defect. Commercial and industrial "functional inutility" and "functional obsolescence" are synonymous for the purposes of this book.

There is great variety in architectural design from era to era, but utility tends to conform for commercial and industrial buildings of the same age. The basic floor plan is of primary importance because its shape will determine degrees of usefulness. A rectangular or square shape lends itself to retail store adaptations more readily than L shapes or other configurations. But in apartment houses and office buildings an L shape or H shape might be advantageous. In a warehouse, a rectangular or a square shape is most often efficient. In a manufacturing facility, a straight-line, unbroken, in-and-out assembly line operation is frequently desirable, or a horseshoe shape of one story may be most efficacious. Modernization of older buildings is often economical and advisable when the location is good and patronage or distribution pattern is assured. Improvements can then be a contribution to net income.

CONSTRUCTION AND MATERIALS

Quality of construction must be measured carefully in your accrued depreciation estimates and on the whole in the Cost Approach. It will also be measured in comparison to similar properties in the Market Data Approach.

Conversely, economy of construction must not be faulted where it is properly applied. Thrifty methods might be most advisable in building a small warehouse or a delicatessen or a retail liquor outlet, which over the term of the lease may produce a good rent. This is better judgment than if such a building were of superior construction quality, built like a branch bank, for instance, which would mean a higher tax assessment and a larger investment against the rent.

Weather pattern influences the type of construction and material used in various parts of the country. Climate affects the capacity of heating equipment and the depth of foundations. Driveways and parking areas must have a heavier base and thicker coat of macadam or concrete where the frost level reaches far down. Pipes and drains must be set deeper. Roofing must be properly sloped for snow load in Alaska; in Florida this is unimportant. But common sense is important in both places.

Availability of materials may bear as heavily as climate on methods of construction. The cost of light aggregate block may be much cheaper in Bridgeport, Connecticut (where it is made portside from lava brought from Greece in ship bottoms) than in Chillicothe, Ohio (where it would have to be transported by truck or rail). The cost of steel in Pittsburgh might be considerably less than in Connecticut where there are no smelting furnaces. The cost of producing aluminum in Vancouver, Washington is less than in other parts of the nation because of relatively cheap power from the Bonneville Dam project.

In evaluating materials and quality of construction, you must judge the locale as it is related to climate, availability of materials, architectural tastes and traditions, and popular purchasing power.

EQUIPMENT

As much as 50% of the total cost of a large office building may be in equipment such as heating, ventilating, air conditioning, lighting, plumbing, water supply, waste disposal, elevators, and telephone cables. In industrial facilities this cost can be much greater.

Equipment is a prime factor in depreciation in a commercial property. Compared to the structure itself, some of the equipment (such as air-conditioning compressors) may have a life of, say, ten years, where the life of the building may be fifty years. So the rate of depreciation on equipment is generally higher than on the structure.

Commercial properties may suffer by loss of tenant appeal when competing properties install improved equipment. Some industrial facilities may comprise as much as 95% equipment in terms of tanks, piping, pumps, and compressors.

When appraising income property, remember that operating and maintenance costs relate directly to the equipment. Shoddy equipment will mean high maintenance and operating costs. Elevator trouble will run up repair bills and tenant dissatisfaction. Breakdowns in the heating or air conditioning systems will do the same.

When evaluating industrial properties, look first to the age and condition of equipment, because a plant without adequate equipment is like a farmer without a plow or a shoemaker without a last.

Study equipment carefully when making your appraisal. You may find signs of equipment shortcomings in the operating expense statement. You may be asked to assist in the selection of a plan for modernizing equipment. But in any event, make a thorough disclosure of equipment operability in your estimate of depreciation.

ESTIMATING BUILDING COSTS

To repeat, *reproduction cost* is the present cost of reproducing a building with one of approximately identical construction. *Replacement cost* is the present cost of replacing a building with one having identical utility. The two terms are frequently juxtaposed in appraisal practice, and by usage have often come to mean the same thing in regard to construction and utility.

Buildings must be valued separately for some of the same reasons that call for separate land valuation:

1. For property assessment purposes (when ad valorem tax laws decree such separation).
2. For accounting and federal income tax purposes (when it is important to show depreciation of structures and equipment).

3. To determine the most likely profitable use of the land and to estimate income imputable to buildings when using the Land Residual Technique under the Income Approach.

METHODS OF ESTIMATING REPRODUCTION COST

Construction cost estimates are never precise. While exact prices of materials and labor can be gleaned from manuals, the cost of putting them together in a finished building cannot be assessed with exactness. The labor and supervision factors and the contractor's appetite for the job can inflate or deflate the cost estimate. When contractors are bidding on a job, cost estimates on the same set of blueprints will often vary by 25% or more. The busy contractor with too many jobs will bid an indifferent high. The contractor starving for work may bid too low.

Estimating reproduction cost means taking an inventory of the materials and equipment in a building under appraisement and pricing these components, plus labor and overhead and architect's fees, to reproduce the property as of the date of appraisal.

Quantity Survey Method

The quantity survey method is the most reliable but most expensive method of cost estimating. It provides a detailed reproduction cost unassailable from any quarter. It is, in effect, a duplication of the contractor's original pricing of the quantity and grade of each item of material used and the estimate of labor involved.

Unit-in-Place Method

Except for use on large, newly constructed buildings, the quantity survey method is impractical and costly. Most appraisers are not builders and, unless they have free access to a recent quantity breakdown, they will find this costly to obtain from a qualified builder. A quantity survey is time consuming and arduous to put together, and too expensive to include in the average appraisal. It should be done by a professional builder who will, of course, want to be compensated for his time and thought.

A quicker, modified version of the quantity survey method is the unit-in-place method, generally used by contractors who are asked by appraisers for supporting evidence on new construction. This consists of using installed prices for materials, employing a convenient unit of measurement, such as cubic or square footage. It eliminates counting the exact number of board feet of lumber, yards of ready-mix cement, bales of shingles, and the like, and facilitates your computation by including labor overhead, insurance, and supervision in the square or cubic foot count. Once basic units are established, the cost of an entire building can be estimated quickly.

You need not qualify as a professional cost estimator since this calls for specialized training and experience. But you should know builders from whom you can obtain cost estimates, the limitations of available methods when applied to your problems, and the nature of the estimate sought in each case. You should be aware that it is most practical to have the cost estimate, the inspection of the building for depreciation, and the rehabilitation cost estimate prepared as a related process under the control of one person. This person does not have to be you, but should be someone working closely with you in whose work you have confidence.

Square-Foot and Cubic-Foot Comparisons

The pros and cons of the square-foot versus cubic-foot methods have to be judged in the light of local custom and individual choice. Most commercial appraisers lean to the square-foot method, which is ideally applicable to warehouses, loft buildings, store buildings, and structures of commercial character. The cubic-foot method is sometimes applied to apartments and frequently to office buildings, that is, structures with a considerable degree of interior finish and partitions.

Two kinds of indirect costs figure in cost estimating: first, the contractor's overhead and profit; and second, the general overhead, including architect's fees and accounting and legal services, taxes, insurance, survey expenses, and interest during the period of construction. With income properties, costs are often incurred after construction while tenants are being solicited and until total occupancy is achieved.

Familiarity with the make-up of the cubic-foot or square-foot cost per unit not only produces more accurate cost estimates, but also figures in estimating depreciation. With proper maintenance, a structure might have a long life. Its equipment might require replacement sooner and can be separately depreciated at an advanced rate.

Cost Manuals and Services

You probably subscribe to one or more of the accredited cost-reporting services, such as Marshall & Swift, Boechk's, F. W. Dodge, R. C. Means, or McElroy or Engineering News Record. Illustrations and alternative adjustments to the standard index example may help you to keener insights on costs. Some manuals provide adjustment in the individual territory in which the appraiser is interested. Some demonstrate cubic-foot costs, some square-foot costs, and some are designed for unit-in-place information. Actual knowledge of local building costs is still the best evidence. Even so, a good cost service is excellent supporting evidence.

As foundation for the Cost Approach, and often as an indicator in the Market Data Approach, the reproduction cost estimate contributes to the estimate of final value. Its accuracy and its presentation must be given careful review. As a rule, one of two general methods is best suited to your use: (1) the modified quantity survey (or unit-in-place method); or (2) the cubic-foot or square-foot (comparative) method. The former is preferred where the builder's testimony in court is important.

PUTTING THE STICK TO DEPRECIATION

In general, there are three classifications of depreciation: (1) deterioration, (2) functional obsolescence (inutility), (3) economic obsolescence. These classifications may be broken down as follows.

1. *Deterioration* is loss in value to a building that occurs by wear and tear in use, from decay, because of structural defects, or from exposure to the elements.

There are generally two kinds of deterioration:

(a) *Curable deterioration* is that which may be controlled by an owner who may cure the decay with good, ordinary maintenance. The amount of accrued curable deterioration is expressed as the *cost to cure* such deterioration. The estimate of cost to cure, however, must be limited by the amount that a prudent owner would be justified in spending.

(b) *Incurable deterioration* is actual loss in strength or in remaining life of the basic components of the structure that cannot ordinarily be reached by a prudent owner for repair and replacement. This is a loss in value occurring as a direct result of age or inferior construction that cannot economically be cured. It is the only type of depreciation that must be estimated on the basis of the age life of the portions of the structure that are not ordinarily maintained by a prudent owner.

2. *Functional obsolescence* is loss in value that occurs within a structure as a result of its inability to perform adequately the function for which it should be used. It may be represented by antiquated design, appearance, overdesign, out-of-date features such as excessively high ceilings or oversized corridors and lobbies, and other structural features that are out of date.

There are two forms of functional obsolescence:

(a) One form of functional obsolescence is *curable,* that is, it can be cured economically by a prudent owner. Examples of curable functional obsolescence include replacement of old-style lavatories and toilets with modern fixtures, the replacement of old-style electrical fixtures with modern recessed fluorescents, the lowering of ceilings, and installation of modern wiring and plumbing, heating and air conditioning. The measure of the amount of accrued curable functional obsolescence is the cost to cure. This estimate is, of course, limited to the amount that a prudent owner would spend in curing the accrued functional obsolescence.

(b) There is, in addition, incurable functional obsolescence. This is functional obsolescence that would be so costly to cure that a prudent owner would find it unreasonable to do so. Examples of this type of functional obsolescence are excessive foundations and buildings that are far too large for a land area. In general, the amount of accrued incurable functional obsolescence is estimated by capitalizing the rental loss suffered because of the inability of the structure to perform adequately the functions for which it was designed. In many cases, the rental loss is measured in reverse, that is, by increased ownership expenses without a corresponding increase in gross income. Sometimes the measure includes the combination of the two. The total amount of loss in value due to incurable functional obsolescence is therefore the capitalization of either the rental loss or the increased ownership cost, or a combination of the two, for the *remaining economic life* of the structure.

3. *Economic obsolescence* is a form of depreciation that contemplates a downward price-level adjustment that is not concerned with the physical condition of real property improvements. It has to do not only with the value of the particular property itself but with all unfavorable economic influences on the value of competing properties. It occurs primarily from a reduction in adaptability to a lower use. Among other causes, it may arise from changes in legislation, the encroachment of noxious enterprises or inharmonious neighbors, shifting business centers and decline in opportunities for gainful employment, poor accessibility, or unfair taxes.

REMAINING ECONOMIC LIFE OF STRUCTURES

All estimates of future depreciation must be based upon the remaining economic life of structures. The remaining economic life is the estimated number of years that a building will produce a net income sufficient to pay a return on, and a return of, its value.

An estimate of remaining economic life can be made only after a careful study of a structure. This study must include not only a complete examination of the physical characteristics of the structure itself, but must also include careful consideration of the probable *future* demands to be made upon the functions that the structure was designed to perform and upon a possible future change in the use of the land. Thus, the estimate of remaining economic life is an estimate of future deterioration, future functional obsolescence, and future economic obsolescence; all reflected by the number of years in the future which, in the judgment of the appraiser, a building can logically be expected to pay a return on and of the value remaining in it as of the day on which the appraisal is made. Such an estimate is only made on an observed-condition basis and is tempered always by experience and by a careful study of a subject property and similar properties.

"Recapture" is the preferred term to define the setting aside of annual sums to recover within a period of years the present value of a structure.

Accrued depreciation, as such, is estimated directly only in the Cost Approach. However, it is estimated indirectly by the market in both the Income Approach and the Market Data Approach. In the Earnings Approach, the loss in value or depreciation is reflected in the income that the property will produce. It results in a lowered income and a consequently lowered value indicated by the Income Approach. Thus, the Income Approach automatically reflects accrued depreciation.

In the Market Data Approach, by comparing the property under appraisement with comparable properties recently sold, all accrued depreciation is deducted from the value of the property as it is actually deducted by actual buyers and sellers of comparable property. Thus, the accrued depreciation is indirectly estimated by the use of comparative sales in which all types of depreciation have been taken into consideration by buyers and sellers in establishing prices.

In giving consideration to accrued depreciation, it is imperative to bear in mind that this is depreciation that has already occurred. Accrued depreciation is estimated only on the basis of observed condition. There is no arbitrary fixed amount per annum that accurately represents accrued depreciation. Such estimates are made only on the basis of what the appraiser actually finds upon inspection of the subject property.

Depreciation may be further described as the difference between the value of a structure and the cost of reproducing it as of the same date.

Accrued depreciation is estimated in the appraisal process by one or more of five different methods, as follows:

1. The capitalized income method, showing *rent loss* or *extra costs* of operation.
2. The market method, showing *sale value* by comparison with similar structures.
3. The straight-line method (age-life depreciation).
4. The engineering method (observed depreciation).
5. The breakdown method (observed depreciation).

Of these, the capitalized income method and the market method are actually indirect systems of estimating depreciation through the Market Data and Income Approaches to value. The remaining three, the straight-line method, the engineering method, and the breakdown method, are direct systems of estimating depreciation employed in the Cost Approach.

The straight-line method assigns a percentage of depreciation, such as 2% or 2 1/2% or 3%, for each year of a building's life. Thus, a building ten years old depreciated at the rate of 2 1/2% will have suffered a reduction in value of 25%.

"Observed depreciation" is the term used for both the engineering and breakdown methods. In the engineering method, percentage deductions are applied to the separate components of building cost. In the breakdown method, deductions (either percentage or in lump-sum amounts) are applied to rehabilitation cost, general deterioration, curable functional obsolescence, incurable functional obsolescence, and economic obsolescence.

The nature of the problem best determines the method and detail you should use in making depreciation estimates.

Legal Basis of Depreciation

Definite legal precedents for the treatment of depreciation have been established. The U.S. Supreme Court has repeatedly held that the *observed-condition method* of estimating accrued depreciation should be accorded the greatest weight. The Court comprehends the intangible nature of the estimate. It has taken the position that the opinion of a qualified witness based upon personal inspection of the property, together with his skill in estimating depreciation, must take precedence over more mathematical computations.

In cases contested by the Internal Revenue Service, you may be called on to set up the foundation figures and premises both as to depreciation and life expectancies. Qualified appraisal opinion is steadily gaining more recognition in income tax procedure and in acquisition and liquidation procedures, per 334B(2), IRS Code of 1954.

Generally, in law and by regulation of the various government agencies, the observed depreciation methods are preferred.

Application

Using the observed depreciation methods, the property is compared with a new property or an index example of a typical modern property. The methods are based upon direction inspection, detailed estimates of accrued deterioration, and studies of functional deficiencies affecting the property and its desirability. Close comparison of the property against a perfect property as a model lends more weight to your judgment of value. Your estimate will stand scrutiny if you report in enough detail so that your reasons are coherent and logical, as well as arithmetically correct.

Analysis of physical, functional, and economic utility, and methods of estimating depreciation are important elements of a full-blown, three-approach appraisal, even though they are to some extent conjectural and must be proven in the Income and Market Data Approaches. Probably the best estimate of use value to an owner is value indicated by the Cost Approach, which is particularly important in evaluating properties owned by industrial users. The estimate should, however, even in this application, be supported by the Income and/or Market Data Approaches.

The Income Approach to value is an appraisal technique in which the anticipated net income is processed to indicate the capital amount of the investment that produces the net income. Therefore, extreme care must be used in estimating the net income to arrive at the value indicated by the Income Approach.

3

A Keener Measure of Value: The Income Approach

For the evaluation of leased commercial (income) properties, such as retail stores, shopping centers, marinas, apartment houses, office buildings, and motels, the Income Approach is the chief indicator of value. For leased industrial properties, such as general-purpose warehouses, research facilities, waterfront dock and rail storage plants, the Income Approach is also the paramount path to value conclusion. Such properties are principally built, leased, bought, and sold by professional investors for income investment purposes.

PROCEDURE: SEVEN KEY STEPS

The seven essential steps to investment analysis under the Income Approach are detailed here (see Figure 1):

1. Set forth the *anticipated annual gross income* from the property.
2. Estimate the possible rent loss due to *vacancies and rental defaults,* and deduct the loss from gross income to arrive at *effective gross income.*
3. Total the amount of the anticipated *operating and fixed expenses* that the property will incur during the time that the income is being received.
4. Deduct the expenses from effective gross income to arrive at an estimate of *net income.*
5. Measure the probable duration of this net income stream. This determination may be based on the economic life of the building or the length of a high-credit lease.
6. Select a *capitalization technique* to process the net income into value.
7. Then find the overall capitalization rate to be applied to the property under appraisal by building an interest (discount) rate and a recapture rate into the

43

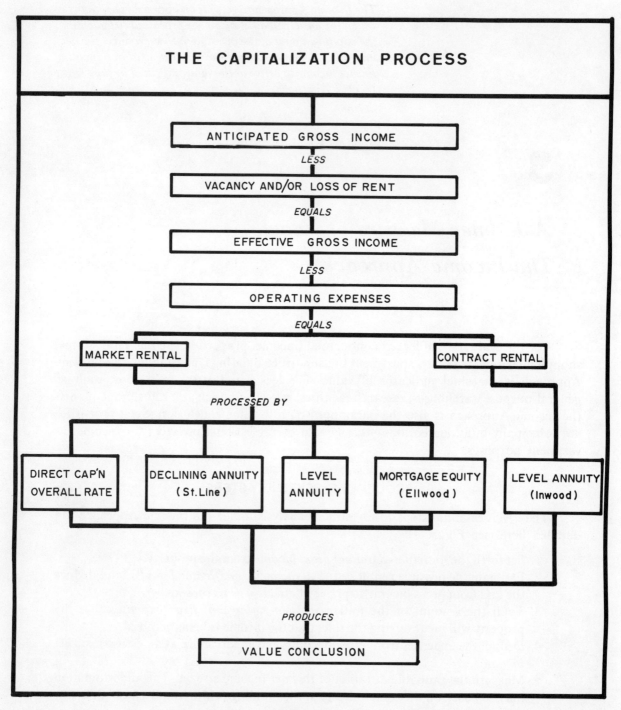

FIGURE 1

overall rate. (Include in this buildup an effective tax rate if the purpose of the appraisal is an ad valorem tax appeal.)

In using this approach, the appraiser is concerned with how much an investor will pay *now* to gain the right to receive the future income that a property may produce. This is generally measured by the *net income* a property can be expected to produce during its remaining economic life.

The seven points above are demonstrated in the following example, showing procedural points 1 through 4 to arrive at *net income*. Points 5, 6, and 7 can be demonstrated after you have been told that the building is new and fully leased; that the rentals are high credit and long term; and that the property is situated in a prime business district downtown and is therefore attractive to investors and hightly mortgageable.

DEMONSTRATION

Net income for a small office building is derived as follows:

Lawyer's Trust Building

Operating Statement for 1976

Rent Roll:

Office rentals	$70,800	
Garage rentals	3,925	
Vending machines	2,600	
(automat cafeteria)		
Gross income		$77,325
Less vacancy and rental defaults (5%)		3,866
Effective gross income		$73,459

Expenses:

Taxes (excluded here because they will be reflected in capitalization rate)	$ 000	
Insurance	6,200	
Fuel (gas)	2,865	
Water	1,250	
Electricity (public use)	4,695	
Maintenance & supplies (includes superintendent's salary)	9,520	
Management (5% of gross)	3,846	
		—$28,376
		$45,083

The tenants include a branch bank and a utility company office on the ground floor on 40-year leases. The floors above are occupied by an insurance company on a 25-year lease and the city's leading law and accounting firms on 10-year leases. The basement garage is operated by building management. The contract rentals here have been found to be economic or better than the average in the neighborhood market.

This situation calls for application of the band of investment method of structuring the discount rate.

Mortgage rate	75% x 9%	= 6.75%
Equity rate	25% x 12%	= 3.00%
Total Interest Rate		9.75% (Discount)

An investor purchasing this property would want his original investment back in 40 years (40/100ths = 2.5%). This is the property's remaining economic life as spelled out by its key leases. The effective tax rate derived by multiplying tax rate x tax ratio = 1.5%. Thus the net income is capitalized into value by applying 9.75% (interest) + 2.5% (recapture) + 1.5% (effective tax rate). Finally, we arrive at an overall rate, 13.75%.

Now, then,

$$\$45,083 \div 13.75\% \ (.1375) = \$327,876$$
$$\text{Rounded to: } \$328,000$$

Value found via the Income Approach for the Lawyer's Trust Building is, therefore: $328,000.

Estimating Gross Income

The first step in processing income to capitalization is to establish a stabilized, realistic *gross income estimate.* In the foregoing demonstration, contract rentals had been found to be *economic* or better than average in the neighborhood marketplace. Suppose they had been lower. How should you estimate a reasonable gross income for the property? By making a careful search throughout the area for:

1. Rentals earned by *comparable properties.*
2. Then matching these comparables against past and present rentals received by the subject. In the demonstration, the Lawyer's Trust Building was new, and so had no *historical rent.* But present rentals were measurable and provided a sound basis for comparison.

The objective is to find what rentals might be attained if the space were currently available in the rental marketplace. This level might be more or less than present actual gross income. The rental the space would attain in the open market at the time of appraisal is called *economic rent,* whether it is lower, higher, or the same as the actual contract rent. Economic rent plus any other income derived from the property is the *stabilized gross income.*

Comparing Rentals in Units of Measurement

To further assure a realistic gross income, convert current rentals into *units of measurement* such as rent per room, per square foot, and per front foot. The unit of measure used will vary with the type of property under appraisal—store, office building, motel, or apartment house. Retail stores are usually measured on a front foot basis, offices by the square foot, and motels and apartment houses by room rentals.

In apartment house appraisals, for instance, the usual application is rent per room per month. If your subject property has 40 three-room apartments totaling 120 rooms that show a per-room rental of $50 per month, this actual rental may or may not be an *economic* rental in the marketplace. The apartment house a block to the north may be renting for $60 per room per month, and the abutting property to the south may be renting for $40 per month per room. It is the appraiser's job to find out why.

The way to go about finding out why, in an organized manner, is as follows:

Setting Up Measurements

Say there are two commercial properties comparable to your subject, although reasonable adjustments are pertinent to stabilizing the economic gross income of the subject property. Keep in mind: the comparable properties are always adjusted to the subject.

Comparative Factors	COMPARABLE #1 $1.30 per sq. ft.	COMPARABLE #2 $1.00 per sq. ft.
Location	Better than subject	Poorer than subject
Age	Newer than subject	Same as subject
Condition	Better than subject	Same as subject
Construction	Same as subject	Same as subject
Air Conditioning	Yes	No
Responsibility of Tenant	Tenant pays extra for parking	Parking is free

Subtract $.10 per square foot for each positive factor; for each negative factor add $.10 per square foot.

For instance, the address of Comparable #1 is superior to subject. Therefore, subtract $.10 in the subject from the rent per square foot of Comparable #1. The location of Comparable #2 is inferior to subject so add $.10 in the subject to the rent per square foot of Comparable #2, and so on through the comparative factors.

Here are a few more factors that must be accounted in apartment house rental comparisons:

1. Built-in stoves and refrigerators
2. Number of rooms per apartment
3. Size of rooms
4. Number of baths
5. Elevators

Effective Gross Income

Always reduce stabilized gross income to allow for vacancy and rental defaults. The percentage deducted for this will vary according to the type of property, neighborhood factors, and local economic conditions. An allowance of five to ten percent is customarily deducted for vacancies, but different types of buildings and varying locations require greater or lesser percentages.

The establishment of gross income less the deduction for vacancy and rental default loss is called *effective gross income. This is the second step in computing value* by the Income Approach.

Your estimate of *effective gross income* can be set forth in your report as follows:

Gross income estimate	$20,000
Less vacancy and rental default allowance, 5%	1,000
Effective gross income estimate	$19,000

There are several factors that influence the percentage of vacancy and delinquency loss. Among the more important ones are these:

1. Present and past income record of subject property.
2. Competitive rentals in the area.
3. An analysis of future economic trends in the area.
4. Length of leases.
5. Tenant credit ratings.

Analysis of Expenses

Expenses are overhead charges to the property that may be classified into three categories: (a) operating charges, (b) fixed expense, and (c) reserves for replacement. These expense categories are detailed here in *appraisal* terms rather than in *accounting* terms.

Operating expenses include wages and benefits of building employees, fuel, utility services, renovations, repairs, management and leasing charges.

Fixed expenses are those costs that are stabilized and recurrent from year to year, such as property insurance.

In ad valorem tax appeals and mortgage-equity appraisals the appraiser should include real estate taxes as an addition to the overall capitalization rate rather than deduct them from income, where accounting practice often puts them.

Reserves for replacement are allocated for replacement of building and equipment items that have a relatively short life expectancy. For example, reserves should be set up for stoves, refrigerators, heating units, elevators, roof replacements, and other items that usually must be replaced before the end of the economic life of the building. The appraiser provides for the replacement of an item by: (1) determining its replacement cost, and (2) estimating its useful life in years. Then the annual charge becomes the cost of the replacement item divided by the number of years of useful life.

Operating Statement Exclusions

Expenses (for appraisal purposes) *do not* include expenditures that are beyond the direct operation of an income-producing property. There are four types of expenses to the owner that are not expenses of the real estate. They are:

1. Mortgage principal and interest payments
2. Income tax payments
3. Depreciation charges (on improvements)
4. Expenditures for capital improvements, i.e., new stoves, refrigerators, storm windows, etc.

The act of excluding these items and realigning pertinent charges as valid to the real property is known as *reconstruction* of the operating statement. Reconstruction of the owner's operating statement, as compared to the one to be made by the appraiser, should look this way:

OPERATING STATEMENT FOR 1976

	Owner's Figures	Appraiser's Reconstruction
Gross income	$100,000	$100,000
Allowance for vacancies	5,000	5,000
Effective gross income	95,000	95,000
Expenses:		
Salaries of part-time superintendents	7,295.40	7,300
Employees' benefits	800.57	800
Insurance	1,849.03	1,800
Gas	3,260.60	3,300
Redocorating	2,545.40	2,500
Payments on unit air conditioners	1,500.00	——
Repairs	2,079.55	2,100
Supplies	692.45	700
Electricity	1,275.20	1,300
Water	563.35	700
Reserves	199.00	4,000
Management	3,000.00	3,000
Real estate taxes	17,500.45	(may be expressed in capitalization rate)
Depreciation—building	12,220.00	——
Interest on mortgage	13,108.00	——
Principal on mortgage	1,510.40	——
Legal and accounting fees	600.60	600
Miscellaneous expenses	——	500
Total expenses	$ 70,000.00	$ 28,600
Net income	$ 25,000.00	$ 46,300

Note that you should omit financing costs, tax payments (if expressed in the capitalization rate), depreciation charges, and payments on capital improvements (such as the air conditioners), but do not make an allowance for "miscellaneous expenses" when the owner does not. Also, drop odd pennies and round dollars to the nearest hundred. If you run across a figure in the owner's accounting that is patently ridiculous, such as $199 for Reserves in an elevator building, as above, investigate and correct the oversight.

VALUE BY INCOME CAPITALIZATION

A composite rate, representing several factors pertinent to the income property and the aims of investors and lenders putting their funds into it, is now divided into the net income to produce capitalized value. This rate is selected by the appraiser after he has considered the following factors.

Investment Aims

Income properties are approached by investors and lenders with several requirements to be met. These are:

1. Rate of return on the amount invested.
2. Security of the amount invested.
3. Capital appreciation.
4. Certainty of a return on the investment.
5. Burden of managing the investment.
6. Ease of liquidation of the investment.

Directly proportional to the *risk* involved is the rate of return to be anticipated. For instance, an investor might be willing to accept a low rate of interest if the risk of losing his investment is low. On the other hand, if the risk were high, he would want a high rate of interest.

The Capitalization Rate

The income property investor purchases two rights:

(a) A return *on* his investment, or the right to receive *interest* on his money.
(b) A return *of* his investment, or the right to get his money back at the end of his term of ownership. Appraisers refer to this as capital *recapture*. It is equivalent to a *depreciation factor*.

For example, when a person buys a $1,000 20-year bond, he expects to receive interest on his $1,000 of say, 6% for the twenty years. And he expects to get back the $1,000 at the end of 20 years. At this end, he has received $1,200 in interest, and he recaptures his $1,000, the whole totaling $2,200, comprising both *interest* and *recapture*.

The sum of these two rates (plus the effective tax rate, if it is included) make up the *capitalization rate*. The effective tax rate is *always* included in ad valorem tax appeals but is *never* included where net leases are calculated as economic rent. In appraisals for still other purposes, it is an optional application.

In income property appraisals, these formulae are axiomatic:

High risk = High capitalization rate = Low value
Low risk = Low capitalization rate = High value

The capitalization rate includes three (if an ad valorem tax appeal is the purpose) separate rates:

1. The interest rate.
2. A recapture rate.
3. The effective tax rate.

If the purpose of the appraisal is for investment or mortgage financing under a net lease, then just the interest rate and recapture rate would make up the capitalization rate. But a third element will enter the picture if the purpose is ad valorem tax appeal. The three elements can be expressed in your appraisal report in this manner:

Interest rate	9%
Recapture rate	2% (50-year life)
Effective tax rate	3%
(Tax rate x tax ratio)	
Capitalization rate	14%

How to Select the Interest Rate

Interest rates should be selected only after careful study. There are two principal methods of developing an interest rate: (1) the *summation* method, and (2) the *band of investment* method.

Summation Method

In the *summation* method, a rate is compiled in a structure of four component parts, assigning a rate to each. The interest rate then is the total of the parts. An example of this is shown below:

	PROPERTY A	PROPERTY B
Safe rate	6%	6.0%
Risk rate	1%	3.0%
Rate for management	1%	1.5%
Rate for nonliquidity	1%	1.5%
Total interest rate	9%	12.0%

The *safe rate* is the foundation element in the summation method of building an interest rate. It is the rate paid by investments of maximum security, highest liquidity, and minimum risk. Usually appraisers apply either the going rate on long-term United States government bonds, the rate paid by banks on savings accounts, or the rate paid by Triple-A Corporate bonds.

The *risk rate* is added to the safe rate as an allowance for the hazards to be encountered in real estate investment. *Axiom:* The safer the investment, the lower the amount added for risk.

The *rate for management* is the component of the interest rate that offsets the responsibility of managing the investment and reinvesting the funds received from the property. This should not be mistaken for the management fee charged against the property as an operating expense, which has no bearing on the interest rate.

The *rate for nonliquidity* is a penalty charge against all real property because of the time necessary to convert real estate to cash. For instance, one can pick up the telephone and sell a good grade bond or listed common stock in a matter of minutes. Negotiations to sell real estate usually last weeks or months.

The interest rate on real estate investments, beyond the base or safe rate of return on U.S. Savings Bonds, is therefore compounded by these factors:

(a) Greater risk
(b) Greater difficulty in converting to cash
(c) Greater burden in managing the investment

Band of Investment Method

Only two conditions affect the interest rate developed by the band of investment method. They are:

(a) The rate of mortgage interest available
(b) The rate of return required on equity

Consider a property in which a first mortgage covering 75% of the value can be obtained at 10% interest and that investors require a 12% return on the equity portion, or 25% of the value of the property. In this situation, an interest rate is developed as follows:

	Percent of Value		Rate	Product
First Mortgage	75	x	10	7.5
Equity	25	x	12	3.0
TOTAL	100%	x		10.5

The interest rate of 100% of value is 10.5%.

If secondary financing is in the picture, the procedure is the same. Assume a first mortgage of 75% obtainable at 9%, a second mortgage of 20% obtainable at 12%, and the equity of 5% requiring a 14% return. Because the equity is reduced and the risk greater, the investor would require a higher rate of return, for example:

	Percent of Value		Rate	Product
First Mortgage	75	x	9	6.75
Second Mortage	20	x	12	2.40
Equity	5	x	14	.70
TOTAL	100%	x		9.85

In most income-investment property situations, the equity owner with a second mortgage watering down his equity would lose his property if net income decreases.

The Rate for Capital Recapture

It has been stated earlier that a sound investment includes two provisions: (a) return on the invested capital, and (b) return of the invested capital, called recapture.

If you are processing income from land only, *no* recapture provision is necessary. Land does not depreciate and so recapture can be realized through resale.

A building, however, is a wasting asset. Its value for accounting purposes decreases with the passing of time. Therefore, add to the interest rate a percentage that will provide for the recapture of the investment in the building. Thus, the words *recapture* and *depreciation* are synonymous.

The Straight-Line Method of Recapture

In this age-life method, the recapture rate is a uniform annual rate (say 5% per annum) at which the depreciating property must be amortized so that all of the investment will have been returned when the building is 100% depreciated (say 20 years) and presumably economically exhausted.

For example, if the appraiser estimates that the building has a remaining useful life of 20 years, he is saying that 1/20 or 5% of the building value should be returned annually out of net income.

Application of the straight-line (age-life) method of recapture calls for appraisal wisdom in regard to the useful lives of commercial and industrial properties. You can get guiding parameters from indices in various cost manuals.

A building most often becomes useless through functional inutility or economic obsolescence rather than just physical deterioration. Thus you should refer to the recapture period as *estimated remaining economic life*. Estimate the remaining economic life after considering the functional and economic factors.

The recapture rate can be expressed in the band of investment method as follows:

Mortgage	75% x 8% =	6%
Equity	25% x 12% =	3%
Total interest rate		9%
Recapture rate: 100% ÷ 20 =		5%
Total interest and recapture rate		14%

How to Compute the Effective Tax Rate

The term "effective tax rate" means simply this: property taxes expressed as a *percentage of full value*. To compute the effective tax rate, you must know two things:

(a) The percentage or ratio of assessment to full value that is being used in your area.

(b) The official (actual) tax rate—the taxes per hundred or per thousand dollars of assessment.

For instance, assume that assessed value of a particular property is 70% of full value and that the official tax rate in the city or town is $50 per $1000 of assessment. The effective tax rate is computed by multiplying the assessment ratio (70%) by the rate per $1000 of assessment (50 ÷ 1000, or 5%). Thus:

$$70\% \times 5\% = 3.5\% = \text{Effective Tax Rate}$$

CAPITALIZATION METHODS

The capitalization process to be used is determined by the *quality of the net income stream* that is anticipated from the property. For example, if the rentals are on a month-to-month or short-term basis, if net income before depreciation is liable to decline, and if the property is generally in mid-life, the straight-line (age-life) depreciation plus the capitalization rate method may be used. In using this method, the number of years of the remaining economic life of the building is divided into 100 to determine the percentage of future depreciation per year. Then the percentage of future depreciation is added to the capitalization rate to arrive at the overall rate that will produce a return on the invested capital for the remaining economic life of the building and the return of the invested capital over this same period.

The value of the building found by this method (as is), plus the value of the land found by the Market Data Approach, becomes the indicated value of the property.

Depending upon the *quality and durability* of income flowing from the property, you can follow either of the following courses of capitalization:

1. Use the straight-line depreciation plus capitalization rate method of capitalization when you anticipate that the net income before depreciation *may decline* in the future. The rate of decline anticipated is represented by this formula:

Annual rate of decline anticipated in the net income before depreciation: $\left\{ \dfrac{\text{Capitalization rate} \times \text{rate of depreciation}}{\text{Capitalization rate} + \text{rate of depreciation}} \right.$

For instance, when evaluating a building having a remaining economic life of 20 years, using a capitalization rate of 5 percent, the annual rate of decline anticipated in the net income before depreciation is as follows:

Annual rate of decline anticipated in the net income before depreciation: $\left\{ = \dfrac{0.05 \times 0.05}{0.05 + 0.05} = 2.5 \text{ percent per year} \right.$

2. But if the net income before depreciation is expected to be level or better, and is *of a contract nature,* if the financial stability of the tenants is substantial and the leases extend over a period of at least twelve years, then the Inwood premise may be used. This premise is used in good, chain-store lease properties. When this method is used, it is only necessary to select the factor in the Inwood table that represents the number of years of

the remaining economic life of the building and the capitalization rate selected. This factor is then multiplied by the net income remaining to the building to indicate the capital value of the building. The value of the building is then added to the value of the land as found in the Market Data Approach, and the sum of the two is the indicated value of the property, as shown here:

Building Residual—Inwood Annuity

```
Value of the land by Market Data ........................$100,000.
Reported annual net before recapture...........................$40,000.
Interest imputable to land value, 9% .............................  9,000.
Annual net income imputable to building  ........................$31,000.
    Remaining economic life 20 years,
    interest rate 9%. Then, the present
    worth of $1 per annum for 20 years,
    discounted at 9%, is found to be
    10.594 (Inwood table factor): Table II
Building value $31,000 x 10.594................................$328,414.
Add Land Value, Market Data Approach ........................ 100,000.
                                                             $428,414.
```

Residual Techniques

The term "residual" means that which remains after all deductions. When it is not possible to find the value of the land by the use of the Market Data Approach, it is best to use the *Land Residual Technique* under a hypothetical *highest-and-best-use* building. After making a careful study of the vicinity, you estimate the type of building that will produce the highest net return to the land. You then estimate the cost of constructing the building, the income that the building will produce, and the expenses that will have to be paid to produce that income. After the estimated expenses are deducted from the estimated effective gross income, the net income to the property is then processed by first finding the amount of the net income necessary to meet the building charges. These building charges include not only a return on the money invested in the building at the proper rate of capitalization but also the return of the capital invested in the building during the remaining economic life of the building.

The income may be processed by the straight-line depreciation plus the capitalization rate method or by the Inwood or Ellwood methods, depending upon the quality of the income stream. The total amount of the annual income necessary to service the building is next deducted from the net income to the property before depreciation, to arrive at the income remaining to the land. The land income is then capitalized at the same capitalization rate to indicate the capital value of the land.

The value of the land found in this method is used in appraisal of the subject property in connection with the *Building Residual Technique*. In other words, the income required by the land on the value found under a hypothetical highest-and-best-use building is deducted from the net income produced by the subject property before depreciation, and the remaining income is considered as the income applying to the existing building. The income applying to the existing building is then processed by the proper capitalization method to indicate the capital value of the building. The capital value of the building found in this way is now added to the value of the land found under the hypothetical highest-and-best-use building, and the sum of the two is the value indicated.

Using the *Property Residual Technique,* land and building are not valued separately, but as a whole. In this process, most applicable to properties leased long term, you capitalize the present worth of the anticipated net income before depreciation for the estimated economic life of the building, or the term of the lease. At the anticipated end of the income, land and building are assumed to revert to the owner. This reversion is valued by discounting its then-anticipated value against its present-day worth. The total value is the sum of the capitalized value of the income plus the present worth of the reversionary interest. Another application of this technique applies an overall rate for the entire net before depreciation with no reversion. It is, in effect, the same as direct capitalization with an overall rate.

ANNUITY AND SINKING FUND
METHODS OF CAPITALIZATION

In the lexicon of appraisal practice, the *guaranteed annual net income* of investment realty is called an *annuity,* whether it is received weekly, monthly, quarterly, or semi-annually. This type of income, guaranteed by a long-term lease from a tenant with a Triple-A credit rating, often has to be evaluated in terms of the *present worth of future benefits.*

For instance, a bank asks for an appraisal of a property leased long term to the U.S. government, for instance, a post office. The lease is only in its third year, with seventeen years to run. The quality and durability of the guaranteed income stream is beyond question. But in order to place a legal limit maximum mortgage loan on the property as of this week, the bank must find the *present worth* of the full amount due from the lease for twenty years. How does the appraiser apply his skill in this situation? He can turn to the Inwood Table.

The Inwood Annuity Table (The present worth of $1 per annum)

This and the Ellwood Tables, as you know, are the most widely used in appraisal work. The Inwood Table is used to determine the *present value* of an income stream or annuity at a specific rate of interest over a given period of time. Finding the present value of an income stream is basically a discounting process. That is, each year's income to be received has a present value that is less than its face value in an amount equal to the loss of interest during the time until it is collected.

For instance, assume you are to receive one dollar one year from today and that 8% is a fair rate of interest. How much should you be paid today for the right to receive this dollar? See Table I in the Appendix and you will find that the answer is $.926.

It should be made clear that the Inwood factors provide for both *interest and recapture* of the investment. The Inwood annuity method of capitalization, therefore, must be used only when processing net income with provision for capital recovery excluded. The Inwood method can be summed up as embracing the following principles:

1. The annual income stream remains constant over the life of the investment.
2. Recapture installments are relatively low to begin with, but increase each year.
3. Interest is received each year on the remaining amount of the investment.

Under the *straight-line method,* capital is recaptured at a faster rate than under the *annuity* method. Therefore, the value of a building under the straight-line method would be *lower* than under the annuity method.

For instance, an appraiser might value a commercial or industrial property today by the Building Residual Technique and straight-line recapture. Ten years later he might appraise the same building, but instead of using straight-line recapture, he might apply the Inwood annuity method. Which method would imply a reduction in risk? Why?

The Inwood annuity method is used when the property's income has taken on the "gold bond" contractual nature of an annuity; in effect, when the property is under long-term lease to a tenant with strong credit. Guarantee of a constant income stream obviously reduces risk.

Sinking Fund Method

Another route that provides for capital recapture is the *sinking fund method.* A sinking fund is created by setting aside an annual amount of the net income that, when invested at a safe rate of interest (such as government bonds), will return the entire building investment in one lump sum at the end of the building's economic life.

The Hoskold 3% sinking fund table (see Appendix, Table VI A) shows factors by which the annual income may be multiplied to obtain the present worth of the building at a specified rate of interest over a given number of years. Note that there are two rates involved: the interest rate, which applies to overall building value, and the sinking fund rate, in this case 3%, which applies to the amount set aside to recapture the investment.

Apply the Hoskold sinking fund method to the following property, for example. Assume the following data:

Net income before recapture—$20,000
Economic life—25 years
Interest on land and building—10%
Effective tax rate—2%
Land value estimate—$100,000

The portion of the net income allocated to the building is:

Total net income $20,000
Interest and tax on land
  ($100,000 x 8%)   8,000
Net income residual to building $12,000

Using the Hoskold sinking fund table, we would value the property as follows:

Net income residual to building $12,000
Sinking fund factor—25 years at 8% = 10.264
Value of building ($12,000 x 9.309) = $111,708
Plus land value   100,000
Value of property   211,708
                                        Rounded to: $212,000

Sinking fund methods are frequently applied to oil wells, mines, gravel pits, railroads, utilities, and other industrial applications where questions of current yield versus eventual exhaustion are paramount. Hoskold is not commonly applied to types of commercial and industrial properties with which this book is concerned, so we will not explore sinking funds beyond this point.

EVALUATING TRIPLE-A TENANCIES

If there is a long-term lease on commercial or industrial property, and the lessee has a Triple-A credit standing, focus is placed on the guaranteed income thereby assured. It becomes a "gold bond deal." The real estate itself is secondary. Financing of the real estate is available on favorable terms to the lessor, and the lessor in turn also has considerably less risk as far as either vacancy or the receipt of rent is concerned.

In this situation, annuity capitalization is always applied via the Property Residual Technique. The net operating income under the lease is capitalized as an annuity until the expiration of the lease. The present worth of the anticipated reversion is added to produce the capitalized value of the property. This produces value of the leased fee, which may or may not be equal to the value of the fee simple. The two are equal only when the contract rental under the lease equals the market rental at the time of the appraisal.

Build-to-suit and sale-leaseback transactions are credit oriented. Financing is not available for specialized or custom construction unless there is a high-credit occupant of the real estate.

One aspect of leased fee versus fee simple valuation is the degree in which the contract rental is different from the market rental as of the date of the appraisal. If the contract rental is greater than the market rental, the lessor has the right to collect more rent than he would receive if the property were leased on an open-market basis at the time of the appraisal. This bonus to the lessor means that the leased fee is worth more than the fee simple would be. Many appraisers object to a lease being universally regarded as an "encumbrance," since it often results in enhanced value to the owners.

If the contract rental is less than market rental, the leasehold estate also has value. This is because the right to occupy the space in question over the remaining period of the lease, at a rental that is less than the going market rate, is a value right. It can have market value because it is negotiable and marketable, unless there is a specific prohibition against subletting in the lease.

The problem of the respective values of the leased fee and the leasehold, and of their relationship to the value of the fee simple, is a subject of considerable debate among appraisers. It may be held that the leased fee and the leasehold estate together must always total the value of the fee simple. This is the position taken by the courts in all condemnation proceedings, and the maximum that will be awarded is the value of the fee simple. The division of the award between lessor and lessee is left to settlement between the claimants.

MORTGAGE-EQUITY AND LEVERAGE

Mortgage-equity analysis starts out with the premise that a long-term lease to a well-rated tenant is an asset rather than an encumbrance on the real estate, at least as far as the money market is concerned. On that assumption, leverage is created.

The credit available through the strength of the lease can maximize financing for the borrower. Moreover, the investor is not interested in accounting income as much as cash flow. That is, the actual cash return on his equity investment that comes to the investor is the basis for his evaluation of the attractiveness of the leased commercial or industrial real estate purchase. Cash throw-off (before tax cash flow) is the difference between net operating income and annual mortgage (debt) service charges.

Debt service is important in mortgage-equity analysis. The appraiser must study the mortgage market terms and conditions to ascertain with as high a degree of precision as possible the type of financing that is most likely to be obtained. All mortgage loan terms influence the constant, and hence the amount that is deducted from the annual net income before recapture in order to develop a cash flow projection.

Before-tax cash flow is then capitalized at an appropriate equity yield rate in order to estimate what the investor would be justified or warranted in paying *in cash* for the right to receive the cash flow. *Capital* recovery is gained in part through mortgage amortization and in part through the proceeds of resale or refinancing at the expiration of the capital recapture or turnover period.

Mortgage-equity analysis can also be used to develop an overall rate by which to capitalize net income to a property value conclusion. This can be accomplished both within and outside the framework of the Ellwood formulation. With information that the income projection is 15 years, and that the investor expects to resell the property at 80% of its present value 15 years hence, the following illustration shows the development and application of a mortgage-equity overall rate. This rate takes into consideration both equity buildup through mortgage amortization over the 15-year income projection period, and capital recovery required to cover forecast capital loss in the reversion.

This technique is helpful in investment decision-making, because it shows the investor or borrower what return he will receive on his cash investment.

TYPICAL EXAMPLE OF A
MORTGAGE-EQUITY OVERALL RATE
(Property Residual Technique)

Mortage:	.75 x .096672	=	0.0725
Equity:	.25 x .110000	=	0.0275
			0.1000

Weighted Average
$\overline{\text{Minus Equity Buildup}}$
.4020 x .75 x .0291   = $\underline{0.0087}$
                                                         0.1087

$\underline{\text{Basic Rate}}$
Plus Recapture .20 x .0291   = $\underline{0.0058}$
                                                         0.1145

OVERALL RATE   = 11.45 %
Net Operating Income = $10,000
Therefore, property value is
developed per
$10,000 ÷ 11.45 %   = $87,336
                                   Rounded to: $87,000

THE ELLWOOD PREMISE

It would call for a separate book in itself to go into all the intricacies of real estate investment analysis as promulgated by the late distinguished L. W. Ellwood. Suffice it to say that the Ellwood method, which is now a *required* technique with most institutional lenders and investors, is more refined than ordinary mortgage-equity analysis in that it includes the *anticipated* reversion as part of the overall rate of return to the investor. It is *direct capitalization* that derives from the investment and financial market rather than the real estate sales market for its standards and basic data. It focuses on the *income* importance of commercial and industrial real estate, rather than its physical qualities.

Input of the reversion as one of two important ingredients in the total return that the investor is seeking makes it possible to grasp the implications of different reversions on the equity return. For instance, within the Ellwood structuring, an appraiser can find the difference it would make to the investor's overall rate of return if the property were to decrease by 10% over the capital recapture period, if it were to remain at its present value level, or if it were to appreciate by 5%. Investment real estate, including leased industrial property, often appreciates; in fact, investors often buy with that expectation. The Ellwood analysis makes it possible for the appraiser to counsel the investor not only about the present worth of the property, but about the likelihood that he will realize a particular overall rate of return at the expiration of his recapture period. This can be called the "projection" period.

The Ellwood premise, therefore, diverges from other compositions of capitalization rate in that it demands:

1. A close approximation of total building depreciation at the end of the projection period.
2. An accurate resale value of the property at the end of the term of ownership.
3. An accurate projection of average net income based on an income forecast during each year of the term of ownership, and reflecting any changes in the economic rent beginning with the next term of ownership.
4. A realistic short-term projection period.

5. An equity yield accurately estimated depending upon the owner's risk position which, in turn, is affected by the building location, its quality of construction, and the type and quality of the building tenants.

Appreciation

Finally, the Ellwood Premise emphasizes the truth that, beyond and above the receipt of an annual cash flow from the property during the term of ownership, investors may garner a lump-sum cash reversion when their properties are sold. This cash reversion will be the difference between the resale value and the remaining mortgage balance on the property. Should the cash reversion on resale be greater than the original cash investment, the owner has then earned an added profit called *appreciation;* and it is a part of the total profit picture that induced him to purchase the property in the first place.

William Shakespeare's Measure for Measure *made the point that "comparisons are oft odious." In the appraisal world, comparisons are odious to owners and assessors who have inflated ideas of the values of their properties. But comparisons are sweet to those analysts looking for fair market value or the price at which a knowledgeable buyer will purchase from a willing seller.*

4

The Uses of Market Data or the Comparative Approach

While all three approaches to value are anchored in the *Principle of Substitution,* the Market Data Approach particularly dictates that *the value of a property tends to be set by the cost of acquisition of an equally desirable substitute property, assuming that no costly delay is encountered in making the substitution.*

This stress on the marketplace where actual, recent sales of closely similar properties can be cited in the appraisal report provides proof positive of the claims of property obsolescence and rent loss that the appraiser may have made against his subject in the Cost Approach. He can measure the economic good and bad in his subject property by finding nearby comparable sales that, by their selling prices, illustrate the functional desirability, or decay, in his subject.

In this approach, you literally measure each component of the subject against a similar component in selected comparables to establish the worth of these components in place, as proved by recent sales, yard improvement for yard improvement, brick for brick, elevator for elevator. In both commercial and industrial properties, look for characteristics comparable to the subject in every detail, such as land-to-building ratio, parking, age, use, design, structural refinement, and foreseeable future benefits. Then place an overall value on the subject that is the result of adjustments in the comparables to the subject. The actual adjustments are made as shown below:

Adjustments (for variations)

Sale Price of Comparable Property	Adjustments	Value of Subject
Sale #1—$102,000	$10,200 (10% x $102,000)	= $91,800
Sale #2—$105,000	$15,750 (15% x $105,000)	= $89,250
Sale #3—$ 98,500	$ 4,925 (5% x 98,500)	= $93,575

Adjustments are not guesswork but are carefully based on such factors as time of sale, location of property, physical characteristics of property, and the financial terms of the sale. The appraiser then selects the comparable or comparables most like the subject as indicated by the adjustments.

The Market Data Approach, as the name implies, depends, of course, directly on sales. The prices at which properties sell in the market indicate the reactions of typical investors and users. This is the sternest test of fair market value and most generally clinches the value estimates made in the Cost and Income Approaches.

Of course, before you can use the Market Data Approach, two conditions must obtain:

(1) There must be comparable properties available. (If they are not available, your alternative routes to value are the residual technique under the Income Approach.)

(2) You must have reliable sales data on comparable properties.

Without reliable data, there can be no evaluation of property. The who, what, where, when, and why principle of news reporting can be effectively used in data gathering and it is recommended as the way to develop a factual, pointed report. First, divide the data required into the following categories, then develop the pertinence of each category.

CLASSES OF DATA

1. General data at the national, regional, and city levels
2. General data at the neighborhood level
3. Specific data about the site
4. Specific data about the building
5. Data relevant to comparable sales and adjustments to subject

Data About the Nation, Region, and City

The value and relevance of general data to a specific appraisal depends mainly on the requirements of the assignment. Normally you will find that the appraisal does not require detailed analysis of national economic data. However, in some cases it will be necessary to analyze national economic trends in order to determine their effect on the property being appraised.

The same thing holds true for data at the regional and city levels. The extent of the data needed at these levels will depend on the nature of the assignment. In some cases, you will find it necessary to gather detailed information concerning the economic, political, and social conditions of the region and/or city and to comment on the effect of these data on the property under appraisal.

Neighborhood Data

The neighborhood, of course, is much narrower in scope than are the city, region, and nation. In the neighborhood, you'll find the physical, economic, social, and political influences that directly affect the value and potential of the property under appraisal. The neighborhood is the point at which you begin to zero in on your target.

Notice that the kinds of information needed at the neighborhood level depend on the type of property being appraised. For example, the availability of parking facilities is an important factor to consider if you're analyzing a commercial or industrial area.

Specific Data

Specific data includes information about the site and the building. It also includes comparative data relating to construction costs, sales, and net income of properties similar to the property under appraisal.

(a) *Data Regarding the Site*—Information about the site includes such things as a description of the land (size, shape, topographical features, etc.) and the presence or absence of public improvement (gas, electricity, water, paved streets, sidewalks, etc.).

(b) *Data Regarding the Building*—Building data includes a comprehensive description of the physical improvement and its condition and an analysis of its layout, style, design, and so on.

SOURCES OF DATA

These are common sources where sales price information can be obtained:

1. Recorded deeds at your municipal or county hall of records.
2. Seller or his attorney.
3. Buyer or his attorney.
4. Broker or builder.
5. Multiple listing systems.

Qualified local opinion is a source of data that may help. Bankers and investors who loan against or trade in real estate will provide background and circumstances bearing on questions of value. One should not overlook any source of information, including the Chamber of Commerce or Local Development Commission. Local newspapers often report real estate transactions; news reports can be verified at city hall. Real estate sales are shown in the public records by the transfer of deeds.

DOCUMENTATION OF DATA

Your appraisal report is no better than the data on which it is based. Inaccurate data can only lead to an invalid conclusion about value. Therefore, you must be certain that the data you collect and use is as accurate and free from error as is possible. Some thought given to each item and to the source of that data will give you the basis for deciding what and how much verification is needed. In some cases, data may be verified by seeking the same information from two different sources.

For example, the physical size and shape of a site taken from a deed can be verified by personally inspecting and measuring the site. Perhaps the area where verification is most important is information on comparative sales. Often the sales price involved in a transaction can be inferred by examining the revenue stamps that have been purchased at the time of the transfer of title. However, the amount derived from this source may be either over- or understated and should be used as a starting point only.

Every sale used in an appraisal must be verified, preferably with the buyer, the seller, and/or the broker.

Accumulating a Data Bank

Generally you will spend much of your time working in the same geographic area. Therefore, it is likely that you have compiled a substantial volume of general data about the nation and about the region, city, and neighborhoods in which you operate. Since this information will be appropriate in many assignments, you can file and keep this information for repeated use, thus saving time and expense on future assignments.

A general data file is important to the appraiser. It must be continually reviewed to keep it up to date. For example, the election of new city administration with strong and differing views about zoning from the previous administration may result in sudden and significant impact on valuation. Or, the move of a major industry in or out of an area could have a great effect on the value of property in the area.

Some typical data-gathering forms in general use with commercial/industrial property appraisers are exhibited on following pages in the order of their positions in the making of an appraisal.

NATIONAL, REGIONAL, AND CITY PROGRAM

National Overview

1. Economic history and trends of the subject business or industry:
   (a) If industrial, what are the prospects for expansion and development of subject enterprise? Where are principal markets and sources of raw materials?
   (b) If commercial, chain store, motel, service station, etc., what are national volume of sales, marketing techniques, number of outlets, management practices, etc.?

2. Government legislation affecting the enterprise nationally, such as tight credit regulations promulgated by the Federal Reserve, plans for gasoline rationing, energy conservation, fair trade employment, etc.

Regional and City Data

1. Prospects. Macro-market influences of area economic situation measured against the micro-market demand for commercial/industrial growth in the city. In measuring local economic conditions, the following factors must be scrutinized:
   (a) Population of the municipality and the area within a 15-mile radius. Forms of transportation within the municipality and to and from subject location. Chief forms of employment within the locale, and estimate of present and future employment levels.

    (b) The amount and substance of commerce and industry in the area, and its contribution to the growth of the locale. The city's importance as an industrial, commercial, or cultural (university) center.

    (c) The planning and zoning practices, the tax policies, and local ordinances affecting the property and the neighborhood must be noted.

    (d) Cultural and recreational facilities provided, including theaters, museums, libraries, parks, sports centers, and clubs.

    (e) Seasonal conditions and the prevailing climate.

2. <u>Market analysis of the neighborhood.</u> Micro-market data concerning the immediate vicinity of the proposed or existing commercial or industrial building should be set forth as follows:

    (a) Assuming that highest and best use (See chapter 5) of the site is confirmed for your subject, with public transportation and automobile parking at hand, and shopping not far away, is the neighborhood conducive to commercial and/or industrial zoning and development? Are there evidences of traffic congestion, air pollution, or other inharmonious elements?

    (b) Describe trends in the district or neighborhood. What is family income level here? What is average family size and composition? Is police and fire service at hand? Are medical services adequate? Is garbage removal service frequent and efficient?

A systematic way to garner such data is exemplified on the following suggested form.

NEIGHBORHOOD DATA FORM

1. AREA ENCOMPASSED BY THE DISTRICT, OR NEIGHBORHOOD:_____

2. LAND VALUE TREND: UPWARD □ DOWNWARD □
    STABLE □ RATE PER YEAR___%

3. ECONOMIC FACTORS:
    a) ZONING_____PERCENT BUILT UP_____
    b) PRICE RANGE OF TYPICAL PROPERTIES:

       FROM $_____ TO $_____

    c) PREDOMINANT TYPE BUILDING:_____TYPICAL AGE:_____TO_____
    d) OWNER OCCUPANCY PERCENTAGE_____
       RENTAL OCCUPANCY PERCENTAGE_____
    e) MARKETABILITY: GOOD □ FAIR □ POOR □

4. UTILITIES
    a) ELECTRICITY   □ e) GAS   □ i) STREET LIGHTING □
    b) WATER   □ f) TELEPHONE   □ j) RAIL SERVICE   □
    c) SEWERAGE   □ g) SIDEWALK   □ k) WATERFRONT   □
    d) STREET SURFACING □ h) FIRE HYDRANT □ l) EASEMENTS   □

5. SPECIAL ASSESSMENT: OUTSTANDING_____EXPECTED_____

6. TAX RATE:_____ RATIO:_____

7. DISTANCE FROM SCHOOLS, CHURCHES, SHOPPING, BANKS, RESTAURANTS, RECREATION_____.

8. PUBLIC TRANSPORTATION: BUS:___RAIL:___SUBWAY:___AIRPORT:___

9. TYPES OF SERVICES OFFERED IN THE NEIGHBORHOOD:
   a) POLICE AND FIRE PROTECTION □   c) DELIVERY SERVICES □
   b) GARBAGE COLLECTION   □   d) OTHERS (specify)_____

10. SPECIAL TRAFFIC PROBLEMS_____

11. ADVERSE ELEMENTS: (smoke, odors, flooding, etc.)_____

12. ECONOMIC BACKGROUND OF RESIDENTS:
    a) MEDIAN FAMILY INCOME $_____TO $_____NO. OF FAMILIES_____
    b) PREDOMINANT COMMERCIAL EVIDENCES:_____
    c) PREDOMINANT INDUSTRIAL EVIDENCES:_____
    d) PREDOMINANT OCCUPATIONS AND SKILLS:_____

13. HIGHWAY ACCESSES FOR (COMMERCIAL) PATRONAGE FROM OTHER PARTS OF CITY AND SUBURBS:_____

14. HIGHWAY AND RAIL LINKS FOR (INDUSTRIAL) RAW MATERIAL IN-TAKE AND PRODUCT DISTRIBUTION:_____

Information collected on the foregoing data sheet should be synthesized, capsuled, and put into terse narrative form so that the client can read it in an easy, comprehensive study. The information herein collected makes up the *initial* part of your market survey (if commercial property) or your labor-distribution survey (if industrial). The site and building data following this completes your survey of supply and demand for land, buildings, goods, and services in the community. You might set up the format for this data as follows.

SAMPLE NARRATIVE
National, Regional, City, and Neighborhood Data

Subject property is situated in the Northeast Corridor (New England shoreline) between New York City and Boston. This area was severely distressed last year by the energy crisis, as there are no oil refineries or pipelines in the area. Consequently, subject plant was forced to switch from oil to gas firing for heat and process refrigeration during the past year. Gas itself is interruptible in this region and subject plant has had to store propane for outages.

The state of the national economy and pressure on the industry itself, as the result of fierce anti-trust activity, has squeezed subject company into deep retrenchments, and subject plant personnel force has recently been reduced by one-third. Late last year, the Justice Department brought suit against subject company. This year could see similar action against other national food processors.

City Data

Telford covers an area of 19.5 square miles
Length: north and south 8.3 miles
Width: east and west 2.5 miles
Geographical center at Main Street and Huntington Road

Population

1950—33,600   1960—45,012   1970—49,775

Transportation*

Central Vermont Railroad
Penn Central Transportation Company
U.S. Route No. 2, Belt Parkway, Connecticut Turnpike
Harbor facilities, navigable river
(Fish are brought in by ship)
Truck terminals
Municipal airport

*Frozen food product distribution to New York, Boston, Albany, and Worcester by refrigerated air, truck, and railroad tank car is thus readily and inexpensively accomplished.

Tax Rate

47.3 mills

City, Neighborhood, and Location

In Rhode Island on the shores of Narragansett Bay. Subject is in Telford Meadows neighborhood, near airport, at about ten feet above sea level.
160 Miles East of New York City
8 Miles East of Providence

Labor

Skilled and semiskilled labor pool, with aircraft, automotive, food products, lingerie, chemicals, and hardware trades in prominence

Fire Department

Central headquarters and two district fire stations
Ten pieces of modern fire equipment
Personnel—98

Police Department

Nine radio police cars equipped as auxiliary ambulances
P.A.L.—youth bureau
Personnel—107

Water

Excellent quality and quantity furnished by
the Telford Hydraulic Company

Gas

Natural gas supplied by
the People's Gas Company

Recreation

15 playgrounds, 14 major parks, 17 small parks (neighborhood)
Three town-owned beaches
Roger Williams Forest (250 acres in natural state)
Waterfront property, boating and fishing facilities
Three yacht clubs
The immediate neighborhood surrounds a Little League field and is bordered
to the south by town dock and boatyard.

Industrial and Business Sites

Competitive sites being developed by
Economic Development Commission (railroad and river facilities)
The immediate neighborhood is in a phase of development, with about half of
available industrial sites improved.

Zoning

Adequate zoning and planning regulations governing
residential, commercial and industrial areas
This immediate neighborhood is zoned M-2, for light Industry, with commercial shopping and professional zone about 500 yards east.

Housing

385 new units under the Telford Housing Authority
Providing for moderate income and elderly citizens
in the immediate neighborhood of subject
Providing ready pool of office help and skilled personnel

Government

Council-manager plan for 52 years

Telford Industries

Ashland Steel Drum Co. —————————————————— containers
Atomic Tool Company ——————————————————tools and dies
Auto Zoom, Inc. ——————————————————hardware
Bevers Rolling Mills —————————————————— foundry
Bluebonnet Dairy—————————————————milk products
Brewer Press ————————————————— printing
Burke Enameled Wire Company, Inc. ————————— insulated wire and cable
Carson Building Materials ————————————————— lumber mill

Chelton Mold Company, Inc. ————————————— plastic molds
Chisholm Oxygen Corporation ————————— welding products
Contract Plating Company, Inc.————————————plating
Diamond-Products Corporation ————————————plastics
E. Z. Heater Company—————————— electrical appliances
Gyromat Corporation————————— paint spray equipment
Jaeger Corrugated Box Company ————————— paperboard boxes
Keyes Equipment, Inc. ————————————— automotive parts
Lariat Division Aero Mfg. Company————————— aircraft engines
Miller Manufacturing Company ————————— sheet metal
Norton Rubber Company ————————————rubber products
Quik Products, Inc. ————————————— aluminum foundry
R & R Diecast Company————————————————machine parts
Salt & Roberts, Inc. ————————————— plastics
Steel Shields, Inc. —————————————————— typesetting
Super Belt Tire Company, Inc. ————————————tire reworking
True Bearing Company ——————————— bearings
U. S. Bevel Corporation ——————————————machine tools
Wellworn, Inc. ———————————————————— lingerie
X. Y. Z. Corporation ———————————————— chemicals

Data Sources

1. Telford Annual Report
2. U. S. Bureau of the Census
3. State Department of Commerce
4. Telford Chamber of Commerce
5. State Department of Environmental Protection
6. State Department of Transportation

In addition to the above listed, your appraisers gathered area information from local bankers, brokers, builders, newspapermen, and registered surveyors.

SITE DATA FORM

1. STREET ADDRESS
2. PARCEL DESCRIPTION:
   a) WIDTH:_____ d) FRONTAGE:_____
   b) DEPTH:_____ e) SHAPE:_____
   c) AREA: _____ f) ROUGHED:_____CLEARED:____
3. UTILITIES:
   a) ELECTRICITY   □   e) FIRE HYDRANTS   □
   b) WATER   □   f) GAS   □
   c) SEWERAGE   □   g) TELEPHONE   □
   d) STREET SURFACING   □   h) SIDEWALK   □
4. TOPOGRAPHY:

   LOT IN RELATION TO STREET GRADE: EVEN □ ABOVE □ BELOW □

LANDSCAPING □ TREES □   ROCK □
TOPSOIL □ THICKNESS_____
SUBSOIL: GOOD DRAINAGE □ POOR DRAINAGE □

5. ZONING:_____

6. DEED RESTRICTIONS: YES □ NO □
         SPECIFY:_____

7. EASEMENTS AND ENCROACHMENTS: YES □ NO □
         SPECIFY:_____

8. TAX RATE:_____
         PROPERTY TAXES AS COMPARED TO THOSE IN COMPETING
         LOCALITIES: HIGH □ LOW □ SAME □

9. SPECIAL ASSESSMENTS: OUTSTANDING_____
                         EXPECTED: _____

BUILDING DATA FORM

1. AGE OF BUILDING(S):_____ 2. OUTSIDE DIMENSIONS:_____

3. NUMBER OF STORIES:_____ 4. TYPE OF CONSTRUCTIONS:_____

5. RENTABLE AREA IN SQ. FT.:_____ 6. USE:_____

7. LAND AREA:_____ 8. PARKING AREA:_____

9. FOUNDATION:_____ 10. BASEMENT:_____

11. FRAME:_____ 12. SIDING:_____

13. WALLS:_____ 14. INTERIORS:_____

15. FLOORS:_____ 16. SUBFLOORING:_____

17. ROOF:_____ 18. GUTTERS:_____

19. LIGHTING:_____ 20. VENTILATING:_____

21. HEATING:_____ 22. AIR CONDITIONING:_____

23. PLUMBING:_____ 24. WIRING:_____

25. PARTITIONS:_____ 26. WINDOWS:_____

27. CRANEWAYS:_____ 28. RAIL SIDING:_____

29. TRUCK DOCKS:_____ 30. WATERFRONT:_____

31. EXTERIOR CONDITION:_____ 32. INTERIOR CONDITION:_____

33. NO. OF LAVATORIES:_____ 34. POWER VOLTAGE:_____

35. CEILING HEIGHTS:_____ 36. YARD IMPROVEMENTS: (such as stand-
37. ELEVATORS:_____   pipes, fencing, signs, outdoor lighting, silos,
                                    storage tanks, paved areas, water wells,
                                    docks, underground piping and wiring,
                                    tunnels, trestles, rail sidings, and
                                    landscaping)

COMPARABLE SALES DATA FORM

1. LOCATION:_____   REMARKS:_____
2. SELLER:_____   _____
   BUYER:_____   _____
3. DATE OF SALE:_____   RECORDED: BOOK___; PAGE_____
4. BUILDING AREA:_____   CONDITION:_____
5. VERIFIED SALES PRICE:_____   VERIFIED BY:_____
6. PRICE PER SQUARE FOOT:_____   _____
7. ZONE:_____   FINANCING:_____
8. LAND AREA:_____   ACCESS:_____
9. DIMENSIONS:_____   ROAD FRONTAGE:_____
10. UTILITIES ATTACHED:_____   RAIL, DOCK OR OTHER:_____
11. PARKING AREA:_____   SPECIAL SERVICES:_____

SALES ADJUSTMENT SHEET

Adjustments to Subject	Sale #1	Sale #2	Sale #3	Sale #4	Sale #5	Sale #6
Date of Sale						
Sale Price						
Area in Square Feet						
Sale Price Per Sq. Ft.						
Time Adjustment						
Location Adjustment						
Site Characteristics						
Composite Adjustment						
Adjusted Price Per Sq. Ft.						

The principles of real property uses are anchored in economics. Because appraising is the valuation of the rights of use of real property, these fundamentals of economics are the basic principles of valuation. A practical knowledge of these principles is necessary to your grasp of the approaches, techniques, and procedures of appraising.

5

Key Principles to Be Weighed in Measuring Value

The term "real estate" denotes the land and all materials permanently attached to it. "Real property" refers to the rights of use of the physical real estate, otherwise known as the "bundle of rights." Included in the bundle are the right to use the real estate, to sell it, to lease it, or to give it away, and the right *not* to do anything with it.

No one possesses *real estate*—the land itself. It is only select property rights—*real property*—that are bought and sold in the marketplace. Some rights, however, have been taken away by the following four powers of government:

(a) *Police*—Power to regulate property for the health and general welfare of the public. Building codes, zoning ordinances, traffic regulations, and sanitary regulations are based upon the police power of government.

(b) *Taxation*—Power to tax the real estate for support of government and to sell the property if taxes are not paid.

(c) *Escheat*—Power to have property revert to the state when there are no legal heirs.

(d) *Eminent Domain*—Power to take property by condemnation for public use, provided just compensation is paid.

THE DIFFERENCE BETWEEN REAL PROPERTY AND PERSONAL PROPERTY

The term "personal property" denotes tangible items not permanently attached to and part of the real estate, such as a window, air conditioner, refrigerator, or forklift truck.

In some states there is a different category of assessable personal property that is intangible in nature, such as cash, securities, patents, and copyrights. We will not discuss further either tangible or intangible classes of personal property in this book. We mention personal property only because there are times in commercial and industrial appraising where judgment is needed to decide whether something is real estate or personal property. Appraisers usually differentiate by deciding:

(1) How the item is attached (permanent or nonpermanent)
(2) The intent of the person who attached it (to leave the item permanently or to remove it at some future date)

Specifically, an item remains personal property if it can be removed without serious injury either to the real estate or to the item itself.

KEY FACTORS IN DETERMINING HIGHEST AND BEST USE

Highest and best, or most likely profitable, use of real property is that use that prudence dictates will, over a reasonably foreseeable period of time, produce for the typical owner the highest net return of use benefits, thus reflecting the highest capital asset value, and will, generally, at the same time preserve the utility of the property.

In general, when buildings constitute a substantial part of the total fair market value of a property, the remaining economic life of the improvements and the preservation of the utility of the property are extremely important factors in determining that use that will produce the highest capital value and in consequence be considered as the highest and best use of the property.

Highest and best use is a most important principle and must always be given primary consideration and dealt with specifically in appraisal reports. It is a major factor of fair market value as pointed out by an 1894 U.S. Supreme Court decision that:

> The value of the property results from the use to which it is put and varies with the profitableness of that use, the present and prospective, actual and anticipated. There is no pecuniary value aside from that which results from such use—the amount and profitable character of such use determines the value.

Example

A 100,000-square-foot-plant sits on 15 acres with a deep and extensive frontage on a major shopping and office boulevard near a metropolitan core. The frontage is zoned commercial to a depth of 400', and the property is abutted on one side by a regional shopping center, and on the other by a major corporate office complex. Both abutting property owners want to purchase the 15-acre site, tear down the plant, and expand their own commercial operations. The owner of the plant hesitates to sell to them because he wants to expand his plant, which is doing well there. He asks an appraiser to guide him as to highest and best use for his property. Commercial land in this neighborhood is worth about $5.00 per square foot, and industrial land with rail service in nearby areas is worth about $2.00 per square foot.

Many things must be considered in estimating highest and best use, including: supply and demand; competitive properties; use conformity; size of the land and possible economic type and size of structures or improvements that may be placed thereon; zoning; building restrictions; neighborhood or vicinity trends. The principle of highest and best use has some of its most practical applications in condemnation procedure under eminent domain powers where purchasing parts or ownership, or flowage, clearance and other types of easements. The value of the part left to an owner, after a partial taking, is governed largely by the highest and best use of the owner's remainder after the taking. It is, therefore, extremely important that great care be used in estimating and supporting an opinion of the highest and best use of the remainder in such cases.

Applying the Principle of Balance

The law of balance, in appraising, holds that value is originated and stabilized in the equilibrium reached through essential uses of real estate. The value of a property is dominated by the balance of the four agents in production, as follows:

1. Labor (wages).
2. Management (entrepreneur coordination).
3. Capital (investment in buildings and equipment).
4. Land.

When the agents in production are in proportionate balance to one another, the property's maximum value is achieved. There is a theoretical point of balance in every property that will produce the greatest net return.

An imbalance obtains when a building is too small or too large for the investment in its site, and now it becomes an *underimprovement or overimprovement.* Imbalance also occurs where the cost of services such as mall maintenance, fancy garden fountains, security guards, and escalators in a shopping center are too little or too much for the building, its class or tenancy, and its rent roll. The principle of balance says that loss in value occurs when there is an excess or deficiency in the contribution of the *four productive agents* as they affect one another.

The principle of balance is used in estimating highest and best use. The proportioning of the agents in production is fundamental if maximum net return is to be produced and maximum land value developed. Because land has last claim on the gross income produced by the careful balancing of the four agents, *the land is residual.*

Example

This technique applies when the value of the land cannot be accurately estimated by the Market Data Approach. It is used to estimate the value of the land by capitalizing the net income imputable to the land at a reasonable rate and would be applied, for instance, to re-evaluating the land under a large shopping center that had achieved its peak percentage of gross rentals above the guaranteed base rentals that originally financed its construction.

The Theory of Surplus Productivity

The net income remaining after the costs of labor, management, and capital have been paid is *surplus productivity*. This surplus can be credited to the land, and it increases the land's value in the use to which it is assigned. Surplus productivity rests upon *the principle of balance,* the law of increasing and decreasing returns, and the proportioning of the four agents in production. It is the greatest net return to the land, which, when capitalized at a reasonable rate, gives value to the land. Highest and best use of the land is shown by the greatest net yield produced by trial and test of proportioning the four agents in production. Referring to the large shopping center again, which has achieved its peak percentages of gross rentals, the owner can now refinance the shopping center for far more than he could at the time of its construction, because his land value has increased substantially.

THE PRINCIPLE OF SUPPLY AND DEMAND

In economic terms, "supply" means the quantity of objects that are offered for sale at various prices in a given market. "Demand" (desire) refers to the quantity of objects that will be purchased at various prices. The price of a property is set by the relation between the supply of its type and the demand for it. If the supply is great as compared with the demand, the price will be low. If the supply is small as compared with the demand, the price will be high.

The poles of supply and demand oscillate with the winds of change. Local changes in population growth, purchasing power, price and wage levels, transportation facilities, taxation and government controls are factors in addition to scarcity that influence the ratio between supply and demand in a given area.

Key Factors

1. Scarcity of labor, and high wage rates, can carry the cost of building beyond the purchasing power of the market, discouraging builders from adding to the supply.
2. Government regulations, such as rent control, tightening of mortgage money, and zoning regulations, affect supply and demand by the restrictions they insist upon.

THE PRINCIPLE OF CHANGE

Change may be slow or rapid, progressive and regressive by turns, but it is always at work. Some changes are mere fad. Some are deep and far ranging, but both kinds affect real property, turning good neighborhoods into poor ones, turning deserts into oil fields, transforming farms into coal fields.

Example

As an appraiser you cannot with absolute precision define all the forces that may appear in the future to change the character of a specific property, a commercial district, or a city. But reasonable interpretations of probable directions, based on your best judgment, are desirable. Is the new hotel in the center of a decaying city core going to fare better than the new motel near the airport? Is the gasoline station on an interior lot in a congested traffic area going to survive?

Look to the market for future benefits. Watch for the pattern of coming events. The market value of a property recently sold is seldom based on a price paid for it in the past, or on the cost to produce it. Its price indicates what the owners believe it will do for them in the future. The marketplace will tell you much about the district's future trend. Income data in the form of rising or falling comparable rentals are sure-fire trend indicators.

THE PRINCIPLE OF SUBSTITUTION

When property is replaceable, its value tends to be set at the cost of acquisition of an equally well-located and useful substitute property. That which may be substituted may be either a replica structure, a similar structure with equivalent functional utility, or an investment having an equal degree of increment opportunity. Thus, the fair market value of a property is to a major extent limited and controlled by the value of similar available properties having like utility and comparable locations, characteristics, and foreseeable future benefits. The Principle of Substitution is important to the Market Data Approach and the Cost Approach.

Example

On one side of the major artery in an industrial neighborhood is a 15-year old, continuous-casting aluminum plant of 400,000 square feet on 20 acres. The owner believes he is overassessed by the County Tax Commission at $10.00 per square foot. He hires an appraiser to evaluate his plant for an ad valorem tax appeal. The appraiser finds, in looking for comparatives, that there is a 12-year old plant about a mile away on the opposite side of the same artery, of similar construction and use, and with almost identical manufacturing, office, and warehouse areas, that has just been sold for $3.75 per square foot, land and buildings. He also finds two other plants further away, but in the same industrial zone, that have sold within the past five years at $3.50 and $4.00 per square foot. The aluminum manufacturer then decides to retain legal counsel; then the attorney and the appraiser go before the Tax Board with their findings, invoking the Principle of Substitution. What conclusion must the Board reach? That the assessment of $10.00 per square foot, land and buildings, for the plaintiff is way out of line, of course. The plaintiff is awarded a reduction in assessment to $3.75. The Principle of Substitution was the vehicle for the Board's decision.

INCREASING AND DECREASING RETURNS

The rule of "diminishing returns" is that larger and larger investments in structures and improvements on land will produce larger and larger net income *up to a certain point* at which the maximum of valuation will be developed and beyond which point any additional investments will not produce a commensurate return for the additional investments.

Bigger is not necessarily better. Floors or wings added to an apartment house or an office building that is short on parking space for tenants, deliveries, and visitors could cause the property to become less desirable to incumbents and prospective tenants, driving down the income from the structure, thus making the investment a waste, diminishing present maximum return.

THE PRINCIPLE OF CONTRIBUTION

This is actually the law of *increasing and decreasing returns,* as it applies to some aspects of real property. It affirms that the value of an item in production is accounted for by its contribution to the net return of the enterprise. In this regard, enterprise connotes the combination of all items in production, such as land, buildings, and other improvements.

The Principle of Contribution has practical application in many valuation problems; it must be considered before undertaking a modernization or remodeling job; i.e., is the future of the property worth the investment?

Example

The owners of an industrial warehouse property are told by the tenant that rental can be increased on a new lease if the owners will install a new, air-conditioned office section. The cost of these improvements amounts to $50,000. The tenant, however, is offering an increase of $10,000 per annum for only five years, which is no real contribution to net income. The problem might be solved, for example, by negotiation extending the lease to ten years at the same rental.

THE PRINCIPLE OF COMPETITION

This principle affirms that profit may excite competition, and that excess profit can attract disastrous competition. Profit is that residue of net income from real property over and above the costs of labor, management, capital, and land.

Example

Merchants who first locate in, say, a new shopping center in a suburban area where merchandising services have long been needed are apt to make unusually large profits. Competing merchants are then drawn to the district, putting up their own structures or leasing new locations, and they begin to share in the total amount of business.

The volume of business originally going to the pioneer merchants declines, and so do their net incomes. This can continue to the point where none of the merchants makes a fair return.

Because the value of land rests upon the use producing the greatest return, competition, in this instance, by spoiling the net return, has reduced the net yield to the land, hence diminishing the value of the land. Profit will evaporate if competitive forces build up beyond economic demand. Too many bowling alleys, too many shopping centers, or too many gasoline service stations in one area result in starvation for many of them.

THE PRINCIPLE OF CONFORMITY

Conformity of use can be seen in the harmonious grouping of retail stores in any primary retail district. Experience has taught the merchant that he can achieve a larger sales volume if his store is located near other stores selling the same type and quality of goods. Have you noticed that Safeway, First National, Shop-Rite, and Pathmark often cluster together within a block or two?

Example

On the contrary, the same teacher has ruled that success rarely comes to the merchant handling an expensive line of merchandise if he locates in a district where the same types of goods are sold but they are of inferior quality. You can bet that Neiman-Marcus in Dallas will not locate across the street from a bakery-stale-goods-thrift-shop, even with unlimited customer parking and a Sheraton Motel built into the picture.

THE PRINCIPLE OF ANTICIPATION

People buy future benefits when purchasing real property. The Principle of Anticipation accounts for value created by benefits expected in the future. It is the future, not the past, that is important in estimating value. The only importance past experience has is when it points to possible future developments in real property. The investor purchasing commercial property has done so *anticipating* income he will receive from the investment, but in deciding to buy the property he had to examine its past income. In examining income history, the buyer had to discover the magnetisms that brought the property that income. He examines the income data to review all influences, adverse or progressive, to form an opinion as to whether the income stream will decline in a few years or is likely to level off or increase in the future.

While "value" may be defined as *the worth of all present and future benefits deriving from ownership,* the quality, quantity, and duration of these benefits in the future must be estimated against past experience, if there is such a history; or measured against start-up probabilities, if there is no history.

Example

For instance, today an investor might build and lease to a major oil company on a near right-hand corner location with good frontage approach at a country crossroads, which he knows from trend indications is going to

82   MEASURING VALUE

become the center of a new suburb in 10 years. He knows that in its first year
it will pump about 150,000 gallons. He also knows that a bank is dickering for
the corner diagonally opposite, and that a restaurant and stores are to be
built directly across the street. On the strength of this knowledge, he has
managed to interest the petroleum company (who also has carefully
researched the market promises of the locale) in a twenty-year lease,
because they now believe that the station will be pumping 400,000 gallons a
year in 10 years, 600,000 gallons a year in 15 years, and 900,000 gallons a
year in 20 years. Thus, everyone interested in the country-crossroads, both
sides of both streets, is applying the Principle of Anticipation to present
worth. Capitalization of the new facility would, therefore, be high in the early
(risk) years, becoming lower as a proven income history develops.

CYCLICAL TRENDS

The appraiser of commercial and industrial property determines the rhythm of a
property's life cycle within its locale and articulates the phase in the life of the district he
is analyzing. He must know a property's age to forecast the life of its income stream. To
this end, the appraiser allows for the *Principle of Integration and Disintegration,* which
avers that the cycles of existence are cadenced in three stages: first, integration, or birth;
second, stasis, or equilibrium; and finally disintegration, or death, after which a renewal
of life on a new foundation is possible, which may be called redevelopment.

The growth factor in a cycle also takes into account trend-making influences such
as the principles of *regression* and *progression,* which are logical extensions of the
Principles of Conformity and Change. *Regression* suggests that the value of a superior
property suffers by the introduction of a less-valuable property as neighbor. *Progression*
holds that the value of the lesser property is enhanced by adjacent association with a
superior property.

CORRELATING KEY VALUE PRINCIPLES

There is a warp and woof relationship among all the principles discussed in this
chapter. They are textured into one another by the same web of social and economic
dynamics listed in chapter 1. Each principle is linked and interwoven into a fabric of
cyclical cause and effect, and each must be applied in a given appraisal with care and
thought, as an influence builds into a trend, and the trend becomes part of a cycle.

Industrial properties are affected by technological changes. Solid-state transistors
eliminated the bulkier tubes of yesteryear, condensing the space needed for their
manufacture. Airports reduced the importance of large railroad terminals. Whole new
cities are being built around airports. Commercial properties are equally affected by
changes in modes of transportation, gasoline shortages, taxation policies, and fads and
fashions.

MODEL TREND STUDY

Over the past 30 years, a huge number of shopping centers sprouted
from coast to coast as eager developers and retailers joined in a race to put

the stores where the people were. However, there have been huge migratory shifts to dislocate many of these centers.

A third of the nation's population moved from the urban and rural areas into the cities' sprawling suburbs, sinking their roots and expanding their families. But for many, these were way-station stops en route to other cities. Quick on their heels came about 15,000 shopping centers, planted in former potato and tomato fields, leading to a new way of shopping, helping local economies, and even creating new socio-economic communities. This also led to the creation of new highways and criticism for massive air pollution.

Some retailers, however, whose business is dominated by suburban branch stores, have been cancelling plans for new stores or are spreading out the opening dates of planned stores. And the centers being planned are more practical, less ambitious, and smaller than their predecessors.

Reasons for the shopping center-building slowdown are sharply increased construction costs, high land costs, high interest rates, a slower rate of retail sales, and increasing environmental and zoning structures by communities.

For developers, the burdensome pressures of difficult economics and erratic sales by many tenants are intensified by numerous store closings. Major closings were made early in this decade by such chains as Arlen's Department Stores, S. Klein, W. T. Grant, the Great Atlantic & Pacific Tea Company, Interstate Stores, McCrory, Mammoth Mart and Bohack. Replacing such tenants is not, of course, easy.

The big problem may be just too many centers and too much competition. In Bridgeport, Conn., Gimbel Brothers announced it was closing its store in a shopping center. The opening of four or five larger centers within a 15-mile radius had created a vast wave of new competition, weaning customers away from the older ones.

As Albert Sussman, executive vice president of the International Council of Shopping Centers, said, "The facts of life are that the tenant's rentals must cover the higher construction costs, higher taxes and higher maintenance costs that the center pays for."

In the years ahead, centers will not only be smaller, but they will also contain fewer small stores, according to industry leaders. Developers will both economize and attempt to eliminate internal competition by cutting back on the amount of space they provide for small shops.

Another, possibly long-term, change will be centers with fewer frills and more practicality, all in the interests of lower construction costs and thus lower rentals. Removal of only one foot in a "cube" dimension—from the space between the roof and the ground—could eliminate as much as $150,000 to $300,000 from the center's building cost.

The shopping-center trend, which may have fostered the suburban way-of-life as much as followed it, is losing momentum. The implications of this stasis may indicate a "back to the big city" trend, with convenient mass transportation to all points, and a surge in big-city neighborhood stores.

The question that must be always uppermost in the appraiser's mind as he approaches any given parcel of land is: Can this location be the right one for the use assigned to it? Can the parcel be subdivided to accommodate several uses?

6

The Underlying Question:
Location and Land Evaluation

Location is the single most important influence on land value in commercial or industrial uses. The apartment house "on the wrong side of the tracks" or the factory not near enough to the railroad tracks and major trucking highways is in trouble.

In the evaluation of vacant commercial and industrial land, the Market Data Approach is employed by gathering comparables and recent nearby land sales on record in the local assessors' office. If the land is vacant this is the *only* way to evaluate a parcel, except for capitalizing the value of any land *leases* nearby and adjusting these values to the similarities of your subject property. If there are no recent recorded sales or leases of nearby land, then the appraiser must extend his radius of comparatives further afield, a mile, two miles, five miles, until he finds likenesses to his subject.

If his subject is improved, however, with a fairly *new* structure, and he cannot find nearby land comparables, then he can turn to the Land Residual Technique to find subject land value. But this is a last resort to land value, and the appraiser should bend every effort to find market data (comparable land sales) before turning to last-ditch positions.

LAND EVALUATION CHECKLIST

In commencing an assignment for the appraisal of land (vacant or improved), you can best organize your procedure by making a checklist as follows:

1. Visit the owner, his attorney, or other representative to whom you are referred, and make a definite appointment with him for your inspection of the site. Tell him that it will make matters easier for him and for you if he will have the following "package" ready for you when you make your inspection. (Invite him to accompany you on this inspection.)

(a) Map, or registered survey of land, with any easements, subdivisions, mineral rights, air rights, or liens duly noted.

(b) Legal description, or assessment reference, with latest paid property tax bill receipted.

(c) Plat plan—that is, a map of the land, with the buildings(s) located on it if the land is not vacant. (If the land is vacant, the survey (a) is sufficient.)

(d) Blueprints of the building(s).

(e) Aerial, bird's-eye view or ground-level photographs.

(f) Any information he may have concerning recent sales or leases of land and/or buildings in the area, and same zone.

(g) Tax data—assessments, tax rate and ratio, special assessments, zone or zones of subject.

(h) How the property is to be appraised—in fee simple or otherwise. That is, are only partial rights or easements to be evaluated?

2. Upon your inspection of the premises, note carefully the type of neighborhood in which the property is situated, and the kind and number of arteries and road accesses serving it.

(a) If the land is not vacant but improved, set up a Depreciation Schedule in your notes: Physical obsolescence, having to do with the age and condition of the building(s). Functional obsolescence, having to do with operational utility or inutility of the improvements, and, if there is inutility or obsolescence, is it curable or incurable? Economic obsolescence, having to do with outside influences on the property, in the neighborhood, in the region, or in terms of regional or national legislation affecting the use of the property.

(b) After checking out the land (vacant or improved), call on one, two, or three prominent local Realtors to ask if they can provide you with recent comparable land sales; sales (if improved) of comparable land and buildings sold as a unit; rentals of similar space, if the land is improved; or land leases of similar parcels, if vacant.

(c) Now go to the town hall, check out your zone, assessments, tax rate, ration, etc., and see if the town clerk has a monograph or other descriptive material on the history and economy of the municipality, including zoning regulations.

(d) Visit the Chamber of Commerce, Board of Trade, or other civic promotion groups like an Urban Renewal Authority, Development Commission, etc., to pick up all *current area data,* forecasts, growth or decline patterns, and the vital statistics of the municipality and/or county and state.

(e) Now check everything you have gathered together. Are your comparable sales truly similar? Have you photographed all your comparables, rentals as well as sales? Is your property description complete? *Utilities? Accesses? Fencing? Paving? Railroad Siding?* Take careful note of the surface and subsoil condition of subject site. Detail the size, shape, topography, and drainage features of the site.

In the evaluation of any commercial or industrial site, use of the foregoing checklist will provide you with the following information:

Commutation (Accessibility and Transportation):
    Range of choice as to mode
    Time
    Costs
    Reliability (on-time performance)
    Safety (of person and property)
    Comfort (environmental qualities)
    Conveniences (surrounding the location)
Taxes: Real property and personalty.
Zoning: Regional and local planning practices.
Shopping: Variety, proximity, banking, and parking
    facilities for these services.
Schooling and Churches:
    Opportunities for further study,
    Ecclesiastical training and social activities.
Cultural Facilities and Proximity:
    Universities, libraries, museums, etc.
Recreational Variety and Proximity:
    Spectator sports
    Participatory sports
    Performing arts, theaters, concert halls
    Restaurants

SPECIAL ASPECTS OF SEPARATING
LAND VALUE FROM BUILDING VALUE

In the evaluation of commercial or industrial property, the improvements must be separately evaluated in order to apply depreciation as a deduction against the property's income under federal income tax regulations. For federal income tax purposes, the owner of improved commercial or industrial property can apply depreciation only to the improvements—not to the land, which physically remains unchanged even though it may rise or fall in value. For this purpose, the depreciable value of the improvements must begin at the time of construction or acquisition. Thus, the appraiser must differentiate between the current market value of land versus improvements.

Moreover, separation of land and building is vital in applying the Income Approach to value. The Building Residual Technique is an avenue of the Income Approach. A rational rate of return on the land value is taken away from the net income earned by the total property in this technique. Therefore, a separate land value is paramount.

Segregated land value may also be needed in the Residual Technique where you are appraising properties with long-term leases. Here one must estimate what the land will be worth at the end of the structure's economic life, or at the termination of the lease. This estimate will be assumed as present value unless there is reason to believe that the land will become more or less desirable.

In most states appraisals made for condemnation purposes require that land and buildings be separately evaluated and that the appraiser testify to separated values of land and improvements. If buildings are destroyed by fire, wind, earthquake, or flood, the owner and his insurers will require a segregated value of land versus improvements. In most part of the nation, local real estate tax ordinances call for land and buildings to be assessed as distinct entities in the interest of uniform land-use levies.

Using the Cost Approach, value of the land is added to the appraiser's estimate of the building's value, based on reproduction cost less depreciation. Therefore, a separate valuation for the land is required. Site valuation is important, too, in determining the degree of economic obsolescence in the improvements.

In sum, the reasons for separate site analysis and valuation are these:

1. Deductible depreciation rates for buildings only on federal tax schedules.
2. Necessary applications of Income Approach techniques.
3. Use in condemnation testimony.
4. Remainder value where buildings are destroyed.
5. Local property tax assessment.
6. Estimating value of improvements only, based on replacement or reproduction cost new, less depreciation.
7. An index to building obsolescence.

The Key Principles in Site Valuation

Among many of the principles described in chapter 5, these are foremost in site valuation:

(a) A site's most likely profitable (highest and best) use is calculated in terms of the income imputable to it after the other agents in production have been satisfied. This is called surplus productivity, attributable to the land.
(b) The larger the surplus, the greater the value of the land.
(c) The Principle of Substitution (comparative sales via market data) is the acid test of value because the value of the site being appraised tends to be ascertained by the price required for an equally desirable substitute parcel.

MODEL APPRAISAL OF VACANT LAND IN THROES OF PARTIAL CONDEMNATION FOR MUNICIPAL AIRPORT CONVENIENCE

The following example demonstrates many of the principles set forth in chapters 1 through 5, particularly those in chapter 4 in the treatment of site data, and it includes techniques that will be elaborated in chapter 7. The format employed in this demonstration is sophisticated and acceptable to any state court condemning property with the power of eminent domain. This appraisal also deals with several types of land: i.e., agricultural, residential, commercial, light industrial, and highway convenience.

XYZ APPRAISAL COMPANY

One Blank Street

Atlanta, GA 30314

October 1, 1976

Spartacus Company of America
660 Madison Avenue
New York, New York 10027

Gentlemen:

We have made an investigation and appraisal of your land parcel of about 50 acres located on Grand Highway (U.S. 140 and State Highway 57) and East Point Road, northeast of the Point Road Interchange, Dashville, Kentucky.

The purpose of this appraisal is to express an opinion of value of the parcel before and after a 4.68-acre parcel in the center frontage is purchased or taken by the City of Dashville for construction of an interchange to the airport on the west side of U.S. 140—State 57; also, the resulting loss and damages to the remainder.

The appraisal includes only the land parcel, without land improvements such as fencing, field tile, or utility easements.

In our opinion, the various fair market values, as of September 15, 1976, are:

1. Entire tract FIVE HUNDRED THIRTEEN THOUSAND DOLLARS ($513,000)
2. Remaining parcel, assuming continued access to the remainder parcel from Grand Highway FOUR HUNDRED TWENTY THOUSAND DOLLARS ($420,000)
3. Loss and damages assuming access continued NINETY-FOUR THOUSAND DOLLARS ($94,000)
4. Remaining parcel, without access from Grand Highway ONE HUNDRED THIRTEEN THOUSAND DOLLARS ($113,000)
5. Loss and damages, assuming no access from Grand Highway FOUR HUNDRED THOUSAND DOLLARS ($400,000)

The term "fair market value" is defined as the highest price a property will bring if exposed for sale in the open market, allowing a reasonable time to find a purchaser who buys with knowledge of all the uses to which it is adapted and for which it is capable of being used.

A personal inspection was made of the property and the surrounding neighborhood and these factors were considered:

1. Location, size, and utility of the vacant land and its value if available for use
2. Sales and asking prices of similar land

Our report consists of:

1. This letter, which identifies the property and summarizes the values estimated
2. A narrative section, including a description of the property, an explanation of valuation procedures, and conclusion of values
3. An exhibit section including:
   A—Photographs
   B—Plats
   C—Identifying descriptions
   D—Certificate of appraiser

We have not investigated the title to or any liabilities against the property appraised.

Respectfully submitted,

s/s _____
APPRAISER

CONTENTS

SUMMARY OF FACTS AND CONCLUSIONS

Property   Vacant land tract owned by Spartacus
                    Company of America

Location   Grand Highway and East Point Road
                    City of Dashville, Kentucky.

Appraisal Date	September 15, 1976
Land Size	Before 50 ± acres (part of larger tract)
	After 45.32 ± acres (part of larger tract)
	Proposed appropriation 4.68 acres
Present Use	Agricultural

Highest and Best Use Before 22.18 ± acres commercial/light
                            industrial
                      27.82 ± acres residential/agricultural
              After with Grand Highway access
                      17.50 ± acres commercial
                      27.82   acres residential
              After without Grand Highway access
                      45.32 ± acres residential

Conclusions	Before	$513,000
of Value	After with access	420,000
	Loss and damages with access	94,000
	After without access	113,000
	Loss and damages without access	400,000

NARRATIVE SECTION

Description of the Area

The property is between Grand Highway and East Point Road adjacent to and northeast of the Point Road interchange at the north central edge of the City of Dashville, Kentucky. Southwest across Grand Highway is the partially constructed terminal building for the Municipal Airport, which serves the immediate area and Dashville, 15 miles north. The property is a few miles from central Dashville and about six miles from central Dixburgh. Grand Highway (also known as U.S. 140, State Highway 57, New Dashville Road, and the Airport Corridor) is a paved four-lane divided road with controlled access, connecting with I-50 at the south edge of Dashville about 15 miles north. Tracks of the Southern Railway cross Point Road about a mile northeast of the property and air transportation is a few minutes away.

Along Grand Highway, north toward Dashville, a strip of new and varied commercial improvements is developing and the trend toward greater land use is accelerating. The area is also developed residentially along Point Road, a paved two-lane road, and on either side of Grand Highway beyond the commercial strip.

Description of the Property

The appraised 50 ±-acre, irregular-shaped parcel is part of a 135.1-acre tract purchased by the Spartacus Corporation in January 1935.

Parcel dimensions are as follows:

2,215.15 feet of frontage along east side of Grand Highway
417.75 feet of restricted access along the northeast line of the
Point Road interchange
68.79 feet of restricted access and 695 feet of accessible frontage
along the northwest side of East Point Road
Other interior dimensions are shown on the plat in Exhibit B.

The gently rolling topography varies about 25 feet in grade, rising in all directions from a low point near the center of the Grand Highway frontage to maximum heights at the northeast and southeast edges.

The parcel, which is now used for agriculture, is supplied with all utilities except public sewer. Plans for sewer service are being formulated. Reported water, gas, and electric easements across and along the property lines were not investigated.

The property is zoned Limited District by the City of Dashville, permitting agricultural and residential uses. No structural improvements are present, and any fencing and field tile are excluded from the appraisal.

Assessments and Taxes

The appraised property is not taxed as a unit, since it is part of a larger area. Assessments are stated as 40% of value determined by the assessor.

The 1976 tax rate was $4.71 per $100 of assessment for the City of Dashville.

Next year an amendment to the state constitution will take effect that classifies real property into four assessment groups:

Property	% of Value
Public utility	55%
Industrial and commercial	40%
Residential and one rental unit	25%
Farm	25%

Highest and Best Use

The trend of commercial development on Grand Highway north to Dashville indicates that highest and best use of the appraised frontage to a depth of 400 feet (22.18 ± acres) is commercial.

Investigation reveals that 400 feet is the median depth of recent sales along Grand Highway. The property also has 695 feet of accessible frontage along East Point Road, in addition to an entry from Edison Street. Because the remaining 27.82 ±-acre parcel is in a residential area, highest and best use is for residential development.

Valuation—Before

In any determination of value, data is sought in the local market on sales of comparable tracts of vacant land. These tracts are analyzed and compared to the appraised property for such factors as location, size, characteristics, and utility. The following sales were reviewed:

Sale 1

Location	East side Grand Highway, north of Susan Street.
Date	November 1975
Type of transaction	Warranty Deed, Vol. 367, Page 202
Sale price	$62,500
Grantor	Tom Phelps
Grantee	Dukum Inn
Land area	10.23 acres
Zoning	None, county agricultural
Topography	Parcel sloped down to east from U. S. 129 frontage. Required fill obtained across street.
Present use	Dukum Inn site
Utilities	Water and gas
Remarks	Smaller site than commercial frontage of subject, 1/4 to 1/2 mile north of airport entry.
Unit price	$6,100 per acre

Sale 2

Location	East side Grand Highway, north of Dukum Inn
Date	September 25, 1975
Type of transaction	Warranty Deed, Vol. 363, Page 115
Sale price	$25,000
Grantor	Dukum Inn
Grantee	Wolf Oil Co.
Land area	1 acre
Zoning	None, county agricultural
Topography	Level and at grade with fronting Grand Highway (U.S. 140—S.H. 57)
Present use	Wolf Oil service station
Utilities	Water and gas
Remarks	1-acre parcel much smaller than subject 22 acres. Location inferior to subject in proximity to airport.
Unit price	$25,000 per acre

Sale 3

Location	East side Grand Highway, 1 1/2-2 miles north
Date	July 13, 1975
Type of transaction	Warranty Deed, Volume 361, Page 434
Sale price	$75,000
Grantor	O'Toole
Grantee	Pincus
Land area	14.5 acres
Dimensions	506 feet on U.S. 140
Zoning	None, county; Commercial, city
Topography	At grade with fronting road, slopes down and away from road.
Present use	Vacant
Utilities	Water and gas
Remarks	More closely approaching size of subject commercial area. Location inferior because farther from airport entry. Transaction for 1/2 interest said to be arm's-length.
Unit price	$10,000 per acre

Sale 4

Location	U.S. 140, west side, north of airport
Date	March 14, 1975
Type of transaction	Warranty Deed, Volume 358, Page 204
Sale price	$70,000
Grantor	Lash Enterprises, Inc.
Grantee	Galt, Inc.
Land area	1.8 acres
Dimensions	200' x 352' x 431' x 215'
Zoning	Commercial, city; None, county
Topography	Land slopes up slightly from Grand Highway frontage
Present use	Vacant, to be commercial
Utilities	Water and gas
Remarks	Smaller than subject. In airport flight pattern, on west side of highway north of airport.
Unit price	$38,900 per acre

Sale 5

Location	West side Route 140, north of airport
Date	October 22, 1974
Type of transaction	Warranty Deed, Vol. 299, Page 12
Sale price	$75,000

Grantor	Lash Enterprises
Grantee	Mertz Ford, Inc.
Land area	5 acres
Zoning	Commercial, City of Dashville
Topography	Slopes up slightly to west from fronting Grand Highway.
Present use	Auto dealership
Utilities	Water and gas
Remarks	Smaller than subject commercial area but short distance north on opposite side of road.
Unit price	$15,000 per acre

Sale 6

Location	Southeast side Route 140, north of Dukum Inn
Date	January 26, 1976
Type of transaction	Warranty Deed, Vol. 388, Page 187
Sale price	$101,000
Dimensions	450-foot frontage
Zoning	None, county; Industrial, city
Topography	Level to slightly sloping down from road frontage
Present use	Vacant
Utilities	Water, gas, and electricity
Remarks	Smaller than subject commercial property. Farther north on Dashville corridor.
Unit price	$18,200

Sale 7

Location	Route 140, northwest side, 1/2 mile north of subject
Date	February 16, 1974
Type of transaction	Warranty Deed
Sale price	$44,000
Grantor	W. M. Farogut
Grantee	Bank of Dashville
Land area	2.24 acres
Zoning	Commercial
Topography	Level, cut to grade
Present use	Branch bank
Utilities	Water, gas, and electricity
Remarks	Smaller parcel, north of subject on opposite side of road
Unit price	$20,000 per acre

Sale 8

Location	County Road, east of Route 140
Date	June 12, 1975
Sale Price	$243,000
Grantor	James P. Clark
Grantee	Silver Lake Golf Club
Land area	160 acres
Zoning	Country residential, agricultural, and recreational
Topography	Rolling
Present use	Golf course
Utilities	None
Remarks	Purchased at distressed price. Now being updated.
Unit price	$1,500 per acre

Addenda:

1. Hoke County Industrial Park—$6,000 to $10,000 per acre. Route 140 south of Louisville.
2. Land for residential development $2,000 to $3,000 per acre with water available.

Based on analysis of these and other sales, and interviews with real estate brokers and informed persons in the area about local market conditions, value of the 50-acre land parcel, before appropriation of 4.68 acres for airport highway improvement, is estimated as follows:

22.18 acres commercial and industrial @ $20,000 per acre $443,600
27.82 acres residential and agricultural @ $ 2,500 per acre   69,550
Total $513,150
                                                                        Rounded to: $513,000

Proposed Expropriation and Effect on Remaining Parcel

The City of Dashville proposes to purchase 4.68 acres of the appraised property to construct ramps to a cloverleaf bridge over Grand Highway from the southeast lane of the highway to the Municipal Airport Terminal complex, now under construction.

As shown on the plat in Exhibit B, the 4.68-acre parcel to be taken fronts 700.03 feet on Grand Highway. Depth varies to a maximum of 400 feet.

The purchase will have the following effects on the remaining property:

1. Reduce present continuous frontage of about 2,215 feet on Grand Highway to split frontage of 750.12 feet to the south and 765 feet to the north, with a 700-foot gap between the two.
2. Reduce utility of about 1.75 acres to the northeast and southeast, which become backland but useful to adjoining parcels with frontage.

An inquiry into access for the remaining frontages revealed the following information. Proposed interchange plans call for a deceleration lane to the on-ramp extending about 200 feet southwest from the acquired parcel and an acceleration or merging lane extending about 700 feet northeast. Although neither the City of Dashville nor the Kentucky State Highway Department reportedly intends to restrict access, the Dashville Land Planning and Zoning Department advises that traffic safety control may require taking access along both remaining frontages.

If reasonable access is permitted to each of the remaining frontage parcels, the purchase will cause no measurable damage other than that caused by the decelerating and accelerating lanes.

If access is no longer allowed to the remaining frontages, the land ceases to have commercial utility since access will be available only from East Point Road. Utility would then be limited to residential use, or, at best, warehouse or industrial purposes, for which indirect access is acceptable.

The 4.68 acres proposed for expropriation along Grand Highway (U.S. Route 140) is valued as part of the whole as follows:

4.68 acres @ $20,000 per acre $93,600

                                                    Rounded to: $94,000

Value—After

Description

Assuming reasonable access from Grand Highway, the remaining 45.32 acres will consist of:

Parcel A—About 9.5 acres, 400 feet deep, with 765 feet of frontage along the east side of Grand Highway north of the interchange site.

Parcel B—About 8 acres, 400 feet deep, with 750.12 feet of frontage along the east side of Grand Highway south of the interchange site, extending south to the corner of the Point Road interchange.

With reasonable access, highest and best use of Parcels A and B is commercial and/or light industrial, i.e. research and development, engineering or laboratory facilities.

Parcel C—27.82 acres with 695 feet of frontage on northwest side of East Point Road and entry via Edison Street as extended northwest from East Point Road. Highest and best use is residential.

Loss or serious restriction of access along the Grand Highway frontage would limit access to the remaining tract to 695 feet along secondary East Point Road and a short section of Edison Street as extended. Consequently, utility of the remaining 45.32 acres would decrease sharply, and highest and best use of parcel would then be residential, with a remote possibility of limited warehouse or light industrial use.

Valuation—After

The same sales and offerings used in the valuation before indicate value after expropriation.

Assuming that reasonable access from Grand Highway is allowed to the remaining land, value is estimated as follows:

Parcel A	Commercial, light industrial	
	9.5 acres @ $20,000	$190,000
Parcel B	Commercial, light industrial	
	8.0 acres @ $20,000	160,000
Parcel C	Residential, agricultural	
	27.82 acres @ $2,500	69,550
Total		$419,550
	Rounded to: $420,000	

Loss and damages would then be $94,000 for expropriation of 4.68 acres. The remaining acreage is considered to suffer no severance damage. Enhancement of value and specific benefits resulting from the proposed expropriation were considered, but such benefits are highly conjectural and could not be proven.

If access along the Grand Highway frontage is no longer allowed, then highest and best use of that frontage changes from commercial to residential, with commensurate loss in value as follows:

45.32 ± acres residential/agricultural land	
@ $2,500 per acre	$113,300
Rounded to: $113,300	

Under this premise, loss and damages to the remaining property result from the expropriation and simultaneous loss of access along the remaining frontages.

Summary of Value

The valuations, as of September 15, 1976, are summarized as follows:

With continued access to Grand Highway frontages:

Value before	$513,000
Value after	420,000
Loss and damages for taking of 4.68 acres	= $ 93,000

Without access to Grand Highway frontages:

Value before	$513,000
Value after	113,000
Loss and damages	= $400,000
Allocated:	
Loss 4.68 acres land	$ 93,000
Damage to remaining 45.32 acres	306,000
	$399,000

(PHOTOGRAPH)

Approximate Location of Parcel to Be Taken
Facing Southeast from Airport Land
Across Route 140/57 from Site

(PHOTOGRAPH)

South Section Northwest Border
Southwest Line of Property Along
Point Road Interchange on Ramp Facing
South Southeast from Airport Land

EXHIBIT B

Note: The appraiser includes as many photographs of the subject before and after
taking as he may deem to be illuminating to the court. A close-up aerial view is
often most comprehensive and effective in testimony.

EXHIBIT C

DESCRIPTION OF 4.68-ACRE PARCEL

Being a parcel of land lying 700 feet along the northeast right-of-way line of
Kentucky State Highway No. 57, and beginning approximately 1876 feet
northeast of the intersection of said State Highway No. 57 and Point Road, all
being in the City of Dashville and being more particularly described as
follows:

Beginning at a point on the northeast right of way of Kentucky
State Highway No. 57, said point bears N21—35E approximately
742 feet from an iron pipe on said right-of-way line, being a
Spartacus Company of America property corner; thence along
the northeast right-of-way line of State Highway No. 57 N21—35E
700.03 feet to a point; thence S33—17E 344.61 feet to a point;
thence following a curve to the right having a radius of 276.00 feet
and an arc length of 697.84 feet, chord bears S39—09W 526.26
feet to a point; thence N68—25W 123.00 feet to the beginning,
containing 4.68 acres more or less. All as shown on Spartacus
Company of America's Drawing No. L823BA, dated 7-6-74.

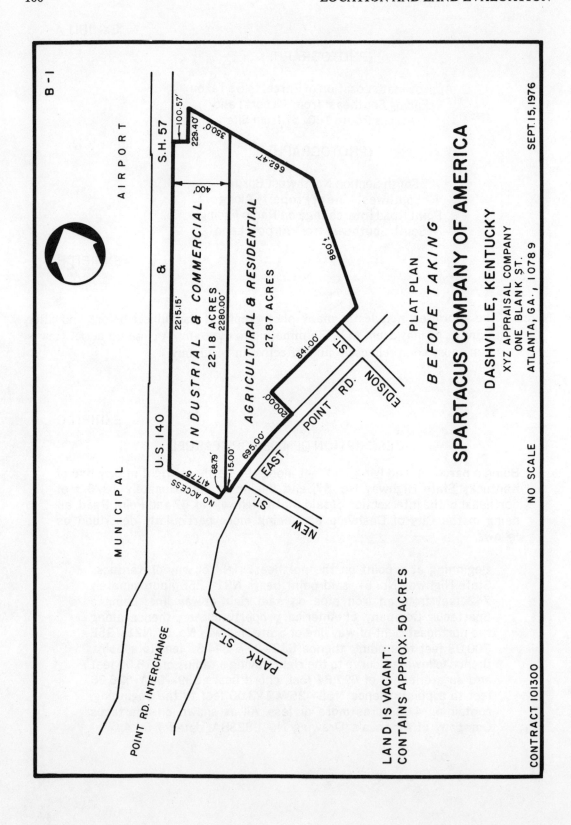

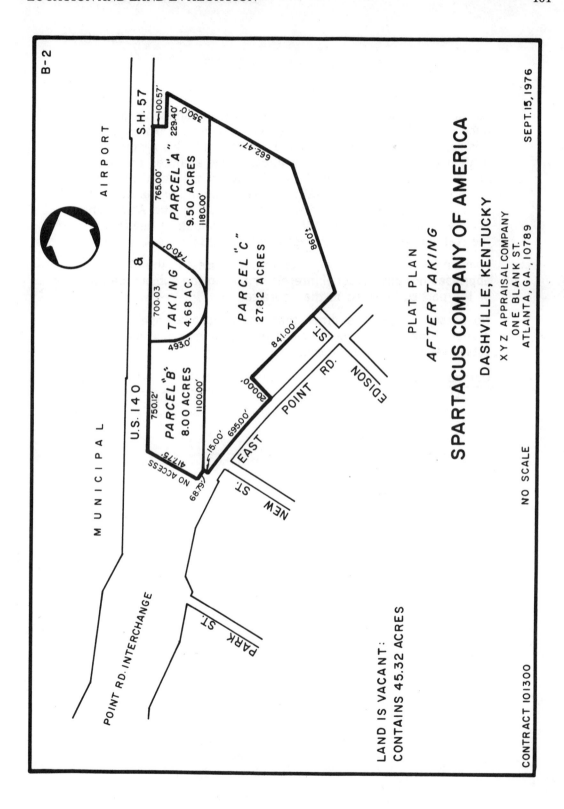

B-2

AIRPORT

MUNICIPAL

S.H. 57

U.S. 140

POINT RD. INTERCHANGE

PARK ST.

NEW ST.

EAST

EDISON ST.

POINT RD.

100.57'

350.0'

229.40'

765.00'

1180.00'

662.47'

PARCEL "A"
9.50 ACRES

740.0'

700.03

TAKING
4.68 AC.

4930'

1098'

PARCEL "C"
27.82 ACRES

841.00'

200.00'

PARCEL "B"
8.00 ACRES

750.12'

1100.00'

417.15'

15.00'

695.00'

NO ACCESS

689.79'

PLAT PLAN
AFTER TAKING

SPARTACUS COMPANY OF AMERICA

DASHVILLE, KENTUCKY

X Y Z APPRAISAL COMPANY
ONE BLANK ST.
ATLANTA, GA., 10789

NO SCALE

SEPT. 15, 1976

LAND IS VACANT:
CONTAINS 45.32 ACRES

CONTRACT 101300

EXHIBIT D

CERTIFICATE OF APPRAISER

I hereby certify that:

To the best of my knowledge and belief, the statements of fact upon which the analyses, opinions, and conclusions expressed in this report are based are true and correct; that this report sets forth all of the limiting conditions affecting the analyses, opinions, and conclusions it contains; that this report has been made in conformity with and is subject to the requirements of the Code of Ethics and Standards of Professional Conduct of the American Society of Appraisers, and of the Society of Industrial Realtors of the National Association of Real Estate Boards.

I have no present or contemplated future interest in the property appraised nor any personal interest or bias in the subject matter or the parties involved in the appraisal.

No person or persons other than those acknowledged below prepared the analyses, conclusions, and opinions concerning real estate set forth in this report.

October 1, 1976
_____
Date

_____
Signature
APPRAISER

This chapter deals with the correlation of the approaches to value that will result in a value conclusion. In addition, methodologies for those special situations, such as severance damage, offsetting benefits, easements and air rights evaluations, that may spring up for solution by the appraiser on short notice, are elucidated here. Applying these tools to the evaluation problem, the appraiser can tackle any task, putting together a coherent and logical articulation of his work.

7

Value Conclusions and
Exceptional Applications

If the appraiser has used all three (Cost, Income, and Market Data) approaches in a given task of evaluation, he now must decide which approach should bear the most weight in his value conclusion.

In terms of bearing most weight, let us eliminate the Cost Approach immediately, unless it is the *only* approach used because the subject is a new, special-purpose, institutional, or otherwise incomparable property. A value conclusion should not be hung on the Cost Approach for all the reasons set forth in chapter 20. The Cost Approach, when the other two approaches are also used, is useful only as a guide to the *upper limit of value range*. It is not a conclusion indicator.

This, then, brings us to a choice between the Income Approach and the Market Data Approach to arrive at maximum weight in our value conclusion. These key factors should be considered:

1. If the property under appraisement is an investment-income property, either presently under lease or of a type customarily built and leased for income, then the Income (capitalized earnings) Approach is the way to go.
2. If the subject is an industrial property, not under lease, owner occupied, built to the specifications of its user, and difficult to lease to anyone else without major alteration, the Market Data Approach is the route to take.

CORRELATION OF THE APPROACHES

The best way to illustrate correlation and the weighting given to each of the three approaches to value is to set forth the conclusion of an actual industrial appraisal report exhibited in court in the course of testimony by the author.

MODEL APPRAISAL:
CORRELATION AND VALUE CONCLUSION

The three approaches to value have produced the following conclusions:

Cost Approach	$965,000
Income Approach	$888,000
Market Data Approach	$895,000

The Cost Approach, which normally sets the upper limit of value, was developed after determining local construction costs from discussions with the plant engineer of the subject property, by reference to national valuation manuals, and from the appraiser's firsthand experience in the building trades. The unit costs applied were derived to include the current costs for labor, materials, profit, and overhead. Depreciation allowances were taken for physical deterioration and functional and economic obsolescence.

In reviewing depreciable items in our Cost Approach and in determining what features were curable or incurable, we looked mainly to dollar value, cost to cure, in our estimates of functional inutility.

Great consideration has been given to whether the buildings are well planned, efficient in operation, and convertible to other modern industrial uses. Since our principal concern in this report is fair market value, we found that large areas of the buildings were antiquated and of little operational value to the owners and likely to require expensive modifications to possible lessees or buyers.

Our arrival at value conclusion has been forged by the following principle:

> The appraiser does not average the indications of value by the three approaches. He selects the one most applicable and rounds to a final figure. He places the most emphasis on the approach that appears to be the most reliable and most applicable, as an indication of the answer to the specific appraisal problem. Then he tempers this estimate in accordance with his judgment as to the degree of reliance to be placed on the other two indications of value.

An economic rental was utilized in order to derive the hypothetical income estimate for the property. The conjectural rental is calculated at the current market. A majority of comparable industrial facilities are being leased on a net basis and that is the approach utilized in the report. The capitalization rate was derived through interest rates applicable to the subject in today's market.

The Market Data Approach has a strong application by way of local and national comparable sales data. A highly probable selling price on the open market was determined through sales of industrial, research, office, and warehouse properties in the same and other areas.

Although the subject property is not presently leased for income and the property is not for sale, we have put reliance on all three approaches; and we have tempered these values into a conclusion. It is the opinion of the appraisers that the value of the subject property as of January 1, 19XX, is:

NINE HUNDRED THOUSAND DOLLARS
($900,000)

EXCEPTIONAL APPLICATIONS

In the course of any given evaluation report, a number of "exceptional" considerations may arise either as part of other evaluations or to be evaluated separately. These include:

1. *Severance Damage*
2. *Offsetting Benefits in Condemnation*
3. *Easements*
4. *Air Rights*

(1) How to Calculate Severance Damage

Severance damage is any loss in value of property remaining to an owner after the condemnation of part of his real estate. It is not a part of the value of the land to be taken. It is a measure of reduction in value as a result of a partial taking of real property. Severance damages are recognized only when there exists identity of ownership and unity of use with respect to parts taken and parts remaining. These damages result when a partial taking lowers the highest and best use or otherwise limits the use of the remainder. Severance damage should never be assumed merely because of partial taking. It always must be fully supported by the facts in each case.

Estimates of severance damages are developed by use of what is known as the "before" and "after" appraisal methods. For example, the "before" (before a taking) fair market value of a neighborhood shopping center of 8 acres is, say, $800,000. The part to be acquired by your state highway department, in fee, say, is 3 acres of parking area with a fair market value of $75,000 at $25,000 per acre. Simple arithmetic would indicate the value of the part left to the owner to be $725,000. Such, however, is not necessarily the case. The "after" appraisal (evaluation of the remainder left to the owner) may indicate a fair market value in fee, of say, $500,000, thus reflecting a severance damage of $300,000. This damage may have occurred from one or more of several causes. The owner may have been left with an imbalance in shoppers' parking-to-building ratio, thus leaving him with decidely "overimproved" land. The damage could be occasioned by the fact that so much of his land was taken that the remainder was appreciably limited as an economic commercial unit due to reduced road frontage and irregular boundary.

This example may be illustrated in a more brief form as follows:

"Before" appraisal, fair market value of shopping center of 8 acres	$800,000
"After" appraisal, fair market value of shopping center left to owner (the remainder) with 5 acres	$500,000
	$300,000
Fair market value, appraisal of part to be taken, 3 acres at $25,000 per acre	$ 75,000
The difference, severance damages	$225,000

As shown in the preceding example, three distinct appraisals are required:

1. The entire property before the taking.
2. The remainder, after the taking.
3. The part to be taken.

Some courts have held that only two steps are essential, that is, the value before and the value after the taking. However, all three evaluations are required in appraisals for most government agencies where partial takings are involved.

Partial-taking appraisals serve to emphasize the use of all of the three approaches to value in the appraisal process as the "remainder" is often rendered entirely dissimilar to lands used as comparable sales. In many cases, you may find the final answer to your problem in your skillful use of the Income Approach. Reasonably accurate maps showing all physical conditions pertinent to the entire property, and to the separate parts, are considered vital.

Here are some typical causes of severance damages:

1. Reduction in highest and best use of the remainder.
2. Resulting insufficiency of the remainder to support normal typical operation.
3. Loss of access to transportation facilities, roads, streets, rails, and water.
4. Distortion in plottage or shape that handicaps use or marketability.
5. Bulwarking the remainder with wall or fence along the taking line.

(2) Offsetting Benefits in Condemnation

The Act of July 18, 1918 (H.R. 10069),(Public No. 200), vol. 40, p. 904 (ch. 55), sec. 6, reads as follows:

That in all cases where private property shall be taken by the United States for the public use in connection with any improvement of rivers, harbors, canals, or waterways of the United States, and in all condemnation proceedings by the United States to acquire land or easements for such improvements, where a part only of any such parcel, lot, or tract of land shall be taken, the jury or other tribunal awarding the just compensation of assessing the damages to the owner, whether for the value of the part taken or for any injury to the part not taken, shall take into consideration by way of reducing the amount of compensation or damages any special and direct benefits to the remainder arising from the improvement, and shall render their award or verdict accordingly.

This language can be applied to offsetting benefits in partial takings by eminent domain condemnors other than the federal government, such as the states, municipalities, and utility companies. Some states, however, still maintain a legal tradition of ignoring offsetting benefits.

As described in the partial-taking process outlined above, if special and direct benefits arising from an improvement increase the value of the remainder, then that increase in value will be offset against the value of the remainder and of the part taken, if necessary.

A special and direct benefit value to a remainder should be reflected in the "after" appraisal of the remainder. Therefore, it is crucial that you become familiar with the developed benefit, its operation, and its effects.

Example

An illustration of net results of an appraisal of a partial taking involving special and direct benefits is as follows:

"Before" appraisal, fair market value, entire property	$120,000
"After" appraisal, fair market value, remainder	36,000
	$ 84,000
Part taken, fair market value	$ 90,000
Enhancement in value of remainder arising from special and direct benefits; to be offset against value of part taken	$ 6,000

Another way to express the same results is this:

"Before" appraisal, fair market value, whole property	$120,000
"After" appraisal, fair market value, including special and direct benefits	$ 36,000
Value of the part taken, offset by benefits	$ 84,000

Benefits must be special and direct, real and imminent. They cannot be speculative or conjectural or for an indeterminate future time.

(3) Easements

An easement denotes ownership of limited real property rights, thus falling short of full fee simple estate ownership. The "before" and "after" method of appraising, described in preceding paragraphs, should ordinarily be employed in their evaluation. The difference between the value of a tract of land and its value with an easement imposed thereon is the value of the easement. For example, the owner of an acre of land that he purchased a year ago sells an easement underground across a corner of his property to a gas-transmission pipeline company for $500 a month later. After two years, he is forced by circumstances to sell the property for $4,500. Thus, the value of the easement becomes $1,000.

(4) Air Rights

All real estate has three distinct physical elements: subsurface, surface, and air space. The right to mine ore or take out gravel (mineral rights) is an example of the first, while the right to traverse the surface (via rail, road, pipe, and cable) illustrates the second.

Since 1949, developers have realized that prime in-city locations were available in quantity above railroad rights of way, highways, schools, post offices, and other low-rise developments. Since then, the treatment of air space (or air rights) as an independent interest in real estate has steadily gathered momentum.

New York has been a leader in creating a market for air rights. Several years ago it set up the New York City Educational Construction Fund, which issues bonds to finance school construction. The fund simultaneously sells or leases the air space above a school to private developers who annually pay it a sum in lieu of real estate taxes. The payments are used to pay off bonds. Two goals are thus achieved: Real estate is kept on the tax rolls and badly needed housing space is made available.

But New York has gone one step further by leasing air space over a public building (the Appellate Division Courthouse) to the developer of adjoining property. In this way, the developer can increase the floor area of the new building since the acquired air space is considered part of the plot for purposes of complying with the zoning ordinance.

Negotiating the Transfer of Air Space

One of four approaches is used, depending upon the particular circumstances:

1. *Sale of Fee Interest:* Air space can be sold just as can real estate in its entirety. However, the buyer must be sure he isn't left up in the air; he must have "support easements" so that he can base a building on columns resting on the surface. Negotiating the terms and conditions of the easement often is the most difficult part of the transaction. Such problems must be resolved as placement of the columns to minimize interference on the ground and the duty of each party to repair and maintain the columns.
   Note: If real estate taxes are imposed on the entire parcel, an allocation must be agreed upon.
2. *Lease of Air Space:* Here, the physical interest (air space) is divided into two legal interests, a fee and leasehold. Sometimes a lease must be used because the owner of the parcel (e.g., a railroad) is not permitted by law to sell any part of the property.

3. *Air-Space Easement:* While in theory an easement in air space may be created, the more common method is for the owner of the parcel to sell the entire physical interest and reserve an easement of the surface. For example, a railroad or highway requires only a right of way at ground level.

4. *Air-Space Condominium:* Here the air space is divided up into "space lots" with all of the lot owners sharing title to the common areas, including the surface. Condominium apartment buildings illustrate this approach.

Examples of Air-Space Development

At one time or another, all of the following have been adopted or proposed:

- Office building over post office
- Commercial building over railroad tracks
- Apartment over street
- Office building over garage
- Building over reservoir
- Building over school
- Railroad tracks over surface use (e.g., connecting links between buildings; here the railroad is using the air space)

Beware the "Navigation Servitude"

One approach that is not feasible is the use of air space over navigable waters. The United States Constitution gives the federal government the absolute right to control navigable waters for purposes of commerce. Thus, any construction over such waters may be taken by the federal government in condemnation proceedings without any compensation. Proposals have been made to limit this "navigation servitude," but so far none of them has met with success.

PART TWO

Methodologies and Model Appraisals for Commercial Properties

There are so many varieties of multi-tenant residences, ranging from a three-family dwelling to the giant complex with thousands of home units, that we have limited this chapter to a demonstration of something in between. The example will concentrate on a middle-income, 17-year old, six-story, elevator apartment house in a bustling urban community. Since this is a type of property that is built, owned, managed, and bought or sold as investment (income) property, the principles applied in its evaluation would be identical to any size of multi-tenant property anywhere.

8

How to Appraise an Apartment House with Retail Stores: Band of Investment Capitalization

KEY CONSIDERATIONS OF VALUE IN APARTMENT HOUSES

The intrinsic value of an apartment house depends heavily on its locale, especially as it relates to the prosperity of the immediate environment and the city or town in which it stands. Micro-market data emphasis in the appraisal of an apartment house is, therefore, placed on the site and neighborhood. But the economic well-being of the area is also important and macro-market statistics on area population and city employment are vital up to a distance of an hour in commuting time.

A well-located and fully rented apartment house is likely to be found in an up-trend zone, where public transportation is available, not too far from schools, churches, and cultural and recreational facilities, and in a neighborhood where stores, restaurants, banks, and professional services are at hand. Off-street private parking or garaging on at least a one-for-one allotment basis is imperative for modern apartments; and in most municipalities this minimum, or a two-for-one allotment, is required by zoning. Tenants usually pay extra for garage accommodations.

The appraisal of an apartment house may be based on plans for a proposed structure on a given site as a *feasibility study* to test highest and best use of the land; or it may be a report on a finished building for mortgage refinancing, with or without a long-term financial history. In any case, rents can be "stabilized" for the subject property by comparison and adjustment with other apartment rentals in the area.

113

How to Prepare a Design and Tenant Profile

If the subject apartment house is proposed and in the planning stage, a design and tenant profile should be developed before the architect reaches the stage of working drawings. The profile may be based on comparative properties in the area and/or a questionnaire based on a direct-mail sampling of apartment dwellers in the locale. Even in the appraisal of an existing apartment house, such as the model illustration following, a tenant profile is important to the owner who may be guided by it in making future alterations, and to the mortgage lender who may be asked for refinancing. This profile should reflect effective demand, the type of units and number of rooms called for, and design preferences in both the micro-market and macro-market. Such a profile might appear in the market survey as follows:

A MODEL OF A
TENANT AND DESIGN PROFILE

(On the basis of 300 neighborhood prospects surveyed)

Element	Aggregate
Average Family Size:	2.29 persons; 45% require 1-BR; 25% 2-BR; 30% 3-BR
Average Age of Family Head:	35 years; 65% are 35 to 70 years of age
Families with Children:	30%
Occupational Activity:	20% professional; 41% executive; 30% retired; 9% other
Places of Work:	58% downtown business core; 18% north side of city; 15% south side; 9% local
Shopping, Schools, Beaches, Churches, and Recreation:	At hand, and within bus distances
Commutation to Work:	50% automobile; 18% bus; 32% train
Commutation Time to Work Less than 30 minutes:	75%; and 25% less than one hour
Former Domicile:	56% from nearby communities
Type of Former Dwelling:	50% single-family; 50% apartment
Average Anticipated Tenancy and Attainable Rent per Room:	3 to 6 years; $90 to $95 per room per month
Summation and Recommendation:	Location is ideal and justifies retail stores with 3 1/2—4 1/2—5 and 5 1/2 room apartments up to 70 units

COMPREHENSIVE CONSIDERATIONS IN EVALUATION OF LAND AND
IMPROVEMENTS IN APARTMENT HOUSE APPRAISAL

Equally important as locale is the *functional design* of the apartment building. For example, rooms should be spacious with ample closet arrangements, but the rooms should be conveniently and economically connected to kitchen and bathroom accommodations, eliminating unnecessarily long or disjointed hall spaces. Maximum window exposure and a balcony when possible add to functional value in an apartment unit and hence to the rental income the unit may command.

Architectural expertise in the arrangement of the living quarters and central placement of lobby, elevators, corridors, and laundry rooms so that these services are readily accessible to tenants is vital. Certain amenity factors, such as prestige, security, and satisfaction in the home, bear on the value of apartment buildings, just as they do on individually owned, single-family residences.

The mechanical equipment of the building—heating, lighting, air conditioning, elevator capacity, plumbing, wiring, and fireproofing—bears heavily on rental return. These elements must be carefully expressed in the Cost Approach.

Management is of great importance to value in an apartment building. Tenants pay for comfort, safety, and quiet enjoyment of the premises, and if they are not provided with responsible maintenance the income from aggrieved tenants will be erratic, if not halted altogether, with less desirable tenants replacing those moving out. The aspects that characterize the property as excellent or poor in design and maintenance dominate the quality of tenant the building attracts, hence the quantity, quality, and durability of the building's income, reflecting finally on land value.

TECHNIQUES AND PROCEDURES

First Step in the Investment Analysis

The *initial step* in evaluating an existing or proposed apartment building is to process its actual or hypothetical income. Decide upon capitalization method, rate, and valuation technique only after examining the quality of the subject's income stream, basing conclusions on the dominant aspects of value that created the situation, namely the ease or difficulty with which the owner has collected his rents, filled his vacancies, reduced his turnover, and kept his expenses in line.

Second Step: The Market Survey and Property Analysis

The next move in evaluating a proposed or existing apartment house is to gather and correlate data that exposes the likelihood of success or failure in renting the building. This information is related to the analysis of the subject property in this manner:

1. *Factors.* Macro-market influences of area economic situation measured against the micro-market demand for apartment space in the locale. In measuring local economic conditions, the following factors must be scrutinized:
   (a) Population of the municipality and the area within a 15-mile radius. Forms of transportation within the municipality and to and from subject location. Chief forms of employment within the locale, and estimate of present and future employment levels.

(b) The amount and substance of commerce and industry in the area, and its contribution to the growth of the locale. The city's importance as an industrial, commercial, or cultural (university) center.

(c) The planning and zoning practices, the tax policies, and local ordinances affecting the property and the neighborhood must be noted.

(d) Cultural and recreational facilities provided, including theaters, museums, libraries, parks, sports centers and clubs.

(e) Seasonal conditions and the prevailing climate.

2. *Relating the Survey to the Neighborhood.* Micro-market data concerning the immediate vicinity of the proposed or existing apartment building should be set forth as follows:

(a) Assuming that highest and best use of the site is an apartment building with public transportation and automobile parking at hand and shopping not far away, is the neighborhood quiet, orderly, and sedate? Is accessibility to the neighborhood easy and attractive? Are there evidences of traffic congestion, air pollution, or other inharmonious elements?

(b) Describe trends in the neighborhood. What is family income level? What is average family size and composition? Is police and fire service at hand? Are medical services adequate? Is garbage-removal service frequent and efficient?

(c) Are churches of several denominations nearby? Are there both elementary and high schools, public and parochial?

(d) Do the amenities of the neighborhood far outweigh any drawbacks? Is the trend for the neighborhood upgrade, static, or downgrade? Is the site the best available in the neighborhood?

3. *Analyzing the Property.* Specific details of the property under appraisement must be clearly delineated:

(a) Recitation of the title, including metes and bounds, assessments and tax levy.

(b) Zone requirements.

(c) Description of the site topography and subsoil conditions, plottage and shape of the land area, together with list of utilities on site or available.

(d) The type of construction, use and condition of the proposed or existing building and its machinery, together with site improvements, planned or existing, such as paved parking, fencing, and outdoor floodlighting.

(e) Each floor of the building must be measured and described.

(f) A summary of the development of the property, if existing, with a five-year history of income and expense, and type of management and maintenance attending the property.

(g) The anticipated useful life of the property must be estimated and allowances made for depreciation and obsolescence.

If the building is proposed or in the planning stage, income and expenses for five years must be projected from knowledge and experience in new apartment house construction. Management and maintenance procedures for the proposed building that are both practical and economic should be recommended.

4. *Comparable Land Sales and Apartment Leases.* List in detail verified data concerning land sales and leases of apartments in buildings similar to the subject property, in the locale of the subject property. These comparables should be inspected and similarities or differences described, as compared to subject land or apartments, summing up the property analysis.

Third Step: The Approaches to Value

Your crucial third step in apartment house evaluation lies in the choice of approaches.

Every apartment house has its own peculiarities in terms of location, land area, and income flow, not to mention age, design, and services. Thus, its nature tends to make it distinct and difficult to compare with sales of other apartment buildings when estimating value. This makes the Market Data Approach generally inapplicable, except for purposes of estimating land value and gauging the apartment rental market.

In the evaluation of an apartment building, the Cost Approach lends better support to the Income Approach than does the Market Data Approach, because the Cost Approach leads the appraiser to a close examination of construction details and the age, condition, and remaining economic life of the property. However, reproduction cost less depreciation only sets an upper limit of value. *The real test is investment value.*

The *Income Approach* is the investor's guide to value, which can rest upon the proper capitalization of net income, less the cost of curing whatever deferred maintenance there may be.

Since the market value of an apartment building depends to a great extent upon the *present worth of its future earnings,* the appraiser must anticipate such earnings and estimate how long they will endure if he is to calculate their present worth.

Fourth Step: Capitalization Rates and Methods

Capitalization rates on apartment properties will vary with circumstances. Choice of capitalization rate and method is the appraiser's critical fourth step in evaluation of an apartment property.

Depending upon the quality and durability of income flowing from the property you are appraising, you can elect to follow either of the following courses of capitalization:

(1) Use the straight-line depreciation plus capitalization rate method of capitalization when leases are short term (less than 10 years) and the net income before depreciation is therefore uncertain for each year in the future. This method is demonstrated in connection with the Building Residual Technique in the model appraisal of an apartment house at the end of this chapter.

(2) But if the net income before depreciation is expected to be level or better and is of a contract nature, say, on long-term leases with security deposits from tenants of financial stability, and there is a long waiting list of tenant applicants for apartments so located that extended popularity is implicit, then the *Property Residual Technique* in conjunction with the Inwood or Ellwood premises can be used as a truly sound means of appraising investment realty. This technique treats the worth of the property as an

undivided entity during the entire economic life of the building, at the end of which the land reverts to its virgin state as vacant and is evaluated as a reversionary interest.

Fifth Step: Procedure for Estimating a Separate Land Value Under the Apartment Dwelling

The Land Residual Technique is best used on a new project where the cost of the apartment building is a known factor. In that case, the appraiser would set up his Cost Approach first and find his land value as demonstrated in the model appraisal. It is a valid application to land under apartment buildings. Estimating land value is the fifth step in apartment property evaluation.

Sixth Step: Procedure for Estimating Value of the Improvements in Apartment House

If the appraiser has established his land value via ample market data, particularly in the case of an older building, then the Building Residual Technique is the best avenue to value of the improvements.

If the value of the building turns out to be near, say, five years, its depreciation cost, then the appraiser should turn back to the Land Residual process in capitalization of net income.

If the worth of neither land nor building is known, then either the building's value for depreciation purposes must be assumed or land value must be assumed for reversionary purposes only, and the Property Residual Technique is employed. When the appraiser has chosen his basic residual technique, his sixth and final step is estimating value of the improvements.

In the following model appraisal of a seventeen-year-old, six-story apartment building, the straight-line method of capitalization is employed as the most common in apartment house valuation, where short leases generally prevail. The capitalization rate has been composed under the band of investment process.

MODEL APPRAISAL OF APARTMENT HOUSE WITH STORES USING COST APPROACH IN SUPPORT OF THE BUILDING RESIDUAL TECHNIQUE UNDER THE INCOME APPROACH

The following is an appraisal of a 1950 apartment house in a suburban neighborhood at the perimeter of New York City. The structure has an established identity as an apartment building for business and professional people and well-to-do retired citizens. Leases are on a three-year term, and there is no available land for competitive apartment construction nearby. Such a property, under present zoning, would represent highest and best use of the land at this location. The apartments are fully rented, and the stores are rented from five to ten years.

XYZ APPRAISAL COMPANY, INC.
201 Haven Road West
New York, N.Y. 10017

January 25, 1977

Mr. John Doe, President
B.E.D. CORPORATION
Suite 330
10 Twelfth Avenue
New York, New York 10025

Re: Halcyon Apartments
101 Blue Hill Boulevard
Blue Hills, X-Borough
New York, N.Y. 10031

Dear Mr. Doe:

Pursuant to your request, I submit an appraisal report relative to this property. A personal inspection of the real estate and of local conditions has been made by me and a member of our staff with analysis of all relevant data being utilized in determining the estimate of market data.

The following report, including exhibits, fully describes the method of approach and contains all pertinent data gathered in our investigation of the subject.

After careful consideration, I have concluded that the fair market value of the subject property as of January 10, 1977, is:

ONE MILLION EIGHT HUNDRED FORTY THOUSAND DOLLARS
($1,840,000)

I certify that we have no present or contemplated financial interest in the subject property and that our employment and compensation are in no way contingent upon the value reported.

Respectfully submitted,

SUMMARY OF FACTS AND CONCLUSIONS

Subject Property   Halcyon Apartments
                                          101 Blue Hills Boulevard
                                          Blue Hills, New York
Date of Appraisal   January 10, 1977
Site Area (300' Front x 250')   75,000 Square Feet
Number of Stores   Four (4)
Number of Apartments   Seventy (70)
Average Rent Per Room $93.37

Number of Garages   Seventy (70)
Number of Rooms (not including Stores) Three Hundred Eighty and
                                                            One-Half (380 1/2)
Date of Completion   1959
Gross Income—100% Occupancy, with
Stores. (Waiting list of 55
applicants) $ 352,946
Net Income 1976 $ 223,287
Site Value $ 525,000
Final Value Estimate of Property $1,840,000

TABLE OF CONTENTS

PURPOSE OF APPRAISAL

The appraisal was made for the purpose of estimating the market value of the subject property, including land and improvements, as of July 6, 1976, as a fair price to a prospective buyer.

MARKET VALUE

For the purpose of this appraisal, market value is defined as "the highest price estimated in terms of money which a property will bring if exposed for sale in the open market, allowing a reasonable time to find a purchaser who buys with knowledge of all the uses to which it is adapted, and for which it is capable of being used. Frequently, it is referred to as the price at which a willing seller would sell and a willing buyer would buy, neither being under abnormal pressure. It is the price expectable if a reasonable time is allowed to find a purchaser and if both seller and prospective buyer are fully informed." (Appraisal Terminology and Hand Book, 5th ed., American Institute of Real Estate Appraisers, Chicago, 1973.)

PROPERTY RIGHTS APPRAISED

The property rights appraised are all rights existing in fee simple as of the appraisal date. These rights are the legal and economic properties of the owner that may rightfully be exchanged for money or equivalent goods. Property rights inherent in the ownership of tangible personal property, and intangible benefits of the property itself, are not the subject of this report.

Areas and dimensions of the property were not physically measured but were taken from plat plans furnished by the principal. No survey has been made of the property by this appraiser, and he assumes no responsibility for the dimensions or areas determined thereby or for any matters legal in nature.

The resultant estimate of market value is predicated on the financial structure currently prevailing.

It is assumed that there is a good and marketable title and that there are no restrictions as to use except those imposed by public ordinance.

Verification of factual matters contained in this report has been made to the extent deemed practicable.

Market data has been taken from sources deemed to be reliable but which could not be verified in all cases.

The apportionment between the land and buildings in the report applies only under the existing program of utilization. The separate valuations for land and buildings may not be used in conjunction with any other appraisal and are invalid if so used.

Neither all nor any part of the contents of this report shall be conveyed to the public through advertising, public relations, news, sales, or other media without written consent and approval of the author particularly as to valuation conclusions, the identity of the appraiser or firm with which he is connected.

The appraiser shall not be required to give testimony or appear in court by reason of this appraisal unless specific arrangements for these services are subsequently made.

LEGAL DESCRIPTION

The property is located in a municipal borough of New York, described on the borough and county tax records as:

Halcyon Apartments
Section A   Volume 8   Block 6070   Lot 46
Dimensions: 300' Front x 250' Rear
Improved with six-story self-service elevator
apartment house; four stores and 70 enclosed
garages on ground level.

All that certain part and parcel of land, together with the improvements thereon, identified by Deed 1047, dated 1/29/57, on the Land Records of Queens County, Liber 183, Page 221.

REAL ESTATE TAX DATA

The subject property is assessed under the auspices of the Borough. The 1975-76 real estate taxes are as follows:

        Assessment:
        Land $ 485,000.00
        Improvements   800,000.00
        Total $1,285,000.00
        1975-76 Tax Rate @   5.00/Hundred
        1975-76 Tax Ratio 65%
        1975-76 Tax Burden $ 64,250
        Effective Tax Rate (Rate x Ratio) = 3.25%

THE APPRAISAL PROCESS

The generally accepted method of obtaining the market value of a parcel of property is by the use of the three approaches to value.

These approaches are the Cost Approach, the Income Approach, and the Market Data Approach to value. The value indicated by each approach is carefully reviewed and that approach, which in the judgment of the appraiser most adequately and accurately reflects all the circumstances in connection with the property under appraisement and the purposes for which the appraisal is being made, will be selected as the best indication of market value. In this appraisal, I shall apply only the Cost and Income Approaches in reference to the improvements since recent nearby sales of comparable retail and apartment buildings are nonexistent. But I shall apply the market Data Approach using comparative nearby land sales to prove land value of subject property.

In the Income Approach, the value of the property will be estimated by the capitalization of the actual net income the property is producing. A reconstructed appraisal operating expense statement will be prepared from the owner's experience in the subject property. The value of the land having been found by reliable market data, the Building Residual Technique will be used to find the value of the improvements.

Capitalization of Income

Chief reliance will be placed by your appraiser on the capitalization of the present net income of the property. I shall, however, apply a Cost Approach to show reproduction cost new, less reasonable depreciation for wear and tear.

The value ascribed to the land in this appraisal will, I believe, materially increase within a short time. A low capitalization rate is therefore indicated.

ZONING AND USE

Property is entirely within the zone of permitted use for multi-family dwellings and retail operations(CR-2). The property is located at the western edge of Community Planning District 6, between Blue Hill Boulevard and City Boulevard.

HIGHEST AND BEST USE

Continuance of present use, as multi-tenant dwelling with retail stores, as consonant with zoning, limiting height to six stories.

AREA AND NEIGHBORHOOD DATA

The premises are located in the X-Borough, Blue Hills, New York. Climate averages mean temperature of 58 year-round, with humidity in the summertime making air conditioning a comfort feature; winter cold requires sound insulation and constant heat in dwellings and stores.

The immediate environs of the neighborhood are predominately multi-family in use with top-grade retail stores along the frontages. Commercial and retail areas are developed all along both sides of Blue Hill Boulevard frontages. Major department stores and a large chain restaurant are nearby subject property; and a new chain store is under construction in the same locale. Retail uses here are at a premium. Neighborhood is uptrend.

Public transport facilities including bus, subway, and train are within two blocks, and schools and churches are located nearby. Conveniences to apartment tenants are first class with an abundance of banks, professional services, and stores immediately at hand. Cultural and recreational facilities include theaters, libraries, parks, and cinema. Public schools are rated good-to-excellent. Parochial schools and state university are nearby.

Borough population is 2,102,751, according to the Borough Chamber of Commerce, 1975. Blue Hills has increased population since 1970 from 48,829 to 54,813. District Six, Blue Hills-Bushey Park, has felt a net gain of 5,984 housing units since 1970.

Retail trade in Blue Hills is flourishing, and the subject property is near the center of this activity.

AREA MAP AND VITAL STATISTICS

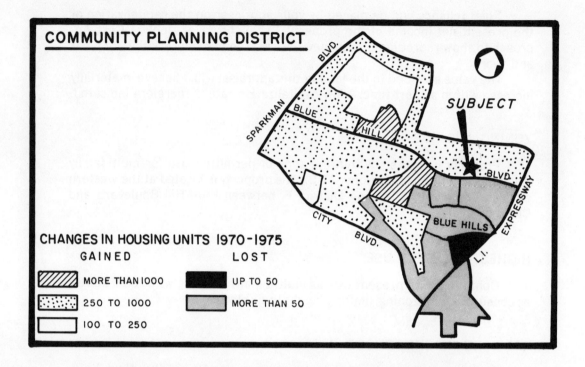

The accompanying map charts housing growth—and, in some cases, losses—during the nineteen-seventies in a vast area of west and southwest borough below City Boulevard and the Long Island Expressway.

Based on official 1970 and 1975 figures, they reflect the change in dwelling unit totals in each of the census tracts, or counting areas, in sections that correspond generally to the city's Community Planning District 6.

During the past five years, the net gain in housing units in all Planning Districts was 16,603. The greatest spurt of building was in the Blue Hills-Bushey Park Section, with a net gain of 5,984 units.

District 6: (Blue Hills-Bushey Park)—A net gain of 5,984 units. Massive construction projects along both sides of Blue Hill Boulevard, on adjacent streets, and in areas bordering Grand Union Parkway.

Data Source: Borough Chamber of Commerce.

SITE DATA

The total site area of 75,000 square feet is level at grade on Blue Hill Boulevard along its frontage, but slopes to the rear where the garages are at basement level. Drainage is good. An open culvert runs along the rear boundary. The site has all utilities connected. Subsoil is hardpan and bedrock. Street frontage is served by concrete sidewalk, street lights, and fire hydrants. Street frontage is 300 feet with a depth of 250 feet. An alley, 14 feet wide, paved with 3" bituminous concrete to the south of the apartment house leads to double-row garages and side parking spaces in the rear yard. Lobby courtyard is landscaped with evergreen shrubs, bordered by grass turf and courtyard center island is well maintained. The site is the best available parcel in the neighborhood for a structure to include stores and apartments.

LAND EVALUATION

All five comparable land sales submitted fall within a narrow range. However, Sale No. 1 comes nearest to the subject in comparable plottage, neighborhood, and location, and has the lowest adjustments. Land value indicated is $7.00 per square foot. Therefore:

75,000 square feet @ $7.00 per square foot = $525,000

[Four or five recent sales of comparable land should be recited below, or referenced in the Addenda Exhibits placed in an Appendix following the entire appraisal.]

IMPROVEMENT DATA

The improvements comprise an attractive steel-frame, horseshoe-shaped building with center set back to form a landscaped courtyard before the marble lobby entrance. The brick veneer over concrete block construction is well maintained. Windows have marble sills, and sash and trim are aluminum.

The accommodations include:

Apts	Rooms	Bedrooms	Baths	
30	3 1/2	1 Each	1	Each
17*	4 1/2	2 Each	1 1/2	Each
12*	5	3 Each	2	Each
10*	5 1/2	3 Each	2	Each
	(Plus Superintendent's Basement Apt.)			
1	5	3	1 1/2	
70	301 1/2	133	101	

*With balconies and/or dens facing Blue Hills Boulevard, all above the ground floor.

Stores	Rooms Including Men's and Women's Lavatories	
4	2 Each	2 Each = 5 Full Baths
Lobby		
1	1 1/2 (Large)	1 Only

(Note: 1/2 bath refers to lavatory with toilet and washbasin, but no bath.)

Totals, therefore, including apartments, ground-floor stores, and lobby with doorman's lavatory are:

70 Apartments
4 Stores
303 Rooms (including lobby)
106 Baths (including stores)

Garage facilities of wood-frame construction on concrete slab are provided for 70 units. The four retail stores are well maintained with attractive fronts. Parking at the rear is available for store employees and deliveries. Customer parking at the rear is limited to 20 marked spaces, but metered parking is available along the street frontage.

The present condition of the premises can only be described as good with conscientious maintenance in effect.

The six-story building has a copper-flashed, flat gravel and tar built-up, 20-year bonded, composition roof, brass and copper plumbing, oil-fired circulating hot-water heat, Otis 1,000 lb. self-service elevator, and exterior fire escapes. The one chimney is double flue. One incinerator serves the building.

Foundation is 18" poured concrete; 220 V-100 amp electric service. Water supply has a capacity of 100 gallons per minute. Air conditioning by Central Chiller System.

Other particulars of construction, layout and equipment are as follows:

TV antenna, bath and kitchen venting system, incinerator, ranges, refrigerators, dishwashers, garbage-disposal units. Coin-operated laundry in the basement. Stoves, oven ranges, and refrigerators, plus dishwashers are furnished to the tenants.

Plumbing is copper and brass. Seventy (70) stainless-steel kitchen sinks; ninety-eight and one-half (98 1/2) porcelain toilets, bathtubs and/or washbasins. Chrome taps and faucets. Seventy (70) Kelvinator kitchen sink garbage disposals, seventy (70) Kelvinator dishwashers, refrigerators, and ranges.

There are seventy (70) units including the superintendent's apartment.

Bath finishes are ceramic tile wainscot and floor, plaster above.

Interior walls are concrete block, plastered.

Interior floors are concrete in the basement; all floors above are hardwood except for the lobby which is terrazzo. The basement floor is covered with asphalt tile in the basement corridors.

Ceilings are plaster.

Effective age: Seventeen (17) years.

A plat plan of the ground-floor area, with garages on level below at rear, and with building accurately located on the site is shown on the next page. Actual blueprints for all levels from basement to roof are placed in the Addenda.

PLAT PLAN

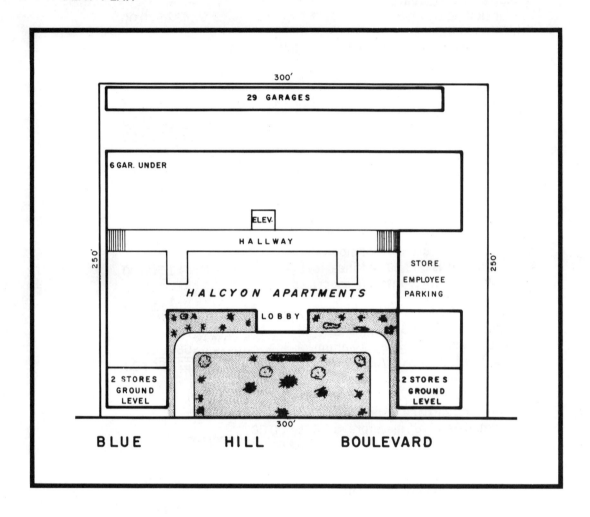

VALUATION OF THE IMPROVEMENTS
VIA THE COST APPROACH

Building contains 13,000 square feet on base. Six stories on excavated basement added = 75,000 square feet.

Building:

Reproduction Cost New Less Depreciation

Using the cost index of an approved valuation service, the following square-foot reproduction cost of building is developed:

$33.30 x 13,000 square feet,
   including elevator = $ 432,900.00
4th, 5th, and 6th floors +2%
each floor = 35.29 x 13,000 x 3 = $1,376,310.00
Basement $7.80 x 13,000 =   101,400.00

Add Location Factor: $1,477,710.00
$1,477,710.00 x 1.02 = $1,507,264.00
                                                                             $1,940,164.00

Plus Garages and Site Improvements:
8,000 square feet, wood frame, unheated
garages on concrete slab @ 5.00 per
square foot = $ 40,000.00
50,000 square feet of bituminous asphalt
paving @ .40 per square foot =   20,000.00
500 feet of courtyard interior sidewalk
paving and curbs @ 3.00 per lineal feet =   1,500.00
Concrete pool with fountain in courtyard
plus floodlighting of same   1,166.00
TOTAL VALUE OF IMPROVEMENTS NEW $2,002,830.00
Less Depreciation of Building and
Site Improvements @ 2% per annum, or 34%   680,962.00
Total Depreciated Value, ALL Real Improvements $1,321,868.00

Extras: (Personalty)
Dishwashers, garbage disposal
units, ranges, and refrigerators = $36,600.00
Less Depreciation @ 10%   3,660.00
(Start-Life Items)
    Total: Personalty   32,940.00
    Total: Personalty and Realty $1,354,808.00
Add Land   525,000.00
Estimated Market Value by Cost Approach $1,879,808.00
                  Rounded to: $1,880.000.00

Explanation of Depreciation

    The improvements are seventeen (17) years old and the care, main-
tenance, and upkeep have been very good. The calculated physical
depreciation includes painting and decorating requirements, new tubing for
the boiler, and fair wear and tear on the exterior walls and roofing.
    There is no observable functional depreciation, and I have not been
able to find any economic depreciation of influences that could cause such
depreciation within the foreseeable future.

Recapitulation

Item	Depreciation	Market Value
Land	—	$ 525,000.00
Apartment Building & Site Improvements		
$2,002,830.00	— $680,962.00 (depreciation) =	1,321,868.00
Appliances		
$36,600.00	— $ 3,660.00 (depreciation) =	32,940.00

Estimated Market Value by Cost Approach $1,879,808.00

Rounded to $1,880,000.00

MARKET DATA APPROACH

After a thorough search I was unable to locate recent sales of comparable improved apartments with stores in the area, although a survey of local, independent stores in a ten-block area proved subject stores have rents slightly higher than economic for the area.

INCOME APPROACH

The Income Approach to the value estimate is an appraisal technique in which the anticipated net income is processed to indicate the capital amount of the investment that will produce net income. It is dependent upon the following: an accurate statement of the actual rental; the deduction of all applicable expenses; the conversion of net income into value by the proper capitalization rate.

Economic rental for the subject property was estimated by analyzing the apartment rentals presently being received and those of comparable apartment complexes in the subject area. The individual apartment rentals are categorized as to number of bedrooms, number of bathrooms, and whether or not a den, balcony, or enclosed terrace are included with the apartment. Income is also received from washer and dryer machines on the premises.

Expense items have been estimated through actual experience in the subject property in conjunction with known expenses of similar apartment properties. Unit estimates and percentages have been utilized to stabilize various expense items.

As the income is projected over an advanced period of time, a rental is applied to include an allowance of five percent for vacancy and rent loss from gross income, although the property was fully tenanted at the time of appraisal.

Wages and salaries of maintenance employees, porters, and handymen, whether full time or part time, are estimated on an expense basis as related to the actual wages paid with free apartment in lieu of wages where applicable.

A verified statement (reconstructed by your appraiser for purposes of true valuation) of income and expenses provided by the owner follows:

Rent Roll (Foreshortened example)

Apt. #	Tenant's Name	Monthly Rental	Lease from:	Dates to:
Basement	Superintendent	$ 00.00		
1A	Parker	$300.00	10/1/74	9/30/77
1B	Dobbins	$300.00	8/1/75	7/31/78
1C	Zukowski	$300.00	11/1/74	11/30/77
1D	Stein	$300.00	2/28/75	2/27/78
2A (with Balcony)	Di Giorgio	$325.00	1/1/76	12/31/79

The 70 garages rent for $30 per month each; the coin-operated laundry averages $2,400 per annum. The stores are leased for $10,000 each, per annum, or $6.60 per square foot.

Explanation of Stabilized Income

Comparable Apartment Rentals

1. Blue Hill Apartments

   One-(1) bedroom apartments to $275.00 per month.
   Two-(2) bedroom apartments to $350.00 per month.
   Three-(3) bedroom apartments to $450.00 per month.
   Garage rentals are additional and range from $20.00 to $30.00 per month depending on location.

2. Bushey Park Apartments

   One-(1) bedroom apartments to $265.00 per month.
   Two-(2) bedroom apartments to $340.00 per month.
   Three-(3) bedroom apartments to $438.00 per month.
   Garage averages from $24.00 to $26.00 per month in covered and enclosed parking spaces.

In the opinion of this appraiser, the stabilized and actual economic rental for the subject is as follows:

30	3 1/2-Room apts.	@ average of $300.00 per month =	$ 9,000.00
17	4 1/2-Room apts.	@ average of $325.00 per month =	5,525.00
12	5-Room apts.	@ average of $400.00 per month =	4,800.00
10	5 1/2-Room apts.	@ average of $440.00 per month =	4,400.00
1	Superintendent's apartment @ gratis	=	000.
Total	. . . .		$23,725.00

Annual Income, Apt. (12 x $23,725) =	$284,700
Annual Income from Garage Rentals (12 x 70 x $30) =	25,200
	$309,900
Annual Income from Coin-Operated Laundry =	3,046
Total Gross Annual Income Without Retail Stores =	$312,946.00

Comments and Adjustments

I consider that the foregoing comparable apartment rentals submitted are nearly at par with subject property actual rentals for this year. Subject rentals are slightly greater, and I believe that this is due to subject's superior location in terms of proximity to public transportation, shopping, schools, churches and synagogues, beaches and recreation.

Both the six-story comparables are within one mile of subject in opposite directions on Blue Hill Boulevard, and both have balconies and dens in the larger apartments above the ground floor. However, neither of the comparables has stores on the ground floor in its buildings.

Blue Hill Apartments (Comparable No. 1) was built 20 years ago, and Bushey Park Apartments (Comparable No. 2) was built 15 years ago, so both are of approximate vintage, with elevators, central air conditioning, garages, and other amenities equal to subject.

The 17-year rental history of subject property has shown consistent annual rental gains, and I believe that this trend has not yet peaked, due to the growth of the community in terms of convenience shopping and ease of access to all points of business, education, and recreation. Public parks, marinas, and beaches are within a three-mile radius of subject location.

Subject apartment property has a waiting list of some sixty applicants for all sizes of apartments, and I can see no decline in rentals in the foreseeable future, even under a national and regional economic climate threatened with "recession."

Therefore, I am stabilizing the current actual rental income of the property, including the store rentals (which could easily be converted to apartments with equivalent income value) as economic in the marketplace of the locale.

The four stores on the ground floor occupy 6,000 square feet and include a high-grade deli-restaurant (The Pickle Barrel); a dry-cleaning and tailoring establishment (D'Andrea's); a travel agency (Travel Consultants, Inc.); and a beauty salon (Pierre and Maurice, Inc.). They possess modern, attractive store fronts, and the interiors are well maintained.

Total Stabilized (Actual) Gross Annual Rental from Apartments, Garages, and Coin-Operated Laundry =	$312,946
Total Actual Gross Annual Rental from Four Retail Stores =	40,000
Total Actual Gross Annual Income from Entire Property =	$352,946

Explanation of Adjusted and Reconstructed Expenses

The care and maintenance of the building has been exceedingly good due to the necessity of presenting an attractive image to prospects. I have accepted the records of the owner's accountant as the stabilized expenses in this appraisal.

Capitalization Rate

I have selected a straight-line method of capitalization to reflect the short terms of the leases and the instability of the income stream.

I have used the band of investment theory of capitalization:

> First Mortgage—70% @ 9.5% =   6.65%
> Equity—   30% @ 12% =   3.60%
> Total   10.25%
> Estimated Remaining Economic Life— 33 years
> Recapture Rate—3.0%
> Interest to Land and Buildings—   10.25%
> Recapture Rate—   3.00%
> Interest and Recapture—   13.25%

The Building Residual Technique is used in the Income Approach to estimate value. While there has been no experience of vacancies since the building was erected in 1960, and few cases of rental default, I will nevertheless allow a 2.5% vacancy and rent loss provision against possible future loss.

Calculations:

> Estimated Gross Annual Income $352,946
> Vacancy and Rent Loss (2.5%)   8,824
> Effective Gross Income $344,122

Expenses:

Taxes	$64,250.00
Fuel, Oil, and Gas	6,245.00
Janitors, Wages, Apt., Grounds, Maintenance and Supplies	11,122.00
Electricity	6,888.00
Water	2,843.00
Elevator Maintenance	1,260.00
Insurance (Fire and Liability)	4,558.00
Rubbish and Snow Removal	1,046.00

Reserves:

Painting and Decorating	2,596.00
Roof	394.00
Boiler	980.00

Ranges, Refrigerators,
   Dishwashers, and Garbage
   Disposals   2,628.00
Management   16,025.00
      Total · $120,835

Net Income to Land and Improvements $223,287
Less Interest to Land ($525,000.00 X 10.25%)   53,813
Interest to Improvements $169,474
$169,474 ÷ 13.25% = $1,279,049.00
Add Land $525,000.00
      Total · $1,804,049
                          Rounded to: $1,804,000

Market Value by Income Approach
One Million Eight Hundred Four Thousand Dollars
($1,804,000)

ANALYSIS, CORRELATION, AND CONCLUSIONS

The Cost Approach usually reflects the upper limit of value. It is a useful guide to reproduction value, not necessarily market value.

I have weighted the Income Approach in this appraisal as the best conclusion of investment value, or the market price that a sophisticated investor would pay for the property.

Conclusion of Land Market Value by Market
   Data Approach . . . .$ 525,000
Conclusion of Reproduction Value by Cost
   Approach $1,880,000
Conclusion of Market Value by Income
   Approach $1,804,000

Fair Market Value of the Property
One Million Eight Hundred Four Thousand Dollars
(1,804,000)

ADDENDA

Photographs, working blueprints, floor plans, basement and roof layouts, and wiring and plumbing details are numbered as Exhibits in the Addenda following the report. They are omitted here for the sake of brevity.

This chapter will deal with a successful plaza of a smaller type, built on surplus land too highly taxed to be held by one of the larger, single-tenancy corporations abutting it. The subject is completely net rented, with restaurant, bank, and stores included with the office structures in the plaza at ground level. It is brand new. Parking is generous in a building at the rear of the plaza.

9

Appraising an Office Plaza (with Stores)

KEY CONSIDERATIONS OF VALUE IN OFFICE BUILDINGS

A properly located and successfully rented office plaza will generally be found in an established top commercial center where public transportation is at hand, where banks and other financial services flourish, and where stores, restaurants, and parking are on the premises or nearby. No two office buildings are ever quite alike in tenant mix and income flow. Each tends to develop its own flavor or character.

Off-street private parking or garaging on a basis of at least one-for-each employee, and more for visitors, is imperative for modern office buildings; and in most municipalities this minimum is required by zoning. Tenants usually have garage accommodations built into their leases, paying higher monthly rentals than they would without parking.

The appraisal of an office plaza may be based on plans for a proposed structure on a given site as a *feasibility study* to test highest and best use of the land; or it may be a report on finished buildings for mortgage refinancing, with or without a long-term financial history. In any case, rents can be "stabilized" for the subject property by comparison and adjustment with other office rentals in the area.

If the subject building or plaza is proposed and in the planning stage, a design and tenant profile should be developed before the architect reaches the stage of working drawings. The profile may be based on comparative properties in the area and/or a questionnaire based on a direct-mail sampling of office professionals in the locale.

Even in the appraisal of an existing office building, such as the model in this chapter, a tenant profile is important to the owner who may be guided by it in making future alterations, and to the mortgage lender who may be asked for original take-out or refinancing. This profile should reflect effective demand, the type of units, and number of offices and services called for.

135

TENANT AND DESIGN PROFILE

(On the basis of 2,000 downtown and airport area prospects surveyed)

Element	Aggregate
Average Office Component:	55% require 8-14,000 sq. ft.; 45% require 50-60,000 sq. ft. There is also a strong demand for retail space in the plaza, looking for 2,500 to 4,000 square feet of store area @ $6-8 per square foot.
Average Credit Rating:	Triple-A
Growth Potential of Firms Interviewed:	Strong
Occupational Activity:	30% airline companies; 25% insurance branch offices; 25% stockbrokers; 20% other
Places of Work:	50% prefer airport area; 50% looking for perimeter of city with free parking
Commutation to Work:	65% automobile; 25% bus; 10% walk
Commutation Time to Work Less than 30 minutes:	65%; and 35% less than twenty minutes
Former Domicile:	60% from nearby communities; 40% within airport area
Average Anticipated Tenancy and Attainable Rent per Room:	25 to 30 years; $6-$8 per square ft. net, per annum in new building, with parking
Summation and Recommendation:	Location is ideal, and justifies restaurant and stores with banks. Garden plaza, four separate buildings placed graciously on 3 acres, best indicated positioning.

COMPREHENSIVE CONSIDERATIONS IN EVALUATION OF LAND AND IMPROVEMENTS IN OFFICE BUILDING APPRAISAL

Equally important as locale is the *functional design* of the office building. Offices should be spacious with ample amenities, such as water fountains and restrooms conveniently and economically connected nearby to office suites, eliminating unnecessarily long or disjointed hall spaces. Maximum tinted window exposure and air conditioning and sprinklering everywhere add to functional value and safety in an office building, and hence to the rental income the unit may command.

Architectural expertise in the arrangement of the working quarters, and central placement of lobby, elevators, corridors and the service core should be centralized in the buildings, so that tenants move about with ease and minimum walking. Certain amenity factors, such as prestige, security, and satisfaction in the home, bear a value to office buildings.

The mechanical equipment of the building (heating, lighting, air conditioning, elevator capacity, plumbing, wiring, and fireproofing) bears heavily on rental return. *These elements must be carefully expressed in the Cost Approach.*

Management is of equal importance to value in an office building. Tenants pay for comfort, safety, and quiet enjoyment of the premises, and if they are not provided with responsible maintenance the income from aggrieved tenants will be erratic, if not halted altogether, with less desirable tenants replacing those moving out. The aspects that characterize the property as excellent or poor in design and maintenance dominate the quality of tenant the building attracts, hence the quantity, quality, and durability of the building's income.

TECHNIQUES AND PROCEDURES

First Step in the Investment Analysis

The appraiser's *initial step* in evaluating an existing or proposed office building or plaza is to process its actual or hypothetical income. He decides upon capitalization method, rate, and valuation technique only after examining the quality of the subject's income stream, basing his conclusions on the dominant aspects of value that created the situation, namely the ease or difficulty with which the owner has collected his rents, filled his vacancies, reduced his turnover, and kept his expenses in line. A properly designed, functional, and well-maintained office building acquaints the appraiser with the rates of depreciation (recapture) that he can reasonably apply to the premises, both in the Cost Approach and the Income Approach.

Second Step: The Market Survey and Property Analysis

The next move the appraiser makes in evaluating a proposed or existing building plaza is to gather and correlate data that exposes the likelihood of success or failure in renting the building at a given location. He relates this information to his analysis of the subject property in this manner:

1. *Macro-market Influence of Area Economic Situation* measured against the micro-market demand for office space in the city. In measuring area vs. local economic conditions, the following factors must be scrutinized:
   (a) Type of city government and its effectiveness politically and economically, together with a synopsis of the city's reason for being (i.e., importance as a rail-head, communications center, harbor and/or airport facility). Indications of growth or decline in such facilities.

(b) Population of the city itself and population of suburbs within a 15-mile radius. Forms of transportation within the city and to and from the suburbs and other cities. Chief forms of employment within the city and within a 15-mile radius.

(c) Principal industries within the city, their growth patterns, and public utilities that serve them. The amount and substance of industry in the area and its contribution, if any, to the commerce of the city. The city's atmosphere as an industrial, commercial, or cultural (university) center, with all three described if necessary.

(d) The planning and zoning practices, the tax policies, and local ordinances affecting the property and its district must be stated clearly.

(e) State the demand for office space within an area of one hour's driving time from subject. Show growth of banks, law and accounting firms, medical services in the macro-market area including branch offices of national corporations, insurance companies, and other rated corporate entities. State the scope and intensity of this demand, or lack of it.

2. *Market Analysis of the Commercial Neighborhood.* Micro-market data concerning the immediate vicinity of the proposed or existing office building should be set forth as follows:

(a) Assuming that highest and best use of the site is an office building, with public transportation and automobile parking at hand, surrounded by banks, stock-brokerages, high-grade shops, restaurants, and other conveniences, state where the tenants for the proposed or existing office building come from. State the rent per square foot in competing office buildings nearby. Note number of vacancies.

(b) Describe trends in the district and block.

3. *Property Analysis and History.* Specific details of the property under appraisement must be clearly delineated:

(a) Recitation of the title, including metes and bounds, assessments and tax levy.

(b) Zone requirements.

(c) Description of the site topography and subsoil conditions, plottage and shape of the land area, together with list of utilities on site or available.

(d) The type of construction, use and condition of the proposed or existing building and its machinery, together with site improvements, planned or existing, such as paved parking, fencing, outdoor floodlighting.

(e) Each floor of the building must be measured and described.

(f) A summary of the development of the property, if existing, with a five- to ten-year history of income and expense, and type of management and maintenance attending the property.

(g) The anticipated useful life of the property must be estimated and allowances made for depreciation and obsolescence.

If the building is proposed or in the planning stage, the appraiser must project income and expenses for five years from his knowledge and experience in new office building construction, and recommend management and maintenance procedures for the proposed building that are both practical and economic.

4. *Comparable Land Sales and Office Leases.* The appraiser must list in detail verified data concerning land sales and leases of office space for buildings similar to the subject property, in the locale of the subject property. These comparables should be inspected and similarities or differences described, as compared to subject land or office space, summing up the property analysis.

Third Step: The Approaches to Value

The appraiser's vital third step in office building or plaza evaluation lies in his choice of approaches.

Usually an office building is somewhat different from any other in terms of location, tenant mix, and income flow, not to mention age, style, and services. Thus its character tends to make it distinct and difficult to compare with sales of other office buildings when estimating value.

This makes the Market Data Approach generally inapplicable, except for purposes of estimating land value and gauging the office rental market.

In the evaluation of an office building, the Cost Approach better supports the all-important Income Approach than does the Market Data Approach, because the Cost Approach leads the appraiser to a close examination of construction details, and the age, condition, and anticipated life of the property, hence the life of the income stream. The ratio of effective age of the building to life expectancy is crucial.

The Income Approach is the chief guide to value and is the proper test of an office structure's ability to throw off a worthwhile investment yield over a long period of time.

Since the market value of an office building depends to a great extent upon the present worth of its future earnings, the appraiser must rationally anticipate such earnings and estimate how long they will endure if he is to calculate their present worth.

Fourth Step: Capitalization Rates and Methods

Capitalization rates on office structure properties will vary with circumstances. Choice of capitalization rate and method is the appraiser's critical fourth step in evaluation of an office building.

Depending upon the quality and durability of income flowing from the property you are appraising, you can elect to follow either of the following courses of capitalization:

(1) Use the straight-line depreciation plus capitalization rate method of capitalization when leases are short term (less than 10 years) and the net income before depreciation is therefore uncertain for each year in the future.

(2) But if the net income before depreciation is expected to be level or better and is of contract nature, say, on long-term leases with security deposits from tenants of financial stability, and there is a long waiting list of tenant applications for offices so

located that extended popularity is implicit, then the *Property Residual Technique* in conjunction with the Inwood or Ellwood premises can be used as a truly sound means of appraising investment realty. This technique treats the worth of the property as an undivided entity during the entire economic life of the building, at the end of which the land reverts to its virgin state as vacant and is evaluated as a reversionary interest.

Fifth Step: Procedure for Estimating a Separate Land Value Under the Office Plaza

The Land Residual Technique is best used on a new project where the cost of the office building is a known factor. In that case, the appraiser would set up his Cost Approach first and find his land value as demonstrated in the model appraisal. It is a valid application to land under office buildings. Estimating land value is the appraiser's fifth step in office property evaluation. However, in the model appraisal that follows, land value was established by market data, and the Property Residual Technique was applied to long-term net income.

Sixth Step: Procedure for Estimating Value of the Improvements in Office Building

If the appraiser has established his land value via ample market data, then the Property Residual Technique or the Building Residual Technique is the best avenue to value of the improvements.

If the worth of neither land nor building is known, then either the building's value for depreciation purposes must be assumed or land value must be assumed for reversionary purposes only, and the Property Residual Technique is employed. When the appraiser has chosen his basic residual technique, his sixth and final step is estimating value of improvements.

In the following model appraisal of a small office plaza on the West Coast, appraised for acquisition and separation from a much larger and less manageable aggregate property, the Letter of Transmittal, Table of Contents, Limiting Conditions, and other introductory requirements of a fully formalized appraisal are omitted because we have already shown in other chapters the complete form required.

MODEL APPRAISAL OF AN OFFICE PLAZA (WITH STORES) AT THE PERIMETER OF THE LOS ANGELES AIRPORT

AREA AND SITE DATA (Macro- and Micro-Market Analysis)

Los Angeles International Airport, second only to O'Hare Airport in Chicago and ahead of Kennedy Airport in New York, is the gateway to Hawaii, the South Pacific, and the Far East, and is one-half mile west of the site. Further, the site is situated within an industrial corridor that is bounded on the north by the Santa Monica Freeway in Los Angeles, on the south by the Irvine Industrial complex in Costa Mesa, and by the San Diego Freeway and

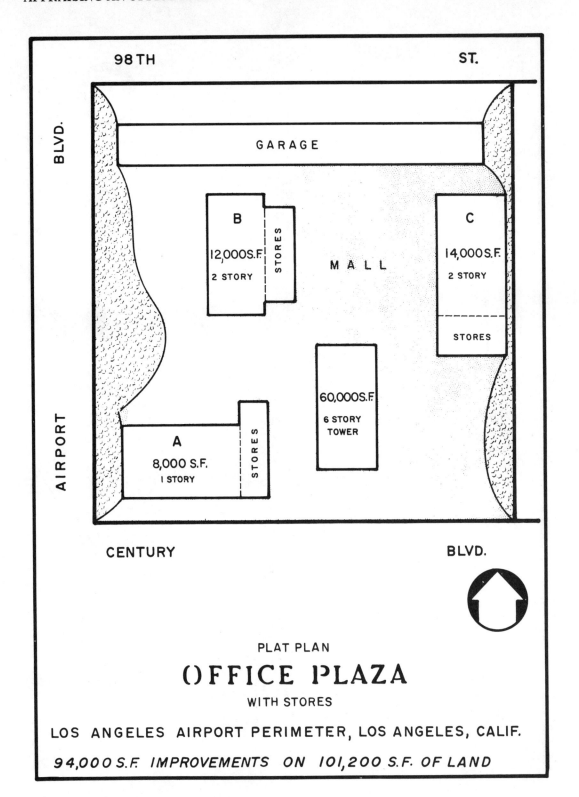

PLAT PLAN

OFFICE PLAZA

WITH STORES

LOS ANGELES AIRPORT PERIMETER, LOS ANGELES, CALIF.

94,000 S.F. IMPROVEMENTS ON 101,200 S.F. OF LAND

VICINITY MAP

L.A. INTERNATIONAL AIRPORT

LOS ANGELES, CALIFORNIA

Pacific Ocean to the east and west respectively. Within or adjacent to this corridor reside several hundred blue-chip industrial firms, two major financial centers (which serve as regional and national headquarters and offices for major banks, financial, industrial, and business concerns), and three commercial airports (Los Angeles, Long Beach, and Orange County Airports).

The subject site is roundly 23 miles southwest of the Civic Center of downtown Los Angeles, approximately 40 miles northwest of Anaheim, California (the home of Disneyland), 15 miles southwest of Beverly Hills (an exclusive residential area and another of the major financial centers in the Los Angeles Metropolitan area), and roundly 20 miles northwest of Long Beach, California (the site of the Queen Mary).

Maps depicting the site layout with buildings and stores plotted related to proximity of the Los Angeles International Airport area follow.

SITE DESCRIPTION

The subject parcel of land consists of approximately 101,200 sq. ft. with 361.11 front feet on the south line of Century Boulevard at the corner of Airport Boulevard.

All off-site improvements including asphalt paved streets, concrete curbs, gutters and sidewalks, underground and overhead utility lines are in place and in use.

The property is zoned for commercial-office development and the completed development conforms to all applicable codes and ordinances for the City of Los Angeles. As completed, the Airport Plaza project achieved an optimum utilization of the land as a development site.

Land Evaluation

After a study of recent site acquisitions and parcel assemblages for new office construction in the airport area, our estimate for the subject site of 101,200 sq. ft. is based on the following conclusions:
1. Century Boulevard frontage running to 361.11 feet. The parcel is approximately square.

Total Land Area, 101,200 sq. ft. @ $7.00 = $708,400

Total Estimated Land Value: $914,788

Rounded to: $915,000

Supporting Data

Three transactions involving major office building sites have occurred in the past four years. [These are cited and summarized at this point in the report, but for brevity will not be detailed in this chapter.]

The subject site was acquired March 10, 1972, for $505,100, or about $5.00 per sq. ft. for the entire parcel. Since 1972, the land value trend for major commercial street frontages in the airport area has approximated 12.5%-13.2% per annum. This trend would justify a current "average" price per sq. ft. for the subject of $7.00.

COST APPROACH

Description of Improvements

1. Garage Building

The three-story garage structure is located to the rear or north side of the main building complex and fronts on 98th Street. Structurally, it is tied into the main complex at its first (entry) level and at the plaza (deck) level. Access from the garage to the tenant areas is by elevator (4-stop) and stairway core opening to the plaza. There are three interior levels and a roof level for parking.

Construction is of reinforced concrete on poured concrete columns and bearing walls. Exterior walls are split-faced concrete block and concrete panels housing ventilator units. Floors are structural concrete slabs as is the half-circle ramp, the latter 8-1/2" on 6-1/2"—10% slope gradient with 8" concrete parapet.

All garage areas are sprinklered and marked for vehicular access, circulation, and parking. Interior space allocations are defined by concrete block walls.

2. Plaza and Store Buildings A, B, & C

The plaza level encompasses the entire project excluding the main garage structure. It surrounds the main (entry) level to all four tenant-occupied buildings and consists of a post-tensioned concrete slab on reinforced concrete columns. The plaza surface is paved with brick tile in a running bond. Four integral, raised planter boxes are located in the open areas flanking the office tower and an additional larger sized planter anchors the plaza's southwest corner. A brick stairway leads to the sidewalk grade along Century Boulevard.

Buildings A, B, & C

Building A is a single-story structure located at the southwest corner of Century Boulevard and Airport Boulevard occupying a frontal position in the project. Buildings B and C are two-story height and are located in a mid-plaza position flanking the office tower. Buildings A, B, and C each have ground-level retail facilities fronting on the mall. The retail space attached to Building A is used as a restaurant; in Building B as a men's and women's clothing store, and in Building C as a branch bank.

All three buildings are of 12" concrete masonry construction on 9" concrete slab. Roofs are 8" concrete slabs with rolled asphalt roof covering.

Exterior wall treatment uses a rough, rock-type facing which is low maintenance and attractive in appearance. All window hardware is aluminum and interior specifications include:

    movable partition walls for tenant space separation
    various tenant-installed floor coverings including
        tile and carpeting
    lighting in fluorescent units set in a suspended
        metal grid and acoustic panel ceiling

Equipment includes central heating and air-conditioning systems on zone controls. Each tenant space is separately controlled and metered for gas and electricity.

3. Office Tower

The office tower was constructed using a system of hydraulic jacks lifting successive concrete slabs into position (from topmost down). Eight jack assemblies worked on a 4 x 2 steel strap that ran vertically up each of the two in-place core units, the strap saddle spliced at the roof of the equipment "penthouses." Each floor slab, once in position, was anchored by its steel frame members to steel pins and welded joints.

The building has a structural steel frame (I-beams) in its lift-slab composition and integration with the two supporting core towers. The exterior is a curtain wall system using interlocking fiberglass modular panels tied to a vertical channel curtain wall frame.

Other basic specifications include:

Seismic damper units installed on the slab/core junctions at plaza level.

All-aluminum window and door hardware on main level and for exterior window units.

Metal channel and vinyl-covered metal frame partition wall system for upper floors; ceilings are suspended metal grid and acoustic panels. Full wall height, solid-core doors are used for all tenant spaces opening to central hall corridors.

Interior specifications include:

Plaza Level Lobby: A 40' x 50' glass-enclosed area with 19' ceiling height and central 528 sq. ft. dropped stainless-steel and pyramirror section over a carpeted seating area. Floors are otherwise same brick tile pavers as for open plaza area. Opens to core units, restrooms, elevators at each end.

Core Units: Core unit A contains two five-fixture restrooms at each level, a janitor's closet, equipment and ducting areas, and stairway.

The restrooms have ceramic tile floors and wainscotting; metal partitions; Formica countertops and porcelain sinks.

Core Unit B contains two elevators—Dover 6-stop automatic control, 2,000-pound capacity by electric overhead traction; elevators are carpeted and paneled. There are also equipment areas and a stairway.

Tower Floors: All wall-to-wall carpeted, vinyl wall covered 3/4" partition walls, and wood trim.

Tenant amenities for the office tower include conference rooms, mail room, decorator fabric drapes for exterior windows, security service.

Equipment: The tower is equipped with a central heating and air-conditioning system incorporating a centrifugal chiller, three-pass cooler system with cooling tower, primary and secondary pumping units for chilled, hot and condensed water, an air-fan system for heating, reheating and cooling coils. Fluidic air-control terminal units are zoned for lobby, mezzanine and each tower floor.

For each zoned space, the system includes a floor-level perimeter air (induction) distribution system with coil units under windows serviced by blowers and circulating ducts located in the air space over the suspended finished ceiling (4-way vent units tied to an air-distribution system located in a Core B ducting shaft).

Electrical service includes a main entry of 480 volt, 3,000 amp, 3 phase with multiple subcircuits and 4 service switching panels of 400 amp to 3,000 amp capacity.

The entire tower structure is monitored by a fire sensor and alarm system with central control panel at lobby level.

Calculated Data—Floor Areas

Garage Areas*

1st Level (extends from Airport Boulevard along 98th Street under plaza)	80,600 SF
2nd Level	26,400 SF
3rd Level	26,400 SF
Roof Level (4th)	26,400 SF
Total Garage Area	159,800 SF
Elevator & Stairway Core	256 SF

*Ramp excluded

Plaza Level

(net of building areas, garage entry core, inclusive of raised planters, entry stairs)	28,200 SF

		Net Usable Areas
Building A (One-Story)		
Gross Floor Area	8,000 SF	6,800 SF
Store Gross Area	3,000 SF	2,000 SF
Building B (Two-Story)		
Gross Floor Area:		
1st Floor:	6,000 SF	4,800 SF
2nd Floor:	6,000 SF	4,800 SF
	12,000 SF	9,600 SF
Stores	2,500 SF	1,500 SF
Building C (Two-Story)		
Gross Floor Area:		
1st Floor:	7,000 SF	5,800 SF
2nd Floor:	7,000 SF	5,800 SF
	14,000 SF	11,600 SF
Stores	3,600 SF	2,400 SF
TOTALS:	43,100 SF	33,900 SF

Office Tower

	Lobby	Service Costs
Entry Level	2,884 SF	(+) 1,440 SF
Tower Floors*	Gross	Net Usable
Per Floor	10,000 SF	10,000 SF
For 6 Floors	60,000 SF	60,000 SF

*The entire tower building is rented on an absolutely net basis for thirty years to a single tenant, Inter-Continental Airlines, so there is no deduction from gross area to net rentable, since they are responsible for maintaining this gross area of the tower in its entirety.

TOTAL COMPLEX—RECAP OF BUILDING AREAS

Garage Parking and Service Areas	159,800 SF
Plaza Level—Open Area, Garage Entry	28,200 SF
Plaza Level Store Space (Gross) (Buildings A, B, & C)	9,100 SF
Two-Level Office Space (Gross) (Buildings B & C)	26,000 SF
One-Level Office Space (Gross) (Building A)	8,000 SF
Office Tower—Six Floors—Gross	60,000 SF
Total Gross Building Area:	291,100 SF

Indirect Costs and Inapplicability of Depreciation

Following this discussion is a summary of our estimated reproduction cost for the subject project. In developing the cost parameters for the various building improvements, we studied data on a number of recent projects of similar size and quality that reflect the most recent construction contracts in the airport area.

All building unit cost figures (shown on a per-square-foot basis) are adjusted to March 1, 1975, or as close to the date of valuation as is possible from our statistical references.

In some cases, our unit cost factors were rounded to the nearest even dollar when the odd cents represented less than 10% of the dollar amount. All factors include contractor's overhead and profit.

Indirect costs at 10% of the total building cost estimate include all architectural and engineering costs, interim financing, property taxes, and other expenditures during the construction phase of the project.

Depreciation is not considered to be a factor in this analysis. The building was completed and ready for occupancy about November 1, 1974, and physical deterioration is not yet a factor to be considered as a deduction from reproduction cost new.

The buildings are functionally perfect, laid out in the most modern manner, 75-foot candlepower lighting at desk level in the offices, 100-foot candlepower in the stores. All areas of each building and retail store are air conditioned and sprinklered. Therefore, no functional obsolesence can be considered here. The extremely busy, attractive, and modern Los Angeles International Airport neighborhood, with good road access and crossover systems, rules out the possibility of economic obsolescence, of course. There are no depreciation factors to be applied to the subject at this time.

REPRODUCTION COST ANALYSIS

Garage Structure (4 stories, elevator)		
	79,200 SF @ $12/SF	$ 948,000
Garage Level Under Buildings and Plaza		
	80,600 SF @ $ 8/SF	644,800
Plaza	28,200 SF @ $ 5/SF	141,000
Buildings A, B, & C (Total)		
	34,000 SF @ $20/SF	680,000
Stores	9,100 SF @ $18/SF	163,800
Office Tower		
Six Floors Totalling 60,00 SF @ $33/SF		1,980,000
TOTAL BUILDING COST ESTIMATE		$4,557,600
Landscaping and Other Site Work		25,500
TOTAL IMPROVEMENT COST		$4,583,100
Indirect Costs @ 10%		458,310
TOTAL		$5,041,410
Land Value:		708,400
TOTAL VALUATION BY COST APPROACH		$5,749,810
	Rounded to:	$5,750,000

INCOME APPROACH
(Applying Property Residual Technique)

Occupancy and Lease Data

1. The garage 4-story parking structure, and the garage level under the buildings and plaza, 159,800 SF in all, are net-leased Byers Bros. Parking Systems for a period of 30 years @ $.50 per square foot per annum. The reason for this low rental is that about 50% of the garage space is committed to tenants in their leases as free parking, the remainder being open to ticket-paying parking visitors and shoppers.

Therefore: 159, 800 SF x $.50 p.s.t.   = $79,900

2. All tenants contribute in their monthly rental payments to the maintenance of the plaza mall, sharing on the basis of the square footage of building space they occupy.

Annually, this amounts to

28,200 SF x $.60 p.s.f. = $16,920

3. Buildings A, B, and C are each net-rented for 30 years to single tenants:

    a. Building A is leased to Smithers, Ferreil and Beam, stockbrokers, for 30 years at $8 p.s.f. per annum, or

      8,000 SF x $8.00 = $64,000

    b. Building B is leased to the Southwestern Farmers and Mechanics Insurance Company for 30 years at $7.00 p.s.f. per annum, or 12,000 SF x $7.00 = $84,000

    c. Building C is leased to Airtech Data Processing for 30 years at $6.00 p.s.f. per annum or 14,000 SF x $6.00 = $84,000

4. Office tower is leased to Inter-Continental Airlines, as their corporate headquarters, for 30 years at $6.00 p.s.f. per annum, or

60,000 SF x $6.00 = $360.000

5. The store space attached to Building A, at the southwest corner of the Plaza on Century Boulevard, is leased for 30 years to The Happy Landing restaurant and cocktail lounge, a high-grade eating place heavily patronized around the entire airport area as well as by the Plaza tenants. The rental is $7.00 p.s.f. per annum, or

3,000 SF x $7.00 = $21,000

6. The store space attached to Building B is also net leased in its entirety to the Fortnum Fashions (men's and women's clothing store) for 30 years at $8.00 p.s.f. per annum, or

2,500 SF x $8.00 = $20,000

7. The store space attached to Building C is leased in its entirety to 2nd National Community Bank. The lease is for 30 years at $6.00 p.s.f. per annum, or

3,600 SF x $6.00 = $21,600

All the net rental leases carry cost-of-living-index escalation clauses. The total of this absolutely net rental income from all sources within airport plaza = $751,420

Operating Expenses and Reserves

The only expense that the owner has to bear are the taxes on the land underneath the airport plaza. However, a reserve for vacancy allowances of 5% per annum must be set aside, even though several of the office tenants are rated triple-A. The stores are not rated concerns, and possible default must be accounted for in these cases.

Therefore: Taxes on the land, plus accruals
for severe anticipated tax increases in future years = $50,000
Vacancy Allowance @ 5% = 37,571
                                                  87,571

TOTAL NET RENTAL INCOME $663,849

Since the purpose of this appraisal is for mortgage financing, the Ellwood factor will be applied to the constant:

Capitalization Rate

Mortgage Constant—————
Term/20 Years Interest Rate/9-1/2%
(Constant) .112 x 75% Mortgage   = .084
Equity Rate—————
14 Percent Equity Requirement
25 Percent Equity Contribution   = .035
Overall Rate: .119
                                                        Rounded to: 12%

Total net rental of $663,849 capitalized at an overall rate of 12 percent equals $5,033,740 ($663,849 ÷ 12% = $5,532,075)

Rounded to: $5,533,100
VALUE CONCLUSION VIA INCOME APPROACH
$5,533,100

CORRELATION AND VALUE CONCLUSION

The three approaches to value were all considered, but no sales of land and building similar to subject were to be found in the Los Angeles International Airport area. Therefore, the Market Data Approach was inapplicable, and only two approaches have been applied. They are as follows:

Cost Approach $5,750,000
Income Approach $5,533,100

The Cost Approach, which normally sets the upper limit of value, was developed after determining local construction costs from discussions with the building engineer of the subject property, by reference to national valuation manuals, and from the appraiser's first-hand experience in the building trades. The unit costs applied were derived to include the current costs for labor, materials, profit, and overhead. Depreciation allowances were omitted for physical deterioration and functional and economic obsolescence.

The contract rentals were applied in order to derive the actual income established for the property. The actual rentals are calculated as economic in the current market.

The Market Data Approach proved to be inapplicable because office and retail land and buildings in the airport are very tightly held and sales of such properties, unless they are very old and ready for demolition, simply are not on the records.

Great consideration has been given to whether the buildings are well planned, efficient in operation, and convertible to other modern office and retail uses.

Our arrival at value conclusion has been forged by the following principle:

The appraiser does not average the indications of value by the three approaches. He selects the one that is most applicable, and rounds to a final figure. He places the most emphasis on the approach that appears to be the most reliable and most applicable, as an indication of the answer to the specific appraisal problem. Then he tempers this estimate in accordance with his judgment as to the degree of reliance to be placed on the other two indications of value. (The Appraisal of Real Estate, published by The American Institute of Real Estate Appraisers, Chicago, Illinois, Fifth Edition, 1971.)

Although the subject property is presently leased for income and the property is not for sale, we have put reliance on two approaches; and we have tempered these values into a conclusion, allowing for future benefits likely to occur under the Income Approach, and for the physical depreciation that will build a tax shelter for the property under the Cost Approach as the subject begins to age. Therefore, it is our opinion that the market value of the subject property as of January 1, 1975 is:

FIVE MILLION SIX HUNDRED THOUSAND DOLLARS
($5,600,000)

Gasoline service stations are an exception to the rule in appraising commercial properties. The reasons for this are the frequency of price wars and giveaways such as glassware, cutlery, and flashlights to achieve a false gallonage gross, which does not show a true percentage of net profit per gallon sold; the personality of the station manager; and tied-in cut-rate tires, batteries, and accessories sales, which again promote gross gallonage, but do nothing to add true value to the station. Even trading stamps affect the value of income produced by gallonage sales, voiding the Income Approach.

10

Appraising Gasoline Service Stations: The Crucial Importance of Market Data

KEY CONSIDERATIONS OF VALUE IN GASOLINE STATIONS

There is no state in the Union with a statute regulation regarding minimum size of the square foot area for gasoline service stations. However, *they are uniform in a front-foot requirement.* Connecticut, for example, requires a minimum of 150 front feet on any state-controlled highway. It is true that many local ordinances set up minimum sizes for commercial sites, but these ordinances serve a different purpose than the frontage requirements dictated by the state for service stations.

Depth is so unimportant to oil companies that it is not at all unusual for appraisers to be requested to value the site required for the service station and treat the balance as excess rear land to be sold. In one example, the rear land was sold as an addition to a shopping center site; in another case, the rear land was sold to a motel chain.

This is what occurs when the appraiser using square feet as a basis for evaluation takes a look at recent sales:

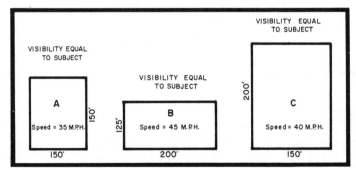

FIGURE 1

153

All sites are interior[1]:

	A	B	C
Area	22,500 sq. ft.	25,000 sq. ft.	30,000 sq. ft.
Selling Price	$150,000.00	$200,000.00	$150,000.00
Sale Price per Front Foot	$ 1,000.00	$ 1,000.00	$ 1,000.00
Sale Price per Square Foot	$ 6.61	$ 8.00	$ 5.00
Subject:	160' x 121' = 19,360 square feet		
	Speed = 40 M.P.H.		

Since minimum frontage is 4 x traffic speed, the subject does not have access frontage.

Then the following results emerge:

Value Range Using Raw Data from Sales

	A	B	C
Front-foot basis:	$160,000	$160,000	$160,000
Square-foot basis:	133,400	160,000[2]	100,000

The error of using a square-foot method is thus demonstrated by raw data and is even more striking with adjusted data. The use of depth tables fails to measure the actual market impact.

Special treatment of front footage of corner properties eliminates use of the hazardous square-foot method and gives an accurate picture of the market.

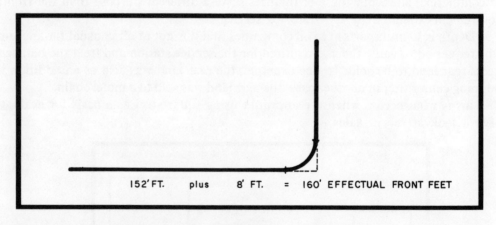

152' FT.   plus   8' FT.   =   160' EFFECTUAL FRONT FEET

FIGURE 2

---

[1]*Note:* Many lots are 300' x 400' deep, which tends to compound the errors and increase margin of error.

[2]Note that the front-foot and square-foot figures coincide only under optimum site size.

The effectual front-foot method brings to light all the errors and miscomputations resulting from lack of consideration of the *true* frontage. Additionally, corner influence (25 to 35 percent depending on many factors) is "hidden" in the square-foot concept.

Another criticized method involves gallonage. Of course, management has much to do with gallonage; but superior management can mislead the appraiser in *every* type of income property. Conversely, *bad* management can be equally misleading.

However, with sufficient data the *median* is rarely misleading, and from our data we have found that service stations sell for from $0.35 to $0.60 per gallon of gasoline sold per year. Frequency of price wars, impact of giveaways and of trading stamps have an influence that can be determined from the market. Thus:

$$
\begin{array}{ll}
\text{400,000 gallons x \$0.30} & = \text{\$120,000} \\
\text{Contribution of improvements} & = \underline{\text{\ \ \ 30,000}} \\
\text{Land value} & = \text{\$\ \ 90,000} \\
\dfrac{\text{\$90,000}}{\text{150 front feet}} & = \text{\$600 \ per\ front\ foot}
\end{array}
$$

which is about what you would expect for a 400,000 gallon/year location, again depending on location, residential backup, adjacency of thruway ramps, speed of traffic, visibility, etc.

Another problem evolves in gasoline alleys where a *share of the market* concept applies. In this case the modification indicated by brand acceptability cannot be overlooked. These figures are available from the various state tax departments.

COMPREHENSIVE CONSIDERATIONS IN EVALUATION OF LAND AND IMPROVEMENTS IN GASOLINE SERVICE STATION APPRAISAL

I. Site Analysis and Value Estimate (factors in appraising)
  A. Discuss importance of careful analysis of the legal description for easements, rights-of-way, deed restrictions, etc.
    1. Type of location
      a. In-town
      b. Interchange
      c. Crossroads and interior lots
      d. Other, such as neighborhood stations
    2. Methods
      a. Front-foot unit (preferred and why)
      b. Square-foot unit
      c. Known gallonage, reduced to unit
      d. Predicted gallonage, reduced to unit
        1. Data re:auto increase in area as well as traffic
    3. Traffic counts and their use
    4. Speed of traffic, analysis
    5. Visibility
    6. Location
      a. Which corner? (Impact of corner location)

            b. The shopping center station
            c. Gasoline alleys
        7. Residential backup
        8. Competition, including discussion of management
            a. Product acceptance
            b. Gallonage, impact of gas wars
            c. Giveaways, trading stamps
        9. Physical characteristics
            a. Frontage, effective vs. effectual
                1. Outside and inside curves
            b. Size
            c. Shape, including triangular lots
            d. Topography
            e. Excess frontage
            f. Excess real land
            g. Utilities
        10. Zoning
            a. Quasi-monopolies (via nonconformity)
            b. Probability of zone change
        11. Permits and licenses
            a. State and local ordinances, curb cuts, distance from corners, distance
               from similar facilities, etc.
II. Service Station Description
    A. Type
        1. Sales outlet (kiosk type)
        2. Two-bay stations: limitations, legal and physical
        3. Multiple-bay stations
            a. Repairer's licenses
            b. Full-service facilities
    B. Constructive
    C. Permanent equipment, when valued
    D. Site improvements
III. Estimate of Value
    A. Cost Approach: discussion of its application in this type of appraisal
        1. Site value estimate
        2. Contribution of site improvements
        3. Contribution of existing building (via cost new depreciated)
    B. Income Approach: discussion of its application and limitations in this type
       of appraisal
        1. Leases, types and analysis
    C. Market Data Approach: describe and illustrate each method
        1. When the station is a proper improvement: Selling price per square foot
           of building to include land and site improvements
        2. When station is under improvement: Selling price of land per unit to
           include building and site improvements

3. When known gallonage: Selling price per gallon, if unit falls within typical brackets. Stations selling for per-gallon figures outside typical market data reflect above-average or below-average management. Use of medians as a basis of adjustment will modify outriders. *All sales must be adjusted to subject* by adjusting unit selling price to subject unit. *All surplus land should be treated as a separate add-on item.* (This is not summation; the excess must be appraised for a value for which it can be readily sold as a separate entity under market value definitions.)

IV. Correlation and Final Value Estimate

APPRAISING THE
USED SERVICE STATION

Many of the major oil companies are today undergoing a re-evaluation of their marketing strategies. The competition for the customer's gallon of gasoline is particularly keen, with the independent marketer attaining a greater share of that gallon with lower-cost facilities, lower-cost land, plus a lower price. The advent of self-serve in various states, fewer oil and lube changes for automobiles, gasoline-dispensing facilities at convenience food stores, and discount prices through chain stores such as Sears and Penney's have also brought about this re-evaluation.

A by-product of this change has been an ever-increasing number of service stations being deactivated by the oil companies and placed on the market for sale, usually for some use other than the sale of gasoline.

While the result of the program is often increased appraisal assignments for the real estate appraiser, the appraiser must in turn use particular care in structuring his appraisal to avoid some of the pitfalls he may otherwise encounter in adequately completing his assignment. These are encountered in the approaches to value, as follows.

The Cost Approach

As a first step, the appraiser should determine from his client whether the property will be sold with a petroleum restriction. In such cases, the value of the building usually becomes marginal, since the service station is primarily a single-use building, requiring extensive modification for other uses. Even when the property is sold without a petroleum restriction, it should generally be discounted substantially through functional obsolescence.

Other major oil companies will generally not buy the outlet, since they use the same criteria in determination of productivity. An independent *may* purchase the facility, but he too will discount the building since he usually has little use for the service bays, and the building may not be ideally located on the lot for his use.

The following comments and illustrations demonstrate the method of arriving at depreciated building value of a station to be continued in service station use. We refer to the sample schedule herewith and comment as follows.

1. Building Cost: Replacement costs of a porcelain and block building will run approximately $26 per square foot in metropolitan areas, and for a newer design station up to $32 per square foot.

2. Deterioration: Deterioration is shown as 40 percent in the example, since most oil companies maintain their older buildings well; if the stations are boarded up, the building should be inspected to be sure of the internal condition of the building and the deterioration rate shown accordingly.

3. Functional Obsolescence: This usually results from the building being too small for modern use, lacking storage room, or being improperly located on the lot; deduction should not be made here for size or shape of lot since this item is a function of land comparables in the land evaluation.

4. Yard Improvements: These are average costs that would vary as to lot size, amount of yard improvements, and types of improvements installed.

In those cases where the property will not be used as a service station, the appraiser will apply a greater degree of functional obsolescence and possibly a greater percentage charge to yard improvements.

In estimating land value in the Cost Approach, the appraiser should be wary of using major oil company land purchases as comparables, as the oil company usually buys larger parcels for their new facility on prime intersections. Also, with their marketing re-evaluation, the major oil companies have, for the most part, retrenched on their acquisition programs currently, or are using extreme selectivity in their site selection. Consequently, the law of supply and demand takes effect and with lesser demand these land prices are beginning to fall.

The appraiser, then, should look for comparables in commercial land sales for a sound Cost Approach.

The Market Approach

The Market Approach is the best approach for the appraiser to use in building a persuasive appraisal report. The market will usually divulge numerous sales of comparable used service stations, due to the increased number of these stations being offered in the market. A tabulation of these sales using square foot value of *both* land and building is often the most effective means of arriving at a valuation estimate.

Only in the smaller communities where there may not be sufficient comparable sales of similar properties should the appraiser revert to the Cost Approach as his primary appraisal tool.

The Income Approach

The appraiser would not ordinarily use the Income Approach in the appraisal of a used service station. The oil company usually is disposing of the station because in their judgment it lacked the capacity of producing adequate income to meet their criteria, with the result that the Income Approach could not be sustained.

It is generally not advisable to use the rental income from the station operator to the oil company as a basis of value for several reasons. For one, competitive pressures, road changes, and the like can result in depressed rentals to the operator. Also, the rental from the operator is not the only source of income to the oil company, who furnish him with various oil products from which they derive earnings, and which information is as a rule not provided the appraiser for his analysis.

An exception to the above would be cases where the oil company is leasing the facility for nonpetroleum use. In this case the rental could be used to reach an estimate of value. For example, if the property were rented for $300 per month, an estimate of value could be reached as follows:

$$\$300 \times 12 \, (mo.) = \$3,600 \div 12\% = \$30,000$$

As the leases written for nonpetroleum purposes are usually short term, a rate above second-mortgage interest requirements is suggested.

There are additional factors the appraiser should research to achieve a well-rounded report; some of these are the following.

Zoning

Many communities have adopted stringent codes regarding closed or abandoned service stations. Often, if the station has been closed for a period of time, the zoning reverts to a higher classification, with the result that the station cannot be reopened for dispensing gasoline. The appraiser should carefully study the applicable codes to determine the exact status of zoning at the time of appraisal.

In other cases the zoning may have previously been changed, placing the property in a nonconforming use. The result may be that the building cannot be remodeled; or at the end of a specified time the zoning reverts to another use; or the zoning may have been changed so that the building now is too close to a church, a school, or other places of public assembly.

Highest and Best Use

The appraiser can often perform a service to his client by determining that the property has substantially greater use for some other purpose than a service station—a used car lot or a dry-cleaning establishment. In areas of high residential density, the property may have greater value as an apartment or condominium, with, of course, a zero or negative value attributable to the building.

Grateful acknowledgment for much of the substance, organization, drawings, and illustrations of this chapter is made here to John A. Rowlson, M.A.I., and John E. Moore, S.R.A., noted specialists in appraising for petroleum companies. Their teachings at appraisal society seminars, roundtable conferences with petroleum company officials, and association with the writer in joint projects have been proven in the writer's own long experience with gasoline service station appraising.

MODEL APPRAISAL
OF A USED SERVICE STATION

PURPOSE OF APPRAISAL

The purpose of this appraisal is to estimate market value of the property located at 145 Paddle River Road, Totamus, New Jersey, as of May 12, 1975.

PROPERTY APPRAISED

All rights inherent in the fee are appraised.

LOCATION OF PROPERTY

The subject service station property is located on the westerly side of Paddle River Road, approximately 500 feet north of the Totamus-Fair Lawn town line in the extreme southern section of Totamus.

LEGAL DESCRIPTION

Grantor: Alfred C. Smith, et al.
Grantee: Tiger Oil & Refining Co., Inc.
Warranty Deed: I.R.S. $65.45; dated May 10, 1960
                       Volume 128, Page 204, Bergen County Hall of Records.
Southwesterly: in westerly line of Paddle River Road, 225 feet;
Northwesterly: by land now or formerly of Bertram Voelker, 150 feet;
Northeasterly: by land now or formerly of Bertram Voelker, 225 feet;
Southeasterly: by land now or formerly of Bertram Voelker, 150 feet.

Northerly, Westerly, and Southerly by Bertram Voelker and Easterly by Paddle River Road.

ASSESSMENT AND TAX BURDEN

Land & Paving	$19,680
Building	12,520
Total Assessment	$32,200
Tax Rate $47.0 per thousand	
Taxes Levied	$ 1,513.40

Assessments are reported to represent 65% of assessed value. The Borough of Totamus is now in the process of a town-wide tax revaluation program which is expected to be completed by October, 1976.

LOCALE

Paddle River Road is a two-lane north-south highway extending to Ramsey, N.J. and New York communities to the north. Traveling south, this highway extends through Route 4 in Fair Lawn.

Between 1965 and 1966, Interstate Route 80 opened and diverted a major portion of traffic from Paddle River Road. Shortly after the opening of Interstate 80, property values along the Paddle River Road took a sharp drop. As a matter of fact, most properties that were placed on the market reflected panic sales. Since the latter part of 1969, and early 1970, property values have been somewhat stablized to a point where some renewed economic confidence has been reflected in this traffic-orientated business strip.

In 1972, the New Jersey Department of Traffic Statistics indicated that 19,900 vehicles passed the subject location per day. This count reflects traffic in both directions on the Paddle River Road, which is a two-lane highway.

Improvements along Paddle River Road include gasoline service stations, restaurants, motels, supermarkets, and discount department stores, industrial operations, and like uses.

Shortly after the opening of Interstate 80, many of these properties were vacated, giving this strip an economically depressed appearance. However, within the last year or so, some of these properties have been purchased or reopened, reflecting a renewed confidence in the area.

Available public utilities include water, sanitary sewers, electricity, storm sewers, and telephone service. Within the last year, sanitary sewers were installed at the rear of the subject property and are now available to be connected to the property.

Gasoline service station competition within close proximity to the subject is not considered excessive. Most of these stations are competitive to the subject in age and utility and most have experienced a similar production history. In 1965, the subject station pumped 518,792 gallons of gasoline and by 1970 it had dropped to 194,612 gallons. In the first four months of 1975, this station had pumped 76,799 gallons of gasoline for an estimated 1975 total figure of 230,397 gallons. The estimated 1975 gallonage may be somewhat optimistic since historically the first four months of the year did not reflect the total year's production when multiplied by three. Therefore, based upon the last four years' gallonage, and considering the first four months of 1975, estimated total gallonage for this year will be 200,000 gallons.

BOROUGH DATA

	1960	1968	% Change City	County	State
Population					
Covered Employment	17,767	22,400	26.0	16.0	16.5
Number of Manufacturing	3,849	10,031	160.6	30.6	25.8
Firms	34	55	61.8	21.5	18.0
Manufacturing Payroll					
(Millions of Dollars)	13.6	51.6	279.4	76.5	67.0
Dwelling Units	5,151	7,433	44.3	43.8	43.4
Motor Vehicles	7.550	13,124	73.8		
Persons/Motor Vehicle	2.4	1.7			
Per Capita Income	977	2,382	34.5	39.4	21.3

ZONING

The subject property is located within an M-1 Industrial Zone.

Bulk Requirements

Maximum Building Height	3 stories, but not to exceed 45'
Minimum Front Yard	25 feet
Minimum Side Yards	2 required, each 15 feet
Minimum Rear Yard	15 feet

Permitted Uses: Gasoline service stations as a special exception, permitted uses as outlined in the B-2 General Business Zone; wholesale businesses, laundries, lumber yards, manufacturing, tire shops, used car sales lots, trucking terminals, etc.

DESCRIPTION OF PROPERTY

The subject property is improved as a gasoline service station operation which, at time of inspection on May 5, 1975, was in operation. The building is a standard-type Tiger station built approximately 20 years ago. It has two bays and is constructed of concrete block on a concrete slab and contains 1,473 sq. ft. of building area. The building contains, besides the two bays, two ceramic tile restrooms, a sales office with asphalt tile floor and plaster walls and ceiling, a utility room, and a fireproof boiler room. There are ample electrical outlets, 100-amp electrical service, and wiring is armor covered.

This one-story, flat-roofed structure, typical of the stations built 20 years ago, is equipped with the standard service station equipment, which includes two single-post hydraulic lifts, air compressor with related piping, copper water piping, office display rack, greasing equipment, etc.

The building is in structurally good condition but should have some minor repairs and decorating within the near future.

The lot is improved with typical service station site improvements such as bituminous concrete paved yard and berm curbing in fair condition, yard lights, two concrete pump islands with two pumps on each island and island lights, underground storage tanks, and air tower.

The lot contains 33,750+ square feet with 225 feet of frontage along Paddle River Road, 225 feet along the rear boundary line and a depth of 150 feet. From Paddle River Road the lot is level and at street grade to an average depth of 100 feet; from this point the lot drops off sharply 20 feet and then is level to the rear boundary line (west).

Public water and sewer are available but not connected to the service station building. At time of inspection, the operator stated that water and sanitary sewer systems consisted of a drilled well and septic system. A recent discussion with the Metropolitan District was made in regard to the water and sewer assessments and is as follows:

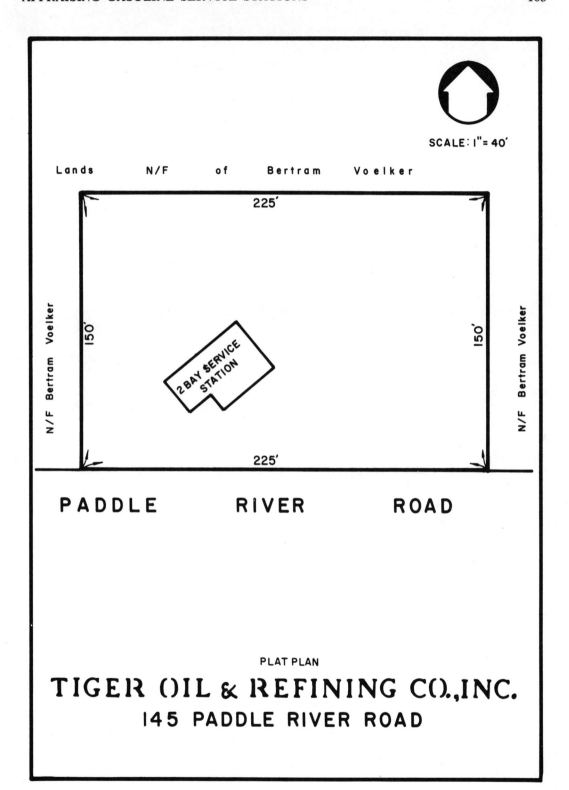

SCALE: I"= 40'

Lands   N/F   of   Bertram   Voelker

225'

N/F Bertram Voelker

150'

2 BAY SERVICE STATION

N/F Bertram Voelker

150'

225'

PADDLE   RIVER   ROAD

PLAT PLAN

TIGER OIL & REFINING CO.,INC.

145 PADDLE RIVER ROAD

Water—not connected; if connected in 1975, it
will cost approximately $2,662.
Sanitary sewer—not connected; assessed at $4,903.

Remarks:

The subject property is located on the west side of Paddle River Road
on the crest of a hill that has excellent exposure to the north of approximately one-quarter mile. To the south it is limited since the identification sign is not of sufficient size or height for good exposure.

The curb cuts and turn radius have been laid out to best utilize the
subject lot. Traffic circulation in and out of this lot has free and easy access
and is enhanced by moderate traffic speed (posted at 45 m.p.h.) and a traffic
light just 200 feet north of the subject location.

HIGHEST AND BEST USE

The highest and best use of the subject property is as currently improved with a major-brand gasoline service station for the remaining
economic life of the property.

It was obvious at time of inspection of this property that it is not being
operated at its capacity due primarily to management. Under current
management, this station will pump approximately 200,000 gallons in 1975.
Based upon relatively good traffic volume and considering competition with
existing service stations, nearby population support, new and proposed
nearby residential construction, the subject station should pump between
250,000 to 300,000 gallons of gasoline per year for the next two to three
years and gradually increase this volume as traffic and nearby supporting
commercial and residential activity increases.

VALUATION ESTIMATE
MARKET COMPARISON METHOD

Sale No. 1

Location:	1818 Washington Boulevard
	Hohokus, New Jersey
Grantor:	George S. Barber
Grantee:	Franklin Oil Company
Date of Transfer:	August 14, 1974
Recorded:	Vol. 160, Page 505, Bergen County
	Records
Sale Price:	$61,000
Lot Size:	14,700 ± sq. ft. with 185 front feet
Topography:	Level at street grade
Utilities:	Electricity and telephone service only
Zone:	Business
Traffic Count:	14,900 vehicles per day in 1974

This parcel of land is improved with an 18-year-old, three-bay gasoline service station that was constructed to Chevron Oil Company specifications. The building at time of sale was in fair to good condition and vacant. The Grantor, Mr. George S. Barber, stated that at time of purchase he estimated this station would pump between 300,000 and 350,000 gallons. Observation of sale property since purchase date leads me to believe that the projected gallonage was somewhat overestimated.

If the projected figure of between 300,000 and 350,000 gallons was the basis of the purchase, the sale price represents $0.17 to $0.20 per gallon paid for the property.

Analysis:

Sale No. 1 is superior to the subject property in respect to having one more bay and although the total traffic exposure is considered less than the subject, this sale is located at a traffic light and crossing which partially off-sets greater traffic volume. Also, the sale property is located in a community that has a more advantageous tax structure. That is, the current taxes on the sale property are $666.45 compared to the subject taxes, which are $1,513.40.

Sale No. 2

Location:	2550 Waldwick Turnpike, Fair Lawn, N.J.
Grantor:	Pentex Oil Corporation
Grantee:	Raymond O. de Bronkart
Date of Sale:	November 28, 1973
Recorded:	Vol. 184, Page 239, Bergen County Records
Sale Price:	$30,500
Lot Size:	55,781 sq. ft.; corner lot with 285 front feet on the Waldwick Turnpike, 289.79 feet on Ann Street, and 134.09 feet on Dunham Avenue
Topography:	Level at street grade
Utilities:	All
Zone:	M-1, Industrial
Traffic Count:	19,900 vehicles per day in 1973

The sale land was improved at time of sale with a two-bay Gulf gasoline service station. The building at time of sale was in fair to good condition and vacant for some time. Since time of purchase, the building has been completely renovated and six more bays added for a used-car operation.

Analysis:

Sale No. 2 is considered slightly superior to the subject since it has more surplus land, is a corner lot and is located in a more active business section of the Waldwick Turnpike. However, strong consideration must be given to the date of sale. At this time, many properties along the Waldwick

Turnpike were for sale and most transactions were based upon an extremely weak market.

Sale No. 3

Location:	1801 North Main Street (Route 25)
	Ramsey, New Jersey
Grantor:	Rich Realty, Inc.
Grantee:	Decker Oil Company
Date of Sale:	March 4, 1974
Recorded:	Volume 523, Page 625 of the
	Bergen County Records
Sale Price:	$22,000
Lot Size:	34,500 ± sq. ft.; with 200 feet along
	Route 25, a divided four-lane highway
Topography:	Relatively level at street grade to
	a depth of approximately 110 feet.
	The rear portion of the property or
	approximately 60 feet is elevated
	above street grade approximately 25-30
	feet and is ledge.
Utilities:	Consists of water, electricity, and
	telephone service only
Zone:	Retail Business
Traffic Count:	12,600 vehicles per day in 1970

The lot is improved with a two-bay, old Texaco service station which has been recently renovated by the grantee, plus two bays were added. This property is currently being used as a used-car sales operation together with a gasoline service station.

This inside parcel has good visibility from the south and north.

Analysis:

This property is considered inferior to the subject since it has less desirable lot utility and the building at time of sale was in relatively poor condition. Also, the sale is located in a stretch along Route 25 that has ex-experienced a great economic slump in business and real estate activity between Dumont to the north and Totamus to the south.

The previous sales are the most recent applicable sales that could be found along the Paddle River area between Ramsey and Totamus, N.J. Although there are many recent known sales within the area of gasoline service stations, these sales were not used since, in the opinion of this appraiser, these sales could not be adjusted within any degree of reliability since they were not exposed to the same economic condition that exists along the Paddle River Road area.

Based upon the preceding sales, the subject property in its present condition has an estimated market value of $45,000.

VALUE CONCLUSION BY MARKET COMPARISON METHOD—$45,000

COST APPROACH

The Cost Approach will not be used since, typically, properties similar to the subject in respect to age and condition are not normally purchased based upon the Cost Approach in this area.

INCOME APPROACH

Due to the lack of sufficient recent rentals and other relevant information in respect to processing the Income Approach, this approach will not be used.

CORRELATION AND CONCLUSIONS

The subject property consists of a two-bay gasoline service station that is currently being operated under poor management. The value of this property is based on the enclosed data and particularly enclosed three recent gasoline service station property sales. These sales were analyzed and compared to the subject property for date of sale, location, physical characteristics, motivation, and other factors that may add to or detract from value.

The result of my investigation and appraisal analysis is that it is my opinion the estimated market value of the subject property in its present condition, as of May 12, 1975 is:

FORTY-FIVE THOUSAND ($45,000) DOLLARS

Since the 1940s, shopping centers have become ubiquitous, mushrooming in all forms and types—regional, community, and neighborhood. In some large cities, the regional types might appear head to head, facing directly across the street, with others but a block or two away, creating competition that becomes disastrous to each. In this chapter, however, our model will be a modest-sized regional center that has no menacing competition in a sixteen-county area, and that represents an ideal investment.

11

Evaluating the Shopping Center for Mortgage Refinancing Using the Land Residual Technique

KEY CONSIDERATIONS OF VALUE IN SHOPPING CENTERS

The modern, successful shopping center is an integrated store group with parking that is planned, developed, owned, and managed as a unit, a fact that often shows itself through an attractive architectural unity. Off-street parking with an area at least four times that occupied by the stores on the property is essential.

Each store tenant in the shopping center was probably selected by the developer to fit into a preconceived pattern of merchandising. Together this group of tenants will supply all of a shopper's daily needs; larger centers will include the shopper's once-a-year needs, too.

The typical customer coming to the shopping center will arrive by automobile and will require 300 square feet in which to conveniently park the car. If parking is not adequate, the customer may be lost to a competing center.

The regional center will have as many as 40 to 100 stores or more totalling 300,000 to 1,000,000 square feet of net leasable area. It will be built around one or more large major department stores, each with not less than 100,000 square feet of gross leasable area. It is designed to accommodate the daily and annual needs of more than 75,000 families. The regional center is the equivalent of a downtown shopping district and offers varieties of apparel and home furnishings, as well as novelties, luxuries, recreational facilities, and often professional services.

The community center is most often built around a junior department store, with as many as twenty to forty stores arrayed around it. It is most often found in flourishing suburbs or at city perimeters. At least 35,000 families must patronize it regularly, and it will contain between 100,000 and 300,000 square feet of net leasable area.

The convenience neighborhood center will usually consist of local or chain supermarket, pharmacy, dry cleaner, hardware store, variety or discount house, and sometimes a beauty salon, barber shop, bakery, delicatessen, branch bank, and gasoline service station, ranging in size from ten to twenty stores. This center will depend on the trade of at least 15,000 families, and generally contains 25,000 to 100,000 square feet of net leasable area.

UNIQUE FEATURES OF SHOPPING CENTER EVALUATION

If the shopping center is already established, or is not yet built but has achieved executed agreements to lease, valuation of the land must be based on capitalization of annual residual net income produced by the yield of the lease rentals; if the shopping center is merely projected and has no lease agreements, valuation of the land can only be based on market data showing comparable sales of similar land in similar situations.

The property must be valued as a whole, and not as separate individual stores or buildings.

The need for the shopping center must be proven by macro- and micro-market surveys. An estimate of rent achievement based on percentage of gross sales must be made, in addition to the minimum guaranteed yield of the leases.

Sales of improved commercial properties in the area cannot be used as comparable in evaluating the subject, because no two shopping centers are ever precisely alike in terms of land area, parking ratio to store areas, tenant mix, goods offered, hours open, lease particulars, gross expenses, and net income produced per square foot of store occupancy.

In these respects, every shopping center is a unique entity and can only be evaluated by capitalization of its guaranteed net income.

TECHNIQUES AND PROCEDURES

First Step in the Investment Analysis

The initial step in appraising a shopping center already established or merely projected is to make a thorough analysis of those land requirements unique to successful shopping center development. The appraiser begins as follows:

Site Analysis: (Micro-market)

1. *Location:* Traffic flow for any kind of shopping center is of prime importance. The neighborhood or community center should be close to public facilities such as churches, libraries, and schools, on or near an intersection of important town roads, and close to state highways.

Proximity to cloverleaf exchanges on express highways is requisite for a regional shopping center, since it embraces a much broader market trade area. Local roads in and out of the center and public transportation are also important.

Pedestrians should be afforded protected, easy access to all three types of center, where they may be carried by bus, train, or subway.

2. Land Area: A regional shopping center with double-decked interior mall and attached multi-level parking can be built on a 10-acre downtown parcel. But in a suburban locale where land is cheaper, a regional mammoth center can be built on one level with surface parking using ten times that area. Community and neighborhood centers require much less area. A vacant tract of the required size usually offers the best opportunity; land improved with buildings to be demolished is too high priced.

3. Cost of Site: Shopping center planners can build on only 25% of their site because of parking requirements. The bulk of the land is assigned to parking, ingress and egress, and delivery areaways for servicing the stores. So they must acquire the site at a cost commensurate with the net income that 25% of the site can produce.

As a rule of thumb for suburban areas, most developers feel that $2.00 per square foot for land is the maximum that can be paid for a shopping center site. In downtown core urban-renewal areas, developers figure on $2.50 per square foot as maximum price, and this only when a high-rise office building can be superimposed over the shopping mall.

4. Zoning: Commercial zoning for the entire tract is necessary to full development of the center. There can be no compromise in this regard with municipal authorities without seriously inhibiting the anticipated value of the property.

5. Utilities: Electric, sewer, and water conduits are necessary attachments to the site. If they are not present, the cost of bringing them in must be in reasonable proportion to budgeted site costs.

6. Topography and Subsoil: Stores can be arranged in a variety of patterns on more than one level, and an experienced architect can often provide both customer convenience and great charm to an irregular site with an uneven surface. However, the costs of site preparation must be compared to acquisition costs of a level site near road grade, if such is available. Poor subsoil conditions can be the cause of flooding, sinking, and cracking of buildings and paved areas, and limitations on expansion of the center. Is subject site free of these flaws? If not, the value of the center is threatened. Test borings are advisable before planning advances.

7. Competition: A new regional shopping center should be five miles or more from a regional center of the same type in the same trade area. Community shopping centers should be at least three miles apart and neighborhood centers two miles apart, subject to density of population where they overlap trade areas; otherwise the value of the center is threatened.

8. Real Estate Taxes: Geographically, tax rates vary. Local real estate assessments and fluctuating mill rates may make the difference between profit and loss in any shopping center. If the site is overassessed to begin with, it is likely that building will also be overtaxed. Tax-escalation clauses commencing upon completion should be included in every lease, in each kind of center, so that the tenant bears his share of tax increases after the first year of occupancy. Without tax-escalation clauses, the value of the center can be washed out.

Second Step: The Market Survey and Property Analysis

The next move in preparing an appraisal report of a shopping center is taken by researching, synthesizing, and writing a comprehensive market survey and forecast of earnings.

Market Survey and Forecast

Its Key Importance: A market survey and forecast must come on the heels of site deliberation in shopping center planning and appraising, because this reconnaissance will take the measure of market strength present and future, and determine the number, size, and mix of stores to be leased and built on the site. It will also become a prime tool in calculating the changed value of the land after agreements to lease on the site have been made.

The survey must include a macro-market study of the prospects and trends in the national, regional, and trade area economic pictures. Further, it must see into the future far enough to predict growth or decline in the customer area, and to assess customer purchasing power over a period of years. It takes about four years for a large center to reach full-tilt operation, so the forecast must cover that period and beyond it if the appraisal is being made at the beginning of the center's life. At that time, the architect will need a survey and forecast to give the center ultimate size and shape, and the banker will need this information to formulate the basis of financing.

The survey and forecast is in itself the major part of a preliminary appraisal of the proposed shopping center on a site under consideration. For the completed shopping center with leases, it means confirmation of existing percentage rents, and a forecast of favorable or unfavorable elements affecting the center's earnings in the future.

The appraiser must have a feel for the developer's sense of timing. Meeting the needs of the marketplace at a given location with specific facilities is an art as well as a science in market research. The developer who owns the right spot at the proper time in the growth pattern of a community is apt to command both the feasibility and success of a shopping center. The right combination of stores in the right place at the right time is the combination for success.

Reach of Market Survey and Forecast: The macro-market survey and forecast must embrace a map of the trade area on which the shopping center under appraisement will depend, showing: (1) number of families in the trade area; and (2) the spendable annual income of total families in the trade area.

The micro-market focus of the survey and forecast is on a fixed location in a definite area, so that all data appended to the trade area map, such as traveling time by automobile from the outer areas, should relate directly to the site.

Appraisals of shopping centers may be required at different phases of their development, from mere conception on a hypothetical site, to intermediate update for temporary financing, or for completed project long-term financing or sale. Whichever the phase, the survey and forecast is of paramount importance.

In the case of shopping centers, the investment analysis method of evaluation is comprised of the site analysis and the market survey and forecast is interwoven in the earnings process, or Income Approach. Except when the site is virgin, comparative market data is of no consequence, because each shopping center has its particular tenant mix, varying percentage leases, and differing numbers of stores and store areas in its make-up.

MODEL MACRO-MARKET SURVEY

City

Effective Buying Income:
Aggregate $417,900,000
Per Household Average   9,287
Number of Households   45,000

Distribution of household by effective buying income:

Over $15,000	35%	$3,000-$6,999	10%
$10,000-$14,999	15%	Under $3,000	11%
$7,000-$9,999	29%		

Greater Trade Area
(Includes contiguous counties)

Effective Buying Income:
Aggregate $999,909,000
Per Household Average   8,620
Number of Households   116,000

Distribution of household by effective buying income:

Over $10,000	53%	$2,500-$3,999	8%
$7,000-$9,999	11%	Under $2,500	8%
$4,000-$6,999	20%		

Source: Board of Trade, 1974.

Third Step: The Element of Evaluation

The next advance in appraising any shopping center, established or proposed, lies in the *element of evaluation:* The center can only be valued as a whole, or single entity, not as separate individual stores or buildings. The center is an aggregate income producer and cannot be evaluated in any other way, since each store has a direct income-producing influence on all the others and is in turn dependent upon the others.

Appraising the Shopping Center as a Single Entity

Factors in Aggregate Property Analysis: Not only because of the income-producing interdependencies of all the stores within it must the center be appraised as a single entity, it must also be aggregated because of its common parking area and because of the senior position of the "hinge" or "key" store or stores around which the specialty stores in the center are arranged. In the larger centers, the hinge will be a junior or senior department store or two; in the smaller centers, perhaps a supermarket. In any event, these hinges are the chief draw of the center without which the surrounding specialty stores would flounder and probably would not sign for leases in the first place.

Micro-market Interdependencies

Parking: A common parking area is used by the customers of all the tenants in the modern shopping center. The convenience attributes of the parking area are of great value to each merchant, whose sales volume is reflected accordingly, and who pays a percentage rent on that volume. Thus, *the parking lot is a production agent of income for all.* You could not separately appraise any one of the stores in the cumulative pull of the center, nor could you separately value the general parking rights underwriting each merchant's success.

Department Stores as Hinges: In large shopping centers, it is common practice that the key department stores first signing up get benefits at a rental below the market, and sometimes even a gift of the land.

However, it is important that the major department store not be permitted to become outsize or to occupy more than one-third of the total shopping center area. The mix of merchants and variety of goods is vital to the specialty store that will be carrying the greater burden of aggregate rents.

Fourth Step: The Approaches to Value

Since shopping centers, large and small, are investment properties primarily built, bought, or sold on the basis of their income production, the fourth step in the appraisal of a shopping center leads us to the Income Approach, which is the emphasis of this chapter, with particular attention focussed on capitalizing income into value. The Cost Approach is employed only in conjunction with residual techniques under the Income Approach. The Market Data Approach is inapplicable, except in the selection of the virgin site before agreements to lease have been signed.

Techniques for Estimating Value of Land and Improvements in Shopping Center Appraisal

Procedure for Estimating Land Value by Capitalizing Percentage Rents. The market survey and forecast sets the mold for determining percentage overrides on minimum guaranteed leases to rated national retailers. Now these percentage rents will help the appraiser to estimate the land value of the center.

Once agreements to lease have been secured, the character of the virgin land changes, because it has become productive in its own peculiar way and is no longer comparable to other sites. Its value can only be deducted as follows:

1. The owner's mortgage commitment, necessary to go ahead with construction, will be based on sufficient minimum guaranteed rentals to pay debt service on

his loan, after subtracting charges for property taxes, insurance, maintenance, and management.

2. The amount of the percentage rents over the minimum guarantees is the surplus income, imputable to the land.

3. The surplus income is now capitalized to create land value.

Fifth Step: Procedure for Estimating a Separate Land Value Under the Shopping Center

If the developer and his appraiser have done their homework carefully, comparing notes on site analysis and market survey and forecasts and the making of the percentage leases, the newly created land value will exceed considerably what the developer paid for the land. Now the new land value will be the developer's equity in the shopping center.

In sum, when the character of the raw land has been made unique by the nature of the particular percentage leases affecting it, the peculiarity of the subject site makes it *nonpareil,* or incomparable. Then the land must be evaluated by capitalization of the residual net income imputable to the land. A front-foot, square-foot, or acreage valuation can be made to satisfy the appraiser's curiosity as to how far his new valuation may be from market data comparables in the vicinity, but land value conclusion must rest on the *Land Residual Technique.*

Sixth Step: Procedure for Estimating Value of the Improvements in Shopping Center

The buildings will be evaluated by the Depreciated Cost Approach if buildings have been completed; or by hypothetical estimate if incomplete. This will be the sixth and final step in the appraisal of subject property.

Appraisal of a Completed Shopping Center: When the shopping center is complete, with a history of say four years, it has a track record of minimum guaranteed rents plus percentage rents based on sales volumes achieved. There are also receipted payments for actual construction costs, fixed interest and amortization on permanent mortgages, and a record of operating expenses. An *updated* appraisal can now be made using a capitalization rate based on experience rather than anticipation. The residual net income for the center, capitalized at a relatively low rate because of good prospects or at a high rate for poor prospects, will give you market value for purposes of sale, refinancing, or other proceedings.

Comparable sales of land or buildings are useless, since the center has established its own track record which has no relationship to sales of other commercial properties in the neighborbood. The Market Data Approach, or comparative method, is inapplicable to shopping centers in operation.

Capitalization Rates: The rate you choose for capitalizing the residual net (surplus) income to find land value must be based on the prospects of the center. An excellent site in a good location in a growing area would call for the lower rate, say 12%; a good site in a competitive location with middling to fair area prospects might be capitalized at 13.5%; a center with very poor prospects for the future of the site, location, or area might be penalized with an extreme rate of 15% to 17%.

Located on an unimpeded site in a good business section, a center for a dynamic area like Atlanta, Baltimore, Boston, Chicago, Dallas, Los Angeles, San Francisco, or Topeka, where the urban region has a strong and expanding economic base, would call for the lowest capitalization rate.

In a deteriorating or static area, where dying industries show a pattern of erratic employment, a shopping center would be nailed with a very high capitalization rate, no matter how impressive its site might be.

Fluctuating interest rates on bonds and mortgages, as in the early 1970s when interest rates jumped from 8% to 10%, also cause capitalization rates to vary. A high interest rate is reflected in a capitalization rate higher than the norm.

The appraiser's common sense and nose for the market must, in the final analysis, be his guide to a precise capitalization rate in a given shopping center situation. But his thought processes must be documented, because a 1% variation in the rate can mean a difference of many thousands of dollars in valuation.

Applications of the Land Residual Technique and the Cost Approach to Building Value

Land Value by Capitalization of Residual Net Income. You reach the residual net (surplus) income attributable to the land by simple arithmetic. Add, subtract, and divide as follows:

1. Add the total of gross annual rents.
2. Subtract from the gross annual rents a vacancy allowance of 5-10%. This will leave you "rents collected."
3. Then total "operating expenses," including building maintenance and repairs, advertising and public relations, insurance, property taxes, and management. Subtract this total from "rents collected." The balance is the sum available for debt service.
4. Now subtract the actual amount of debt service from the amount available for debt service. The balance is the net residual (surplus) income imputable to the land.
5. Divide the net annual income imputable to land (by percentage leases) by your chosen capitalization rate, between 10% and 13%, depending upon your interpretation of the facts revealed in the site analysis and market survey and forecast in your appraisal.

Building Value—Cost Minus Depreciation: Steep changes upward in building costs during the past few years require that up-to-date reproduction figures be used in any appraisal as of a current date. These figures can be obtained from various reliable manuals, such as Marshall & Swift, F.W. Dodge, and Boechk's Cost Indices. Realistic depreciation rates can then be applied to deduce current value of improvements.

A shopping center built in 1948 might have been put together for as little as $8 per square foot. Today, the same center might cost $45 per square foot.

Occasionally, all store utilities including fixtures are installed at owner expense, but this occurs only when the developer is having difficulty promoting national big-name tenants in an area where competition is keen. The average tenant will receive only the shell of a store from the developer; that is, the bare floor, four walls, and ceiling. The tenant will then install utilities, fixtures, and decorations at his own expense as leasehold improvements.

Large regional centers must include nonrentable areas for heating and air-conditioning plants serving the mall or plaza covered spaces, with public services such as elevators, escalators, and restrooms. Usually the merchants are asked to share the maintenance of such areas along with the owner. If an escalator or elevator is inside the department store, it is usually built and maintained at the owner's cost. Truck delivery tunnels servicing the merchants are also normally built and maintained at the owner's cost. Police security forces are usually hired and directed by the merchant's association where each tenant contributes on a pro-rata space basis.

National chain tenants usually require that parking areas at least four times their store area be provided. The parking areas must be readily accessible to highway entrance and exit, macadam paved, and floodlighted at night.

As an appraiser computing all the developer's costs on the basis of each square foot of building area, you would also include architect's and engineer's fees, the contractor's profit, and interest on the interim mortgage financing during construction.

In the following model appraisal, the Letter of Transmittal, Table of Contents, Limiting Conditions, and other introductory requirements of a fully formalized appraisal are omitted since they have been shown in previous models.

MODEL APPRAISAL OF REGIONAL SHOPPING CENTER FOR MORTGAGE REFINANCING PURPOSE: THE LAND RESIDUAL TECHNIQUE

SUMMARY OF FACTS AND CONCLUSIONS

Type Center: Enclosed Mall
                                               Regional Shopping Center

Address: 2100 Santa Fe Avenue
                                               Topeka, Kansas 66612

Number of Tenants: Forty-six (46)
    As of May 1, 1976 (not in-
    cluding Shears but includ-
    ing gasoline service station)

Land Area:

Santa Fe Tract (owned by subject)	1,042,390.8 SF	24.42 Acres
Shears Tract (not owned by subject)	505,536.2 SF	11.61 Acres
Total	1,547,927.0 SF	36.03 Acres

(Only the Santa Fe Tract will be appraised here)

Gross Square Footage, Improvements: 343,095 SF

Square Footage Leased: As of May 1, 1976 (not including Shears but including gasoline service station)	291,731 SF
Parking Stalls: As of May 1, 1976	
Santa Fe (Owned by subject)	1,649
Shears (Owned by Shears)	941
Total	2,590
Gross Income:	$1,193,412
Net Income:	$ 848,997
Site Value:	$1,407,862
Value Conclusion by Cost Approach: Applied to Income Approach via Land Residual Technique	$7,310,000

PURPOSE AND FUNCTION OF APPRAISAL

The appraisal was made for the purpose of estimating the market value of the subject property, including land and improvements, as of May 1, 1976. The function of the appraisal is to provide a basis for first mortgage refinancing of the Santa Fe Shopping Center, excluding the abutting Shears property.

MARKET VALUE

For the purpose of this appraisal, market value is defined as "the highest price estimated in terms of money that a property will bring if exposed for sale in the open market, allowing a reasonable time to find a purchaser who buys with knowledge of all the uses to which it is adapted, and for which it is capable of being used. Frequently, it is referred to as the price at which a willing seller would sell and a willing buyer would buy, neither being under abnormal pressure. It is the price expectable if a reasonable time is allowed to find a purchaser and if both seller and prospective buyer are fully informed."

REAL ESTATE TAX DATA

The property is subject to the assessment and taxes as promulgated by Shawnee County. The current assessment and taxes levied against the subject property are as follows:

Assessments—1975-1976

Atchinson Development, Inc.—Area 22, Sec. 16, Bl. 4, Pcl. 1.

	100%	25%
Total Land Value	$1,250,350	$ 312,588
Total Value Improvements	5,999,850	1,499,963
Total Appraised Value	$7,250,200	$1,812,551

Tax Structure

Valuations in Metropolitan Topeka overall:

Real Estate: $165,983,875   Personal Property: $48,519,716
Utilities and Rail: $26,051,040   Total: $240,554,631
Tax Levy:_____
City 31.71 mills; County 17.20 mills; School 50.37 mills;
Total 120.28_____
Ratio of assessed valuation to true value: 25%
Remarks: 21 mills are levied for special purposes such as Washburn
University, Public Library, Recreation Program, etc._____

ZONING AND USE

The subject site is situated in a "C" commercial zone, city of Topeka, Shawnee County, Kansas. This zoning permits retail establishments, office buildings, and other conforming commercial uses, such as restaurants, theaters, etc.

An analysis of the site and surrounding economic conditions indicates that the subject is improved to its highest and best use.

AREA DATA

Topeka, Kansas
Latitude: 39 degrees, 3 minutes north.
Longitude: 95 degrees, 41 minutes west.
Elevation: 876' in valley to 971' in southwest part of the city.
National: In the approximate geographical center of the United States, close to the western edge of the prairie lands cornbelt, the southern edge of the glacial drift, and about the middle of the temperate zone.
State: In the east-central portion of the state of Kansas.
County: In the approximate center of Shawnee County.
Highways: Near the junction of Interstate 70 and 470, U.S. Highways 24, 40 and 75, State Highway 4, and the Kansas Turnpike.
Cities: Located in highway miles in proximity to key nearby cities, Topeka is:
           68 miles west of Kansas City, Missouri, on U.S. 24 and 40, Interstate 70, and the Kansas Turnpike.
           175 miles south of Omaha, Nebraska, on U.S. 75.
           221 miles north of Tulsa, Oklahoma, on U.S. 75.

160 miles northeast of Wichita, Kansas, on the Kansas Turn-pike.

541 miles east of Denver, Colorado, on Interstate 70.

290 miles northeast of Oklahoma City, Oklahoma, on the Kansas Turnpike and Interstate 35.

Topeka is an attractive city with a population of 150,000 in the metropolitan area. The downtown area is lined with modern stores and businesses. The city's expansion to the suburban areas is due to new and modern shopping centers and industries that are increasing in number. An additional 181,760 people live in Shawnee County. There are more than 1,200,000 people in the sixteen-county trade area.

Form of Government

Topeka has the mayor-commission form of government, whose elected members serve two-year terms.

Housing

The 1970 census reported a total of 43,700 dwelling units in Topeka, 72.7 percent of which were one-family units and 60.4 percent of which were owner occupied. This high percentage of owner-occupied homes is an indication of the stability and character of the local labor force. There has been about a 5% growth in single-family dwelling units in the city since 1970.

Topeka is keeping pace with demand for dwelling units as the population increases both in the city and the metropolitan area. Building permits issued by the city from 1970 through March, 1975, indicate approximately 2,185 new dwelling units, either as individual houses or apartments, have been completed. Building permits were issued by Shawnee County from January 1, 1974 to March 31, 1975, for 338 one-family houses outside the city, but within Shawnee County.

Climate

Temperatures: In 1975, temperatures in Topeka ranged from extremes of —20 degrees on February 8th to 99 degrees on September 10th. The record low was —25 degrees in February of 1899, and the record high was 114 degrees in July of 1936.

Precipitation: Average annual rainfall is 33.26 inches. Extremes since 1900 were 19.30 inches in 1966 to 48.60 inches in 1951.

Average annual snowfall is 19.3 inches ranging from 4.5 inches.

Hospitals and Health

Number of Hospitals in City: 7   Beds: 3,109

Number of G.P. Doctors: 42   Surgeons: 45

Specialists: 127

Number of Dentists: 73   Registered Nurses: 1,098

Remarks: The Topeka hospitals are: 1. Memorial Hospital, 2. C.F. Menninger Memorial Hospital, 3. St. Francis, 4. Stormont Vail, 5. Veterans Hospital, 6. Children's Menningers Hospital, 7. Kansas Neurological Institute.

Financial Data—1974

Banks:

Deposits	$ 504,723,710
Debits	$66,811,182,724
Clearings	$ 1,510,166,044
Resources	$ 619,590,654

Savings Associations:

Assets	$ 1,082,507,000
Mortgage Loans of Record	$ 975,151,000
Savings	$ 861,232,000

Construction

Building Permits	898
Building Permits and Value	$ 21,366,888
Permits (New Dwellings)	166
Total Living Units	265
$ Value	$ 6,198,138
Value of Bldg. Permits (County)	$ 12,019,808

Utilities

Electric supply from Kansas Power and Light is ample in the trade area. Natural gas is supplied by the Gas Service Company. Water is provided by the city of Topeka. The city has an activated sludge sewage treatment plant.

News and Advertising Media

Newspapers: Daily—Topeka Daily Capital and Topeka State Journal Weekly, Pictorial Times; Highland Park News; Forbes Sky Schooner.
Radio: KEWI; KSWT FM; K-TOP AM-FM; WIBW AM-FM; WREN.
Television: WIBW-TV; KTSB-TV; KTWU-TV (Educational Television).

Schools and Colleges

There are 53 elementary schools, 17 junior high schools, six high schools, and 2 area vocational-technical schools in the Topeka area. Four unified school districts—Shawnee Heights, Washburn Rural, Seaman, and Topeka.

Washburn University, a municipal university, is recognized for its school of Law and Liberal Arts College. A new Law School and Fine Arts Center have recently been completed on the 160-acre campus in mid-Topeka. Enrollment at Washburn is around 5,200 students.

Recreation and Entertainment

The Topeka Civic Theater, Topeka Civic Orchestra, Broadway Theater of Topeka, Community Concert Series, Broadway Theater, and Mulvane Art Center offer a variety of entertaining programs.

Manufacturing Firms

Goodyear Tire & Rubber Company, Inc.
Atchinson, Topeka, & Santa Fe Railhead; Repair & Machine Shops; Marshalling Yards; & Rail Research Center.
American Yearbook Company, a Division of Josten's, Inc.
Stauffer Publications, Inc.
E.I. DuPont deNemours & Company, Inc.
Hallmark Cards, Inc.
Adams Business Forms, Inc.
Seymour, Inc.
Allis-Chalmers Manufacturing Company, Inc.

Topeka has a total of approximately 275 firms that do some manufacturing or processing. The "Directory of Topeka Manufacturers and Processors" available from the Economic Development Division, Greater Topeka Chamber of Commerce, lists most of these firms, number of employees, and products produced.

Services Provided by the City

Following is a partial list of services and departments provided or maintained in or by the city:

Fire Protection	Police Protection
City Parks & Recreation Centers	Water Treatment Plant &
Sewer Systems & Treatment Plant	Distribution System
City Scales	Forestry Department
Housing Authority	Municipal Airport
Municipal Parking Garages	Public Library
Refuse Dept.—trash & garbage collection	City Traffic Engineer
	Human Relations Commission
City Engineer	Street Lighting
City Building Inspector (Elec., Plumbing, Building Permits)	Police Court
	Weights & Measures Inspector
City-County Health Department	City-County Zoning Commission
Municipal Auditorium	City Attorney
Humane Shelter & Dog Pound	Street Department
City-County Planning Commission	Civil Defense
Urban Renewal	Recreation Commission

Natural gas for Topeka is sold and distributed by Gas Service Company, electricity by Kansas Power and Light Company, telephone service by Southwestern Bell Telephone Company, water by City Municipal Plant, trash and garbage pickup by the city or private handlers, public transportation is provided by Topeka Transportation Company.

Local Transportation

Topeka public transportation is provided by two taxicab companies, eleven car rental and leasing agencies, and the Topeka Transportation Company, which operates 24 buses that cover all portions of the city from 5:45 a.m. to 6:30 p.m. six days a week. The buses run on an approximate schedule of 20- to 25-minute intervals during peak hours and 30- to 45-minute intervals during off-peak hours.

Rail, Air, Bus, and Motor Freight Service

Topeka is served by four railroads, the Santa Fe, Union Pacific, Rock Island, and Missouri Pacific, with reciprocal switching between the four lines within the city. Rail passenger service is provided by Amtrak on the Chicago-Houston route.

Air service is provided by Frontier Airlines, a first-class carrier, and a third-class carrier, Allen Aviation. In addition, charter service is available through four local firms. The municipal airport has two main runways, each 5,100 feet in length. The airport has an instrument landing system, weather service on the field, FAA control tower, direct line to flight service, and an airport cafe. Several new hangars and an improved and enlarged service and maintenance building are in the planning stage.

Kansas City Muncipal Airport, a distance of approximately seventy-five miles from Topeka by the Kansas Turnpike, which can be reached in about one hour and fiteen minutes by automobile, provides service in all directions by many of the major airlines.

Passenger service by bus to and from Topeka is provided by Continental Trailways and Greyhound, plus local lines operating into local areas.

Topeka is served by approximately 23 regular route motor common carriers, with 22 of them maintaining docks in Topeka. Motor carriers provide overnight service to Chicago, St. Louis, Indianapolis, Omaha, Denver, Dallas, Fort Worth, and many other points.

Survey and Forecast: (Macro and Micro-market Combined)

On the following page see the map of the market area magnetized by the Santa Fe Shopping Center. There is no other shopping center with the merchandising magnetism of the Shears-Tenney combination in Topeka or in the marketing area, and since Shears and Tenney are both in subject centers (Shears locked in by owning its premises), the forecast for subject must be characterized as dominant for the foreseeable future.

While there are other shopping centers approximately equal to subject in size, they are not menacing competition to the tenant mix of subject shopping center, and will not detract from its present or foreseeable-future patronage.

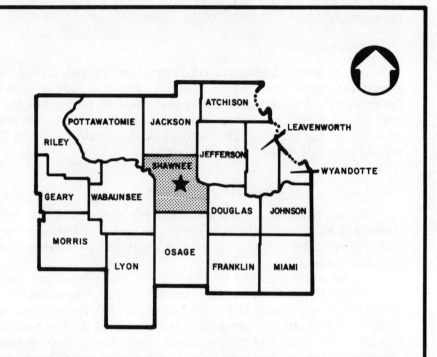

DAILY SHOPPING TRIPS TO TOPEKA, KANSAS FROM
16 SURROUNDING COUNTIES
WITHIN ONE HOUR DRIVE VIA AUTOMOBILE OR BUS

SUBJECT SHOPPING CENTER DRAWS OVER 550,000 CUSTOMERS FROM
16 COUNTIES IN THE MARKETING REGION.

NEAREST COMPETING METROPOLIS IS KANSAS CITY, 75 MILES AWAY.

TRADE AREA MAP
MACRO-MARKET SURVEY
TOPEKA, KANSAS

Appendix to Map
Apportionment of Family Income Spent in Each
Kind of Store in the Trade Area

	1974	Percent of Total
Total Retail Stores:	$999,909,000	100.0
Food stores	259,976,340	26.0
Eating, drinking places	79,992,720	8.0
General merchandise	99,990,900	10.0
Apparel, accessories	74,993,175	7.5
Furniture, home furnishings, appliances	56,994,813	5.7
Automotive	141,987,078	14.2
Gasoline service stations	52,995,177	5.3
Lumber, building materials, hardware, farm equipment	38,996,451	3.9
Drug and proprietary	53,995,086	5.4
Liquor stores	20,998,089	2.1
Jewelry, novelties, gifts	78,992,811	7.9
Recreational and amusements (travel, books, sporting goods)	39,996,360	4.0

Source: Board of Trade

THE APPRAISAL PROCESS

The generally accepted method of obtaining the market value of a parcel of income property is by the use of the three approaches to value. These approaches are the Cost Approach, the Income Approach, and the Market Data Approach to value. However, in the case of an operating shopping center complete and with a long income history, market data becomes inapplicable.

Sales of improved commercial properties in the area cannot be used as comparable in evaluating the subject, because no two shopping centers are ever precisely alike in terms of land area, parking ratio to store area, store mix, goods offered, hours open, lease particulars, gross expenses, and net income produced per square foot of store occupancy.

In these respects, every shopping center is a unique entity, and can only be evaluated by capitalization of its guaranteed net income.

In the appraisal, the improvements will be evaluated by the Depreciated Cost Approach. The land must be evaluated by the Land Residual Technique under the Income Approach.

SITE ANALYSIS

The subject property is an irregularly shaped plot consisting of 24.42 acres. It has frontages on Santa Fe and Atchison Avenues. On its westerly border, subject site abuts 11.61 acres owned by Shears, Buckroe and

Company with which it enjoys common usage and general rights-of-way. All public utilities are connected on site.

The site is at grade level with the surrounding public streets rising to a slight crown at its center, so that natural surface drainage is evident. Key tenants in the complex are Shears and J. B. Tenney Regional Department Stores. There are forty-four other stores in the plaza, which is fully occupied. The site is in the fast growing southern sector of the city, and is surrounded by modern residential and commercial developments.

SITE VALUE

When the character of the raw land has been made unique by the nature of the particular percentage leases affecting it, the peculiarity of the subject site makes it incomparable. Then the land must be evaluated by capitalization of the residual net income imputable to the land.

The buildings will be evaluated by the Depreciated Cost Approach.

Since subject shopping center is complete, fully rented, with a history of eight years, it has a track record of minimum guaranteed rents plus percentage rents based on sales volumes achieved. There are also receipted payments for actual construction costs, fixed interest and amortization on permanent mortgages, and a record of operating expenses. This appraisal will be made using a capitalization rate based on experience rather than anticipation.

So-called comparable sales of land or buildings are useless, since the center has established its own track record which has no relationship to sales of other commercial properties in the neighborhood. The Market Data Approach, or comparative method, is inapplicable to shopping centers in operation.

Value of the 24.42 acres is developed in the Land Residual Technique via the Income Approach.

IMPROVEMENT DATA

The improvements existing on the subject site consist of eight different buildings, five of which are closely connected. Building D, a free-standing J.B. Tenney TBA* Service Center is separate and for that use only. Building G is also free-standing. The building areas are as follows:

Key Tenant†	Main Building Area	Square Feet	
Woolwich	Building A (Single Story)	30,600	
PCPI & Woolwich	Building A (Lower Level)	21,600	
Local Stores	Building B (Single Story)	32,400	
J.B. Tenney	Building C (Three Stories)	63,600	
J.B. Tenney	Building C (Second Level)	54,600	
J.B. Tenney	Building C (Penthouse)	4,500	
J.B. Tenney TBA	Building D (Single Story, F.S.)	24,000	
Walburn Drugs	Building E (Single Story)	30,660	
Finney Shoes	Building F (Single Story)	29,095	291,055

*Tires, Batteries, and Accessories, as well as gasoline.

		Main Mall Area		
		North (east-west) mall	11,400	
		North court	6,600	
		Center mall	10,600	
		South court	9,440	
		South (east-west) mall	12,300	50,340
Pentex Oil Gasoline		Building G (Land lease,		
Station		Building owned by Gulf)		1,700
		Total Square Feet Gross		343,095

†Note: Shears, Buckroe and Company own their two-story building at the north end of the subject's enclosed mall. The Shears Building is approximately 158,000 square feet, which added to subject's 343,095 square feet brings the total gross in the center to 501,095 square feet.

Description of the Buildings

The buildings are constructed of fireproofed structural steel frame with reinforced concrete floors, poured concrete foundations and brick veneer exteriors. All buildings except Building A are constructed on slab, no excavation.

Roofs are built-up tar and gravel composition with cast-iron interior drains. Maintenance is excellent.

The enclosed mall is spacious and attractive, with ample room for additional kiosks or stall-type stands, should they be desirable as tenants. Public toilets and restrooms are tiled, clean, and well lighted.

The store fronts along the mall are well designed for retail sales and display. Lighting is high intensity, troffered fluorescent, and spot.

Near the Atchison Avenue entrance to the west parking area, there is a metal-paneled prefabricated mini post office, put up, owned, and operated by the U.S. Post Office Department on a land lease from subject owners at $1.00 per annum. The building's foundation and electrical connections were at expense of subject owner.

Truck delivery is handled by four outlets, walled courtyards, paved and well maintained, with ample room for truck turnaround. Areas of these yards are also as follows:

Service Court Area	Square Feet	
A-B Court	5,400	
C Court	3,600	
D Court	6,570	
E-F Court	5,105	20,675

Heating and Air Conditioning

Hot and cold water system hydronic, through coils over which air is blown by fan propulsion into the mall. There is a 200-ton capacity for air conditioning the mall.

Boiler is Cleaver-Brooks, gas-fired; pressure 30 P.S.I.—275,000 BTU.

Flapper valves induct fresh air activated by fans. The cooling condensers are Worthington Pump and Machinery Corporation. Pump controls are by McDonnell. Switchgear is Square-D. Wiring is BX cable.

Sprinkler System

One hundred percent coverage throughout the buildings. Installation and maintenance by Mid-West Automatic Sprinkler Company, Inc., of Des Moines, Iowa. Plumbing is copper and brass.

Utilities

Electric: 440 volts, transformed to 270, through three east-west-south transformers owned by Kansas Power & Light Company.
Gas: From Gas Service Company, Topeka. Boiler is gas-fired.
Water: City connected, pressure 60 pounds, P.S.I.
Sewers: City connected.

Excavation

21,600 square feet under Woolwich section of Building A only. Mechanical room uses 1,247 square feet of this area. The remainder is leased to Woolwich and a number of local tenants, including the center's management office.

COST APPROACH

The estimation of the reproduction cost of the improvements was derived through consultations with area builders and developers, and supplemented with construction cost manuals. Cost figures from Marshall and Swift's Valuation Service and Boechk Building Cost Calculator have been adjusted to the local conditions of Topeka. The unit prices include all elements of cost to reproduce the improvements including direct and indirect costs, profit and overhead.

The subject improvements were constructed during 1967-68. A physical inspection of the property indicates that the improvements are in excellent condition. Physical depreciation has been taken in relation to the age of each building, and in relation to the excellent maintenance control the property has experienced. No deduction was made for functional or economic obsolescence as the improvements are suitably well designed for the site and economically sound.

Building A
Single story and basement,
ground floor   30,600 SF @ $23.67 = $ 724,302
Basement (incl. mechanicals)   21,600 SF @ $21.35 =   461,160
                                                                    $1,185,462

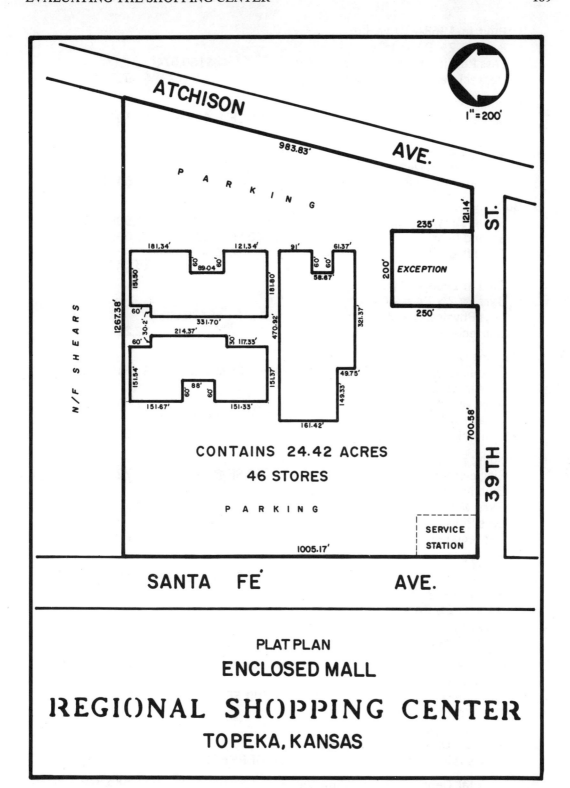

ATCHISON AVE.

983.83'

P A R K I N G

121.14'

235'

EXCEPTION

200'

250'

181.34'   121.34'

60' 60'

89.04'

181.80'

91'   61.37'

60' 60'

58.67'

151.50'

1267.38'

N / F   S H E A R S

60'

331.70'

470.92'

321.37'

30.2'

214.37'

60'   30'   117.33'

151.37'

49.75'

151.54'

149.33'

700.58'

39TH   ST.

60'   88'

60'   60'

151.67'   151.33'

161.42'

CONTAINS 24.42 ACRES

46 STORES

P A R K I N G

SERVICE
STATION

1005.17'

SANTA FE' AVE.

1" = 200'

PLAT PLAN

ENCLOSED MALL

REGIONAL SHOPPING CENTER

TOPEKA, KANSAS

190   EVALUATING THE SHOPPING CENTER

Built in 1968—50 yr. life
8 yrs. @ 2% PA = 16%
Less Physical Depreciation $189,674
Depreciated Building Value $ 995,788

Building B
Single story   32,400 SF @ $23.67 = $ 766,908
Built in 1968—50 yr. life
8 yrs. @ 2% PA = 16%
Less Physical Depreciation $122,705
Depreciated Building Value $ 644,203

Building C
Three-story ground floor   63,600 SF @ $23.67 = $1,505,412
Second floor   54,600 SF @ $20.07 = 1,095,822
Third floor   4,500 SF @ $13.63 =   61,335
                                                         $2,662,569

Built in 1968—50 yr. life
8 yrs. @ 2% PA = 16%
Less Physical Depreciation $426,011
Depreciated Building Value $2,236,558

Building D
Single story, free-standing   24,000 SF @ $25.83 = $ 619,920
Built in 1968—50 yr. life
8 yrs. @ 2% PA = 16%
Less Physical Depreciation $ 99,187
Depreciated Building Value $ 520,733

Building E
Single story   30,660 SF @ $23.67 = $ 725,722
Built in 1968—50 yr. life
8 yrs. @ 2% PA = 16%
Less Physical Depreciation $116,115
Depreciated Building Value $ 609,607

Building F
Single story   29,095 SF @ $23.67 = $ 688,678
Built in 1968—50 yr. life
8 yrs. @ 2% PA = 16%
Less Physical Depreciation $110,188
Depreciated Building Value $ 578,490

Building G
One-story, free-standing
gasoline service station   1,700 SF @ $NO COST $ -------
This structure is built,
owned and operated by
Arabian Oil on a land lease
from subject owners   NO DEPRECIATION

    Total Depreciated Building Value $5,585,379

Site Improvements

697,000 SF of bituminous macadam pavement in parking areas @ $.40 =	$ 278,800
Floodlighting	23,527
Post office mat and electrical connections	3,667
(Prefabricated post office building is owned by U.S.)	
Curbing and sidewalks, storm drains	15,444
Brick walls, lighting and paving in four service courts	22,444
Total Cost New, Site Improvements	$ 343,882
Less Depreciation, All Causes @ 2%/annum	27,511
	316,371
Total Depreciated Cost—All Improvements	$5,901,750

INCOME APPROACH

The Income Approach to the value estimate is an appraisal technique in which the anticipated net income is processed to indicate the capital amount of the investment that will produce net income. It is dependent upon the following: accurate estimation of the economic rental; the deduction of all applicable expenses; the conversion of net income into value by the proper capitalization rate. A low capitalization rate will be applied to reflect subject property's dominance in the locale. There is no other shopping center with the cumulative magnetism of subject in Topeka; and, of course, subject has locked in the cream of tenants in the city.

Economic rental for the subject property was estimated by analyzing the space rentals, at the present rate per square foot. It was determined that the minimum lease rentals, together with the percentage rentals, common area maintenance charges, and tax participation paid by various tenants produced an overall economic rental rate of space in the subject shopping center, which may be increased in 1978 when the leases for several of the stores have expired.

The income and expense illustrated are taken from the actual experiences of this shopping center. Unit estimates and percentages have been utilized to stabilize these items. This is done according to common appraisal practices. The overall capitalization rate is arrived at by the summation method and acknowledged as a sound appraisal technique. This method is double-checked by the projected mortgage constant, using the Ellwood factor under the band of investment theory.

Income

Guaranteed Rentals	$ 854,008.
Percentage Override	244,770.
Reimbursement Property Tax	25,014.
Common Area Charges	60,284.
Speaker Rental	2,501.

Coin Machines	241.
Telephones	3,334.
Xerox Machine	3,260.
Total	$1,193,412.

Gross Income		$1,193,412.
Allowance for Vacancy and Rent Loss		
Five Percent (There has never been		
a vacancy in the center since open-		
ing day, October 1968)		59,670.
Effective Gross Income		$1,133,742.

Expenses

Maintenance	$	5,684.
Building		41,500.
Mall		28,047.
Parking		4,873.
H.V.A.C.		6,810.
Security		15,836.
Real Estate Taxes		136,912.
Insurance		14,416.
General Administration		25,818.
Amortization of Leasing Costs		4,849.
Total	$	284,745.

| Net Income | | $ 848,997. |

Valuation of Land and Improvements via Income Approach
(Using Land Residual Technique)

Depreciated Cost of the Improvements	$5,901,750	
Effective Net Income per Annum		$ 848,997
Interest Imputable to Improvements		
$5,901,750 x 12%)		$ 708,210
Interest to Land		$ 140,787
Therefore, $140,787 ÷ 10% = $1,407,870		
Depreciated Cost of the Improvements		$5,901,750
Add Value of the Land ($57,652 per acre)		1,407,862
Estimate of Market Value of the Property		$7,309,612
	Rounded to:	$7,310,000

Explanation of Capitalization

This method is used to estimate a proper interest rate. This method builds a rate by adding together component parts that are considered appropriate to constitute a total interest rate. See the following bracket:

        Safe Rate or Nonrisk Rate   8.25%
        (Interest paid by Savings Bank

or Government Bonds)
Rate for Lack of Safety   .75%
Rate for Nonliquidity   .50%
Rate for Burden of Management   .50%
                        Total   10.00%

Recapture Rate

The expected economic life of the building improvement is influenced by the anticipated durability of the income stream, which in turn is anticipated from the credit of the tenant or lessee, the location of the improvements, and the permanence of usage. The tenancy herein could be expected to last for a period of 50 years, therefore, the recapture rate would be 50/100ths, or 2.00 percent; therefore, interest and recapture on the improvements are 12 percent.

Fluctuating interest rates on bonds and mortgages, as in the 1970s, when interest rates jumped from 8 percent to 9 or 10 percent, caused capitalization rates to vary. A high interest rate is reflected in an overall rate higher than the norm. In this market, 9.5 percent seems justified.

Since the purpose of this appraisal is for mortgage financing, the Ellwood factor will be applied to the constant as a double-check on the applied overall capitalization rate of 12%:

Mortgage Constant ----------
Term/20 years Interest Rate/9-1/4%
(Constant) .108 x 75% Mortgage   = .081
Equity Rate -------------------------------
14 Percent Equity Requirement
25 Percent Equity Contribution   = .035
Overall Rate: (Ellwood factor
                        includes built-in
                        depreciation
                        (recapture rate)   .116

Total net rental of $848,997 capitalized at an overall rate of 11.6 percent equals $7,309,620 ($848,997 ÷ 11.6% = $7,318,939). Rounded to: $7,310,000.

CORRELATION AND FINAL VALUE ESTIMATE

As the subject property is income producing and an investment property, greater consideration must be given to the Income Approach. An investor would base his purchase on the potential net income that may be derived from the property. It is my opinion, based on the data contained in this report, that the fair market value of the subject property as of May 1, 1976 is:

SEVEN MILLION THREE HUNDRED TEN THOUSAND DOLLARS
($7,310,000)

The Principle of Competition has become more acute in this type of retail outlet, particularly small food stores, supermarkets, and discount stores, than in any other types of merchandising enterprises in the nation, including gasoline stations. The truth is there are just too many of them fighting one another for the same market in the same community. The result has been the recent overwhelming bankruptcy of W.T. Grant Co. and the closings of the White Front Stores on the West Coast, of many A & P's across the nation, and the selling out of the Grand Union Stores in the East. However, there are exceptions to the rule in some areas; the model appraisal at the end of this chapter will demonstrate an exception.

12

Appraising a Free-Standing Retail Store

KEY CONSIDERATIONS OF VALUE IN SINGLE RETAIL STORES

Step 1

The procedural steps, approaches, and techniques in evaluating land and building in this type of property, be it supermarket, fast food stand, dry cleaners, shoe store, or ice cream drive-in, are precisely as outlined in the foregoing shopping center chapter (and so will not be repeated again here); there is one exception to this context, however. The market survey for the single retail store does not have to reach as far geographically for predictable patronage. A single store can succeed in a trade area of more or less one square mile if population density is heavy, or within a three-mile radius if population is scattered. But parking ratio to building area must remain generous, with easy accessibility for pedestrians as well as automobiles. The model appraisal within will illustrate these points.

Step 2

As distinct from shopping centers, single retail units must attract shoppers by their own and their neighbors' pulling power. They are sometimes affected adversely in competition among themselves, by rivalry from nearby shopping centers, or by traffic congestion in downtown areas. They are sometimes gems, in locations protected from competition.

The Income Approach is the chief guide to evaluation of income-bearing, investment properties, with Market Data and Cost Approaches used, when applicable, as supporting evidence of value.

Step 3—Special Features of Retail Unit Evaluation

Retail store properties are usually established by risk-taking entrepreneurs in the urban core and environs, in perimeter districts along arteries leading to suburbs, and in outlying rural places where the only mark of commercial activity may be the general store and gasoline pump at the crossroads.

In any case, valuation of such income-bearing property must begin with the appraiser's estimate of its highest and best use (i.e., "most likely profitable use") in supplying desirable goods and services at retail to a demanding public convenienced to the spot by relatively easy access, paying close attention to the competition existing in the neighborhood or likely to appear in the future on zoned vacant lots nearby.

To determine highest and best and most productive use of land and building, the appraiser must first collect and absorb all economic data having any bearing on the operation of the retail store property under appraisement. The initial question uppermost in the appraiser's mind must be: *Is it the proper store in the proper place at this time?* Timing is perhaps the most important ingredient.

Without the answer to this question, the appraiser cannot begin to forecast the earnings expectancy of the subject property. He must determine the likely type, quality, and permanence of tenant business (for instance, a rated, national chain store long-term lease vs. a month-to-month fly-by-night) in order to establish the basis of a capitalization rate that will produce a fair net return on the equity invested.

The dominant kind of value possessed by a retail property is *investment value.* This is its market value, and it is measured by the *investment analysis method* (i.e., earnings expectancy of the property). It is then possible to compute the present worth of a number of years of annual dollar benefits at a yield rate commensurate with the risk involved in purchasing the property at his appraised value. The likely length and strength of the lease guarantee is vital in this calculation. Free-standing, triple-A rated food stores, such as shown in the model appraisal of this chapter, are usually leased long term to the food company by the landowner and/or builder, with a capitalization based on the prime rate, plus 2% to 4% for recapture. Very often, a percentage rent is paid over the base lease.

The appraiser's forecast of annual net dollar returns and his selection of the yield rate are modified by comparative market data, which must be carefully collected by him during his examination of the district in which the subject property is lodged. He will have to make a comparative analysis of rentals of similar properties throughout the district in order to determine an average yield rate. (See model appraisal following.)

Intricate mathematical formulae and tables can be useful tools in the Income Approach, but not unless they are based on common-sense application of rental data collection and a practical feeling for the pulse of the marketplace. Only then can the approaches, techniques, and procedures for value estimate be rationally employed.

MODEL APPRAISAL
SUMMARY OF SALIENT FACTS AND CONCLUSIONS

Subject Property:

Super Stores, Inc.
Newtown Turnpike
Westerville, Conn.

Date of Appraisal:	July 25, 1975
Site Area:	26,752 ± Square Feet
Building Area:	11,329 ± Square Feet
Date of Construction:	1950
Site Value:	$392,180
Improvement Value (Depreciated):	$178,000
Value Conclusion via Income Approach:	$498,860
Final Value Estimate:	$500,000

PURPOSE AND FUNCTION OF APPRAISAL

The appraisal was made for the purpose of estimating the market value of the subject property, including land and improvements, as of July 24th, 1975. The function of this report is to provide subject owners with true cash value for intercorporate accounting and depreciation schedules.

REAL ESTATE TAX DATA

The property under appraisement is subject to the assessments and taxes by the town of Westerville. The assessments and taxes are promulgated by this taxing jurisdiction for 1975 as follows:

Parcel No. 1		Parcel No. 2	
Land	$191,100.	Land	$91,600.
Improvement	168,800.	Paving	4,220.
Total	$359,900.	Total	$95,820.

Grand Total: $445,720
Tax Rate: $330   Ratio: 100%
Tax Burden: $12,857.

LEGAL DESCRIPTION

The subject property is found on the maps and records of the town of Westerville, as follows:

Lots 1 and 2
Map-56
Block-407
District 10

(See Plat Plan Following)

ZONING AND USE

The subject property is situated in the CB, Central Business District of the town of Westerville. The zone permits only retail business-type uses as set forth in Article 15 of the zoning ordinances of the town. The present improvement conforms to the zoning requirements of the town.

HIGHEST AND BEST USE

Highest and best use for the subject property is its present use, which conforms to the present zoning.

AREA DATA

The town of Westerville is located in the southern portion of the state of Connecticut, approximately six (6) miles north of the New York State border. The area is residential in nature, with high-priced homes predominating. Transportation facilities are unusually good for both Stamford and White Plains commuters with excellent rail and bus service to these cities, and the Merritt Parkway and I-95 will help speed easy access to all shore points.

The population of Westerville is 20,000 in 13,560 households with a median income of $16,200 per household head, far above national, state, and county averages. The area is growing, is within minutes of the Westchester County Airport, and chief employers within 5 miles are The American Can Company International Corporate Headquarters and AVCO Corporate Headquarters. The environment is extremely attractive.

THE APPRAISAL PROCESS

The generally accepted method of obtaining the market value of a parcel of property is by the use of the three approaches to value. These approaches are the Cost Approach, the Income Approach, and the Market Data Approach to value. The value indicated by each approach is carefully reviewed and that approach that in the judgment of the appraiser most adequately and accurately reflects all the circumstances in connection with the property under appraisement and the purposes for which the appraisal is being made will be selected as the best indication of market value. In this appraisal, we shall utilize only the Cost and Income Approaches since recent nearby sales of comparable sites and buildings are nonexistent in this highly restricted zone and small shopping district.

In the Income Approach, the value of the property will be estimated by the capitalization of net income that the property could produce.

Capitalization of Income

Full reliance will be placed by the appraiser on the capitalization of the economic net income of the property rather than on a market estimate due to the fact that it is impossible to estimate the value of this raw land without comparable sales. There are no other parcels of land but one in Westerville zoned for this use; the other is a complete 12-store neighborhood convenience shopping center, with bank and post office, about three miles northeast. We will, therefore, apply a Cost Approach and find our land value by use of the Land Residual Technique.

SITE DATA

The subject site is irregular in shape and in two (2) separate lots, measuring 71' x 212' and 78' x 150' for a total of 26,752 ± square feet. The site also includes 11,700 ± square feet of paved parking. Pavement is 3" bituminous asphalt concrete.

The site is serviced by all utilities including gas, electricity, sewers, and telephone.

The site is level at road grade, with slight decline to its borders for drain-off purposes into dry wells in each corner of the lot. Subsoil is gravel over hardpan and highly compacted, and there has been no settling or heaving in front since 1951.

IMPROVEMENT DATA

The subject site is improved with a one-story plus partial basement building constructed in 1951. There has been some remodelling since 1958. The building comprises a total ground floor area of 11,329 ± square feet, a basement area of 6,875 ± square feet, and a mezzanine of 512 ± square feet.

The building is constructed of steel frame with foundation walls of masonry. The interior of the building has reinforced concrete floors, sheetrock and wood-panelled walls with hardwood trim, suspended grid ceiling with recessed fluorescent lighting.

The roof is flat with tar and gravel cover. The heat is forced hot air with air conditioning. Plumbing facilities are adequate, with the entire building sprinklered.

The building is trimmed out in authentic Colonial sash, door jambs, and gabled overhang above surrounding sidewalks, which are laid out in 2" slate mortared paving blocks. The building is brick-faced on all sides, and presents an inviting approach from the road front. Evergreens flourish along the property borders, screening it from neighboring properties.

COST APPROACH

The subject improvement has a gross floor area of 11,329 ± square feet.

The cost method of the improvements has been calculated based on information supplied by builders and developers, and valuation and cost services. The unit costs derived have been adjusted to reflect the building conditions in the Westerville area.

A physical inspection of the property indicates that the improvements are in fair condition. Physical depreciation has been deducted from the reproduction cost new to reflect the age and condition of the improvements. The deduction of the total amount of depreciation from the cost new results in a depreciated cost for the building.

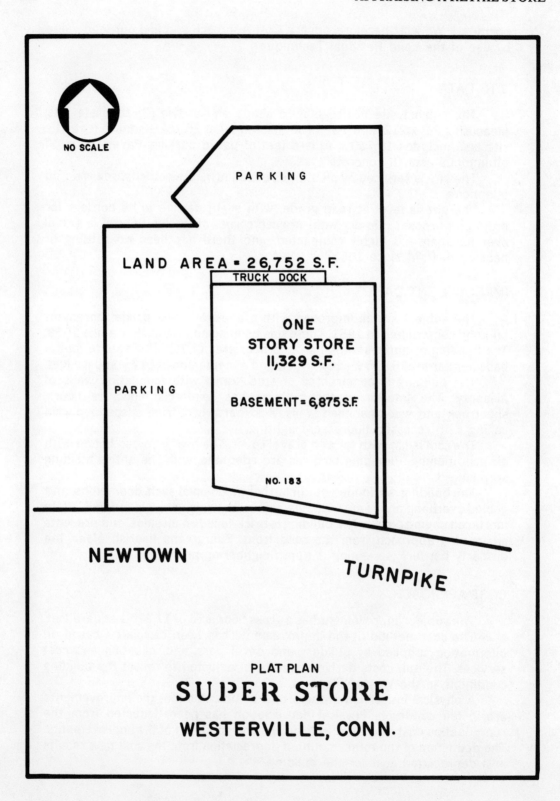

NO SCALE

PARKING

LAND AREA = 26,752 S.F.

TRUCK DOCK

ONE
STORY STORE
11,329 S.F.

BASEMENT = 6,875 S.F.

PARKING

NO. 183

NEWTOWN   TURNPIKE

PLAT PLAN
SUPER STORE
WESTERVILLE, CONN.

VALUATION OF THE IMPROVEMENTS VIA THE COST APPROACH

Improvement—11,329 ± square feet;
Base cost includes basement, air
conditioning, excavation, and sales
area: $30. p.s.f.

Improvement
11,329 ± square feet @ $30./s.f.   = $339.870

Sprinklers
11,329 ± square feet @ $1.00/s.f.   = $ 11,329

Site Improvements
Blacktop paving
15,000 square feet @ .30/s.f.   = $ 4,500
Reproduction Cost New $355,699

Less Depreciation
    Physical   50%
    Functional   -0-
    Economic   -0-
    Total   50% $177,850
Depreciated Cost of Improvement $177,850
                              Rounded to $178,000

Explanation of Depreciation

The Cost Approach was used to estimate the depreciated cost of building and site improvements new. The Land Residual Technique will be used to estimate the value of the land at its highest and most profitable use. Since the building and site improvements are 25 years old, and we estimate the effective life of the improvement at 50 years, 50/100th = 2% per annum as a constant straight-line depreciation factor.

We will, therefore, apply the depreciation as of the date of the report at 50%.

Remaining economic life is estimated at 25 years, or 50% of useful life expectancy.

INCOME APPROACH

The Income Approach to the value estimate is an appraisal technique in which the anticipated net income is processed to indicate the capital amount of the investment that will produce net income. It is dependent upon the following: an accurate statement of the economic rental; the deduction of all applicable expenses; the conversion of net income into value by the property capitalization rate.

The property is owned by Super Stores, Inc. and is leased to W.J. Riggins Enterprises, Inc. The lease dated January 1, 1970 is for thirty years commencing April 1, 1970 and terminating on December 31, 2000. The contract rental is $39,000 per annum, net, net, net, with no percentage override.

Moreover, a comprehensive study of rentals paid for similar food stores within a 10-mile radius, even in more competitive neighborhoods, indicates that $5.00 p.s.f. absolutely net would be economic in the marketplace as of this date.

Economic Rental

11,329 + square feet @ $5.00/sq.ft.   = $ 56,645
                                          Rounded to: $ 57,000

Valuation of Land and Improvements via Income Approach
(Using Land Residual Technique)

Depreciated Cost of the Improvements = $177,850
Effective, Absolutely, Net Income Per Annum = $ 57,000
Interest Imputable to Improvements   =
   ($177,850 x 14%)   24,899
Interest to Land $ 32,101
Therefore, 32,101 ÷ 10% = $321,010
Depreciated Cost of the Improvements $177,850
Estimated Value of the Land   321,010
Estimated Market Value of the Property $498,860
                                          Rounded to: $500,000

Explanation of Capitalization

The summation method is used to estimate a proper interest rate. This method builds a rate by adding together component parts that are considered appropriate to constitute a total interest rate. See the following illustration:

Safe Rate or Nonrisk Rate	8.50%
(Interest Paid by Savings	
Bank Rated; Corporate Stocks	
Preferred, or Government	
Bonds)	
Rate for Lack of Safety	0.50%
Rate for Nonliquidity	0.50%
Rate for Burden of Management	0.50%
Total	10.00%

Recapture Rate

The remaining economic life of the building improvement is influenced by the anticipated durability of the income stream, which in turn is anticipated from the credit of the tenants, the location of the improvements, and the permanence of usage. The tenancy herein could be expected to last for a period of 25 years; therefore, the recapture rate would be 25/100th, or 4.0 percent. Thus, interest and recapture on the improvements are 14 percent.

RECAPITULATION OF VALUE CONCLUSIONS

Value of Site	$177,850
Value of Improvements	$321,010
Total	$498,860
Rounded to:	$500,000

Estimated Market Value of Subject Property

FIVE HUNDRED THOUSAND DOLLARS
($500,000)

The motor-hotel industry depends upon travel. Travel is occasioned by: (1) business activity; (2) government activity; (3) vital happenings in individual or family affairs; (4) leisure time and discretionary income for vacations, exploring, and touring. The velocity of these four elements in travel movement varies at different times and in different directions. But it is a force of constant expansion with population growth, spreading wherever airlines, new highways, and a viable economy allow it to penetrate. In this chapter, we will treat with a 150-unit, leased motel at the perimeter of the Seattle-Tacoma Airport that was one of the first to arrive on the scene, but which has become surrounded with intense competition from big chain motels and is suffering property "taxitis" as well.

13

Motel Leasing:

A Tax-Appeal Appraisal Using the

Land Residual Technique

KEY CONSIDERATIONS OF VALUE IN MOTEL PROPERTIES

The aspects that dominate value in a new motel (or an older unprofitable one) are as follows:

a. *Room sizes.* The motel customer now requires larger rooms and often housekeeping facilities as well. Former room sizes of less than 200 square feet are now obsolete. Today's travelers get 250 square feet without a kitchenette and approximately 360 square feet with housekeeping facilities.

b. *Number of units.* Motels are larger; 100 units or more is the rule for chain management.

c. *Area for expansion.* The new motel pattern also includes room for expansion (especially high-rise). Enough land is acquired initially so the motel can grow with success and with the growth of the community (for instance, the St. Francis Motel in San Francisco). The new units frequently constitute a completely separate building from the original.

d. *Public facilities.* Sufficient public space is now a must for the new motel that caters to businesspersons as well as tourists. The old rule of 100 square feet per room of public space (meeting rooms and conventions) is now increased to 200 square feet per room. The growth in public space in motels has been so great that competition is becoming a major factor, as is the ability to obtain trained personnel. Furthermore, the competition is not merely within the community, but also is intercity, state, and national. That is another reason why the motel chains have an edge over the single-ownership operations; the chains can offer a choice of cities, and, more recently, of countries.

e. *Height increase with land costs.* Of necessity, the height of a motel is a function of land costs, e.g., the Holiday Inn in midtown Manhattan must be high-rise to justify land costs.

f. *Architecture and design.* Modern design must incorporate features for built-in operating economy. Gadgetry that is expensive to maintain is out. Plumbing and other utility lines must be available for easy repair. This means they must be accessible without the need to tear down a wall, which puts rental space out of use for significant periods of time. Floor and wall redecoration is standardized and simplified. Furniture and fixtures must be durable as well as aesthetic and be resistant to ordinary wear and tear. Single kitchens should be used to service all of the eating facilities in the motel with, at most, serving pantries on other floors.

Today's motel should return 14 percent on a free-and-clear basis (i.e., operating income as a percentage of total investment). Financing today is available to 75 percent of value and at an interest rate of about 9 1/2 percent. Recognizing the increased stability in the industry, lenders will extend 20-year terms, which may still require a balloon at the end in order to prevent a negative cash flow to the investor.

Demand for hospitality space remains relatively constant. Growing demand caused by increased travel is offset by speedy air transport that eliminates much of the former need to be away from home for extended periods. A motel should not be built unless there presently is a greater demand than can be supplied in the community.

TECHNIQUES AND PROCEDURES

First Step in the Investment Analysis

The appraiser's *initial step* in evaluating an existing or proposed motel is to process its actual or projected income. He decides upon capitalization method, rate, and valuation technique only after examining all the circumstances surrounding his subject's location, competition, design, and service, basing his conclusions on the dominant aspects of value that contribute to its operation.

In amplification of the foregoing paragraph, we introduce an article written by James E. Liek, an SRPA member of the Society of

Real Estate Appraisers, which has since become "bible" to those who specialize in motel appraisals. The article was entitled "The Income Approach Applied to Motel Leasing." It appeared in the Society's periodical "The Real Estate Appraiser" in the January-February issue of 1970, and it is a format used today not only by appraisers, but by bankers, builders, developers, franchisers, and accountants.

THE INCOME APPROACH APPLIED TO MOTEL LEASING [1]

The motel business is an important and steadily growing segment of the travel accommodations industry. It has doubled* in size in the last ten years. With its ability to adjust to changing highway patterns and with the emergence of large national motel chains, such as Holiday Inn, Howard Johnson, Ramada Inn, Downtowner, and others, motels have grown and prospered. This is in contrast to the hotel business which continues to decline in size, occupancy rate, etc. due to aging physical plants, depreciated locations, and rapidly increasing costs.

As the motels have grown, especially the chain units, there has been an increasing demand for motel loans. We have noticed in recent years an increase in the number of motel installations built by local real estate investors and leased either directly to the motel chains or to independent motel operating companies.

For example, in our lending area (the Midwest), we have recently financed or participated in the financing of motels leased to each of the above-mentioned chains and are now negotiating financing for a motel franchised by a national chain, but leased to one of the nation-wide motel operators which include such firms as Inn Operations, Innkeepers, Inc., and many others.

The trend to motel leasing has, in our opinion, greatly simplified both the appraising and financing of motels. The typical motel lease covers real estate only, the lessee having agreed to provide the required furnishings and removable equipment. Thus, the chore of abstracting income attributable only to furnishings and/or real estate is eliminated.

Typical leases provide for net rents based on a percentage of the sales of motel rooms, food, and beverages respectively, but often stipulate a guaranteed minimum rental. This provision, of course, enables us to readily determine minimum income and cash flow for loan underwriting purposes. Since most of the acceptable operating and/or franchising chains demonstrate a substantial net worth and the management expertise of the firms is

---

[1]Reprinted, with permission, from *The Real Estate Appraiser,* Jan-Feb. 1970, from the Society of Real Estate Appraisers, 7 S. Dearborn, Chicago, Ill., 60603.
*Tripled since this article was written.

well established, the guaranteed minimum income stream is considered to be reliable. We have often been able to arrange additional secondary financing on a commercial (non-real estate) basis, relying on the assignment of the excess amount of guaranteed rental after deducting required first mortgage loan debt service.

The appraisal of the property requires additional analysis, of course.

The Cost Approach has presented few problems since the chain motels are generally of 100-room size, or more, and bidding has tended to be on a "turn key" basis by well-established general contractors. We have also found the national cost estimating data services such as Marshall-Stevens, Boechk's, and others to be highly reliable when properly used.

The Market Data Approach has in the past, and still does, presented validity problems due to the relatively few sales of large motel properties.

As lenders, we have relied heavily upon and concerned ourselves particularly with the Income Approach. Prior to the emergence of motel leasing patterns, we laboriously constructed detailed stabilized income and expense statements in order to estimate net income in the Income Approach. In this effort we have relied almost entirely on the "gold mine of information" provided by the national accounting firm of Harris, Kerr, Forster, in their annual publication *Trends in the Hotel-Motel Business*. The firm audits a number of the motel chains and major independent facilities. Their data is well organized for our use and we have found it to be exceptionally valid and reliable.

Happily, the typical motel lease is written on an "absolute net" rental basis; i.e., the rental is absolutely net to the lessor, all expenses including real estate taxes, maintenance, utilities, franchise fees, insurance, etc., are paid in full by the lessee. Thus the estimation of net income requires little more than properly estimating the probable performance of the subject facility in the motel market.

The leasing pattern which prevails nationally is as follows:

National motel chains will pay rent based on:

25% of room sales
 5% of beverage sales*
 5% of food sales*

National motel operators will pay:

28% of room sales
 5% of beverage sales*
 2% of food sales*

(Note that in the above-listed situations furnishings for the motel rooms as well as the restaurant, bar, and meeting room area are provided by the tenant. In the event the landlord provides fur-

---

*Inflationary increases in these rates since Mr. Liek wrote his article are about 1%.

nishings, food and beverage percentage rates are typically increased to 10% each for the first ten years of the initial lease term.)

The problem now becomes one of estimating the probable net rental based on probable sales of rooms, food, and beverages. In this estimating process, we rely implicitly on trends in hotel-motel business for motel properties of 50 units or more. For motels of less than 50 units we have found the data published by the *Tourist Court Journal* (Temple, Texas) to be easiest to use. Both sources categorize their data on the basis of unit size, geographic area, and rate group. In the case of a typical two-story, 120-unit Holiday Inn located in the Midwest, we would employ the following procedure to estimate annual rental.

First we consult the current issue of "Holiday Inns Directory," which is readily available at any Holiday Inn. This booklet lists the current room rates for each Holiday Inn operating in each state. Next we consult *Trends in Hotel-Motel Business* for data relating to motels with restaurants in the following categories: (1) $10.00 to $12.50 base-rate group, (2) 75 to 150 room-size group, (3) North Central geographic division.

We then can conclude by interpolation of the available data that the motel, if in existence now, would probably enjoy the following experience:

Single rate (prevailing locally)	$11.00
Double rate (prevailing locally)	14.00
Average number of guests per occupied room	1.5
Average sold room rate per day	$12.50
Annual percentage of rooms sold	75%
Food and beverage sales as percentage of room sales	80%

The food and beverage sales category is most difficult to estimate if the lease provides for rentals based on a percentage of sales of these items. The above-80% estimate is an "industry average," but better-than-average bar and restaurant management may well produce income in that category equal to 100% of room sales, or more. Considerable judgment must be exercised by the appraiser in estimating not only the relationship between room sales and food and bar sales, but the proper average room rate as well. Surveys of competition are the best basis for such estimates. There is some leeway, perhaps $1.00 to $2.00, in average rate per day considering the influences of location (in the subject area tourist travel patterns are important) and the upward trend of motel rates. In new construction cases, we have found that motel rates generally increase 50¢ to 75¢ by the time construction is completed and the motel is in actual operation.

The probable sales of the typical 120-unit Holiday Inn can now be estimated. In this example we will assume a proposed construction situation with operations of the completed unit expected to begin about twelve to fifteen months hence. We believe the following projection would be both reasonable and accurate.

Estimated Annual Sales:

```
    120   Available Rooms
  x 365   Calendar Days
 43,800   Possible Room Sales
   x .75   Occupancy (Sales) Rate
 32,850   Sold Rooms
   x $13   Average Daily Room Rate
$427,050  Gross Annual Room Rate
   x .80   Ratio of Food and Beverage Sales
$341,640  Gross Annual Food and Bar Sales
```

Estimated Annual Rental:

1. Leased to Motel Chain

Annual Room Sales (Rounded)	$427,000	
Percentage Rent Factor	x .25	
Rent Attributed to Room Sales		$106,750
Annual Food & Beverage Sales (Rounded)	$342,000	
Percentage Rent Factor	.05	
Rent Attributable to Food & Beverage Sales		$ 17,100
Total Estimated Net Annual Rent		$123,850
	Rounded to:	$124,000

2. Leased to Operating Company Chain

Annual Room Sales	$427,000	
Percentage Rent Factor	.28	
Rent Attributable to Room Sales		$119,560
Annual Food Sales	$225,000	
Percentage Rent Factor	.02	
Rent Attributable to Food Sales		$ 4,500
Annual Beverage Sales	$117,000	
Percentage Rent Factor	.05	$ 5,850
Total Estimated Net Annual Rent		$129,910
	Rounded to:	$130,000

The two leasing patterns produce net rent estimates that differ in the amount of $6,000 per annum. But the value conclusions may or may not differ radically, depending on the capitalization rate applied by the appraiser in each of the above examples. It is not within the scope of this paper to discuss selection of the proper capitalization rate, but the appraiser may well feel that investors would apply different capitalization rates in each of the above situations depending on the financial posture of the lessee. As mortgage lenders, we prefer the Ellwood method and have found it to be highly satisfactory for our purposes.

Applying our current mortgage terms of 9% interest, 20-year amortization, 75% loan-to-value ratio, and assuming 5% depreciation in the first 5 years and applying equity yields ranging from 10% to 12%, we obtain value indications by the Ellwood overall capitalization method as follows:

Net Income Estimate	Equity Yield	Indicated Value
$124,000	10%	$1,257,606
$124,000	11%	$1,222,879
$124,000	12%	$1,190,019
$130,000	10%	$1,318,458
$130,000	11%	$1,282,051
$130,000	12%	$1,247,600

Thus it appears that value by Income Approach will probably be about $1,250,000 to $1,300,000 depending on the final selection of net income estimate and capitalization rate.

Although construction costs are rising rapidly at this writing, it appears that a two-story, 120-unit motel can still be constructed (including indirect costs) on reasonably priced land for that amount *exclusive* of furnishings. Thus the proposed improvement seems economically appropriate in view of the fact that expected net rental income will produce a reasonable return to equity after debt service and before tax depreciation benefits. If we further assume a minimum or guaranteed rent of $1,000 per unit, or $120,000 per year, (which is reasonable), a mortgage loan in the $925,000 to $975,000 range can be comfortably serviced by the guaranteed rental.

The above net income estimation is also applied by our appraisers in the valuation of strictly franchised or independent (owner-operated) motels. It is our feeling that the typical lender, after acquiring a motel property through borrowers' default, would attempt to rent the property to a motel chain or operating company while acquiring title or seeking a purchaser. Thus the rental value technique is considered to be particularly appropriate if the function of the appraisal is to assist the lender in mortgage loan underwriting.

In summary, we find the motel business trends to be indicative of a healthy, growing industry, and one which requires a substantial real property investment and financing. There is a considerable amount of current, reliable and well-organized data available on motel operations which provides a sound basis for motel appraisal and loan underwriting. The recent trend to motel leasing provides data and "norms" which further simplify use of the especially important Income Approach in property appraising or loan underwriting. Thus, we believe lenders, appraisers, and investors alike can rely heavily on this simplified Income Approach and can proceed with confidence in this important area of activity applying the above-illustrated income-estimating technique.

Mr. Liek was, at the time of writing the foregoing classic review, vice president of the Mortgage Loan Division, First Wisconsin National Bank of Milwaukee, Milwaukee, Wisconsin. He received his master's degree from the State University of Iowa. He is currently Executive Vice President, Institutional Property Advisors, Inc., investment advisors to Institutional Investors Trust (R.E.I.T.).

Second Step: The Market Survey and Property Analysis

The next move the appraiser makes in evaluating a proposed or existing motel is to gather and correlate data that points up the likelihood of success or failure. He relates this information to his analysis of the subject property in this manner:

1. *Prospects.* Macro-market trends and travel patterns in the nation, region, and area measured against the micro-market demand for a motel in the locale. In measuring regional vs. local economic conditions, the following factors must be scrutinized:
    (a) Highway arterial system feeding the locale and the site; the business, tourist, and sport travel using these arteries; and the nearest airport facility.
    (b) Chief forms of employment within the locale, and the amount of local commercial patronage on which the motel can count.
    (c) The amount and substance of industry in the region and its contribution, if any, to the commerce of the locale. The area's atmosphere as an industrial, commercial, and resort center, with all three described if necessary.
    (d) The planning and zoning practices, the tax policies, and local ordinances affecting the property and its district must be stated clearly. Ingress and egress permits from and to frontage highways are vital.
    (e) Assuming that highest and best use of the site is a motel, with good roads, automobile parking on site, restaurants, and other conveniences, state the likely competition to be met from motels nearby. Overbearing competition can affect highest and best use adversely.
2. *Property Analysis and History.* Specific details of the property under appraisement must be clearly delineated:
    (a) Recitation of the title, including metes and bounds, assessments and tax levy.
    (b) Zone requirements.
    (c) Description of the site topography and subsoil conditions, plottage and shape of the land area, together with list of utilities on site or available.
    (d) The type of construction, use and conditions of the proposed or existing building together with site improvements, planned or existing, such as paved parking, swimming pool, other recreational facilities.
    (e) Each floor of the building must be measured and described.
    (f) A summary of the development of the property, and type of management and maintenance attending the property.
    (g) The anticipated useful life of the property must be estimated and allowances made for depreciation and obsolescence.
    If the building is proposed or in the planning stage, the appraiser must project income and expenses for five years from his knowledge and experience in new motel construction, and recommend management and maintenance procedures for the proposed building that are both practical and economic.
3. *Comparable Land Sales and Leases.* The appraiser must list in detail verified data concerning land sales and leases similar to the subject property in the locale

of the subject property. These comparables should be inspected, and similarities or differences described, as compared to subject land and/or buildings, summing up the property analysis.

Third Step: The Approaches to Value

The appraiser's *third step* in motel appraisal lies in his use of all three approaches: Cost, Income, and Market Data, if possible.

Usually valuation of a motel is first gauged by its *Depreciated Cost,* with land, site improvements, furniture, equipment, and housewares added. An approved cost index service will provide square-foot or cubic-foot multipliers for a variety of classes of motels.

The Income Approach applied to a leased motel is laid out precisely in accordance with Mr. Liek's formula. The bottom line is *net income* which is accordingly capitalized into value.

The Market Data Approach can be applied to motels on a selling-price-per-unit basis where recent sales of motels similar to the subject have taken place. The comparables should be taken from nearby areas, with type of operation and room rates that are closely similar. If these don't exist, then chief reliance for value conclusion should be put upon the Income Approach.

Fourth Step: Capitalization Rates and Methods

Capitalization rates on motel properties will vary with circumstances. Choice of capitalization rate and method is the appraiser's critical fourth step in evaluation of a motel property.

Fifth Step: Estimating a Separate Land Value Under the Motel

As the fifth step in motel evaluation, it is necessary to determine land value. Market data on sales of vacant land is usually abundant, since land sales do not have to be close by, but similar in respect to area, location, highway conditions, and topography.

Sixth Step: Estimating Value of the Improvements in a Motel

Property Residual Technique Under the Income Approach. A sound motel may develop net income that, capitalized, proves investment or market value greater than depreciated reproduction cost can show. It may also show capitalized value greater than market data indicates.

Therefore, the Income Approach is generally the best proof of investment value, with close support from the Market Data Approach.

In the following model appraisal of a proposed airport perimeter motel building, the Property Residual Technique is employed for value conclusion with the Cost Approach and Market Data Approach in close support. Since the value of the land has been established via market data, the Property Residual Technique under the Income Approach solves the remaining questions concerning market value.

MODEL APPRAISAL
SUMMARY OF SALIENT FACTS AND CONCLUSIONS

Subject Property:	Skyline Inn
	Amelia Earhart Drive
	Seattle, Washington 98104
Site Area:	3.0 Acres—130,680 Sq. Ft.
Assessment——————————Land @ 100%	$ 556,200
———Improvements @ 100%	1,249,200
——Total Assessor's Market Value	$1,805,400
Market Value by This Report:	1,400,000
Difference:	$ 405,400
Net Rentable Area: (Excluding	150 Units with
Corridors, Service Areas	70-Seat Restaurant and
& Outdoor Swimming Pool)	65-Seat Cocktail Lounge
Gross Area of Building:	67,625 Square Feet
Value Conclusion via	
Cost Approach:	$1,461,000
Value Conclusion via	
Income Approach:	$1,400,000
Value Conclusion via	
Market Data Approach	$1,395,000

PURPOSE OF APPRAISAL

The appraisal was made for the purpose of estimating the market value of the subject property, including land and improvements, as of January 1, 1976.

FUNCTION

To provide a fair and reasonable full cash, or market value, as the basis of an ad valorem tax appeal to the Board of Equalization.

THE APPRAISAL PROCESS AND VALUATION PREMISE

The generally accepted method of obtaining the market value of a parcel of property is by the use of the three approaches to value. These approaches are the Cost Approach, the Income Approach, and the Market Data Approach to value. The value indicated by each approach is carefully reviewed and that approach that in the judgment of the appraiser most adequately and accurately reflects all the circumstances in connection with the property under appraisement and the purpose for which the appraisal is being made will be selected as the best indication of market value.

In the Cost Approach, valuation is made of the cost new of the improvements based on up-to-date construction costs in the area and supplemented by recognized national valuation services. Deductions are made from the replacement cost of the improvements for physical deterioration and functional and economic obsolescence. Then the value of the land is added.

In the Income Approach, the value of the property is estimated by the capitalization of the estimated net income the property is capable of producing. We have utilized an overall capitalization rate to obtain the market value of the subject property.

The Market Data Approach to value is the method of appraisal in which the value of property is inferred from sales of comparable property. Value is measured by observing what comparable properties are selling for in the market.

REAL ESTATE TAX ASSESSMENTS

Tax assessments and levies are promulgated and collected by the King County Treasurer, King County Administration Building, Seattle, Washington.

Market value as determined by the Board of Equalization is as follows:

Land	$ 556,200
Improvements	1,249,200
Timber & Minerals	- 0 -
Total	$1,805,400

Ratio is at 100%
The 1976, Payable 1977, Levy Rate is 27.013 per $1,000
Tax Burden to Be Paid in 1977 = $44,528

HIGHEST AND BEST USE

We are of the opinion that the motel use of subject property constitutes at present the highest, best, and most profitable use. Subject property possesses the disadvantage of being one block south of the heavy traffic intersection of Pacific Highway at So. 188th Street, approaching either from the I-5 Freeway or the airport, and therefore misses the mainstream business and tourist automobile visibility from these approaches.

A further hardship against earnings is the intense competition from ten other motels within a mile or so of subject. One block north, on the opposite corner, located at a more convenient and visible corner approach from the freeway and the airport is the luxurious Sea-Tac Thunderbird Inn, which siphons off the approaching tourist from Skyline Inn. Other hostelries in nearby competition are the following:

Hyatt House	Jet Inn
Hilton	Sandstone Motel
Holiday Inn	Motel Six
Royal Inn	Travelodge, International
Swept-Wing Inn	Sheraton Renton

As a result, Skyline Inn stands at the bottom half of this list in earnings, and best and most likely profitable use is threatened if subject motel should be eliminated by financial collapse. Tax relief might prevent that eventuality.

ZONING

Zoning is for commercial and business use. The present use conforms with zoning bylaws.

UTILITIES

City water, electric, sanitary, and storm sewers are connected on site. Streets are lighted; 50 feet wide and paved; and fire hydrants are nearby.

AREA DATA

The Seattle-Tacoma area is richly endowed with scenic beauty and recreational opportunities. There are miles of ocean beaches for hiking or beachcombing; rivers, lakes, and streams for boating and fishing; and magnificent mountains for skiing or just plain viewing. Population of the combined cities is approximately 800,000.

SEA-TAC AIRPORT

Construction

After several years of intensified construction under the multi-million-dollar expansion and modernization program, building activity slackened in 1974. The total amount of contracts in force, including those commenced, completed, or continued through the year, came to $7,603,800.

The major ones were completion of the central control facility ($3,599,700); completion of the northeast cargo area taxiway ($918,440); purchase of three additional vehicles for the underground transit system ($1,305,807); and expansion of the air traffic-control tower ($681,200).

Economic Impact

The importance of Sea-Tac Airport to the economy of King County was graphically underscored by a study made in June by the airport's Planning and Research Department. This survey showed that more than 15,200 jobs, accounting for a gross annual payroll of $160 million and a yearly business activity of $390 million in the county, are related to the traffic and business activity at the airport.

The airlines were responsible for a major portion of the economic impact, producing $91 million in wages and purchasing $48.6 million in goods and services in the state of Washington.

The study estimated that some 38,000 residents of King County depend directly or indirectly on the commercial traffic at Sea-Tac for their livelihood.

Sea-Tac Plan

The Sea-Tac/Communities Plan neared its implementation phase by year's end. Action by the port of Seattle, King County, and the Federal Aviation Administration, and others will be necessary to accomplish the goals and principles developed by the plan. In close cooperation with citizens in the area environmentally impacted by the airport the study has defined problems and recommended solutions for Sea-Tac Airport and its surrounding communities.

The Airport Master Plan, following an FAA procedure format, predicts growth and requirements for 1978, 1983, and 1993. It indicates that Sea-Tac Airport will be able to handle all of the 15.2 million passengers forecast for 1993 with the terminal expansions already identified. No additional runways will be needed and no major land acquisition for strictly airport purposes is necessary. Increasing air cargo and maintenance demand will require gradual development of the west side through the study period, and facilities for those uses, as well as corporate/general aviation and a public viewing park, will be required.

Some potential future problem areas at the airport involve ground access—getting to and around the airport—and employee parking. Increased emphasis on public transportion and remote parking areas may alleviate some of the pending conflicts. Good coordination between port, county, and state agencies will be required, however, to monitor further development needs, especially beyond 1985.

Sea-Tac Airport is the largest single major land use in southwest King County. In order to help minimize the impacts generated by the airport on its residential neighbors, a program of citizen involvement and participation has generated plans for areas around the airport. Open meetings, workshops, and technical discussions have produced community development concepts that can be compatible with aircraft impact and community needs.

Most land-use plan changes are to the west and directly north of Sea-Tac Airport. State Highway 509 and the airport surround an area for which a change in use appears appropriate. This residential land adjacent to Port of Seattle property is recommended to be developed into higher density residential and commercial uses. Airport land use on the west side will eventually be needed for maintenance and air-cargo facilities; some additional land area is recommended for airport acquisition because of its potential runway orientation. In general, the area west of the airport is the only direction that the Burien commercial center can grow. Future west side development on the airport itself can also lead to an increased community orientation to Sea-Tac Airport.

SITE AREA

Subject corner site encompasses an area of 3.00 ± acres, with a frontage of 506 ± feet on the west side of Pacific Highway South, a main thoroughfare between Seattle and Tacoma, and somewhat less frontage on Amelia Earhart Drive. The site is with the rear or northerly boundary running about parallel the length of the Pacific Highway frontage.

The tract is slightly above road grade, on filled soil.

All public utilities, electric, city water, and sewers are connected on site.

Approximately 45,000 square feet of the area is asphalt paved for roadways, walks, and parking areas. Unpaved areas are grass covered and shrubbed.

The site is at the extreme outer edge of Seattle city limits in the town of Burien, within one mile of the Sea-Tac International Airport Terminal.

Maps of the site and its relationship to the airport are shown on the following pages.

LAND EVALUATION

Land in the immediate vicinity of subject in the same zone is very closely held, but your appraisers were able to procure records of some recent transactions that we feel are most indicative of value.

Overall, we have encompassed a radius of several miles, but we have found land similarly zoned and on or near the arterial route shared by subject.

Adjustments have been made to consider size, shape, topography, zone, access, and date of sale.

[Five recent comparable vacant land sales in the same zone as subject, one to four years old, are cited in this space, and after careful adjustments to the subject, they reflect a value of $3.00 per square foot as land value of the subject.]

Summation

The foregoing small acreage land acquisitions indicate a sale value of $3.00 per square foot for subject property. These comparables all have the same utilities attached as subject; that is, city water, gas, electricity, sewers, lighted and paved streets, and fair access to downtown arteries. As such, they have a strong influence on value indications to subject.

After balancing all the factors implicit in these comparables and gauging the qualities of each in the marketplace with a view toward elements affecting their value as a whole, we estimate that the fair market value of land for the subject property is $3.00 per square foot. Subject property embraces 3.0 ± acres, which equals 130,680 ± square feet. Therefore:

$$130,680 \text{ SF} \times \$3.00/\text{SF} = \$392,040$$

COST APPROACH

Property Description

The improvements are composed of five buildings forming a quadrangle, or inner court, where the swimming pool is centered. The pool itself is surrounded by an attractive, landscaped patio.

Three of the five buildings, which house 150 units of sleeping rooms, are two storied.

The lobby, attached to Building No. 1, is single storied, with a mezzanine. Building No. 2 is two storied, entirely sleeping quarters. Building No. 3 is a free-standing, single-story, housekeeping and maintenance structure, with guest laundromat. Building No. 4 is two storied and entirely sleeping quarters. Building No. 5 is single storied and houses the restaurant, cocktail bar and lounge, and meeting rooms. Roofing is gabled, asphalt shingle over ply-score and tar paper, insulated.

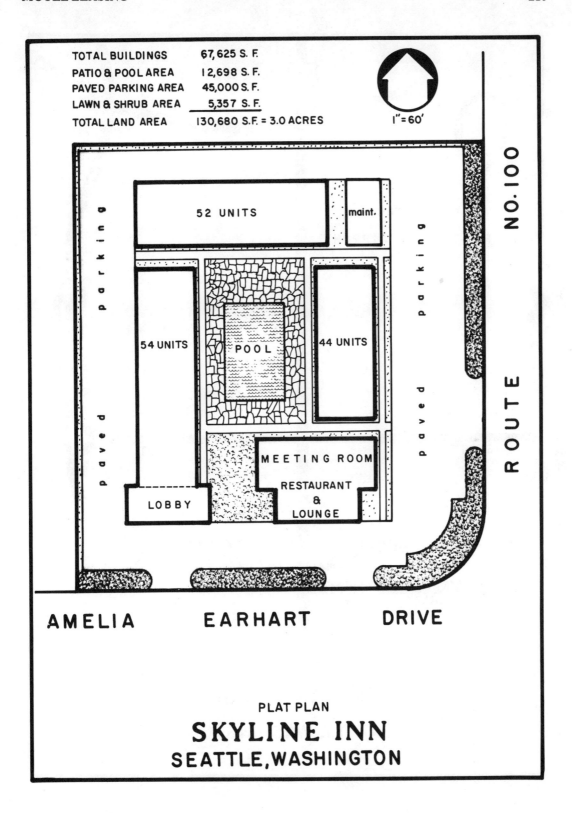

TOTAL BUILDINGS   67,625 S.F.
PATIO & POOL AREA   12,698 S.F.
PAVED PARKING AREA 45,000 S.F.
LAWN & SHRUB AREA   5,357 S.F.
TOTAL LAND AREA   130,680 S.F. = 3.0 ACRES

1" = 60'

52 UNITS

maint.

54 UNITS

POOL

44 UNITS

parking   parking
paved   paved

NO. 100

ROUTE

MEETING ROOM

RESTAURANT
&
LOUNGE

LOBBY

AMELIA   EARHART   DRIVE

PLAT PLAN
SKYLINE INN
SEATTLE, WASHINGTON

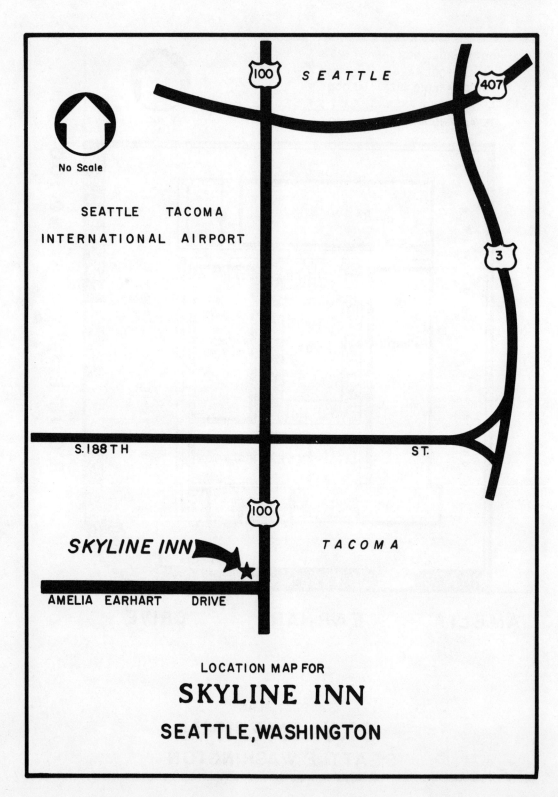

LOCATION MAP FOR
SKYLINE INN
SEATTLE, WASHINGTON

All the buildings are masonry, Colonial in style, brick veneer over cement block, and steel framed. Second-story sleeping quarters are reached by balconies running the full length of the dormitory buildings.

There are no basements. The only excavated portion of the structure was for the swimming pool. Foundations for the buildings are reinforced nine-inch concrete slab on poured concrete footings.

The structures are well maintained and in excellent condition. Maintenance is first rate. However, the buildings have settled two or three inches into the soft, filled surface, with the result that connections with city water and sewer mains, below road grade, have become disjointed and are presently under repair.

The buildings house 150 sleeping units (small by common standards), a 70-seat restaurant (small by common standards), and a 65-seat cocktail lounge. Rooms are 196 SF in area, under par by competitive standards.

The current reproduction costs of the improvements were obtained by the use of nationally known construction cost manuals. These have been adjusted and modified by judgment and experience.

Depreciation of the improvements is defined in the following categories.

1. Physical Deterioration—Loss of value resulting from wear and tear, disintegration, use in service, and action of the elements.
2. Functional Inutility—Loss of value caused by factors inherent in the property itself, such as undercapacity, inadequacy of room and restaurant sizes, and lack of full-sized 300-seat banquet room.
3. Economic Obsolescence—Loss of value caused by factors external to the property itself, such as accessibility and intense competition, those over which the property has no direct influence. Excessive taxes could cause economic obsolescence as could economic trends.

Considering the previously mentioned possible causes of loss in value, we believe the property has been affected by all three types of depreciation. We find that a building of the type under review has an economic life of approximately 33 years. This is supported by the various construction cost manuals such as the ones previously mentioned.

Physical Deterioration

The structure under review was originally constructed in 1969 and finished ready for operation early in 1968. Normally, the depreciation on buildings such as the subject is approximately 3.33 percent per year. These factors are the norm derived from actual mortality studies of buildings of the type and class of construction as the subject. These factors, in our opinion, are reflective of the condition of the subject at the time of review.

The conditions of such components as foundation, floors, roof, windows, doors, and interiors were noted. These factors were studied to arrive at an overall physical deterioration factor for the subject under review. We have found that the subject has received excellent care through the years. We have attributed a deterioration factor of 26.4 percent total for the subject structure.

To the yard improvements we have given an overall rate of 50 percent physical deterioration, since the asphalt paving takes a heavy beating from rapid in-and-out turnaround of cars, and the outside pool and patio require heavy maintenance and constant upkeep.

Functional Inutility

We found room sizes to be exceptionally small in comparison to motel norms. The 70-seat restaurant is also exceptionally small for motel norms. For these two inadequacies in layout, we have penalized the property by 20 percent after physical depreciation.

Economic Obsolescence

The crossover approach from the airport and second corner position in approach from I-5 at intersection of Pacific Highway South puts the location in awkward neighborhood traffic position. The Sea-Tac Thunderbird on the immediate right-hand corner approach from I-5 intercepts this business. Add intense competition of ten other motels within one-mile radius. Further, excessive taxes overburden the net income to the property after payment of land and building rental. We have, therefore, accounted for a 20 percent economic obsolescence factor to the subject.

Depreciated Reproduction Cost New

Building Improvements

67,625 ± Sq. Ft. @ $33 per Sq. Ft. =	$2,231,625	
(The original cost of the building was $1,500,000 in 1968, according to Skyline Inn auditors.)		
Less: Physical Deterioration—26.4%		
(8 Yrs. @ 3.33% Based on 33-Year Life)	589,149	
	$1,642,476	
Less: Functional Inutility—20%	$ 328,495	
	$1,313,981	
Less:Economic Obsolescence—20%	$ 262,796	
Depreciated Cost of Building Improvements		$1,051,185

Yard Improvements

Asphalt Paving		
45,000 ± Sq. Ft. @ $.40 per Sq. Ft. =	$18,000	
Less: 50% Depreciation	9,000	
		$ 9,000
15' x 35' Swimming Pool Sloping Floor 3' to 9' Depth; 12' Perimeter Patio and Retaining Wall above Drive-In	$18,000	
Less: 50% Depreciation	9,000	$ 9,000
Depreciated Cost of Yard Improvements		$ 18,000

Total Depreciated Value of Building &
  Yard Improvements $1,069,185
Add: Land Value   392,040
Total Indicated Value $1,461,225
                                    Rounded to: $1,461,000

Value Conclusion via Cost Approach
$1,461,000

INCOME APPROACH

The Skyline Inn is net leased from General Land & Development Co. (at arm's length) with a base annual rental, plus override gross percentage of gross business overall.

As the motel operation derives its income from real estate, personal property, and management, it is necessary to arrive at a realty rent based on the gross income the property is producing. Established methods utilized in the hotel/motel industry indicate that 25 percent of room sales, six percent of food sales, six percent of beverage sales, and five percent of miscellaneous income is attributable to the real estate.

In analyzing the income and operating statements of the subject, we found that the 1975 occupancy rate has dropped to 74.45 percent from 80.70 percent in 1974. The month of January, 1973, however, only showed an occupancy rate of 53.58 percent.

The above decrease in income was caused in part by the national gasoline shortage and rationing program which was instituted during the winter of 1973-74. The 1975 slowup in construction and development of the Sea-Tac Airport also may have affected the occupancy rate for 1974-75.

Since the gasoline shortage has now mostly subsided, we find that the subject should regain the clientele it had temporarily lost during the crisis. Based on the foregoing, we have projected an income for the future based on the past operations of the subject property.

An analysis of the gross income and net income derivation, together with an explanation of capitalization, appears on the following pages.

Capitalization Methodology and Process

The formula delineated below is readily accepted by both lessors and lessees in the industry and is evidenced in the many leases examined by the authors.

Net Rental

25% of Total Room Sales
5%* of Total Food Sales
6%* of Total Beverage Sales
5% of All Other Income

Room Sales   = $540,824
Net Rental   25%
                                     ───────────
                                                    $135,206

Food Sales	= $258,604	
Net Rental	6%	
		15,516
Beverage Sales	= $222,110	
Net Rental	6%	
		13,327
Other Income	= $ 75,022	
Net Rental	5%	
		3,751
Total Net Rental		$167,800
	Rounded to:	$168,000

*Note slight inflationary increase in percentage rates over those prescribed by Mr. Liek in his 1970 article.

Capitalization Rate Explanation

Mortgage Constant————————
Term/20 Years Interest Rate/9 1/2%
(Constant) .112 x 75% Mortgage =   .084
(Ellwood Tables)

Equity Rate————————
14 Percent Equity Requirement
25 Percent Equity Contribution =   .035

Overall Rate: .119

                                                              Rounded to: 12%

   Total net rental of $168,000 capitalized at an overall rate of 12 percent equals $1,400,000. ($168,000 ÷ 12% = $1,400,000)

Value Conclusion via Income Approach
$1,400,000

MARKET DATA APPROACH

   Your appraiser has researched sales of motor hotel properties in not only the immediate Sea-Tac Airport area, finding no recent recorded transactions. Therefore, we extended our search within a five-mile radius north and south in similar areas of business, leisure, and comparative circumstances. We found two that compare closely with subject north toward Seattle and two more southwards toward Tacoma. They are listed below:

Sale No. 1—The 100-room, 2-story motel at 1035 Parkside Drive, Georgetown, just off I-5. Sold 1/10/74, Book 4022, Page 565, for $945,000 or $9,450 per unit. Built in 1970, slightly larger rooms than subject. About 5 miles north of Sea-Tac Airport, north toward Seattle; less competition than subject. Situated on 3.56 acres.

Sale No. 2—The 140-room, 2-story motel at 888 Jones Road, Highland Park, near junction of Routes 509 and 599. Sold 9/8/73, Book 3996, Page 782, for

$1,046,000 or $7,471 per unit. About 4 miles north of subject. Bar and restaurant have been enlarged since time of sale, adding value in today's market. 2.98 acres.

Sale No. 3—The 175-room, 2-story motel at 22 Burning Bush Boulevard, just south of Normandy, in the city of Tacoma, on Route 508. Sold 2/14/75, Book 5001, Page 28, for $1,592,500 or $9,100 per unit. Same room sizes as subject, but 5 years older than subject. On 4.8 acres.

Sale No. 4—The 200-room, 2-story motel at 1211 Rainier Avenue, South Center, south of I-5 intersection with I-5, in City of Tacoma, about 3 miles southeast of subject. Overbuilt for size and community and tourist access. Sold 7/15/74, Book 5000, Page 808, for $1,806,000 or $9,030 per unit. 6.86 acres.

Adjusting the foregoing sales for room sizes, amenities, location, access, and accounting for the present slump in tourist trade, subject value is reflected at $9,300 per unit, or 150 x $9,300 = $1,395,000.

Value Conclusion via Market Data Approach
$1,395,000

CORRELATION AND FINAL VALUE CONCLUSION

The value conclusion from the two approaches that were utilized are as follows:

Cost Approach	$1,461,000
Income Approach	$1,400,000
Market Data Approach	$1,395,000

The Cost Approach normally sets the upper limit of value. The reproduction cost indicators were developed after determining local construction costs from references to national valuation manuals and from the appraiser's experience. The unit costs applied were derived to include the current costs for labor, materials, profit, and overhead. Depreciation allowances were taken for physical deterioration, and the subject was found to be affected by functional and economic obsolescence as well.

The Income Approach indicates a value for the subject based on the ability of the property to produce income and a return to the investor. The actual income and operating statement of the subject was utilized in order to determine a hypothetical economic rental for the property. This rental was capitalized into value by the use of interest rates applicable to the subject at the time of appraisal.

The Market Data Approach was applied as this value reflection hinges on the process of measuring value by the comparison of current unit-sale prices of similar properties. Due to the fact that four sales of similar properties were recently recorded within five miles north and south of the subject, or its environs, this approach cannot be completely discounted.

Since the Cost Approach by its inherent nature tends to set the upper limit of value, this approach has been discounted. The Cost Approach, however, provides the evaluator a check on the other values derived. Income-producing properties are not bought or sold on the basis of their cost, but rather on their ability to produce an adequate income to give the investors a return on their investment.

Consequently, greater weight is given to the Income Approach to arrive at a final value conclusion.

It is the opinion of the appraisers that the value of the subject property as of January 1, 1976 is:

ONE MILLION FOUR HUNDRED THOUSAND DOLLARS
$1,400,000

Convalescents, the chronically or recurrently ailing who do not need the intensive medical attention a hospital provides, are the people occupying beds in this definition of a "nursing home." Homes for the elderly, medical clinics, and those institutions treating alcoholics, drug addicts, and victims of contagious diseases are excluded from this definition. There are two types properly designated "nursing homes": (1) Those owned and managed for a profit, called proprietary nursing homes; and (2) those operated by nonprofit eleemosynary groups such as churches and charitable societies.

14

Appraising a Nursing Home:
A Special-Purpose Commercial Property

KEY CONSIDERATIONS OF VALUE IN NURSING HOMES

Nonprofit nursing homes seldom enter the real estate market, and appraisals are required infrequently. The appraiser is more likely to make an appraisal of a proprietary nursing home, and his task is to estimate the market value of the facility. The appraisal report is usually requested by a prospective purchaser to guide him in arriving at a fair price or by an owner negotiating for a mortgage loan.

KEY FACTORS
INVOLVED IN NURSING HOME APPRAISALS

The appraiser must be aware of the special-purpose nature of the proprietary nursing home when approaching all the parts of its intrinsic value. It has some similarities to a motel, also special-purpose, also more dependent on occupancy rate and income than land and building value. It differs from the motel, however, in the precise type of hospitality services offered; and where the motel depends on room count, the proprietary nursing home depends upon bed count for its income. But both are income or investment properties. The following are the special factors to be considered in evaluating the proprietary nursing home:

227

1. A proprietary nursing home provides certain services to its occupants as part of the charge for occupying a bed. These include food, nursing care on a 24-hour basis, and some recreational outlets.

2. Beds, mattresses, furniture, and equipment must be provided for the use or care of the nursing home occupants, and may represent an investment ranging from 20% to 25% of the total value of the facility.

3. Because it may take as long as one year of operation for a nursing home to reach a profitable occupancy level, initial working capital of about 25% of one year's operating expense is needed to carry the project. This is considerably more than is required in other types of income-producing real estate, such as an apartment or office building.

4. The owner-operator or the lessee-operator expects a "business profit" for running the nursing home and for assuming the risk inherent in a venture of this type. This is a profit after compensation for time spent in personal attendance at the nursing home, and after a return on his investment in the facility.

5. Since the proprietary nursing home is a special-use property, its marketability is quite limited. The special design limits alternate uses for the real estate. A prospective borrower may find it difficult to assure a lender that he can provide long-term, specialized management for operating the facility. This makes many lenders reluctant to take mortgages on such risks. Some who do so make loans only on the value of the real estate (land and buildings) and disregard the value of the personal property and the "business profit" for mortgage purposes. For these reasons, even though the proprietary nursing home has value as a going concern, it is appraised more frequently as a real estate entity.

6. Therefore, the real estate alone is not the least important income-producing aspect of the evaluation, and location and a standing application list of occupancy prospects is very important.

In the following model appraisal, long-term financing was successfully achieved for a proposed proprietary nursing home. The key considerations and procedures apply to established nursing homes as well.

MODEL APPRAISAL OF A PROPRIETARY NURSING HOME

SUMMARY OF SALIENT FACTS AND CONCLUSIONS

Subject:	Mardel Nursing Home
	Maryland Avenue and
	Madison Street
	Mardel Township,
	Delmar, Delaware
Date of Appraisal:	December 9, 1975
Site Area:	2.50 Acres
Improved Area:	.1886 Acres

Zoning:	Approved
Building Area:	16,900 Square Feet
Gross Annual Income (Estimate):	$374,309
Net Annual Income (Estimate):	$ 83,428
Economic Life of Building	35 Years
Estimate of Site Value	$ 40,000
Indicated Value via Income Approach:	$695,000
Indicated Value via Cost Approach:	$680,000
Final Value Estimate:	$695,000

REAL ESTATE TAX DATA

The current assessed valuation is not material to the report since it reflects unimproved vacant land. It is the opinion of the owner, who has reflected taxes in his budget to Medicare, that the tax burden will total $2,800 annually, or about $4,000 per bed (52 x $4,000 = $208,000; $208,000 x $1.35 per one hundred dollars of A.V. = $2,808.00). This opinion also reflects the estimate of the local assessor who recites assessments on three nearby nursing home facilities.

(1) Roberts Nursing Home	
Assessed Valuation	$ 150,000
Number of Beds	50
Per Bed Assessment	$ 3,000
(2) Calvert Manor	
Assessed Valuation	$ 249,400
Number of Beds	75
Per Bed Assessment	$ 3,325
(3) Parkhurst Manor Home	
Assessed Valuation	$1,436,000
Number of Beds	274
Per Bed Assessment	$ 5,241
(4) The Subject	
Estimated Assessed Valuation	$ 208,000
Number of Beds	52
Per Bed Assessment	$ 4,000

AREA DATA

Delmar is a border community sharing about half of its size and population with Maryland. It is centrally located within Delaware and about equidistant from the Atlantic Ocean and Chesapeake Bay. Washington, Baltimore, and Wilmington, three major cities, are within 100 miles, and New York City is about 200 miles via Route No. 13 and the New Jersey Turnpike. This is predominantly an agriculture-farming area, sparsely populated but scenically serene and attractive. There is a wide variety of crops and a large poultry industry, and mixed but minor industrial concentrations. The accessibility of the shore and its proximity via the splendid vehicular parkway system provide unparalleled recreational facilities within short driving distances.

SITE DATA

The ample, block-front site is on a paved street at the quiet northwest corner of the town. Subsoil is hardpan under about 4' of compacted gravel. It will be fully developed as a proprietary nursing home with rooms for expansion and ample parking. The site is level, at road grade, and accessible to sewer, water, gas, electricity, and telephone. A slight crown in the center of the site provides excellent surface drainage.

HIGHEST AND BEST USE

The proposed use of the ground as the site for a nursing home is considered the "highest and best use," or that use that will produce the highest net return to the land, in this section of town at the present time.

DESCRIPTION OF IMPROVEMENTS

The subject property consists of a proposed one-story, fire-resistant nursing home containing 23 individual rooms and 52 beds. It will be erected in accordance with plans and specifications prepared by Thomas Francis Couzens, Associates. The architecture is contemporary, functional with a three-wing concept, each wing having a 15° angle of departure from the main stem.

Layout

West Wing:
  (6) one-bed rooms
  (8) two-bed rooms
  (1) common bath
      lounge
      administration office

East Wing:
  (1) two-bed rooms
  (4) three-bed rooms
  (4) four-bed rooms
      toilet and bath
      reception area
      waiting room
      medical storage room

North Wing:
      patient dining room
      employees' dining room
      kitchen
      employees' locker room
      receiving-storage room
  (2) storage—mechanical room
      storage room
      beauty shop

      examination room
      therapy room
      morgue
      maintenance-storage room
      trash room
      laundry
      barber shop

The central core will contain an entrance foyer-lobby and a nurses' station.

Room Count Summary

(6) one-bed rooms	=	6 rooms, 6 beds
(9) two-bed rooms	=	9 rooms, 18 beds
(4) three-bed rooms	=	4 rooms, 12 beds
(4) four-bed rooms	=	4 rooms, 16 beds
Total		23 rooms, 52 beds

The building will have concrete foundation footings, walls and slabs, structural concrete frame; concrete block enclosure walls, stuccoed; concrete floor slab; precast concrete plank, insulated room with a 20-year bonded finish; 8" concrete block partition walls; aluminum sliding sash and glass; large plate glass areas in central core; complete plumbing system with cast-iron soil and waste lines, copper risers and crotons, drained to the town's central sewer system; wet sprinkler system throughout with chrome heads; electrical cooling and heating elements augmented by a roof-mounted gas-fired unit; modern ceramic tile floors and wainscot in baths and toilets; suspended acoustical ceilings; resilient and carpeted floors; vinyl wall finishes; ramp corridors with side-wall railings; special bathroom accessories, guards, grips, safety railing; miscellaneous fixtures, equipment, appliances common to nursing homes; incandescent light fixtures in individual units with switches and outlets. Fluorescent lighting in lobby, community rooms, and passageways. Fire alarm system, nurse call, emergency lighting system. Patient built-in closet units, nursing stations, cabinets for storage and work area, etc.

COST APPROACH

A cost breakdown per trade has been prepared by the general contractor and is submitted herewith:

Site work & paving	$ 38,000
Landscaping & paving	10,000
Street (municipal) connections	6,250
Concrete & masonry	82,000
Insulation	3,800
Structural steel & erection	48,200
Roofing & sheet metal	22,200
Windows, glass & glazing	26,800
Toilet partitions	2,150
Wood doors	6,200
Lumber, mill work & carpentry	36,500
Interior-exterior painting	12,000
Gypsum walls & metal studs	22,000
Acoustical ceilings	12,500
Hardware	17,500
Kitchen equipment	22,500
Vinyl & asphalt tile	8,200
Caulking & waterproofing	1,800
Ceramic & quarry tile	6,200
Folding partitions	4,500
Sprinkler system	18,500
Plumbing	35,000
Heating, ventilating & air conditioning	47,000
Electric	65,000
Plaster & exterior installations	22,000
Construction Cost	$576,800
Plus overhead & profit (11%)	63,448
Total Construction Costs	$640,248

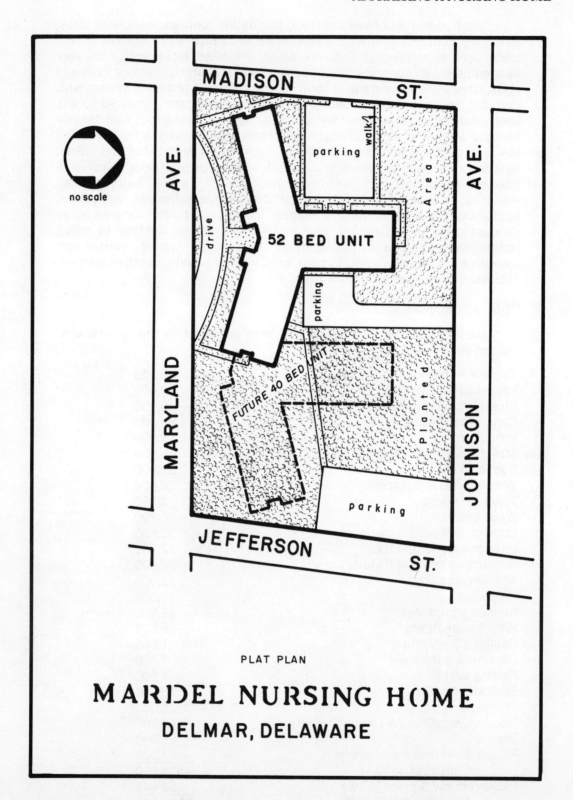

PLAT PLAN

MARDEL NURSING HOME
DELMAR, DELAWARE

In the Cost Approach the land value is added to arrive at a total figure. The land value in this instance was so inconclusive, based upon land value research, that the appraiser has used the Land Residual Technique to arrive at an estimate of land value. This is computed as follows:

Net Income		$83,428
Capital Requirements of Structure		
Interest	= 9.25%	
Recapture	= 3.33%	
Total	12.58%	
$640,248 x 12.58%		80,543
Net Residual to Land		$ 2,885
Capitalized Land Value		
$2,885 capitalized at 7.5%		$ 38,467

Summation

Total Construction Costs	$640,248
Land Residual Value	38,467
Total Cost Estimate	$678,715

Rounded Value Summation

Improvements	$640,000
Land Value	40,000
Total	$680,000

INCOME AND EXPENSE ANALYSIS AND VALUE ESTIMATE

A budget of anticipated income and expenses has been prepared for state and federal agency consumption. These are based upon experienced ratings, medicare and social service standards, and comparable accommodations. A projection of 50 percent private patients and the remainder under the auspices of medicare and social services are accordingly set forth.

Income

52 beds x 365 days = 18,980 patient days of full occupancy at an average of $19.72 per bed equals $374,286, approximately $374,309 annual gross. Subdivision of these charges are allocated as follows:

Private Patients

Category (1) Private rooms — 6 beds x $26.00 daily =	$	156.00
		x 365
Per Annum	$	56,940.00
Category (2) Semiprivate — 9 beds x $20.50 daily =	$	184.50
		x 365
Per Annum	$	67,343.00

Category (3) Three-bed   — 6 beds x $18.50 daily $ 111.00
            ward   x 365
                           Per Annum $ 40,515.00

Category (4) Four-bed ward— 5 beds x $17.50 daily = $ 87.50
                                                              x 365
                           Per Annum $ 31,938.00

Medicare and Social Services Patients

Category (5) Medicare   — 7 beds x $22.00 daily = $ 154.00
   (semiprivate)   x 365
                           Per Annum $ 56,210.00

Category (6) Social Services
   Semiprivate   — 2 beds x $17.50 daily = $ 35.00
   3-bed ward   — 6 beds x $17.50 daily =   105.00
   4-bed ward   — 11 beds x $17.50 daily =   192.50
                                                      $ 332.50
                                                              x 365
                           Per Annum $121,363.00

Income (Recap) Per Annum
Category (1) $ 56,940
Category (2)   67,343
Category (3)   40,515
Category (4)   31,938
Category (5)   56,210
Category (6)   121,363

   Gross Annual Income All Sources $374,309

(Comparable Competitive Charges)
Barkley Nursing Home

	Theirs	Subject
4-bed room	$17.75	$17.50
3-bed room	$19.75	$18.50
Semi-private	$21.00	$20.50
Private	$27.00	$26.00
V.I.P.	$30.00	None

Gross Annual Income All Sources $374,309
Less Vacancy and Collection Loss (10%)   37,431
        Effective Gross Income $336,878

Expenses
Salaries $145,200
Food and Kitchen Supplies   34,200
Repairs/Maintenance   5,000
Laundry, Linen & Bedding   5,100
General Administration   17,000

Utilities	8,500	
Miscellaneous/Supplies	2,500	
Replacement Reserve	4,200	
Management & Supervision	25,000	
Realty Taxes	2,800	
Insurance	3,950	253,450
Net Income		$ 83,428

Capitalization Process
Mortgage: 20-year loan at 9.25% = 11% Constant

75% Mortgage at 11%	=	8.25%
25% Equity at 15%	=	3.75%
Capitalization Rate		12.00%
Capitalized property value:		$ 83,428
Capitalized at 12%		= $695,233
Rounded to:		$695,000

CORRELATION & CONCLUSIONS

Cost Approach Value	$680,000
Income Approach Value	$695,000
Market Approach Value	Inconclusive

Your appraiser has examined, in detail, the presentation of plans, specifications, nursing home income and expenses, land values, location, and the multitude of detail involved in an appraisal of this character. He has examined periodicals relevant to nursing homes, operational costs, the unique assets that a skilled administrator and professional staff lend to this most required social benefit. He is personally disturbed at the pathetic conditions involved, but thankful that the need for such a modern, attractive installation is recognized by local, state, and national authorities. This is a splendid social asset.

While the Cost Approach usually sets the upper limit of value, it does not in this case. The Cost Approach and Income Approach are within close proximity and average at $687,500. Anticipating increments beyond 100 percent occupancy, your appraiser has used the Income Approach as his final value estimate:

Land	$ 40,000
Improvements	655,000
Total	$695,000

PART THREE

Methodologies and
Model Appraisals
for Industrial Properties

*One of the distinctions between the commercial and in-
dustrial categories of real property is that commercial
properties are generally income or investment types and
industrial properties often are not. Usually, the special-
purpose industrial facility is owned and occupied by one
proprietor who uses the premises for his own productive
processes, financing the plant from his working capital
fund. In the model appraisal later demonstrated in this
chapter, however, the undercapitalized owner has applied to
a local bank for a mortgage loan against his unusual and
valuable industrial-service facility; the bank, interested in
his application, has asked an independent appraiser to
make a fair market value judgment on which the lender can
base his risk.*

15

Appraising a Special-Purpose Cold-Storage Plant for Mortgage Financing

KEY CONSIDERATIONS OF VALUE IN SPECIAL-PURPOSE PLANTS

The Cost, Income, and Market Data Approaches are applied to the appraisal of an industrial plant just as rigorously, when possible, as in the evaluation of commercial properties.

Special-purpose facilities, such as a food-processing plant, a bonded warehouse, or refrigerated storage plant, can be evaluated by the application of the Cost and Income Approaches, even though the appraiser may have to reach to other locales for rental income comparables. Because the very nature of the special-purpose plant is special and *unique* in the area, the Market Data Approach is usually inapplicable, except for the purpose of finding the value of the industrial land under the improvements.

Highest and Best Use

Modern industrial properties of all types are usually established in zones that provide easy access to rail, air, sea, and express highway facilities, in or near areas close to skilled labor pools and/or raw materials. The most modern and ideal plants are single-story, straight-line-of-production buildings, or U-shaped, to allow for uninterrupted processing of raw materials coming in at one end and finished products being shipped out at the other end (unless, of course, the manufacturing process calls for gravity flow; in that case a high-rise building is a necessity).

A preliminary investigation of such property must begin with the appraiser's estimate of its highest and best use in processing products it was, is, or will be designed to deliver.

Highest and best use embraces the *functional utility* of the physical plant, the economic future of the end product or service, and the potential alternative uses of the real estate. Especially if the evaluation is for mortgage-financing purposes, the real estate appraiser is at least as much a credit and financial analyst as he is an evaluator of the industrial facility itself.

To determine highest and best and most productive use of land and building, the appraiser must first collect and absorb all economic data having any bearing on the operation of the industrial property under appraisement. The initial question must be: *Is it the proper plant in the appropriate location at this time?*

Without the answer to this question, you cannot begin to forecast the *economic life* of the subject property. Guidelines for calculating the effective age of industrial facilities are as follows.

Effective Age of a Building

"Effective age" and "actual age" are substantially identical in an industrial (or commercial) building that has had average care and maintenance, no remodeling, modernization, or additions, and that has a normal life expectancy. Where major alterations or modernization definitely increases the remaining life expectancy of a building, the effective age should be adjusted.

An important market viewpoint is that prices tend toward the same level within neighborhoods of comparable properties. The tendency is equally strong for buildings to tend toward the same effective age within a particular era. *As an example:* Assume that the actual years built for industrial facilities in a given neighborhood dated from 1961 through 1969, inclusive. The effective year built for the early sixties era may be the same for all the properties, resulting sometimes in effective year built being 1 to 8 years less than the actual year built.

Location is of prime importance to the value of an industrial plant, but chiefly in the *convenience sense* as it relates to the immediate environment in which it stands. Data emphasis in the appraisal of an industrial plant is therefore placed on the zone and district, on the municipality, and to an *important* degree on the *labor-pool area* immediately surrounding the city and the site. The arterial accesses to airport, rail, and waterfront shipping are equally important.

A properly located and successfully operated industrial facility will generally be found in an established industrial district where public transportation is available, where rail and other transportation services are on site, and where banks, restaurants, and parking are near the premises.

The appraisal of an industrial plant may be based on plans for a proposed structure on a given site as a feasibility study to test highest and best use of the land; or it may be a report on a finished building—brand new, recent, middle-aged, or old—with or without a long-term financial history. In any case, rents can be stabilized for the subject property by comparison and adjustment with other industrial rentals in the area.

TECHNICAL CONSIDERATIONS IN EVALUATION OF LAND AND IMPROVEMENTS IN INDUSTRIAL APPRAISALS

It is essential in the evaluation of any industrial facility, large or small, that the technical layout results in the greatest *functional utility for economic production* for the gross area. Architectural expertise in the arrangement of the plant and placement of freight handling, laboratories, corridors, and utility rooms is of vital significance. Column spacing should be designed to allow uninterrupted product flow. The *mechanical equipment* of the building—heating, lighting, air conditioning, elevator capacity, plumbing, wiring, fire equipment and soundproofing—bears heavily on functional utility as well as on comfort and safety. Producers pay for the efficient, safe, and economic enjoyment of the premises, and if they are not provided with these services, the income from, or market value of, the deficient plant building will be poor.

These elements must be carefully expressed in the Cost Approach in a technical essay narrating the history and development of the plant and its product(s) and explaining the calculations applied to physical construction costs new and depreciation, and technological or economic obsolescences.

These observations of age, maintenance, and depreciation can then be proved in the Income and/or Market Data Approaches by values found in the marketplace for rentals or sales of buildings in similar condition, using the Principle of Substitution in the comparatives.

TECHNIQUES AND PROCEDURES

First Step in the Evaluation of an Industrial Facility: Comparable Sales and Leases

The *initial step* in evaluating an existing or proposed industrial building is to look for sales (of land and buildings separately) and rentals of similar properties in the same zone as his subject. You thus develop parameters of value in the marketplace for the subject and find the penalties against obsolescences in the comparables. Later in the appraisal this will help you to properly measure the degrees of functional and economic obsolescences that will be placed in percentage terms or dollar adjustments against the subject. These comparables should be inspected and photographed, with similarities or differences described as compared to subject land and plant space. Sale and lease transactions should be dated and verified.

Second Step: The Economic Survey and Property Analysis

Next, gather and correlate data that exposes the likelihood of success or failure in the life of an industrial facility at a given location within the city. Relate this information to the subject property in this manner using the following factors.

1. *Location.* Influences of area economic situation measured against the labor pool available in the area. In measuring area vs. local economic conditions, the following factors must be scrutinized:
   (a) Type of city government and its effectiveness politically and economically, together with a synopsis of the city's reason for being (i.e. importance as a railhead, communications center, harbor and/or airport facility). Indications of growth or decline in such facilities. Credit financing available from city and state.
   (b) Labor population of the city itself and labor reserve in suburbs within a 15-mile radius. Forms of transportation within the city and to and from the suburbs and other cities. Chief forms of employment within the city and within a 15-mile radius. Data on unions.
   (c) Principal industries within the city, their growth patterns, and public utilities that serve them. The amount and substance of industry in the area and its contribution, if any, to the commerce of the city. The city's atmosphere as an industrial, commercial, or cultural (university) center, with all three described if necessary.
   (d) The planning and zoning practices, the tax policies, and local ordinances affecting the property and its district must be stated clearly.
   (e) Where is the demand for industrial growth coming from? State the scope and intensity of this demand, or lack of it.

2. *Analysis of the Industrial District.* Data concerning the immediate vicinity of the proposed or existing plant facility should be set forth as follows:
   (a) Assuming that highest and best use of the site is an industrial plant with public transportation and automobile parking at hand, surrounded by express highways, restaurants, and other conveniences, where will the labor for the proposed or existing plant come from? State the rent per square foot in similar competing industrial facilities nearby. Note number of vacant plants in the area.
   (b) Describe trends in the district. Is the district growing or decaying? Is redevelopment underway? How far away is city hall, the public library, hospitals, medical clinics, the newspaper plant, public utility offices? Is the district served by main highways and a sensible traffic pattern? Is it readily accessible to other important districts within the city? What are utility rates in the area, and can special rates be effected for subject industry?

3. *Property Analysis and History.* Specific details of the property under appraisement must be clearly delineated:
   (a) Recitation of the title, including metes and bounds, assessments and tax levy.
   (b) Zone requirements.
   (c) Description of the site topography and subsoil conditions, plottage and shape of the land area, together with list of utilities on site or available.
   (d) The type of construction, use, and condition of the proposed or existing buildings and its affixed equipment, together with site improvements, planned or existing, such as paved parking, fencing, outdoor floodlighting.

(e) Each floor of the building must be measured and described.

(f) A summary of the development of the property, if existing, with a five- to ten-year history of income and expense, and type of safety and maintenance attending the property.

(g) The anticipated useful life of the property must be estimated and allowances made for physical depreciation, functional utility, and economic obsolescence.

4. *Adaptability.* Many industrial buildings, especially those designed for manufacturing purposes, are peculiar in nature. They are built to embrace the specific requirements of a particular user or process. The more specialized the plant, the greater the difficulty in adapting it to the requirements of another user. Much appraisal analysis of existing industrial properties, therefore, focuses on fitting or changing the structure to suit new occupants. The adaptability of the property must be considered from the point of view of both function and investment feasibility. This brings in considerations of the feasibility of renovation and usually involves the estimation of both market value and investment value for comparative decision-making purposes.

Because ready marketability is often lacking, much existing industrial real estate is appraised for investment value, value in use, or even going-concern value, as well as market value. The differences among the estimates help the current owner-occupant decide whether to vacate a plant or keep it in production.

Carefully measure market absorption rates because discounts for waiting periods are often required. The marketplace, in the ordinary sense of the term, may not exist for a large or special-purpose property.

5. *Functional Utility.* Users of industrial space demand operational efficiency above all. Even location may be a secondary consideration of the functional utility of the improvements.

It is therefore pressed on the appraiser to know the space standards of the subject industry, and particularly what the most probable user of the space being appraised needs and wants. To achieve this, he must be familiar with industrial processes and their technical requirements, including the needs of varying industrial users as to floor loads, ceiling heights, loading bay sizes, elevator capacities, marine and rail service, freight rates, power rates, and the geography and economy of his subject's environment.

If his subject plant is functionally obsolete the appraiser must be able to define what part of the functional inutility is curable and what part is incurable.

Because of the emphasis on function and efficiency, industrial real estate is particularly susceptible to functional obsolescence as a result of innovation and technological change. For example, shortly after World War II an electronics plant with ceilings 40 feet high was built in New Jersey to manufacture communications panels the size of boxcars. Today that same plant makes the same-purpose communications panels, only they are now the size of cigarette lighters due to the invention of the transistor. Consequently, the plant now needs ceilings of only 18 feet and has had to drop ceilings and "box in" space for air-conditioned and dust-proof laboratories. So its cubic area, in height above 18 feet, is *idle, wasted,* and *obsolete.*

To a large extent, the utility of any industrial property is subject to technological change, and in these days of revolutionary science and invention, last year's modern building is often left in the dim past by technological change. Radical change in product development can take place overnight in any industry.

6. *Access.* Transportation services bear on the value of industrial properties more than any other type of real estate. This means not only highway access, but also rail, ship, or air facilities at or near the site. The functional utility of any industrial complex is greatly enhanced for a large-volume shipper and receiver if more than one means of transportation is available at the site. Many industrial firms have paid premium prices for sites with rail facilities, even though they rarely use railroads for shipping and receiving. The rail siding or spur is insurance for the firm in the event of a truckers' strike. The greater the volume of materials handled and the further they must travel (either to or from the plant), the more likely the existence of multiple-transportation outlets will increase value.

7. *The Complexion of the User.* Industrial real estate evaluation is much more user-oriented than other real estate appraisement. The peculiar nature of much industrial real estate and the emphasis placed on functional utility presses the appraiser to estimate who the most likely user, or what the most probable use, may be. This calls for much more specific analysis than required in other areas of real estate appraisal, and is complicated by the wide variation in types of uses and users possible in the industrial field.

There is a close relationship between the success of the industrial occupant and the value of industrial real estate. This depends in part on the market acceptability of the occupant's product, and in part on his credit rating. The type and terms of available financing, in turn, influence the return on the investment to the owner, and hence the value of the real estate to him. The appraiser, therefore, cannot ignore the economics of the most probable user's industry, nor the financial and economic status of the firm itself when there is a long-term lease on the property.

8. *The Market.* The market within which industrial space is traded is frequently geographically wider than the market for other real estate. A plant on the West Coast may be ideal and just what the doctor prescribed for a manufacturer on the East Coast, and there may be nothing like it existing in the East or Midwest.

But that very market can also be termed economically sparse, because there is only one user for such a plant—the manufacturer on the East Coast.

The market can be sparse in the sense that there are few participants in it. Because of the specialized nature of industrial real estate, few users may be available to bid for the space under any circumstances. There are often also few speculator-investors because of tightness in the financing situation. In this imperfect market framework, wide variation in the prices of seemingly similar or competitive properties will often result.

9. *Unity of Use.* The value of industrial properties is sometimes influenced by the uses and users in the area surrounding the property in question. The difference, however, lies in the fact that the specific users can have a major impact on the utility of the property in question, and therefore directly on its value. The profitability of many industrial operations is dependent on easy access to and from interrelated uses. This phenomenon has been termed "unity of use." Ship terminals, truck depots, even petroleum plants may be worth very little standing alone; however, they may be quite valuable as part of an industrial complex.

Third Step: The Approaches to Value

The appraiser's *third step* in an industrial plant appraisal lies in his choice of valuation approaches.

Although a plant is often different from any other in terms of location, age, style, and product, by adjustment and the appraiser's articulation similarities can be found to compare with sales of other plant buildings when estimating value. This is where the appraiser can prove his talent.

The Market Data Approach is the chief guide to evaluation of an *owner-occupied* plant, which is adaptable to other, subdivided uses. Developers, speculators, and users looking for a bargain will be in the market for older plants of this type.

The Income Approach is the stronger indicator of value for a *leased* plant, or an owner-occupied plant adaptable to no other uses, when the rental is proved to be economic, or nearly so, by rental income data. This is particularly true for general-purpose facilities such as general-purpose warehouses, but it also applies to some special-purpose properties.

The Cost Approach usually proves the upper limit of value in the appraisal of an industrial plant. But when the plant is brand new and of *special* or *single-purpose* use, the Cost Approach could conceivably coincide with available market data to form a positive indication of market value.

When the Income Approach is the chief guide to value and is the proper test of a plant structure's ability to throw off a worthwhile investment yield over a long period of time, capitalization of net economic income is paramount. It is also of maximum importance when appraising for purposes of mortgage financing, since the lender wants to know what net income it could produce even if a present owner should default and the lender had to foreclose and rent it to another user to retire the bank's investment in the facility.

Since the market value of a leased industrial plant could depend upon the *present worth of its future earnings,* the appraiser must rationally anticipate such earnings and estimate how long they will endure if he is to calculate their present worth.

Fourth Step: Capitalization Rates and Methods

Capitalization rates on industrial buildings will vary with circumstances. Yield percentages will differ. Choice of capitalization rate and method is the appraiser's critical *fourth step* in evaluating an industrial plant.

Capitalization Methods. Depending upon the *quality and durability* of income (see chapter 5) flowing from the property you are appraising, you can elect to follow either of the following courses of capitalization:

1. Use the straight-line depreciation plus capitalization-rate method of capitalization when you anticipate that the net income before depreciation *will decline* regularly each year in the future.

2. But if the net income before depreciation is expected to be level or better and is *of a contract nature,* for instance, with a triple-A concern in the plant, or if the financial stability of the tenant is substantial and the lease extends over a period of at least *fifteen years,* the Inwood premise may be used. This premise is used only on prime industrial buildings with rated corporations as tenants on long-term leases.

Fifth Step: Procedure for Estimating a Separate Land Value Under the Industrial Building

As the *fifth step* in industrial building evaluations, it is best to estimate land value, particularly where market data on nearby vacant land is sufficient.

On occasion, such market data may be scarce, but the appraiser may know from the outset the value of the buildings, particularly if the structures are new or recent and the builder's costs are competitive and at hand. In that case, the appraiser would set up his Cost Approach first and find his land value using the Land Residual Technique.

Methods of Evaluating Land. Land value may be estimated by: (1) recent sales of nearby vacant land; (2) recently executed land leases; (3) the Land Residual Technique. This chapter will emphasize the first method, recent sales of nearby vacant land, with adjustments of comparables.

Sixth Step: Procedure for Estimating Value of the Improvements in Industrial Appraisals

Residual Techniques Under the Income Approach. An older plant may be (unusually) leased for rentals that, capitalized, prove investment or market value greater than depreciated reproduction cost could show, which is contrary to the fact that on new or recent buildings the Cost Approach is usually the upper limit of value.

Therefore, we will turn to other means of finding the value of industrial building improvements when the value of the land is already known through market data. These means are provided by the Residual Techniques under the Income Approach. This is the *sixth and final step* in the appraiser's road to valuation of an industrial plant.

MODEL APPRAISAL OF COLD-STORAGE PLANT

XYZ Appraisal Company
Real Property Valuations
20 Church Street—Suite 705
New York, N.Y. 10009

April 18, 1976

Mr. Robert Spector
Chief Mortgage Officer
Second National State Bank
280 Franklin Street
Hackensack, N.J. 07720

Re: Market Value Appraisal
Property Located At:
999 Sparkman Avenue
Bay City, New Jersey 04230

Dear Mr. Spector:

Pursuant to your request, we submit an appraisal report relevant to this property. A personal inspection of the real estate and of local conditions has been made by a member of our staff with analysis of all relevant data being utilized in determining the estimate of market value.

The following report, including exhibits, fully describes the method of approach and contains all pertinent data gathered in our investigation of the subject.

After careful consideration, we have concluded that the fair market value of the subject property as of April 18, 1976, is:

ONE MILLION SIX HUNDRED THIRTY-SIX THOUSAND DOLLARS
($1,636,000)

We certify that we have no present or contemplated financial interest in the subject property and that our employment and compensation are in no way contingent upon the value reported.

Respectfully submitted,

Vice President
Senior Appraiser

SUMMARY OF SALIENT FACTS

Subject Property: 999 Sparkman Avenue
Date of Appraisal: April 18, 1976
Date Construction Began: 1965
Completed and in Operation: 1966
Plant Site Area (Lot A):   65,000 Square Feet
Parking Area with Rail Siding (Lot B):   25,000 Square Feet
Rail Siding: 250 Linear Feet
Plant Area: 50,000 Square Feet
Site Value (Lots A & B): $460,000
Indicated Value—Cost Approach: $1,680,500
Indicated Value—Income Approach: $1,635,000
Indicated Value—Market Data Approach: Inapplicable
                                                   (Except to Land)
Final Value Estimate: $1,635,000

TABLE OF CONTENTS

ADDENDA

PURPOSE OF APPRAISAL

The appraisal was made for the purpose of estimating the market value of the subject property, including land and improvements, as of April 18, 1976, toward establishing a safe equity position in proposed mortgage financing for the subject to give the lender a sound risk position.

MARKET VALUE

For the purpose of this appraisal, market value is defined as "the highest price estimated in terms of money which a property will being if exposed for sale in the open market, allowing a reasonable time to find a purchaser who buys with knowledge of all the uses to which it is adapted, and for which it is capable of being used. Frequently, it is referred to as the price at which a willing seller would sell and a willing buyer would buy, neither being under abnormal pressure. It is the price expectable if a reasonable time is allowed to find a purchaser and if both seller and prospective buyer are fully informed." (Appraisal Terminology and Hand Book; 7th ed., American Institute of Real Estate Appraisers, Chicago, 1973.)

PROPERTY RIGHTS APPRAISED

The property rights appraised are all rights existing in fee simple as of the appraisal date. These rights are the legal and economic properties of the owner that may rightfully be exchanged for money or equivalent goods. Property rights inherent in the ownership of tangible personal property, and intangible benefits of the property itself, are not the subject of this report.

LIMITING CONDITIONS

Areas and dimensions of the property were not physically measured but were taken from plat plans furnished by the principal. No survey has been made of the property by this appraiser, and he assumes no responsibility for the dimensions or areas determined thereby or for any matters legal in nature.

The resultant estimate of market value is predicated on the financial structure currently prevailing.

It is assumed that there is good and marketable title and that there are no restrictions as to use except those imposed by public ordinance.

Verification of factual matters contained in this report has been made to the extent deemed practicable.

Market data has been taken from sources deemed to be reliable but which could not be verified in all cases.

The apportionment between the land and buildings in the report applies only under the existing program of utilization. The separate valuations for land and buildings may not be used in conjunction with any other appraisal and are invalid if so used.

Neither all nor any part of the contents of this report shall be conveyed to the public through advertising, public relations, news, sales, or other media without written consent and approval of the author particularly as to valuation conclusions, the identity of the appraiser, or firm with which he is connected.

The appraiser shall not be required to give testimony or appear in court by reason of this appraisal unless specific arrangements for these services are subsequently arranged.

REAL ESTATE TAX DATA

The property under appraisement is subject to the assessments and taxes promulgated by Bay City. The 1976 assessments and taxes are as follows:

Land	$ 450,000
Improvements	1,200,000
Total	$1,650,000
Tax Rate	$12.20/Thousand
Tax Ratio	100%
Taxes Levied	$ 20,130

LEGAL DESCRIPTION

The subject property is described on the assessor's map as 999 Sparkman Avenue, Bay City, New Jersey, Block No. 2230, Lots Nos. A and B. Lot A is at the northeast corner of Sparkman Avenue and Turcott Street; Lot B fronts on Turcott Street and is traversed by a spur from the trunk line of the Pennsylvania Railroad. Lot A fronts 250' on Sparkman Avenue; Lot B fronts 100' on Turcott Street running to a depth of 250' northeast.

ZONING

The subject property is located in a zone described as Light Industrial District, permitting warehouse, packaging, light assembly, and receiving and shipping of industrial products.

HIGHEST AND BEST USE

The present use as a cold-storage warehouse conforms to the zoning ordinances of the town and is considered the highest and most profitable use of the property. The plant is not adaptable to any other industrial use, and the cost of demolition to completely change its character would make site value prohibitive to any other type of industrial use that might replace it.

THE APPRAISAL PROCESS

The generally accepted method of obtaining the market value of a parcel of property is by the use of the three approaches to value. These approaches are the Cost Approach, the Income Approach, and the Market Data Approach to value. The value indicated by each approach is carefully reviewed and that approach, which in the judgment of the appraiser most adequately and accurately reflects all the circumstances in connection with the property under appraisement and the purpose for which the appraisal is being made, will be selected as the best indication of market value.

In the Cost Approach, valuation is made of the cost new of the improvements based on up-to-date construction costs in the area and supplemented by recognized national valuation services. Deductions are made from the replacement cost of the improvements for physical deterioration and functional and economic obsolescence. Then the value of the land is added.

In the Income Approach, the value of the property is estimated by the capitalization of the estimated net income the property is capable of producing. We have utilized an overall capitalization rate to obtain the market value of the subject property, land and building, under the Property Residual Technique.

The Market Data Approach utilizes sales of comparable properties. This approach has been found inapplicable to the subject property due to its specialized use, except for evaluating the raw land alone before site improvements.

AREA DATA

The subject property is located in Bay City, County of Hudsex, New Jersey. The town is served by five major railroads, seventy-three bus routes, and is surrounded by major highways: U.S. Routes 1, 9, and 22 going north, south, east, and west. The New Jersey Turnpike runs through the city with the Garden State Parkway running along the town's western border. There are two interstate highways under construction—Route No. 78 serving nearby Newark Airport, and Route No. 280 featuring direct access to the central business district. Newark Airport is located between the New Jersey Turnpike and U.S. Route No. 1 just fifteen minutes from downtown Bay City. All major airlines use this facility. Port Newark, located adjacent to Bay City, adjacent to the New Jersey Turnpike and the Newark Airport, boasts one of the nation's finest container ship terminals. The ports are served directly by a highway-air-rail complex that reaches over the entire country and into Canada and Mexico. All major railroads serving New York provide services to and from the ports of Bay City and Elizabeth.

The semiskilled labor pool reserve in a 25-square-mile radius from subject is about 55,000 at the present time, according to the New Jersey State Labor Department. The term "semiskilled" includes truck drivers, packers, shippers, forklift operators, clerks, warehousemen and dispatchers, i.e., precisely the chief groups generally employed at subject plant.

Population: 1970 U.S. Census—382,417
1960 U.S. Census—405,220

AREA MAP

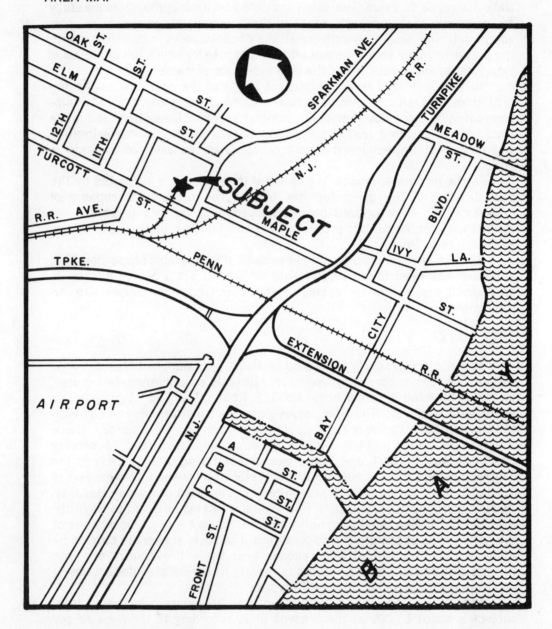

NEIGHBORHOOD DATA

The subject property is located at 999 Sparkman Avenue, corner of Turcott Street. This thriving area is one of commercial and industrial development. It is characterized by the presence of the multistoried Penquin Company, Banta Company, General Pigment Division of Colorama Chemical Industries. The Pennsylvania Railroad is situated one block from the subject with a spur running to the site (the on-site railroad siding is owned by subject property). Two blocks east a major cloverleaf leads to all major highway arteries. Newark International Airport and Port Newark are within two miles.

Adjacent properties include the Mace Tool and Die Company and the Mestor Manufacturing Company along with several other small manufacturing firms located on Turcott Street.

One block north on Sparkman Avenue a branch bank of New Jersey State Bank & Trust Company is located within a small neighborhood shopping center also containing a gasoline service station and a restaurant, enabling Bay City Refrigerating Company employees to cash their pay checks, shop for groceries and variety items, and get automobile service easily.

The neighborhood has no ambiance to reflect any economic obsolescence on subject. It can only be described as readily accessible for incoming raw materials and outgoing packaged products, convenient and safe for employee comings and goings. Public transportation by bus stop at the corner of Turcott and Sparkman Avenue is available at half-hour intervals to Newark, Elizabeth, Fort Lee, Clifton, and New York City.

SITE DATA

The subject site including both Lots A & B is rectangular in shape and occupies 90,000 square feet. The topography of the property slopes gradually from the front to the loading dock areas where the remaining property is level at road grade. The property is located on a corner lot with 250 foot frontage on Sparkman Avenue and a depth of 360 feet on Turcott Street, which includes the frontage of the parking lot and rail spur access on Lot B.

The site is serviced by all utilities (gas, electric, water, and sewer). Electric service is 440V, 200 amps, on an uninterruptable basis.

Drainage appears to be excellent (the property was inspected on three different occasions, once in heavy rain and sleet weather, and surface runoff was excellent). The parking area is paved with bituminous asphalt and crowned in the center with included run to sideline guttering. The sloped truck-receiving area on the plant site is paved with scored concrete, sanded in the wintertime, with cast-iron drain along its entire deepest run, connected directly to city sewers.

The streets, Turcott and Sparkman Avenue, are well lighted at municipal expense, and a fire hydrant stands at the corner of Turcott and Sparkman.

The streets are 40' wide, curb to curb, with concrete sidewalks, storm sewers, and are regularly policed by motor and foot patrol. The district firehouse precinct station is three blocks west on Turncott Street.

Floodlights in clusters at each of the top corners of the plant illuminate the parking area, rail siding, and front truck inclined apron on Sparkman Avenue.

TABLE OF COMPARABLE LIGHT INDUSTRIAL LAND SALES
(All in Bay City)

No.	Grantor Grantee	Address	Date	Sale Price	Area	Price Per Sq. Ft.
1	Andrew Benton to Public Service Gas & Electric Co.	2 Penquin Rd. Block 10 Lot 4	9/30/73	$230,000	110,000 Sq. Ft.	$2.10
2	Charles Zukowski to Oriental Petroleum Co.	909 Turcott Road Block 6 Lot 8	1/25/74	$180,000	60,000	$3.00
3	Pasquale Italiano to Penquin Corp.	10 Penquin Rd. Block 9 Lot 2	5/28/74	$290,000	75,000 Sq. Ft.	$3.86
4	Ajax Distributing Co. to Perkins, Welton et al.	Zink Avenue Block 6 Lot 10	2/3/75	$510,000	128,000 Sq. Ft.	$2.96
5	Technex Corp. to Board of Education, Bay City	Block 8 Lot 12	1/20/76	$626,000	156,500 Sq. Ft.	$4.00

Summary

The foregoing comparable sales are all relatively close to subject, approximately within one mile in any direction. They show a consistent rise in Light Industrial Zone land values since 1973 in Bay City, with the most recent sale recorded only four months before the date of this appraisal.

254

SITE VALUATION

We recognize that subject owners paid $100,000 for 25,000 square feet, or $4.00/square foot, for Lot B of his parcels, and accept it because of its plottage increment to the whole land value; but we cannot reflect this in the city-wide current land market since it was paid as a premium to provide the abutting subject premises with necessary parking for their visitors, salespersons, and employees, and to provide a strip for the rail siding necessary to bring refrigerated raw materials in bulk to be processed in the plant, packaged, and shipped out by truck. This provided the original plant site a unity of use for rail services and parking.

Based on a study of numerous sales and from discussions with local developers active in the area, we are of the opinion that land values comparable to the subject plant (Lot A) site ranged from $2.10 per square foot to $4.00 per square foot allowing for five percent annual inflationary increase over the nearby Benton purchase to PSG & E sale of 110,000 sq. ft. at $2.10 per square foot on September 30, 1973. We concluded the value of the Lot A site (raw land) to be $4.00 per square foot. Therefore:

Lot A = 65,000 square feet at $4.00 per square foot = $260,000
Lot B = 25,000 square feet at $8.00 per square foot = $200,000
                                                              Total = $460,000

Site Value $460,000

(Including Lots A & B)

IMPROVEMENT DATA

The subject site is improved with a one-story cold-storage building including a two-story office area and loading dock with ten (10) bays. The building comprises 63,751 square feet of ground area which includes loading docks and ground floor office area. The improvement was constructed in 1963. An office of 1,250 square feet on the small second floor superstructure brings total gross square footage to 65,000 square feet.

The building is constructed on a reinforced poured concrete foundation, with spread footings. Exterior walls are stucco over concrete block in the front with the sides and rear being brick over concrete block. The roof is flat, built-up tar and gravel composition over steel deck.

The office area consists of four separate offices containing a total square footage of 1,800 square feet. Three of the offices on the first floor comprising 1,200 square feet have asphalt tile flooring, acoustical tile ceiling, paneled walls, and fluorescent lighting. The fourth office, on the second floor, has wall-to-wall carpeted floors, ash paneled walls with exposed beamed ceiling. There are four lavatories each with two basin and toilet fixtures for each office. There is a full concrete basement under the office area on the ground floor. The 1,250 square feet on the second floor is reached by rubber-treaded steel stairs. There is an outside fire escape on the northeast side of the second-floor area.

LAYOUT OF SITE AND IMPROVEMENTS

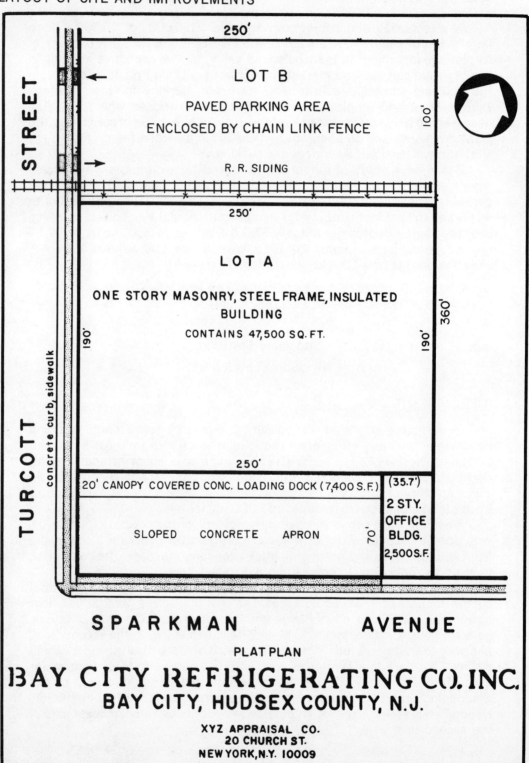

PLAT PLAN

BAY CITY REFRIGERATING CO. INC.
BAY CITY, HUDSEX COUNTY, N.J.

XYZ APPRAISAL CO.
20 CHURCH ST.
NEW YORK, N.Y. 10009

The loading dock consists of ten bays with ten fiberglass-paneled, electrically operated overhead doors, and ten four-strand fluorescent lights. It has a total square footage of 7,400.

There are six cold-storage areas containing a total square footage of 30,000 square feet. The refrigerated (cooled) areas are kept at 32 degrees. The sharp-freeze areas are maintained at 40° below zero. Ceiling heights are ten and twelve feet with twelve-inch concrete floors. There are six stainless-steel freezer doors measuring 6' x 8'. Ceiling and wall insulation consists of four-inch polyurethane over cork with concrete and plaster on top. The sharp-freeze area totals 12,500 square feet.

The remaining areas consist of two dry-storage rooms (one measuring 60' x 35' and the other measuring 60' x 40') and a compressor room measuring 25' x 20'. Total space in dry-storage area, including the compressor room = 5,000 square feet.

There is a concrete paved parking and inclined loading area measuring 100' x 100', to a depth of 8", reinforced with wire mesh.

There is cyclone fencing on four sides of the parking lot (B) with two gates eight feet high (5 strand).

Maintenance of the improvement appears to be excellent with depreciation cited as minimal.

Because of the original monolithic reinforced concrete construction, the conscientious maintenance and repairs, and the added service facility gained in the acquisition in 1971 of Lot B, we have accorded the building an economic life of 66.6 years. Actual age of the plant on Lot A is 20 years, but actual age of the Lot B acquisition and site improvements reduces effective age to 19 years.

On the basis of 66.6 years of economic life, and applying against it an effective age of 19 years, a remaining economic life of about 47 1/2, rounded to 48, years is indicated.

COST APPROACH

For reproduction cost new calculations, reference is made to Blank Valuation Service, Section 58, Page 1, September 1975.

Structure: Basic (without sharp-freeze, cold-storage, and dry-storage warehouse, 10 loading docks), no basement, and interior refrigerated railroad car off-loading on interior platform at rear of building.

	47,500 SF @ $12.56/SF	$596,600
Ground Floor Office Space:	1,250 SF @ 15.25/SF	19,063
2nd Floor Office Space:	1,250 SF @ 17.81/SF	22,263
Totals	50,000 SF	$637,926

Site Improvements:

700 Lineal Ft. of Chain Link Fence and 2 Reinforced Gates and Posts on Lot B @ $6.60 L.F.	4,620
17,500 SF of Concrete Sloping Dock Approach @ 4.68/SF and bottom drains	81,900
250 Lineal Ft. of R.R. Siding @ $22.00/L.F.	5,500
22,500 Sq. Ft. of 3" Bituminous Asphalt Paving (Lot B)	10,000

Refrigeration: (Special Plumbing and Electrical
                         Including Compressors)

Freezer:	12,500 SF @ $29.26/Sq. Ft.	365,750
Cooler:	30,000 SF @ $19.43/Sq. Ft.	582,900
Dry Storage:	5,000 SF @ $11.00/Sq. Ft.	55,000
Reproduction Cost New in Total:		$1,743,596

Depreciation:

Less Physical @ 30%: (20 yrs. x 1.5% per annum)   523,079
   (No functional or economic obsolescence was
   observed as affecting the real estate)
Total Depreciated Value $1,220,517

Add Land:

Lot A—65,000 SF @ $4.00/square foot = $260,000
Lot B— 25,000 SF @ $8.00/square foot =   200,000

                                                              $ 460,000
         Indicated Value—Cost Approach $1,680,517
                                            Rounded to: $1,680,500

VALUE INDICATED BY COST APPROACH $1,680,500

MARKET DATA APPROACH

Despite considerable research in the immediate area of Bay City, we found there to be a dearth of recent sales on record of comparable properties of cold-storage buildings.

Furthermore, even traveling to other cities, we found no two cold-storage plants to be alike in structure, size, and use of sharp freeze/cooler ratio of space. We consider, therefore, that subject special-purpose facility is unique in the state of New Jersey and cannot be accurately compared to the sale of any other cold-storage facility in the state. We, therefore, relied on the capitalization of economic net rent in the Income Approach for our final value conclusion.

The building is not adaptable to any other use, including general-purpose warehouse, because the ceilings are not high enough for general-purpose pallets (most such dry warehouses require ceiling heights of 20'-24' for racking or palletizing materials and packaged products).

The functional utility of subject is chiefly designed for sharp-freeze, cold storage and the separation of bulk parts of meat, poultry, and fish into small packages to be wholesaled to retailers.

While there are other facilities of smaller or larger design in the state of New Jersey, none has been sold in recent years, though some sections of these cold-storage plants have been leased to other wholesalers from time to time. From such leases we have derived rental values of component parts of cold-storage facilities, applying these rentals to the Income Approach, which follows.

INCOME APPROACH

The Income Approach to the value estimate is an appraisal technique in which the anticipated net income is processed to indicate the capital amount of the investment that will produce net income. Although subject property is user-owned and not leased, an accurate hypothesis of a likely economic rental that could be achieved, and the conversion of this net income into value by the proper capitalization rate, is essential to valuation for mortgage purposes.

The economic rental for the subject property was estimated by analyzing comparable rentals presently being received in the area of the subject, with reference to statements made by J.E. Dolberg, Manager, Penquin Refrigerating Company Cold Storage Warehouse, two blocks south of subject; and by C.M. Thayer, Manager, Frozen Products Processors, Inc. of Trenton, New Jersey. A composite rental was adduced as follows:

12,500 SF Freezer Space	@ $5.00/Square Foot =	$ 62,500 Per Annum
30,000 SF Cooler Space	@ $3.50/Square Foot =	105,000 Per Annum
5,000 SF Dry Storage & Docks	@ $1.00/Square Foot =	5,000 Per Annum
2,500 SF Air-Conditioned Offices	@ $8.00/Square Foot =	20,000 Per Annum
Economic Net Rental		$192,500

Property Residual Technique

Capitalization

The capitalization rate was based on the mortgage equity method. It was based upon a 15 percent yield rate for the investor, included a depreciation rate of 22.5 percent, 1.5 percent per year over a projected 15-year holding period and supported by mortgage financing equivalent to 75 percent of appraised value at 9 percent interest for 15 years.

The actual formula for the determination of the overall capitalization rate is:

$$R = Y - MC + Dep.1/S_n$$

Of this formula, "C" (the mortgage coefficient) can be found in table "C" of the Ellwood Tables for Real Estate Appraising and Financing. (R = Capitalization Rate; Y = Equity Yield Rate; M = Loan Ratio; C = Mortgage Coefficient; $1/S_n$ = Sinking Fund Factor)

The actual calculations are as follows:

R = .15 — .75 (.049275) + .225 (.021017)
R = .15 — .036956 + .004728
R = .117772

Therefore:

Net Income: $192,500 Capitalized @ .117772 = $1,634,514
Rounded to: $1,635,000

Value Conclusion by Income Approach $1,635,000

CORRELATION AND VALUE CONCLUSION

Two recognized approaches to value have been applied in estimating the fair market value of the subject property. The following is a summary of the various approaches:

Cost Approach $1,680,500
Income Approach $1,635,000

The Cost Approach reflects the upper limit of value. We have examined all three approaches to value, finding only two to be applicable, and from this analysis have based our final value conclusion on the Income Approach. Therefore, fair market value as of April 18, 1976 is:

ONE MILLION SIX HUNDRED THIRTY-FIVE THOUSAND DOLLARS
($1,635,000)

LOAN RECOMMENDATION

We recommend that such a loan would be sound and equitable for a term of not more than 15 years, because of the possibility of technological changes in the equipment of the industry that cause the borrower to revolutionize his present processes.

ADDENDA

1. In this section, the appraiser can place his qualifications and photographs of his subject property, front, rear, and side views, including one of the roof and several of the interior division, freezers, coolers, railroad siding, and parking area.

2. Then he should include photographs of the land comparables and the rental comparables, together with an economic survey of the cold-storage industry on a regional and national basis and such other maps, charts, graphs, and projections as to give the lending institution and the borrower a complete overview of the risk and terms of the mortgage loan applied for on subject premises.

*Keeping in mind all of the considerations of value in
special-purpose plants, as set forth in the foregoing chapter
(which will not be repeated in this one), we will in this
chapter bring out one very important additional feature:
substitution to eliminate functional inutility.*

16

The Principle of Substitution
Applied to a Multi-Storied Plant:
An Ad Valorem Tax Appeal Employing the
Building Residual Technique

THE PRINCIPLE OF SUBSTITUTION

When property is replaceable, its value tends to be set at the cost of acquisition of an equally desirable and valuable substitute property. That which may be substituted may be either a revised plan, a similar structure with equivalent functional utility, or an investment having an equal degree of increment opportunity. Thus, the fair market value of a property is to a major extent limited and controlled by the value of similar available properties having utility and comparable locations, characteristics, and foreseeable future benefits. The Principle of Substitution is important to the Market Data Approach and the Cost Approach in appraisals.

KEY CONSIDERATIONS OF VALUE IN SUBSTITUTION
OR REPLACEMENT BUILDINGS

If it can be shown that the layout of a single-story plant can eliminate double-handling of materials, elevators, ramps, and waste space that might occur in a two- or three-story, or split-level plant, and produce at the same or greater capacity, then obviously the single-story plant should be substituted for the multilevel plant, even though it may turn out to be *smaller* in floor area than the multilevel.

It usually requires a qualified architect-engineer working closely with the plant manager to work out the process-flow of products in the replacement plant, as it did in the model appraisal that follows.

261

The space saved in the substitute (replacement) plant is proof of functional obsolescence in the multilevel plant and proof of maintenance money being wasted on excessive heating, electrical, and cleaning costs. It means closer contact between personnel, more immediate labor supervision, and faster handling of products to the finishing and delivery point.

In the model appraisal following, all these points are proved, showing that a replacement single-story plant of 196,950 square feet could produce more effectively, at less cost, than the existing multilevel building of 237,000 square feet (see drawings). Thus, some 40,050 square feet of expensive waste space has been eliminated.

The plant in the model is a computer-assembly facility, beautifully landscaped into a very expensive, sloping parcel in the heart of one of the nation's most expensive residential and office-park neighborhoods. However, the sloping lot required three-level, split-section construction which could have been eliminated on a level lot condensing plant operation into five-sevenths the space actually required for optimum efficiency.

MODEL APPRAISAL

(With Letter of Transmittal, Table of Contents, and preambles omitted.
See foregoing chapter for these forms.)

VITAL STATISTICS OF THE PLANT

Street Address------------ Data Avionics Corporation
Computer Assembly Plant
121 Sierra Magdalena Avenue
North Hollywood, California

1. Year Built: 1955----------In Operation 1956
Acquired by Subject Owner 1956

2. Construction: Brick and Block on Steel Frame on Three Levels

3. Land Area: 9.609 ± Acres

4. Floor Space Area Within Plant:
(a) Assembly Area & Mfg. 71,424 SF
(b) Storage & Warehousing 42,572 SF
(c) Offices and Cafeteria (Including Penthouse, Corridors, Utilities) 107,208 SF
(d) Laboratories 13,996 SF
Subtotal 235,200 SF
(e) Outside Docks & Patio 1,800 SF
Total Area 237,000 SF

5. No. of Employees: Averaged----------900
Period From------5/1/60 to 5/1/75

6. Types of Products: The plant is used for the assembly of computers and the manufacture of small parts.

7. No. of Truck-Loading Docks: Three

8. Paved Parking Area: 185,069 Square Feet
9. Land Available for   None-----The plant occupies
   Plant Expansion: 237,000 square feet of the
                            422,069 square feet total land
                            area. This leaves 185,069
                            square feet for parking on the
                            north side of the building.
                            This is minimal parking for
                            900 employees. The usual
                            space provided for one car is
                            205 square feet.

THE APPRAISAL PROCESS AND VALUATION PREMISE

In the valuation that follows, we have relied not only on a Cost Approach using the Principle of Substitution, but have combined it with an Income Approach based on appropriate rental data, incorporating therein a reflection of the market behavior of depreciated structures in relation to the subject plant through application of the Building Residual Technique.

We have also applied a Market Data Approach to reflect sales of used buildings the size of the subject. The Market Data Approach has strong application to the subject, as the property under appraisement is similar in aspects to others in the area. Thus, all three approaches in the appraisal process show their close indications of value.

In summary, we have employed an overall test of value based on construction costs and adjusted to incorporate market behavior; but it is a tempered value derived from all three approaches that most accurately reflects its true value as it is presently used.

Proper deductions have been made from the cost of the improvements for applicable forms of accrued depreciation: physical deterioration and functional obsolescence. The depreciated cost, when added to the land value, will complete the Cost Approach to value which has been attained in consideration of the overall view supported by the other two approaches.

REAL ESTATE TAX DATA

The subject property is listed on the real property identification map for the County of Los Angeles, California, as shown hereunder:

Map Book 8135—Page 654—Parcel 231

	Assessor's M. V.	Assessment
Land	$1,555,000	$ 388,750
Improvements	2,545,000	636,250
Total	$4,100,000	$1,025,000
Total—Land & Buildings Excluding Fixtures—		$4,100,000

Tax Rate for Land and Buildings

$11.3339/$100

Tax Ratio

25%

Tax Liability at Present Assessment	$116,172
Tax Liability at our Market Value of $2,500,000	70,827
Difference	$ 45,345

ZONING

The property is under the planning jurisdiction of the City of North Hollywood and is zoned for industrial uses (M-1).
The present use is consonant with zoning by-laws.

HIGHEST AND BEST USE

We are of the opinion that the present facility is reflective of optimum use at the present time. The property is not readily convertible to an occupancy by one user because of its three-level layout and may be designated as a single-purpose building because of its low ceiling heights and special wiring. Further, elevators are required to lift process materials from one level to another, necessitating double-handling in the process flow, unnecessary waiting for elevator space from time to time, thereby adding to labor and time-saving costs. A single-level plant would have saved space, time, and money if the slope to the rear had been filled or built on piles with garage space underneath.

UTILITIES

Heating
    Fuel   — Natural Gas; No Alternate
    Type   — Direct Fired in Duct
    Boiler   — 352,000 BTU
Air Conditioning
    Capacity   — 237,000 Square Feet; 1,300 Tons
    Areas   — Entire Building
Electricity   — Primary Voltages---4,160 KV
                             Secondary Voltage--120 V, 208 V,
                                          277 V, 480 V;
                                          5250 KVA
                             Distribution System: Motor Control
                             Centers and Breaker Panels; Individ-
                             ual Voltage Regulators for Special
                             Applications; Fix-Tap Manuals on
                             Transformers

Gas	— Natural
Water	— Municipal; Two 4"-6" Meters, 95 PSI
Sewer	— Municipal Sanitary and Storm
Compressed Air	— 120 PSI; 80 CFM (40 HP - 120,000)
Sprinklers	— Wet Type, Monitored; Cover Entire Plant; Municipal Water Source
Special Utilities	— Deionized Water, Soft Water, H_2, O_2, LN

EMPLOYEE FACILITIES

Office	— Condition and Style Good
Cafeteria	— Counter Service Seating Capacity 200 Condition and Appearance Good
Cloakrooms	— Inadequate
Lockers	— 568------377 Full Length, 191 Small
Washrooms	— Adequate and in Good Condition
Parking	— One Lot---797 Spaces Bituminous Concrete Surface Fenced, Lighted

SHIPPING FACILITIES

No rail siding; three truck doors; adequate truck docking and turn-around.

CITY AND AREA DATA

Location

North Hollywood is located in the northwest area of the rich, semi-arid San Gabriel Valley, ten freeway miles north of the Los Angeles Civic Center. It is a rapidly developing high-class residential community, which followed on the heels of a few very modern industrial and sophisticated engineering laboratories moving out there from Los Angeles Center over 20 years ago. It is now a most desirable place in which to live, work, and find recreation. All major truck lines serve Pasadena and provide overnight delivery schedules to San Diego, San Francisco, and points in Arizona and Nevada. Scheduled air transportation from Ontario International, Los Angeles International, and Hollywood-Burbank Airports with limousine service between Pasadena and the latter two. Executive aircraft accommodations at the three airports listed plus El Monte Airport. Continental Trailways and Greyhound Bus Lines have local depots in Pasadena. Nearest port facilities at Los Angeles and Long Beach Harbors.

The Santa Fe and Southern Pacific Railroads serve North Hollywood, with reciprocal agreements with other lines.

Industrial Sites

There are only 625 acres in the city limits zoned for light industry—a small percentage is vacant and available in small parcels. Typical sales prices range from $109,000 to $260,000 per acre. The terrain is generally level. Drainage is excellent. Subsoil is clay and loam, and piling is sometimes required. Sizes of water mains range from six to twelve inches. Sizes of sewer lines range from minimum to eight inches.

SITE DATA

The site comprises an aggregate of 9.609 ± acres. The site fronts on Magdalena Avenue for a distance of 454.17 feet providing ingress and egress to the improved lot. Mean depth is 720 feet.

The subject site slopes gently to the east, at the intersection of Beaumont Boulevard and Olive Street, and is well drained. All utilities are attached.

The site is paved with three-inch bituminous asphalt in all areas not grassed, planted, or improved with structures.

The land is leased for 52 years from February 4, 1955, ending February 4, 2007; and the tenant has an option to purchase the site (by a supplement dated in February, 1956) for $425,513 at any time after February 1, 1960.

Copies of the lease and its supplement appear in the Addenda to this report.

LAND EVALUATION

After completing our study of vacant land sales of similar shape and topography in this section of North Hollywood, we are convinced that raw land value for subject property is as follows as of current date:

9.609 Acres at $160,000 per Acre = $1,537,440
Rounded to: $1,537,500

COST APPROACH

Cost Analysis

The cost analysis in this report will be used in conjunction with the Income (hypothetical) Approach to develop a building residual, and it will also show cost of reproducing the single-purpose utility of the premises at current prices deducting depreciation from all sources.

In the subject structure, there exists, besides the physical depreciation factor, functional obsolescence created by the use of the premises.

The entire structure, which dates from 1955, is burdened with physical and functional obsolescence. Conversion of this building to alternate or multiple uses would require large amounts of input capital and the decentralization of the primary sources of heat, light, power, water, and sprinkler systems.

Therefore, the existing single-purpose facility will be depreciated according to its functional problems in addition to the physical erosions of time, wear, and tear.

Utilizing cost indices from accepted manuals, such as Marshall & Swift, we have reviewed the total area of the premises, amounting to approximately 237,000 square feet, and the range of original construction dates and will adapt a unit value of cost to the building.

Depreciation

Building areas are calculated on the basis of exterior dimensions. In order to facilitate the description of the structure, we attached a layout sketch of the floor plan on a following page.

Physical Depreciation

Physical depreciation is based on age, condition, and original construction. The process used is based on our field inspection of building's parts such as foundation, flooring, wall sections, roof framing and roofing, windows, doors, and interiors. Each of the aforementioned factors was studied to arrive at a total physical depreciation factor which has been substantiated by age, erosion, use, and deterioration of materials. Maintenance and repair is so governed that we have placed a physical life of 50 years or two percent per annum for the building.

Functional Obsolescence

Functional obsolescence is defined as the loss in value due to decreased utility of the building caused by the combined effect of inadequacies or excesses.

This two-story and basement structure suffers from functional as well as physical obsolescence. Its three-level design hampers both material and personnel movement. Much square footage is lost as a result of excessive corridor space which would not be necessary on a more modern single-level design.

Ceiling heights are low, making all warehouse and storage uses a functional drawback. Ceiling heights in the basement and lower level are 8'6"; on the upper, ceiling height is 10'. The stacking process requires 14'.

The property is further penalized from the cost point of view in that it could presently be constructed with much simpler and more economical components (e.g., insulated steel or tilt-up concrete versus brick walls). Its "superadequacy" construction is unnecessary and merely results in higher cost figures that make up the assessment.

The Principle of Substitution will be applied later in this report to show the dollar amount of functional inutility loss calculated herein.

Economic Obsolescence

This is a form of depreciation ensuing from deleterious elements in the neighborhood off the premises. None was present near subject. Excessive taxes, however, can be considered a form of economic obsolescence. We have chosen to ignore this possibility in this case, since we feel the burdens of proof of excessive taxation must be proven by our effort.

Description of Improvements

The premises may broadly be described as comprising 237,000 square feet of a three-story industrial building, erected in 1955, and offering manufacturing, assembly, warehousing, laboratory, and office facilities. The improvements are comprised largely of brick, block, steel, and reinforced concrete construction with a paved parking lot on all sides of the building.

Following is a breakdown of improved areas:

Manufacturing and Assembly Area	71,424 Square Feet
Storage and Warehousing	42,572 Square Feet
Offices & Cafeteria (Including Corridors, Utilities, Washrooms, Penthouse, and Vault)	107,208 Square Feet
Laboratories	13,996 Square Feet
Total	235,200 Square Feet
Plus Outside Docks and Patio	1,800 Square Feet
Total Area	237,000 Square Feet

Impaired Use—Functional Inutility

Warehouse and Storage Area	42,572 Square Feet

Construction
Type, Age, and Condition

A Class "C" structure, reinforced concrete floors, brick exterior over block walls, composition and gravel roofing on 1/2-inch ply sheathing with tapered steel beams, batt insulation, standard plumbing, conduit-wired electrical system, sprinkler system, and combination heating and air-conditioning system.

Built—1955-56
Condition—Fair

The Plant

The plant has a total gross floor area of approximately 237,000 square feet on three levels. The overall building, along with miscellaneous construction, is described as follows:

Two Story and Basement
Brick, Reinforced Concrete, and Steel Frame Construction

Upper Level: 200 Feet x 609 Feet	=	121,945 Square Feet
Lower Level: 200 Feet x 420 Feet	=	84,000 Square Feet
Basement: 200 Feet x 110 Feet	=	22,000 Square Feet
Penthouse and Vault	=	9,055 Square Feet
Total	=	237,000 Square Feet

                Story Heights: Upper   = 14 Feet
                               Lower   = 12 Feet
                               Basement   = 12 Feet

Floor Live Loads Range from 150 lbs. to 350 lbs.
Trucking Docks: 20 Feet Wide x 30 Feet Long x 10 Feet High
Metal-Clad Steel Frame Enclosure on Reinforced Concrete and Timber-Piled
Bents with Reinforced Concrete Floor Slab.

Elevators and Boilers

Building Elevators   —2 Otis, 10,000 lb. Capacity Electric
                            Freight. Three landings each.
Boiler Room   —One-Story, Brick, Steel-Frame Construction
                            on Upper Level.
                            18 Feet to 40 Feet wide x 50 Feet Long x
                            37 Feet High--------Irregular Shape
                            Gross Floor Area------1,806 Square Feet
Boilers   —2 Ajax 200L/P Package Type
                            Scotch Marine Generator
                            Gas Fired including auxiliary equipment

NOTE: There would normally follow here a detailing of doors and
windows, interior finish, lighting, plumbing, heating and ventilating, roofing, sprinkler system, etc., too lengthy to be
described in this chapter. We will, therefore, continue with a
summary of construction costs without this list.

Electricals and Mechanicals

The building contains a full complement of plumbing, sewerage, heating
and ventilating, air conditioning, electric lighting, sprinkler system, fire alarm
system, Autocall system, and central clock system facilities necessary for the
required functions for which the plant was originally designed.

Yard Improvements

Gas Meter House—Brick, Steel-Frame Construction
Blacktop Yard Paving
Concrete Walks and Curbs
Brick Wall with Two Gates (North and East Side)
Chain Link Fence (North Side)
Water and Sewer Lines

Calculations

Reproduction Cost New of Foregoing Detail
Measured as 237,000 Square Feet of:
Finished Office, Laboratory, Manufacturing,
Assembly and Warehouse Area
Including Electricals and Mechanicals and
Underground Wiring and Piping

235,200 Sq. Ft. x $12.40 per Sq. Ft.   = $2,916,480
Reproduction Cost New of Outside
Docks & Patio: 1,800 SF @ $5.50/SF   = $ 9,900
Reproduction Cost New of Yard
Improvements   =   75,000
    Total Reproduction Cost New   =   84,900
Total Cost New of Main Structure,
Docks & Patio, and Yard Improvements   = $3,001,380
                       Rounded to: $3,000,000

VALUATION VIA THE PRINCIPLE OF SUBSTITUTION

The buildings and certain building equipment under review, exclusive of production equipment, represent only a part of a business enterprise; but their true value, as with most industrial property, normally reaches its highest level only when associated with the business for which designed or built. The buildings under review were constructed for a single purpose—to house a computer assembling and packaging operation.

It follows, also, that the characteristics of the related business enterprise may limit the investment justified in the property appraised. When sales of similar single-purpose properties are infrequent or lacking, market value must necessarily be construed as the value of the property to the owner and may be further defined as that amount of money that would justly compensate the owner for its loss. This may also be stated as the amount at which ownership would be justified.

After careful review, our opinion of fair market value was based on:

1. A personal inspection and inventory of the buildings, structures, and certain equipment comprising the property under review.
2. An estimate of the cost of reproduction new in like kind.
3. An estimate of the cost of replacement new with a modern plant building of comparable capacity to measure functional obsolescence by the Principle of Substitution.
4. An estimate of accrued depreciation resulting from physical deterioration.
5. A study of the history of the operation and the influences affecting its development and future investigation.
6. A review and correlation of all factors affecting the fair market value of the buildings and structures under investigation.

To measure functional obsolescence, the cost to construct a substitute plant of comparable capacity using modern practices and materials was developed to estimate the excess construction inherent in the subject property.

The modern replacement building of comparable capacity would be a one-story structure measuring 480.37 feet x 410 feet with a gross floor area of approximately 196,950 square feet. Ceiling heights would range from 12 feet high in the office and cafeteria areas, 16 feet high in computer chassis and packing areas, and 20 feet high in packed stock area. On a following page is a layout of the substitute modern replacement building.

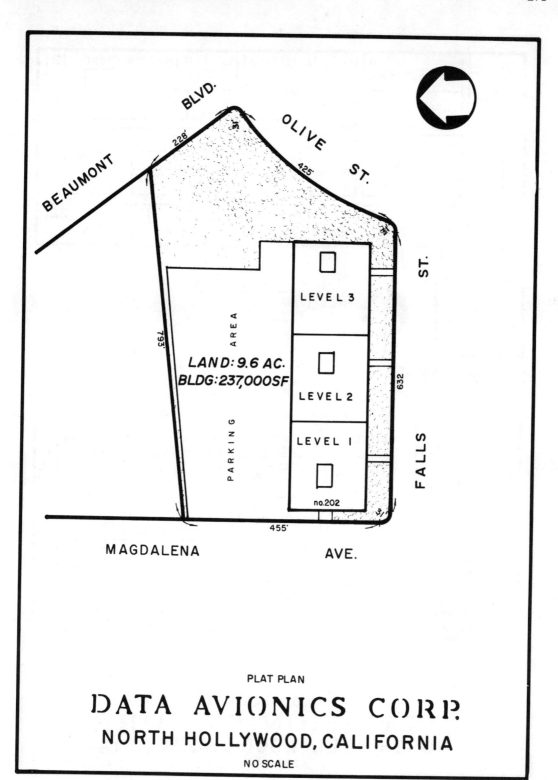

PLAT PLAN

DATA AVIONICS CORP.
NORTH HOLLYWOOD, CALIFORNIA
NO SCALE

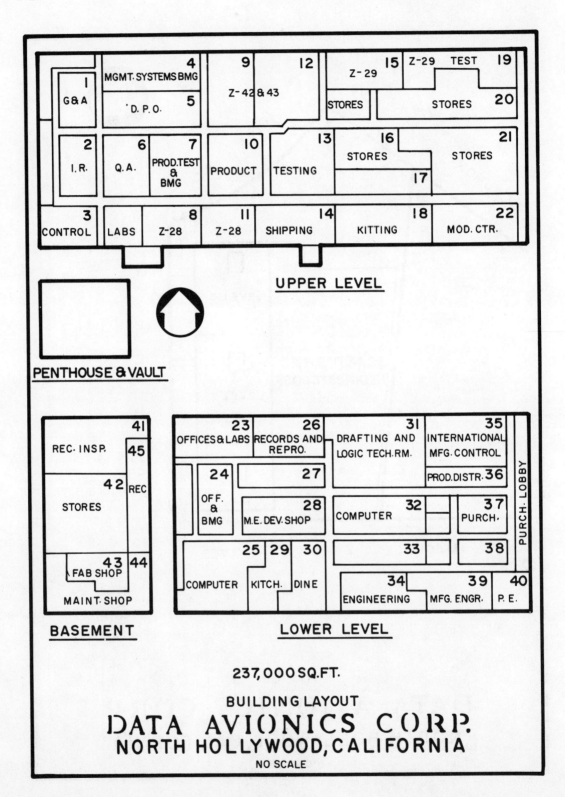

UPPER LEVEL

PENTHOUSE & VAULT

BASEMENT   LOWER LEVEL

237,000 SQ.FT.

BUILDING LAYOUT

DATA AVIONICS CORP.
NORTH HOLLYWOOD, CALIFORNIA
NO SCALE

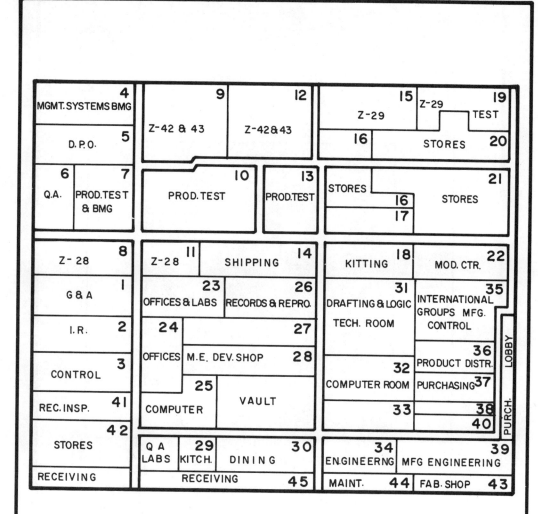

EXISTING BUILDING 237,000 S.F. (gross)
REPLACEMENT BUILDING 196,950 S.F. (gross)
NET USABLE INTERIOR 195,428 S.F.

MODERN REPLACEMENT BUILDING ON 10 ACRE LOT

DATA AVIONICS CORP.

NORTH HOLLYWOOD, CALIFORNIA

NO SCALE

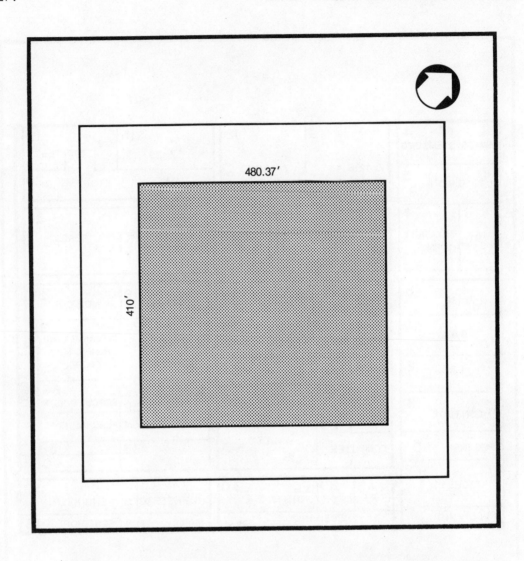

Materials and construction and general specifications are as follows:

Reinforced concrete foundations and floors with loadings ranging from 175 lbs. to 500 lbs. per square foot—four feet above grade
Concrete panel tilt-up walls six inches thick with exposed aggregate exterior
Structural steel long-span framing with 40 feet minimum bays
Roof of ribbed metal deck with two-inch insulation, built-up four-ply tar and gravel roofing
Aluminum sash
Concrete block partition walls ranging from 6" to 12" thick

Air conditioning in offices, cafeteria, locker rooms, toilets,
recreation room, and packing area
Gas-fired unit heaters
Electric lighting system ranging from 12-foot candles to
100-foot candles per square foot
Power wiring
Plumbing and sewerage
Sprinkler system throughout
Fire alarm system
Autocall
Yard improvements including paving and fencing

A modern substitute replacement facility represented on the foregoing
pages would require about 10 acres of usable land. The present plant
building and improvements are located in an area between Margarita
Avenue and Beaumont Boulevard and Olive Street which contains approximately 9.609 acres. The easterly slope of this land dictated the three
levels of construction. A new site should be level at road grade permitting
single-story operation. There is such a site available within two miles at
about equal land value.

Based on prices for labor and material in the North Hollywood area on
December 1, 1975, including an allowance for contractors' overhead and
profit and architect and engineering fees and contingencies, the estimated
cost of modern computer assembly and packaging building _substitute_ is:

$2,250,000

Functional obsolescence of the _existing_ building and yard improvements determined by the Principle of Substitution is 25 percent,
calculated as follows:

Cost of Reproduction @ $12.65
Including Yard Improvements   = $2,998,050
Rounded to: $3,000,000
Cost of Replacement @ $11.42
(196,950 x $11.42)
Including Yard Improvements   = 2,250,000
Excess Construction ($3,000,000 — 2,250,000) = $ 750,000
$750,000 ÷ $3,000,000   = 25 Percent

Conclusion

Based upon our investigation and after considering all factors, it is
believed the depreciated cost of the property appraised as of March 1, 1974,
is fairly represented in the amount of $2,933,000 determined as follows:

Calculations

Cost of Reproduction Inc. Yard Imp. $3,000,000
Less Physical Depreciation at 38%   1,140,000
                                           $1,860,000

Less Functional Obsolescence at 25%
     (Incurable)   465,000
Depreciated Cost—New $1,395,000
Add Land   1,537,500
Total $2,932,500
     Rounded to: $2,933,000

Value Conclusion via Cost Approach
$2,933,000

INCOME APPROACH

The Income Approach to the value estimate is an appraisal technique in which the anticipated net income is processed to indicate the capital value of the asset by capitalization. Since subject property is owner occupied, we have established an economic rental reflective of the current market on which to base a hypothetical lease.

As a precursor to the development of the income analysis, we examined the land-to-building ratio existing within the subject property and found this to be land, 9.609 acres; buildings, 3.245 acres. Normal industrial requirement varies, land to buildings, from 3.0 to 4.0; and we consider, therefore, that there is no surplus land in excess of normal requirement. In fact, there is limited space for a two-story addition on the north side of the present building if parking area is excavated and paved under the structure.

We examined industrial net rental values prevailing in the Los Angeles area in 1972 and 1973 and found that newly developed industrial premises of moderate size (25,000 to 100,000 square feet) rented at eight cents to ten cents per square foot net per month dependent on the lease term and lessee covenant, the type and use of the structure, its age, and its location. We adjusted these comparables (which are manufacturing, warehouse, and office in make-up) to embrace a rental value for subject office/warehouse and manufacturing usages, bringing rental value of subject to .1125 cents per square foot net per month or $1.35 per square foot net per annum. We could find no comparable rentals in the city of North Hollywood, so your appraisers went countywide in their market study. The subject enjoys quiet neighborhood, wide street front, landscaped environment close to downtown Los Angeles metropolitan value influences. For these reasons, we have given subject a plus adjustment of 25 cents per square foot on an annual net rental basis.

Having tested the area market for current net rentals for tenants with satisfactory credit ratings, our investigation divulged the following comparable net rentals which, we believe, are economic in subject locale:

(*Six long-term rentals of comparable space to rated tenants would be cited here, but in the interest of chapter brevity they will be capsulated as adjusted to the subject. All were photographed, mapped, inspected, and verified.*)

The foregoing rentals were verified by Mr. Dan Moore of The Seeley Company, who was broker in the transactions.

It is our opinion, based on these rentals, that the annual rental value of the subject property is $1.35 per square foot of building, net, which is at par for the current market in the Los Angeles metropolitan area. Comparable rentals applied are all single story, and plus adjustments to the subject have been made because the rental comparables similar to subject in quality were further out from the metropolitan area, with public transportation facilities more remote.

Calculations

Net Income Attributable to Property
237,000 Sq. Ft. at $1.35/Sq. Ft., Net	$319,950
Less Return to Land (11.3% x $1,537,500)	173,737
Net to Improvements	$146,213

Capitalization Rate

Interest	8.5%	
Effective Tax Rate	2.8%	
Recapture (Depreciation) (25-Year Remaining Economic Life)	4.0%	
	15.3%	
$146,213 Capitalized @ 15.3%, Overall		$955,640

Recapitulation

Value of the Land	$1,537,500
Value of Improvements	955,640
Total	$2,493,140
Rounded to:	$2,493,000

Value Conclusion via Income Approach
$2,493,000

MARKET DATA APPROACH

The Market Data Approach is employed to compare sales of land and buildings of comparable industrial properties to determine a unit selling price. These sales are adjusted to compare with the subject and are used to indicate a value for the subject property.

An investigation of the local market in the Los Angeles area revealed the sales on the following pages.

(Five comparable sales of similar construction, on similar shaped land with same type of topography, zoning, and arterial access would be cited here, but are eliminated in the interest of brevity. They were two- and three-story masonry buildings of an age close to subject, spread across nearby communities.)

We have analyzed all pertinent information and have studied Los Angeles County figures for comparable size improvements, which range in value from $4.71 to $10 per square foot for land and building, and have related the subject property to the comparables submitted and made adjustments for time of sale, location, size, acreage, and overall comparability. Based on these facts, we estimate that fair market value of subject on a per square foot basis would be $10. Therefore:

237,000 ± Square Feet at $10 per Square Foot = $2,370,000

Value Conclusion via Market Data Approach
$2,370,000

CORRELATION AND VALUE CONCLUSION

The three approaches to value have produced the following conclusions:

Cost Approach	$2,933,000
Income Approach	$2,493,000
Market Data Approach	$2,370,000

The Cost Approach, which normally sets the upper limit of value, was developed after determining local construction costs from discussions with the plant engineer of the subject property, by reference to national valuation manuals, and from the appraiser's first-hand experience in the building trades. The unit cost applied was derived to include the current costs for labor, materials, profit, and overhead. Depreciation allowances were taken for physical deterioration and functional obsolescence, as measured against a substitute building of equal production capacity.

An economic rental was utilized in order to derive the hypothetical income estimate for the property. The conjectural rental is calculated at the current market. In the Income Approach, the capitalization rate is derived through interest rates applicable to the subject in today's market.

The Market Data Approach has a strong application by way of local and national comparable sales data. A highly probable selling price on the open market was determined through sales of industrial, research, office, and warehouse properties in the same and other areas.

In reviewing depreciable items in our Cost Approach, and in determining what features were curable or incurable, we looked mainly to dollar value cost to cure in our estimates of functional inutility.

Great consideration has been given to whether the building is well planned, efficient in operation, and convertible to other modern industrial uses. Since our principal concern in this report is fair market value, we found that some small areas of the building were inutile and of questionable functional value to the owners and likely to require moderately expensive modifications to possible lessees or buyers.

Although the subject property is not for sale, we have put reliance on all three approaches; and we have weighted these values into conclusion. It is the opinion of the appraisers that the value of the subject property as of December 1, 1975, is:

TWO MILLION FIVE HUNDRED THOUSAND DOLLARS
($2,500,000)

The property owner should recognize at once that the insurance policy he has paid for is a contract between him and the underwriting insurance company. The intermediary agent or broker ordinarily has no binding responsibility for the compliance or enforcement of the conditions of the policy. Furthermore, the policy conditions remain inoperative until there is a cause to make a claim for loss. Until that time, the property owner pays the insurance company (a premium), but at the time of a loss claim it becomes a matter of arranging for the insurance company to pay the property owner for the loss sustained. Another fundamental of insurance underwriting and loss settlement is the valuation basis of the property involved. Throughout insurance policies and practices, the term used to describe the valuation basis for the insured property is "actual cash value." In practice, this term does not ordinarily mean what those individual words connote. In practice—buying insurance, compliance with a co-insurance clause, or settlement of a loss—the basis of value ordinarily applied is cost of reproduction new less physical depreciation.

17

How to Appraise for Insurable Value: A General-Purpose Warehouse

PROCEDURAL STEPS TOWARD
INSURANCE APPRAISAL REPORT

The insurance appraisal report of valuation for replacement purposes consists of the usual letter of transmittal and supporting data. The letter of transmittal is a concise statement identifying the property appraised, showing the date of valuation, a statement of values found, any conditions that may qualify the use of the figures submitted in the light of insurance considerations, and a clear description of what is included and excluded in the values. The supporting data consists of identifying photographs and/or maps, descriptive details, and the reproduction costs, depreciations applied, and 100% insurable values developed. The amount of supporting data will vary in accordance with the desires of the client. The extent of detail required by him should be understood clearly before the appraisal is undertaken. Naturally, the insurance appraisal excludes land excavations, foundations below ground, and other indestructibles, which will be demonstrated in the model appraisal report for insurable real property concerned with the general merchandise warehouse (but not its contents) embraced in this chapter.

CONSIDERATIONS OF VALUE FOR INSURANCE PURPOSES

Step 1

The appraiser may be called upon to estimate the value of a building and its contents in order to determine the amount, type, and scope of insurance to be carried by the owner to protect him against loss by fire or *other* property damage. To serve his client effectively, the appraiser must understand: (a) the nature of value for insurance purposes; and (b) the process used in estimating value for insurance purposes.

This chapter deals with these aspects of insurance valuation. It also discusses the manner in which the appraiser's findings must be conveyed to his client in the model appraisal so that the client will comprehend the proper application of the values found.

Step 2

Consideration of Co-insurance. A large amount of insurance carried on buildings and their contents is underwritten on a "co-insurance basis." Such policies contain a "co-insurance," or "average," clause wherein the assured agrees, in return for a reduction of premium, to carry an amount of insurance at least equal to a stated percentage of the insurable value of the property at the time of a loss. In the event of a partial loss under these policies, if the amount carried does not equal or exceed the required percentage as agreed in this clause, recovery by the insured will be limited to the proportion that the amount of insurance carried bears to the amount required.

The following demonstrates the operation of the co-insurance, or average, clause in event of loss:

Example: 100% Insurable Value at time of Loss—$1,000,000
                   80% Average Clause in Policy (Insurance required—$800,000)
Settlement: In event of total loss, entire amount of policy is paid.

In many states, co-insurance is compulsory and insurance cannot be secured without it. Even when it is not necessarily imposed, its use often results in a net premium saving to the insured. This is due to the fact that the insurance rate with co-insurance, compared to that without co-insurance, is usually low enough to overcome the difference in cost between the amount of insurance necessary to meet the co-insurance requirements and the amount that the insured must carry to provide reimbursement to him for the maximum probable loss that may take place. We will not dwell on the co-insurance any further here, because our model appraisal is on a 100% basis.

Step 3

100% Insurable Value. Reproduction cost less exclusions and depreciation: When the essentials of restoration or reimbursement and co-insurance are understood, it is obvious that the beginnings of an estimation of value for insurance purposes is the cost of reproducing the property under appraisement. This is termed *reproduction cost*. In the insurance field, it is often referred to as "replacement cost," but the latter term is sometimes confusing, as *substitution* can be implied by use of the word "replacement." Insurance does not refer to substitution.

Exclusions in insurable value are those indestructibles consisting of excavation and foundations, and plumbing below the underside of the lowest floor or grade, whichever is lower. Their cost is deducted from total reproduction costs to develop a reproduction cost less exclusions, or reproduction cost of the insurable portion of the property.

Depreciation for insurance purposes is an estimate of physical deterioration present at the time of appraisal. It represents the theoretical cost of restoration of the property to new condition.

Actual cash value is a term used in fire, storm, and flood insurance policies, and is the reproduction cost of the insurable portions of the property, less depreciation, as described above. For the purposes of this chapter, and to avoid the misconception that this term implies a relationship to a "market value," it is referred to hereafter as "100% insurable value."

Step 4

Relationship to Market Value. The difference between a *market value* appraisal and an *insurance appraisal* exists in the presence of obsolescence, both economic and functional. In an insurance appraisal, the general application is that where a property is being used for the purpose for which it was designed, or is usable for that or another purpose, *obsolescence is not a factor in determining insurable value.* Most losses are partial.

The total loss is rare, and under the terms of policies, the insurance carrier is obligated to restore with like kind and quality, or to reimburse for the cost thereof, damage caused to the insured property, regardless of the extent of obsolescence or overimprovement present. Therefore, in an insurance appraisal normally no allowance for obsolescence as part of depreciation is made. In a market value appraisal, both economic and functional obsolescence can be applied where found to exist.

Step 5

Insurance on "Replacement Cost" Basis. It will be noted that a distinction has been made between "value for insurance purposes" and "100% insurable value" or "actual cash value." The reason for this is that insurance is sometimes written on a "replacement cost" basis (as in the model following). In such event, the insurer would be liable, in the event of loss, for the cost to repair or replace using materials of like kind and quality without deduction for physical depreciation. The property, however, must be repaired or replaced, and the insurer's maximum liability would be the cost of such repair or replacement using identical materials. In the event that the insured does not desire to repair or replace, the collectible loss is based upon the actual cash value, or, in other words, the depreciated value of the destroyed property.

Depreciation insurance. In this type of coverage, the amount of the physical depreciation of the property being appraised is calculated and insured separately, in addition to the actual cash value, and both figures are shown in any valuation for insurance purposes. The result, however, in its combined form should represent the same amount of coverage as insurance written on a "replacement cost" basis.

Because the following model appraisal is in itself a revelation of the principles of restoration or reimbursement for loss against fire and other causes on a total basis, we will present the full replacement report as its own proof of soundness and validity, bearing out the foregoing explanations.

Because our merchandising warehouse is high-ceiling, one-story masonry on asbestos-coated steel frame, the fire risk is very low. The building is fully sprinklered. Even at 100% insurable replaceable value, the premium is low because noninflammables such as china, glassware, hardware, and soft beverages are stored here. Thus we begin the model appraisal with the Letter of Transmittal.

MODEL APPRAISAL

December 14, 1975

Mr. John J. Burke, CPCU
Director of Corporate Insurance
General Distribution Corp.
100 Park Avenue
New York, New York 10017

Re: Merchandising Warehouse
20 Mack Drive
East Rutherford, N.J. 07073

Dear Mr. Burke:

We hereby certify that we have personally and thoroughly inspected the above reference property. An analysis of all relevant data was utilized in determining the estimate of replacement costs and insurable value.

We are presenting this report to you in four separate sections:

Section I——Definitions and explanations of insurance appraisal terminology.
Section II——Describes the pertinent facts affecting the subject property.
Section III——Replacement cost breakdown by item with applicable exclusions.
Section IV——Building plan of subject property.

After careful consideration of all factors, it is our opinion that the insurable value of the property as of August 31, 1974, is:

FOUR HUNDRED TWENTY-SIX THOUSAND DOLLARS
($426,000)

We certify that we have no present or contemplated financial interest in the subject property and that our employment and compensation are in no way contingent upon the value reported.

A duplicate copy of this appraisal is retained in our files. Should the necessity arise, this report may be made available for use in our office by you or any authorized representative.

By retaining a copy of your appraisal, it is possible for us to revise and update this report. To obtain the most effective use, we recommend that this be done from time to time as conditions indicate.

Respectfully submitted,

Senior Appraiser

Section I—Definitions and Explanations

A. This report has been compiled on a replacement cost basis. The insurer would be liable, in the event of loss, for the cost to repair or replace using materials of like kind and quality without deduction for physical depreciation.
B. Replacement cost of the various items of construction has been determined as of the date of this appraisement on the assumed basis of replacing the entire property as a complete unit at one time.
C. The insurance exclusions used in this appraisal are items that are commonly excluded from fire insurance coverage or that are specifically excluded under terms of your policies. The decision as to which categories of property should be excluded is a matter for determination by the insured in consultation with his insurance broker or agent. The insurance exclusions scheduled in this appraisal are prepared as a convenience to the user. It should not be considered as suggesting that these categories are not liable to damage by fire nor that they should be excluded from insurance coverage.
D. This appraisal is subject to limiting conditions and assumptions, which include the following: no investigation of title to the property has been made; existing liens and encumbrances, if any, have been disregarded and the property appraised as though free of indebtedness; responsible ownership and competent management of the property is assumed; specifications and engineering data furnished to us are assumed to be reliable.

Section II—Pertinent Facts

Property:

Merchandising Warehouse
20 Mack Drive
East Rutherford, N.J. 07073

Building Area:

50,000 S.F. (250' x 200')

Type:	One-Story Concrete Block and Steel Structure
Ceiling Height:	24' under Truss
Erected:	1964
Use:	General Merchandise Warehouse All-purpose and convertible to manufacturing use

Building Description

Excavation:	Trench & Pier Excavation
Foundation:	Concrete Footings and Foundation Walls
Frame:	Steel; Steel Columns
Floor Structure:	Concrete on Ground
Exterior Walls:	Concrete Block Brick Face on Two Sides
Roof:	Built-up on Steel Deck on Steel-on-Steel Bar Joist
Heating and Cooling:	Gas-Fired Space Heaters
Electric:	Wiring in Rigid Conduit; Strip Fluorescent Lighting Fixtures
Plumbing:	Miscellaneous Average Lavatory Fixtures
Sprinkler:	Dry System
Partitions:	Plasterboard Walls/Office Four Separate Offices
Miscellaneous:	ADT System

Section III—Replacement Cost

Excavation	$ 1,798	
Foundation	22,922	
Frame	116,067	
Floor Structure	49,018	
Interior Construction	4,866	
Plumbing	15,666	
Sprinklers	25,267	
Heating, Cooling, Ventilating	14,150	
Electrical Lighting	17,182	
Exterior Walls	64,274	
Roof Structure	88,941	
Roof Cover	19,708	
Trusses and Girders	31,837	
Miscellaneous	2,500	
Architect Fees	28,452	
Total Replacement Cost		$502,648

Less Exclusions:
    Excavation $ 1,798
    Foundation Below Ground   22,922
    Floor Structure   49,018
    Piping Below Grade   1,567
    Architect Fee   1,423
    Total Exclusions   76,728

Insurable Value $425,920
                           Rounded to: $426,000

Section IV—Photographs*
and
Building Plan

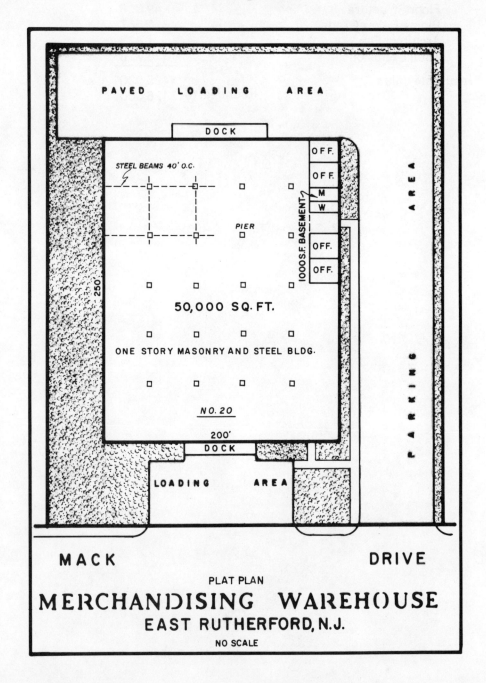

*An unencumbered property in fee simple is historically
known in law as a freehold in which the owner has full right
of use and enjoyment. A lease is a contract by which an
owner conveys an interest in this property, usually for a
term of years at a specified rent. When a freehold is leased,
it changes status and becomes encumbered to the extent of
the rights conveyed in the lease. Subleases are further
encumbrances on the property, although the sublease
position will not be encountered in the model appraisal
demonstrated in this chapter.*

18

How to Evaluate Leasehold Estates and Leased Fees

KEY CONSIDERATIONS OF VALUE
WHERE MORE THAN ONE INTEREST IS INVOLVED

When the value of leased property is to be estimated, two or more interests are in question, designated as follows:

(1) The owner, as lessor, retains a leased fee interest.
(2) The direct tenant, as lessee, owns rights to a leasehold estate equity, which is an encumbrance on the owner's title in fee simple.
(3) If the direct tenant has, in turn, subleased to others, the interest of the direct tenant becomes a "sandwich lease interest," because it is now sandwiched between the interest of the owner and the interest of the sublessee.

OTHER CONSIDERATIONS IN THE VALUATION OF LEASEHOLDS

The theory of leasehold valuation has developed over a period of two thousand years in Europe and Britain, where it was introduced by the Romans who had taken it from the Greeks. Long experience in the marketplace here has made it clear to owners and lessees, their attorneys and appraisers, and the courts, that there are two hinges on which value swings in leasehold appraisals:

1. Leasehold value is established by rental market conditions, or through a capital investment by owner or lessee, and by a combination of each of these factors.

2. Leasehold value is enhanced when the market rental (economic rent) becomes greater than the contract rent; or when the lessee constructs an improvement or makes a substantial capital investment in rehabilitating an existing structure.

This creates the framework of the "two-property concept" familiar to many appraisers, which holds that when there is a lease favorable to the owner, then the owner has, in effect, two properties: the leased fee interest (the real estate itself), and the bonus in the lease.

The reverse situation will be true when the direct tenant obtains a lease to his own advantage, that is, at a rental lower than the market rent, or when because of improvements made by others he is getting the bonus. This situation was dramatized in the discussion of the "sandwich tenant" in condemnation.

There is a bonus submerged somewhere in every contract between humans. In the leasehold contract, the bonus must be revealed by the diligent appraiser seeking to estimate fair market value.

Types of Leases

There are five types of commercial property leases in general use today made for brief or long-term periods. They are as follows:

1. The straight, fixed-sum net lease, with in-advance monthly rental payments is the most common form in commercial use.
2. The graded lease, with periodic "step-ups" in rental payments, is sometimes made where tenant's start-up cost is heavy, but his future is assured.
3. The percentage lease, usually applied to retail gross sales annually, sometimes with monthly minimum guarantee.
4. The security-advance lease, sometimes applied to special new construction, with the tenant advancing rent for a year or more in order to gain long-term advantages in the lease.
5. The revaluation lease, where revised rentals are established by arbitration. This is the weakest form of lease, holding perils for both owner and tenant. Lending institutions steer away from it.

Reversionary Right (Repossession)

The owner's interest in the leased fee consists of his right to collect the stipulated rental from the tenant monthly, quarterly, or based on another time period, in payment for his release of the use of the premises, which he nevertheless continues to own in fee simple. In this title he also retains the right to repossess the premises at the expiration of the lease, which is legally known as his reversionary right. Unless otherwise specified in the lease instrument, this right gives the owner recapture title to all physical improvements on the premises, even if he must pay the expiring tenant a depreciated part of their cost.

The Tenant's Rights

The lessee's primary interest in a commercial leasehold is his right to transact business on the premises in a profitable enterprise, which entitles him to the excess of any net gain over expenses for the duration of the lease after payment of rent to the owner. The tenant is also entitled to rental income from the property ensuing in leases to subtenants, which is the right to the difference between the contract rent payable to the owner and any higher market rentals current at the time of valuation. Further, the tenant retains an interest in the market value of any improvements to the property that he may have created during the term of the lease. While he must leave these improvements attached to the property at the end of the lease, he will be compensated for their depreciated cost unless the provisions of the lease instrument state otherwise.

In evaluating the leasehold, the appraiser must estimate the present worth, or market value, of rental increment (if any) above the contract rent and the lessee's interest in any improvements, being guided by the provisions of the lease.

The value of a leasehold is that amount of money for which a tenant can sell his leasehold in the prevailing market.

Provisions of the Lease Instrument

The first step in the evaluation of a leasehold requires that the appraiser obtain and carefully study all the provisions of the lease instrument. These may be highlighted as follows:

1. *Term of lease and renewal options.* A long-term lease generally has greater value to a tenant than a short-term lease would afford. It is a hedge against inflation. It gives the tenant time to amortize expensive improvements. It is insurance against the "penalties of success," i.e. burdensome rental increases constantly stepped up. And options to renew the lease at the same, or slightly increased rental, add to the value of the leasehold.

2. *Rental.* To return to the two hinges on which value swings in leasehold appraisals: "Leasehold value is established by rental market conditions ... Leasehold value is enhanced when the market rental becomes greater than the contract rent." When the contract rental is higher than the current market rental, the value of the leasehold is depressed.

3. *Condemnation.* This all-important clause can be written to protect both owner and tenant in the event of eminent domain proceedings against the property. Its absence as a provision can be damaging to the owner's leased fee interest and highly speculative in value to the leasehold.

4. *Termination.* Specific language as to the owner's obligations to reimburse the lessee for depreciated value of improvements that the lessee may have installed, together with a statement of the lessee's obligations to the owner as to condition of premises to be quitted, disbursement of any security deposit, and other matters pertinent to termination of the lease will add to the value of the leasehold.

5. *Purchase option.* The right to purchase the property at a set price can be an important provision in a long-term lease, particularly where it will be exercised after the owner's tax shelter in depreciation has run out, and where the tenant benefits by insuring permanence to his place of business and recapture of his investment in improvements.

Other provisions of a commercial lease, such as clauses for assignment of the lease, tax participation, maintenance and building improvement, insurance, forfeiture in event of default by lessee, mortgages on the leasehold, and use of the property, are equally important to both owner and tenant, and vital to evaluation of the leasehold.

The Special Effects of Sale and Leaseback

A popular gambit in financing sound industrial properties on a long-term basis is the sale and leaseback transaction, whereby a user-owner will sell his property to an investor, simultaneously taking back a lease on the premises which guarantees income to the investor for many years. It is a good move for an owner-user whose property has outrun its depreciation factor.

When the contract rental from such a lease is under the prevailing rental market, the leasehold may have great value. When the rental is greater than actual market, the leasehold may be valueless and purely a paper transaction as a tax benefit to the seller.

If the lease contains a recapture clause, giving the property back to the seller-lessee after a period of years, the Internal Revenue Service will view the sale and leaseback as a mortgage in disguise. To be valued as a true leasehold, the seller-lessee must maintain an enduring arm's-length position with the buyer.

LEASEHOLD AND PROPERTY ANALYSIS

The *second step* the appraiser takes in preparing evaluation of a leasehold is to condense the provisions of the lease in their significant aspects, with a detailed statement of rental income and the details of any subleases involved. The format of the report is developed in the investment-analysis manner:

Market Survey and Property Analysis

1. *Identification.* A complete legal description of land and (proposed or existing) building is set forth. Terms of the lease are stated in connection with description of the property. The following macro-market influences should be noted:

   (a) Type of city government and its effectiveness politically and economically, together with a synopsis of the city's reasons for being (i.e. importance as a rail head, communications center, harbor and/or airport facility). Indications of growth or decline in such facilities.

   (b) Population of the city; forms of transportation within the city and to and from the suburbs and other cities; chief forms of employment within the city.

(c) Principal industries within the city, their growth patterns, and public utilities that serve them; the amount and substance of industry in the area, and its contribution, if any, to the commerce of the city; the city's atmosphere as an industrial, commercial, or cultural (university) center, with all three described if necessary.

(d) The planning and zoning practices, the tax policies, and local ordinances affecting the property and its district must be stated clearly.

2. *Micro-market Data of the Industrial District.* Factual data concerning the immediate vicinity of the proposed or existing property and leasehold should be set forth as follows:

(a) Highest and best use of the property should be sharply emphasized. If a change in highest and best use is recommended, it may render present improvements valueless. State the rent per square foot in competing properties nearby. Note the number of vacancies.

(b) Describe trends in the district or park. Is the district growing or decaying? Is redevelopment underway? Is the industrial park the best one in the area? How far away is city hall, the public library, hospitals, medical clinics, the newspaper plant, public utility offices? Is the district served by main highways and a sensible traffic pattern? Is it readily accessible to other important districts within the city?

3. *Description of the Improvements.* Specific details of the property under appraisement must be clearly delineated:

(a) The building's layout, design and construction, together with assessments and tax levy.

(b) Zone requirements.

(c) Description of the site topography and subsoil conditions, plottage and shape of the land area, together with list of utilities on site or available.

(d) Use and condition of the proposed or existing building and its machinery, together with site improvements, planned or existing, such as paved parking, fencing, outdoor floodlighting.

(e) Each floor of the building must be measured and described.

(f) A summary of the development of the property, if existing, with a five- to ten-year history of income and expense, and type of management and maintenance attending the property.

(g) The anticipated useful life of the property must be estimated and allowances made for depreciation and obsolescence.

4. *Method of Evaluation.* Usually the property is first evaluated in fee simple, as if there were no lease involved. Then the value of the leasehold is separately estimated by capitalization of net income, and this amount is subtracted from the value of the whole property. The difference is the value of the leased fee (or lessor's interest). But the reverse is operable: The value of the lessor's interest may be estimated and subtracted from the value of the whole to produce the value of the leasehold. Choice of method should be made clear.

5. *Feasibility Reports.* If the building is proposed or in the planning stage, the appraiser must project income and expenses for five years from origination of

the proposed lease, and recommend management and maintenance procedures for the proposed building that are both practical and economic.

6. *Comparable Land Sales and Leaseholds.* The appraiser must list in detail verified data concerning land sales in the area. If sales prices of other comparable leaseholds can be obtained, these should be exhibited. These comparables should be inspected and similarities or differences described, as compared to subject land or space, summing up the property analysis.

THE APPROACHES TO VALUE

The appraiser's *third step* in leasehold appraisal lies in working up his approaches as to both the property as a whole and the leasehold.

The Market Data Approach may be useful only for purposes of estimating land value and gauging the rental market.

In the evaluation of both leasehold and property as a whole, the Cost Approach may lend better support to the Income Approach than the Market Data Approach, because the Cost Approach leads the appraiser to a close examination of construction details and the age, condition, and anticipated life of the property, hence the life of the income stream. The ratio of effective age of the building to life expectancy is crucial.

The *Income Approach* is the chief guide to value and is the proper test of the lessee's ability to deliver a worthwhile investment yield over a long period of time.

Since the market value of a leasehold depends absolutely upon the *present worth of its future earnings,* the appraiser must tabulate such earnings from the provisions of the lease if he is to calculate their present worth.

Capitalization rates will vary with circumstances. Yield percentages will differ. Choice of capitalization rate and method is the appraiser's critical *fourth step* in evaluating a leasehold.

CAPITALIZATION METHODS

Depending upon the *quality and durability* of income flowing from the property under appraisement, one can elect to follow either of the following courses of capitalization:

1. Use the straight-line depreciation plus capitalization-rate method of capitalization when you anticipate that the net income before depreciation *may decline* regularly each year in the future.
2. But if the net income before depreciation is expected to be level or better and is *of a contract nature,* with rated tenants and the leases extended over a period of at least *twelve years,* then the Inwood premise may be used. This premise is used only on prime properties with rated corporations as tenants on long-term leases.

TECHNIQUES FOR ESTIMATING VALUE OF LAND AND IMPROVEMENTS IN LEASEHOLD APPRAISAL

Procedure for Estimating a Separate Land Value in a Leasehold Estate

As the *fifth step* in a leasehold evaluation, it is best to estimate land value, particularly where market data on nearby vacant land is sufficient.

On occasion, such market data may be scarce, but the appraiser may know from the outset the value of the building, particularly if the structure is new or recent and the builder's cost are competitive and at hand. In that case, the appraiser would set up his Cost Approach first and find his land value using the Land Residual Technique. It is a valid application to land under a leasehold.

Methods of Evaluating Land. Land value may be estimated by: (1) recent sales of nearby vacant land; (2) recently executed land leases; (3) the Land Residual Technique. This chapter will emphasize the first method, recent sales of nearby vacant land, with adjustments of comparables.

Procedure for Estimating Value of the Improvements in Leasehold Appraisals

Residual Techniques Under the Income Approach. An aging leased property may produce a rental that, capitalized, proves investment or market value greater than depreciated reproduction cost could show.

Therefore, one can employ other means of finding the value of building improvements when the value of the land is already known through market data. These means are provided by the Building Residual Technique under the Income Approach. This is the *sixth and final* step on the appraiser's road to valuation of a leasehold.

In the following model appraisal of a property leased as a general distribution warehouse, the *Building Residual Technique* is employed as stronger proof of value than the Cost Approach could show. The whole property is evaluated first, as a fee simple. Then, the equity in the leasehold is evaluated as part of the whole, or freehold, using the Discount Tables.

MODEL APPRAISAL: LEASEHOLD ESTATES AND LEASED FEE

(*This appraisal will omit Letter of Transmittal, Table of Contents, and other preliminaries, which have been demonstrated in other parts of the book.*)

ASSUMPTIONS AND LIMITING CONDITIONS

1. No responsibility is assumed for matters that are legal in character, nor is any opinion rendered as to title. The title to the subject property is assumed to be good and marketable.

2. The property has been appraised after consideration of all liens and encumbrances as specified in the lease exhibit.

3. Average competent management has been assumed in the analysis of the income and operating aspects of the property.

4. No survey has been made. All sketches and plat plans in this report are only for illustrative purposes.

5. Information furnished by others is believed to be reliable and has been investigated as fully as possible, but cannot be guaranteed.

6. The appraiser is not required to give testimony or attendance in any court of law or before any commission or board by reason of this appraisal, unless specific arrangements for these services are subsequently arranged.

7. That the net income attributable to the first lessee, after meeting the terms and conditions of the lease, remains at $39,725, or more, during the projection period.

8. The economic value of the leasehold estate is reported in dollars on the basis of the currency prevailing on the date of the valuation. The current purchasing power of the dollar is the basis for the value reported. No adjustments have been made to compensate for inflationary trends.

PURPOSE OF THE REPORT

The purpose of this report is to furnish an estimate of the fair market value of the land and improvements, and to estimate the amount attributable to the first lessee's leasehold interest in the real estate located at 5000 Silver Lane, East Hartford, Connecticut.

DEFINITION OF VALUES

Fair market value may be defined as the highest price estimated in terms of money that the property will bring if exposed for sale in the open market by a seller who is willing but not obliged to sell, allowing for a reasonable time to find a buyer who is willing but not obliged to buy, both parties having full knowledge of all the uses to which it is adapted and for which it is capable of being used.

Leasehold Value—The leasehold interest may be defined as the economic interest held by the first lessee. "The leasehold estate, consisting of the use and occupancy of the property, the value of which arises from the margin of the economic productivity of the property, subject to meeting the terms and provisions of the lease."

IDENTIFICATION OF PROPERTY

The subject property under appraisal is located at 5000 Silver Lane, East Hartford, Connecticut.

COMMUNITY DATA

East Hartford, encompassing an area of 18.2 square miles, is contiguous to Hartford and is located at the intersection of two major highways, I-84 and I-91, with Bradley Airport about ten miles distance.

The subject property enjoys accessibility to Routes 5 and 15, leading south to New York and north to Boston.

The 1970 population estimate indicates the population at 69,086. The subject is located in the Greater Hartford area, which has large and diverse manufacturing industries, and where some of the nation's largest insurance companies have their headquarters.

East Hartford industries include National Building Supply, Admiral Corporation, Pratt & Whitney, Continental Baking Company, Westinghouse, and United Aircraft Corporation.

ZONING AND UTILITIES

Zoning: Industrial, the existing improvements conform to the zoning ordinances.

Utilities: All utilities are available, including water, electrical power for industrial use, gas, and sewer.

HIGHEST AND BEST USE

After an analysis of existing land-use patterns in the area, stage of development, future potential and current zoning ordinances, it is apparent that the highest and best use of the site, which would produce the greatest net return to the land over a given period of time, would be for light industrial and/or warehouse development.

SITE DESCRIPTION

The subject site consists of 5.32 acres of level land with good soil-bearing capacity and apparently good drainage; there are no known problems with comparable improvements on similar land in the area.

DESCRIPTION OF IMPROVEMENTS

Buildings: Improvement consists of a one-story masonry and steel building with an aggregate floor area of 121,175 square feet, including 1,225 square feet of attached office area.

Layout: Building consists of three units. Unit "A" measures 150' x 266'. Unit "B" measures 150' x 267'. Unit "C" measures 150' x 267'. Unit "B" has an attached office area which measures 35' x 35'.

Foundation & Footings: Concrete

Superstructure: Steel beams and girders with light steel joists.

Exterior Walls: Masonry.

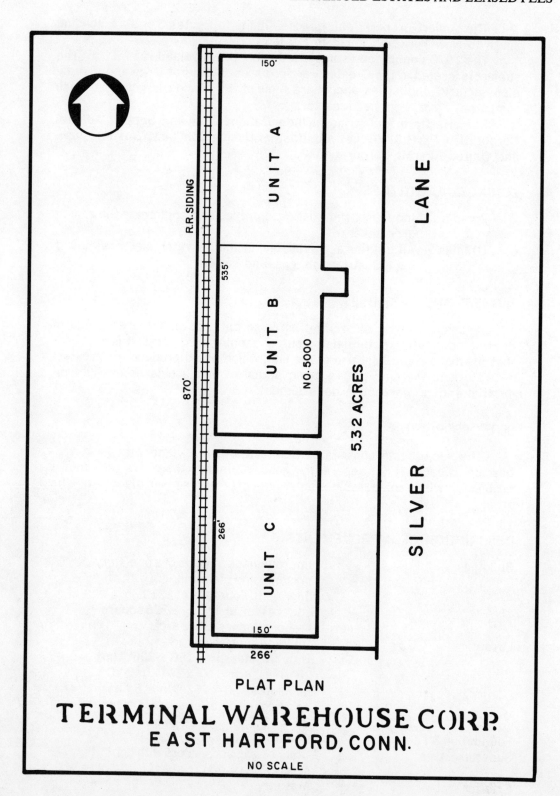

PLAT PLAN

TERMINAL WAREHOUSE CORP.
EAST HARTFORD, CONN.
NO SCALE

Roof:	1-1/2'' steel deck with 1/2'' insulation and 15-year built-up bondable type roofing.
Interior Finish:	Warehouse area: masonry walls, exposed steel joists, sprinkler room painted concrete block, plywood ceilings.
Plumbing:	Adequate plumbing and hot water heater to service facilities.
Electrical:	400 Amp. service, fixed lights in warehouse area, exterior floodlights. Wiring conduit type.
Sprinkler:	A dry system equipped with an automatic air-pressure maintenance device providing protection to all areas.
Heating:	Gas-fired, ceiling-mounted unit heaters.
Miscellaneous:	Metal gutters and leader and gravel stops will facilitate rapid drain-off of rain water.
Comments:	The improvements, constructed in 1966, are of good quality and workmanship. Maintenance and repairs have been adequate. The improvements are presently in good condition.

VALUATION ANALYSIS

Valuation of the total property rights and the allocation of the amount attributable to the first lessee's position necessitates three phases:

The first phase is to estimate the value of the total property in fee simple, including a Cost and Income Approach.

The second phase involves determining the amount of the whole attributable to the leased fee position.

The third phase involves subtracting the value of the leased fee from the overall property value in order to determine the residual value attributable to the leasehold position.

OVERALL PROPERTY VALUE

Cost Approach

The Cost Approach consists of estimating the value of the land plus the estimated development costs of the building and land improvements, less accrued depreciation.

The land value was derived from the Market Data Approach to vacant nearby land sales in the same zone and area.

Estimated development costs were obtained from builders and developers currently active in the Hartford area. The original construction costs in 1966, and such published cost data as Marshall Stevens Valuation Service, Dodge Reports, Dow Building Costs Calculator, and Boechk, were analyzed and considered in estimating the current building cost.

Land Value

Sale #1—Located on the north side of Roberts Street, East Hartford, Connecticut. Site contains 14.61 acres purchased in June of 1968 for $175,500, or $12,012 per acre, by Morrone, et al. Adjustments were necessary to compensate for time of sale, no rail, and location.

Date of Sale:	1968
Adjustments:	Time 1.30, rail 1.10, location 2.50
Comparability Index:	3.57
Adjusted Price Per Acre:	$42,900

Sale #2—Located on New State Road and Adams Street, Manchester, Connecticut. Site contains 5.401 acres purchased in November 1970 for $80,130, or $14,836 per acre, by James Melo and Howard Miller. Adjustments were necessary to compensate for location, topography (property is low and wet), and no rail.

Date of Sale:	1970
Adjustments:	Location 3.00, topography .80, rail 1.10
Comparability Index:	2.64
Adjusted Price Per Acre:	$39,200

Sale #3—Located on Skitchewaug Street, Windsor, Connecticut. Site contains 9.33 acres purchased in February 1969 by American Standard for $100,000, or $10,718 per acre. Adjustments were necessary to compensate for time, location, and no rail.

Date of Sale:	1969
Adjustments:	Time 1.20, location 2.75, rail 1.10
Comparability Index:	3.63
Adjusted Price Per Acre:	$38,900

Sale #4—Located on the west side of Brainard Road, in the Brainard Industrial Park, Hartford, Connecticut. Site contains 6.25 acres purchased in July 1969 for $300,000, or $48,000 per acre, by Harry Simon. Adjustments were necessary to compensate for time and location.

Date of Sale:	1969
Adjustments:	Time 1.20, location .70
Comparability Index:	.84
Adjusted Price Per Acre:	$40,300

Summary of Land Value

Sale #1	$42,900
Sale #2	$39,200
Sale #3	$38,900
Sale #4	$40,300
Adopted for Use:	$40,000

Building Value

Warehouse and office area 121,175 sq. ft. at $9.20 per sq. ft.	$1,114,810
Land Improvements:	
Asphalt Paving—80,000 sq. ft. at $.45 per sq. ft.	36,000
Rail Siding—870 lineal feet at $16 per lineal foot	13,920
Total Estimated Improvement Value	$1,164,730
Less Accrued Physical Depreciation—10%	116,473
Total Estimated Improvement Value	$1,048,257

Land Value

5.32 Acres at $40,000 per Acre	$ 212,800
Estimated Land Value (Rounded)	$ 213,000
Estimated Improvement Value	$1,048,257
Estimated Land Value	$ 213,000
Total Estimated Value by Cost Approach	$1,261,257
Rounded to	$1,261,000

INCOME APPROACH

The Income Approach consists of estimating the economic rent, deducting vacancy allowances and other expenses, and translating the resulting net income into an indication of value using accepted capitalization procedures.

The following is a sample list of recently leased, newly developed one-story industrial buildings in the general area:

Location:	Ledyard Street, Hartford, Conn.
Size:	20,000 square feet
Tenant:	Allied Aluminum Company
Terms:	5 years from 1970
Rental Rate:	$1.65 net, with tax stop
Comments:	Location is superior to that of subject property.

Location:	Murphy Road, Hartford, Conn.
Size:	21,000 square feet
Tenant:	Kaiser Aluminum & Chemical Co.
Terms:	5 years from 1970

Rental Rate: $1.45 net
Comments: Location is superior to that of
                                    subject property.

Location: 218 Murphy Road, Hartford, Conn.
Size: 20,000 square feet
Tenant: Sperry Rand Corporation
Terms: 5 years from 1970
Rental Rate: $1.50 net
Comments: Location is more centralized than
                                    that of subject property.

Location: 121 Meadow St., Hartford, Conn.
Size: 8,000 square feet
Tenant: Automatic Distributors
Terms: 5 years from 1971
Rental Rate: $1.87 net, with tax stop
Comments: Location is superior to that of
                                    subject property.

Due to the height (the subject building has 26'-28' clear ceiling height offering substantially more cubic contents per square foot of ground area), design (the building is designed to facilitate the rapid handling of storage items), and location (in close proximity to major interstate highway systems), it is estimated that the net economic rent for the warehouse area is $1.10 per square foot by comparison.

The average rental for office area of this type has a net economic rental of $2.50 per square foot by comparison to other office space in the metropolitan Hartford area.

Net Income Estimate (Economic Rent)

Warehouse Area: 119,950 sq. ft. at
    $1.10 per sq. ft. $131,945
Office Area: 1,225 sq. ft. at $2.50
    per sq. ft. $ 3,062
Net Income Before Capital Requirements $135,007

Analysis of Capitalization Rate

The capitalization rate used in processing the net income attributable to the property into an indication of value represents the relationship between the value of the capital investment and the residual net income.

The rate represents a synthesis of current equity investment requirements, and the existing financing rate, term, and constant. It is assumed that the property would be sold on a cash-over-existing-financing basis.

The property was originally financed with a 6%, $650,000 direct reduction mortgage, fully amortizing in 15 years. Remaining balance as of the appraisal date approximates $493,994.

Basic elements of the capital structure are projected as 60% equity with a 12% return, the balance being secured by the existing 6% mortgage with 15 years' amortization by level installments.

Basic Capital Requirements

Interest Rate	6%
Equity Rate	12%
Amortization	15 years

.60 x .12 (equity dividend)   .0720
.40 x .1013 (annual constant)   .0405
Capitalization Rate   .1125%
$135,007 capitalized at 11.25% = $1,200,062

Rounded to   **$1,200,000**

Summary

Indicated Value by Cost Approach	$1,261,000
Indicated Value by Income Approach	$1,200,000

The subject property is income producing in nature, its value being directly related to the net income it produces and the cost of acquiring financing and equity capital for its acquisition.

After consideration of the aforementioned data, the indicated value of the total property rights, in fee simple, as of the appraisal date, is in the amount of:

$1,200,000

LEASED FEE VALUATION

The Terminal Warehouse Corp. has leased the property from the fee owner at the following terms and conditions:

Annual Rent: $95,832 (1st 16 years)
$95,832 (1- to 10-year option)*
Period: 4/1/67 to 3/31/87 (20-year lease) plus one ten-year option at same rate and terms
Terms: Net to fee owner

*The demand for the subject property can be reasonably expected to continue for a minimum of 26 years from the appraisal date. Although the lease agreement provides for one additional 10-year option, a prudent purchaser would tend to discount any benefit to be received past the 26th year period.

Hence, the fee owner's position includes the right to receive $95,832 per annum for the first years, and $95,832 per annum for 26 years, and the reversionary value of land and improvements at the end of the 26th year.

The interest rate selected as being applicable to the leased fee was determined after analysis of the overall rate, equity rate, and sale-leaseback transactions involving leased fees on properties exactly comparable to the subject.

The leased fee position is considered generally comparable to that of the first mortgage with the major difference lying in the relationship between the value of the leased fee and the overall property value.

First mortgage positions are limited by statute to a fixed percentage of their total value, usually ranging from 70-80% with 75% being the median. In the case of newly created leased fee positions, the ratio occasionally exceeds that of a first mortgage, hence requiring a higher rate than that of a first mortgage to compensate for the additional risk.

Market analysis has indicated that leased fee positions typically command a rate approximately 1% less than the overall rate which has been developed after consideration of the capital structure comprising the investment, and due to the fact that the property is leased to a major corporation on a long-term basis.

Indicated Leased Fee Rate—10%

For the purpose of determining the anticipated reversion at the end of the lease period, we have assumed that the improvements will be worth approximately 40% of their replacement value, plus a reversion of the present land value.

Due to the unknowns involved in projecting value over a long term, we have assumed that the improvements will depreciate on a straight-line basis. As the income is guaranteed by lease, it has been treated as an annuity. In all probability, the decline in building value will be offset by the increasing land values.

Actual Rental (1st 26 years)		$ 95,832
Present Worth Factor, 26 years 10% (Inwood)		x 9.161
Present Total Value of Income		$877,916
Reversion of Land, taken as	$213,000	
Reversion of Improvements, 40% of present value ($1,164,730)	$465,892	
	$678,892	
Present Worth Factor, 26 years at 9.5% (Inwood)	.0839	
Indicated Value of Reversion	$ 58,372	
Present Value of Income Stream		$877,916
Present Value of Reversion		$ 58,372
Total Value Leased Fee		936,288
	Rounded to	$936,300

VALUATION OF LEASEHOLD INTEREST

An indicated value of the leasehold can be obtained by deducting the present value of the leased fee from the total property value.

Present Total Property Value	$1,200,000
Present Value Leased Fee	$ 936,300
Indicated Value of Leasehold Interest	$ 263,700

The interest rate applicable to the leasehold interest can be determined by analyzing the relationship between the net income attributable to the leased fee position and the fair market value. The average annual net income attributable to the leasehold over the projection period is $39,725, which, when related to the value of the leasehold indicates a return rate of approximately 14.78%, which is slightly higher than the present equity rates that would attract prudent capital to this type of property.

Due to the fact that the leasehold position has a higher degree of risk as compared to the leased fee position, a prudent investor would require a greater return. The risk inherent in the leasehold position is usually reflected in the return rate which ranges from 30-50% greater than that of the leased fee rate.

CORRELATION AND VALUE CONCLUSION

Indicated Value of Leasehold Interest	$263,700
Indicated Value of Leased Fee	$936,300
Indicated Total Property Value (Fee Simple Interest)	$1,200,000

The indicated total property value is the result of processing the net income attributable to the whole by a capitalization rate selected by a mortgage/equity band of investment.

The indicated value of the leased fee position is the result of processing the contract rental for 26 years at 9.5% interest plus the reversionary value of the improvements and land at the end of the lease period.

The indicated leasehold value was determined by deducting the present value of the leased fee from the indicated overall property value.

The resulting interest rate of 14.78% accurately reflects the risk inherent in this position when compared to first mortgage and equity rates.

Based upon the aforementioned data, as well as the general economic conditions and demand for this type of property, we are of the opinion that the value of the leasehold position attributable to the Terminal Warehouse Corp. as of February 1, 1971 is in the amount of:

Two Hundred Sixty-Three Thousand Seven Hundred Dollars
($263,700)

CERTIFICATION

1. We have appraised the property in fee simple.

2. We have no interest present or contemplated nor is compensation contingent on the amount reported.

3. A member of the firm has made a physical inspection of the site and the surrounding area.

4. No representation is made concerning the validity of title.

5. We certify that the appraisal has been made in accordance with the standards of good appraisal practice.

6. The total estimated leasehold value of the subject property as of February 1, 1971 is in the amount of:

Two Hundred Sixty-Three Thousand Seven Hundred Dollars
($263,700)

_____
Staff Appraiser

The subject of this chapter is a group of electronic specialty buildings constructed during World War II and the Korean War when military communications panels were built the size of boxcars, requiring 40- and 50-foot ceilings with overhead cranes to move the heavy equipment. Since 1958, these huge circuit conductors have been reduced to the size of postcards, some as small as cigarette lighters. The new, smaller products are far more delicate than the old, and require dust-proof, perfect climate control rooms housing delicate laboratory equipment. This has only been accomplished at great cost by lowering ceilings, boxing in sound-proofed clean space, narrowing corridors, and keeping the converted space spotlessly clean. This is an excellent example of "convertibility."

19

Appraising a Special-Purpose Factory with Convertible Features

KEY CONSIDERATIONS OF VALUE IN CONVERTING OBSOLESCENT SPACE

The conversions to modernity mentioned above have still left 20% to 30% overall of inutile, barnlike, obsolescent, old-fashioned space, particularly in the basement areas and high-roof areas. Therefore, the problem of what to do with the functionally inutile space is a difficult one for company engineers and planners who might hope to rent out at least some of the unused areas, possibly all of it. For instance:

1. A heliport on the rooftop with lounges and guest accommodations in the high-ceiling areas.
2. A compatible, clean, fumeless industry in the unused basement areas. (This might be difficult to find, but not impossible.)

Alternatives:

   (a) If the older space now unusable to the owners proves to be unrentable over a long period of time, the owners should file an ad valorem property tax appeal with the local taxing jurisdiction, basing their case on *functional obsolescence* for the unusable areas. If they are turned down, their next consideration might be:

(b) To put the entire plant up for sale. If they do this and it fails to sell over, say, a five-year period, the only remaining alternative is to:

(c) Live with the situation and file a property tax appeal each and every year meanwhile.

It is the appraiser's duty to counsel the owners after handing them his report on each of these alternatives. Before giving such advice to his client, the appraiser has, of course, written and delivered a full-blown, three-approach appraisal. To accomplish that, he has gathered and reflected on rental and market sales data of similar buildings in the area. He has inspected and photographed these comparables and is now tuned in on the pulse of the market in the vicinity. The following model appraisal will demonstrate what the appraiser has accomplished before counseling his client.

MODEL APPRAISAL

In the appraisal following, whose function is to provide company engineers and planners with some possible solutions, the difficulties encountered in making the most of the plant's convertible features will be demonstrated, with evidences of effort to salvage nonconvertible, special-purpose, original parts of the structures that are soundly built and very well located, within four miles of the Lincoln Tunnel into Manhattan.

SUMMARY

Subject Property	General Electronics
	Elgin Drive
	Clift View, New Jersey
Site Area	60 Acres
Improvement Area	
(Nine Structures Totaling):	924,725 ± Square Feet
Obsolescent Area 9 Structures:	247,288 Square Feet
Converted Features:	677,437 Square Feet
Market Value via Cost Approach:	$11,700,000
Market Value via Income Approach:	$10,500,000
Market Value via Market Data	
Approach:	$10,000,000
Final Conclusion of Value:	$10,000,000

PURPOSE AND FUNCTION OF APPRAISAL

The appraisal was made for the purpose of estimating the market value of the subject property, including land and improvements, as of October 1, 1974.

The function of the evaluation, made for subject management, engineers, planners, real estate consultants employed by the company and prospective lessees of waste space, is to break down the functional or useful parts of the plant now modernized versus the inutile areas, and to discover what curable functional obsolescence might be achieved.

REAL ESTATE TAX DATA

	1975 Assessment
Land	$ 3,987,000
Buildings	13,572,000
Total	$17,559,000

HIGHEST AND BEST USE

We are of the opinion that the present use of the subject property is, at present, its highest, best, and most profitable use, if the curable functional inutility can be overcome.

LEGAL DESCRIPTION

The subject property is defined in the assessor's records of Clift View as Block 22-A, Lot No. 4.

We have not included a detailed legal description within this report due to its length, but consider that the references to the assessment parcel recorded and the plat and building plans will serve as adequate identification.

ZONE

M-2, General Manufacturing, Heavy Industry.

UTILITIES

Gas, water, and heavy power (26KV) on site. Sanitary and storm sewers connected.

AREA DATA

Clift View is located in Bergen County, northern New Jersey, within the metropolitan area and only 14 miles from Times Square in New York City. It comprises 11-3/4 square miles, is one of the largest cities in area in the state, and has a population of approximately 90,000.

Governed by council-manager, the city is being operated economically on a strictly "cash basis" showing an excellent financial condition with a steadily declining "capital debt."

Clift View has one of the most remarkable diversifications of industry of any community of its size. Some of the larger firms are Tallmark-LaGrande; Belmont Laboratories, Pentex Corporation; and many others.

Clift View public schools house 12,500 pupils in 18 buildings, including a special Cerebral Palsy School, and is the seventh largest school system in the state of New Jersey.

In addition to local transportation facilities, Clift View has great advantages for the manufacturer, the businessperson, and home seekers such as railroad services for shippers and commuters; many direct bus lines to New York City and other nearby cities such as Paterson, Passaic, and Newark; and direct highways to the George Washington Bridge, Holland Tunnel, Lincoln Tunnel, Garden State Parkway, and the New Jersey Turnpike.

SITE DATA

The subject site encompasses an overall area of 60 acres fronting on Elgin Drive and running through to Route 3 between River and Paddle Brook Roads. It is located in the southeasterly corner of Clift View on the Passaic town line.

The overall tract is level at road grade, sloping off to the rear. Formerly farmland and later a golf course, it has a rich loam and gravel surface in its varying sections with a hardpan subsoil. Drainage appears adequate.

The site is largely in grass with planting well kept. Three approaches to the buildings on site are paved in bituminous macadam; and paved areas, including parking, total 800,000 square feet.

The location offers easy access to main arteries, and the site is afforded public transportation by bus to New York. The environs are spacious and well landscaped.

All public utilities are connected on site.

LAND EVALUATION

We have noted in the Addenda five industrial land sales in Clift View occurring in the foregoing four years. These comparables range in price from $51,823 to $75,150 per acre. Careful research of available land records in the area of subject reveal no sales showing increase over these sale prices. We believe that subject land, overall, ranging from, say, $85,000 along the Route 3 frontage to $50,000 along Elgin Drive, averages in value at an average of $60,000 per acre.

Therefore: 60 acres @ $60,000 per acre produces an overall land value of:

$3,600,000

COST APPROACH

Description of the Improvements and Cost New

In order to facilitate the description of the improvements, we will refer to them by letter as they appear on the attached plat plan following.

In referring to reproduction cost new calculations, we applied square-foot base figures taken from Section 14, Page 11, Industrial Buildings (Calculator Method), Marshall & Swift Valuation Manual, November, 1974. We defined subject buildings in general within that manual as Industrial Buildings, Class B, ranging between good and average.

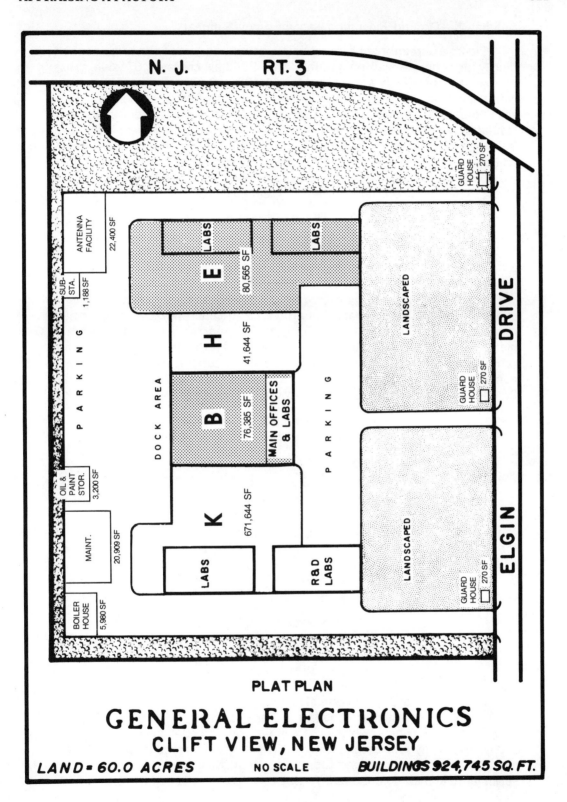

PLAT PLAN

GENERAL ELECTRONICS
CLIFT VIEW, NEW JERSEY
LAND = 60.0 ACRES   NO SCALE   **BUILDINGS 924,745 SQ. FT.**

Building K—Ground Floor and Second Floor Summary

Floors are reinforced concrete slab, beam and girder supports, asphalt tiled with concrete slab on ground. This building contains 671,644 gross square feet of which approximately 510,000 square feet are used for manufacturing. The walls are steel frame bonded to concrete block with steel sash. Roof is flat, reinforced concrete slab with beam and girder supports, is insulated, and built up. Exterior is face brick veneer over concrete block. The building has, in part, recessed fluorescent lighting and drop ceilings, and is heated and partly air conditioned. Completely sprinklered, brass and copper plumbing, buss ducts, and cast-iron drains. 30% of this building is unused. About 70% has been modernized at great expense.

Reproduction Cost New

671,644 SF @ $16.50/SF = $11,082,126

Building B Summary

Floor is concrete slab on ground and over basement portion with part asphalt tiling. Walls are steel frame bonded to concrete block. Roof is flat, reinforced concrete slab, beam and girder supports. The building is completely sprinklered. The exterior is brick veneer over concrete block. Fully air conditioned, cast-iron interior drains, brass and copper plumbing, and buss ducts are included in Building B. Total gross floor area is 76,385 square feet. 25% is unused; the balance has been modernized at heavy capital input.

Reproduction Cost New

76,385 SF @ $18/SF = $1,374,930

Building H Summary

Floor is reinforced concrete slab. Walls are steel frame bonded to concrete block. Roof is flat, reinforced concrete slab. Built in 1944 and renovated in 1958 and is in good condition. Beam and girder supports. Exterior is brick veneer over concrete block. Cast-iron interior drains. Brass and copper plumbing, buss ducts, fully sprinklered, and partly air conditioned. Total gross floor area is 41,664 square feet. 25% of this space is archaic and unused. The balance has been modernized at heavy investment.

Reproduction Cost New

41,664 SF @ $18.25/SF = $760,368

Building E Summary

Floor is reinforced concrete slab supported by beam and girder, except for shed extension which is wood frame. Partly asphalt tile flooring. Walls are steel frame over concrete block. Roof is flat, reinforced concrete slab, beam and girder. Partly suspended ceiling with recessed fluorescent lighting. Cast-iron interior drains, brass and copper plumbing, buss ducts. Building is fully sprinklered and air conditioned. Total gross floor area is 80,565 square feet.

20% of this 1944 building is unused. The balance has been modernized with expensive laboratories and heavy wiring for experimental processing.

Reproduction Cost New

80,565 SF @ $19/SF = $1,530,735

Antenna Facility Summary

Floor is concrete slab on ground. Walls are painted concrete block over steel frame with stucco exterior. Roof is 20-gauge steel sections, one-inch insulation, tar and gravel. Wall height is 22 feet with a total gross area of 22,400 square feet. No functional obsolescence. Modern equipment.

Reproduction Cost New

22,400 SF @ $15/SF = $336,000

Oil and Paint Storage Summary

Floor is reinforced concrete slab, beam and girder support. Steel plate and steel frame. Walls are reinforced concrete, asbestos board and steel frame in parts. Roof is flat, reinforced concrete slab supported by beam and girder. Exterior is brick veneer. Concrete loading dock, 8 feet x 40 feet. Total gross area, including loading dock, is 3,200 square feet. Serviceable and functional structure. No obsolescence.

Reproduction Cost New

3,200 SF @ $11.26/SF = $36,032

Maintenance Building Summary

Floor is reinforced concrete slab. Walls are concrete block with brick veneer exterior. Roof is flat, reinforced concrete slab. Partially air conditioned with units in office areas. Adequate toilet facilities. Copper and brass plumbing, buss ducts. Total gross area is 20,909 square feet. No functional problems.

Reproduction Cost New

20,909 SF @ $12.15/SF = $254,044

Boiler House Summary

Floors are reinforced concrete slab, beam and girder. Walls are reinforced concrete frame, cement block fill, with brick veneer exterior. Roof is flat, reinforced concrete slab. Contains three Wickes Boilers, four air compressors, burners (Bunker C). Pumps, piping, and accessories affixed to the realty. Total gross area is 5,980 square feet. Performing its function as designed.

Reproduction Cost New

5,980 SF @ $60/SF = $358,800

Substation Summary

Structure is 18 feet x 66 feet, overall exterior dimensions. Floor is concrete slab on ground. Walls are cement block fill, concrete frame. Roof is flat, reinforced concrete slab on reinforced concrete beams. Contains sheltered panels and equipment for the transformation of heavy power. Total gross area is 1,188 square feet. Excellent performance. No obsolescence.

Reproduction Cost New

1,188 SF @ $150/SF = $178,200

Guardhouses (Three) Summary

Structures are brick veneer over cement block on concrete slabs, flat gravel composition roofs. All three structures are heated, but only the main entrance guardhouse has toilet facility. Total gross area is 810 square feet. Simple structures performing their designed purposes.

Reproduction Cost New

810 SF @ $15.10/SF = $12,231

Description of Yard Improvements and Cost New

Fencing—4,950 linear feet of eight-foot high chain link fencing and gates.

Reproduction Cost New

4,950 LF @ $6.85/LF = $33,908
(Including Posts and Gates)

Paving—800,000 square feet of bituminous macadam.

Reproduction Cost New

800,000 SF @ $.40/SF = $320,000

Recapitulation

Total Reproduction Cost New of Buildings =	$15,923,466
Total Square Feet Involved =	924,725
Average Cost New of Buildings	
$15,923,466 ÷ 924,725 SF =	$17.22/SF
Total Reproduction Cost New of Yard Improvements =	$ 353,908
Total Reproduction Cost New of All Improvements =	$16,277,374

DEPRECIATION SCHEDULE

Building	Date Built	Total Sq. Ft.	Price/ Sq. Ft.	Reprod. Cost	Physical Deprec.	Depre. Cost	Funct. Obsol.	Deprec. Value
K	1948	671,644	$ 16.50	$11,082,126	27% $2,992,174	$8,089,952	30% $2,426,985	$5,662,967
B	1944	76,385	18.00	1,374,930	31% 426,228	948,702	25% 237,175	711,527
H	1944	41,664	18.25	760,368	31% 235,714	524,654	25% 131,163	393,491
E	1944	80,565	19.00	1,530,735	31% 474,528	1,056,207	25% 264,052	792,155

Note: Ancillary buildings are advanced to 1.5% physical depreciation because they are of less durable construction than the prime buildings and suffer a heavier wear and tear life.

Building	Date Built	Total Sq. Ft.	Price/ Sq. Ft.	Reprod. Cost	Physical Deprec.	Depre. Cost	Funct. Obsol.	Deprec. Value
Antenna Facility	1952	22,400	15.00	336,000	34.5% 115,290	220,080	- 0 -	220,080
Oil and Paint Storage	1948	3,200	11.26	36,032	40.5% 14,593	21,439	- 0 -	21,439
Maintenance Building	1948	20,909	12.15	254,044	40.5% 102,888	151,156	- 0 -	151,156
Boiler House	1948	5,980	60.00	358,800	40.5% 145,314	213,486	- 0 -	213,486
Substation	1948	1,188	150.00	178,200	40.5% 72,171	106,029	- 0 -	106,029
Guardhouse (3)	1948	810	15.10	12,231	40.5% 4,953	7,278	- 0 -	7,278
Totals		924,725		$15,923,466	$4,583,853		$3,059,375	$8,279,608

Summary

Total Depreciated Cost of Improvements		$ 8,279,608
Total Reproduction Cost New of Yard Improvements	$353,908	
Less 50 Percent Depreciation—All Sources	176,954	176,954
Total Depreciated Cost of Buildings and Yard Improvements		$ 8,102,654
Add Land Value		3,600,000
	Total	$11,702,654
	Rounded to:	$11,700,000

Value Conclusion via Cost Approach
$11,700,000

INCOME APPROACH

The Income Approach to the value estimate is an appraisal technique in which the anticipated net income is processed to indicate the capital value of the asset by capitalization. Since subject property is owner occupied, we have established an economic rental reflective of the current market on which to base a hypothetical lease.

As a precursor to the development of the income analysis, we examined the land-to-building ratio existing within the subject complex and found this to be land, 60 acres; building, 21.23, say 21 acres. Normal industrial requirement varies from 2.5 to 3.0; therefore, the ratio, land-to-buildings in this case is 2.85 and there is no excess land.

We examined industrial rental values prevailing in the general Clift View area and found that newly developed industrial premises of moderate size (100,000 to 169,000 square feet) rented at $1.00 to $1.32 per square foot net per annum dependent on the lease term and lessee covenant.

In considering the rental value of the subject complex, it is necessary to be cognizant of the lessee/purchaser reactions. These might vary as follows:

1. The complex has been developed over a substantial period of time, and, especially adapted to the needs of the present user, would have limited appeal to a future lessee/purchaser.
2. The location of the various structures is presumably to accommodate the work flow of the present occupant and might require considerable reorganization to meet the needs of any other industry.
3. An industrial complex of this magnitude would only be of attraction to a major industry; and major industry, being possessed of financial strength, does not often acquire buildings especially built for others.
4. If, indeed, a single occupant were not attracted to this complex, the alternative use is one of adaption to meet the needs of a small user, which would itself reflect on the head rent/purchase price, the cost of conversion, the delay in the production of revenue, and entrepreneurial reward.

Six economic comparable net rentals of office/warehouse/manufacturing space in the North and Central New Jersey area surrounding the subject property that show a typical inflationary trend of industrial rental values in the past several years, including 1974 (in spite of recessive tendencies in other areas and other types of industry) would be cited at this point, but in the interest of brevity will be omitted and summarized.

These rentals ranged from $1.20/square foot to $1.40/square foot for comparable space with equal functional inutilities, and were of approximately the same age and in the same zone with close approximation of locational value.

Therefore, we have selected $1.30/square foot as a fair net rent for subject, as follows:

924,745 Square Feet at $1.30/Square Foot = $1,202,168
Annual Net Rental Value, Rounded To: $1,202,000

Valuation of Land and Improvements via Income Approach
(Using Building Residual Technique)

Value of the Land = $3,360,000
Net Income $1,202,000
Interest Imputable to Land
  ($3,600,000 x 9%)   324,000
Interest to Improvements $ 878,000
Therefore, $878,000 ÷ 13% = $6,753,846
Add Land   3,600,000
                            Total $10,353,846
                            Rounded to: $10,500,000

Value Conclusion via Income Approach
$10,354,000

Explanation of Capitalization Rate

A responsible investor would expect to be able to procure a mortgage of 65 percent of the value of the subject property as if leased to a rated tenant at an interest rate of 8.50%
the product of which is 5.53%
and Equity of 35 percent at 10 percent return 3.50%
                                        Total 9.03%
                                        Rounded to: 9.00%

Recapture

On acquiring buildings of the age and type of the subject, an informed investor would expect a recapture of investment in 25 years, or at the rate of four percent per annum; then,
Interest on Land 9.00%
Interest and Recapture on Improvement 4.00%
                                        Total 13.00%

MARKET DATA APPROACH

The Market Data Approach is employed to compare prices paid for land and buildings in relation to subject building areas, both locally and areawide. We have found five sales of properties comparable to subject property, two larger than subject selling at $5 and $6 per square foot, and three about half the size of subject selling at $7.50 and $9.75 per square foot. However, we accord the subject a certain superiority over the market because of its location, its relationship to divisional offices in Passaic, and its ready access to Manhattan. The following sales are submitted. We have adjusted for the amount of functional inutility in subject, but also for capital input to modernize its best areas.

Here the five sales would be cited, Book, Page and Record, date of sale, price per square foot, etc. We omit them here for brevity.

Analysis and Summary

We have analyzed all pertinent information and have studied sale prices for comparable size improvements. In relating the subject property to the comparables submitted, we have made adjustments for time of sale, location, size, acreage, and overall comparability. Based on these facts, we feel that all of the comparables are inferior in quality to subject and have made the necessary adjustments. Therefore:

924,745 ± Square Feet @ $10.50/Square Foot = $9,709,822
Rounded to: $9,710,000

Value Conclusion via Market Data Approach
$9,710,000

CORRELATION AND VALUE CONCLUSION

The three approaches to value have produced the following conclusions:

Cost Approach	$11,700,000
Income Approach	$10,500,000
Market Data Approach	$ 9,710,000

The Cost Approach, which normally sets the upper limit of value, was developed after determining local construction costs from discussions with the plant engineer of the subject property, by reference to national valuation manuals, and from the appraisers' first-hand experience in the building trades. The unit costs applied were derived to include the current costs for labor, materials, profit, and overhead. Depreciation allowances were taken for physical deterioration and functional obsolescence.

An economic rental was utilized in order to derive the hypothetical income estimate for the property. The conjectural rental is calculated at the current market. A majority of comparable industrial facilities are being leased on a net basis and that is the approach utilized in the report. The capitalization rate was derived through interest rates applicable to the subject in today's market.

The Market Data Approach has a strong application by way of local and national comparable sales data. A highly probable selling price on the open market was determined through sales of industrial, research, office, and warehouse properties in the same and nearby areas.

In reviewing depreciable items in our Cost Approach and in determining what features were curable or incurable, we looked mainly to dollar value cost to cure in our estimates of functional inutility.

Great consideration has been given to whether the buildings are well planned, efficient in operation, and convertible to other modern industrial uses. Since our principal concern in this report is fair market value, we found that large areas of the buildings were antiquated and of little operational value to the owners and likely to require expensive modifications to possible lessees or buyers.

Our arrival at value conclusion has been forged by the following principle:

"The appraiser does not average the indications of value by the three approaches. He selects the one which is more applicable, and rounds to a final figure. He places the most emphasis on the approach which appears to be the most reliable and most applicable, as an indication of the answer to the specific appraisal problem. Then he tempers this estimate in accordance with his judgment as to the degree of reliance to be placed on the other two indications of value." (The Appraisal of Real Estate, published by The American Institute of Real Estate Appraisers, Chicago, Illinois, Fifth Edition, 1971.)

Although the subject property is not presently leased for income and the property is not for sale, we have put reliance on all three approaches; and we have tempered these values into a conclusion. It is the opinion of the appraisers that the value of the subject property as of October 1, 1974 is:

TEN MILLION DOLLARS
($10,000,000)

Occasionally, a client will ask an appraiser for a report involving more than one kind of value, perhaps three, as is evidenced in the model appraisal in this chapter. This does not necessarily make for great complication in the report, since most often one kind of value is a direct cue to the next. The reason for such a request is that various departments of the client organization, i.e. Insurance, Corporate Accounting, and the Tax Director may want differing values all wrapped in one, easy-to-hand-around report (for one fee!). Appraisers: Beware bargain hunters; the hours are long and hard.

20

Industrial Appraising for More Than One Purpose

PROCEDURAL STEPS WHEN EVALUATING FOR MORE THAN ONE PURPOSE

Step 1

When you are appraising a property for more than one type of value, begin with the simplest form of value; in the model appraisal at the end of this chapter it is insurable value.

Step 2

Insurable value has thus given you the skeletal outline of the Cost Approach, but without land value, site preparation, excavation, and underground wiring and piping. Now you must find these values to add to the picture for market value. Rental data must be collected and adjusted to the subject. Market data such as sales of similar buildings will have to be brought in. Thus, Step 2 is going to be the most formidable task among the three values asked for in this model appraisal.

Step 3

Finding assessment value is the easiest of the three values sought because the tax ratio is often 100% of market value. But, if the taxing jurisdiction ratio were 75% of market value, or 25% of market value, then those percentages would be assessment value.

You might be asked, on occasion, to define three or four *other* types of value for a property: value in use, market value as of some date in the distant past, mortgage value, and/or rental value. Here again, you select the simplest form of value first, which, in this case, would be rental value gathered from the marketplace; then, as in Step 2, build your report into the most difficult valuation, which would be value in use.

CONSIDERATIONS OF VALUE FOR VARIABLE PURPOSES

Because the following model appraisal demonstrates all the practices, principles, procedures, and techniques already set forth in preceding chapters, and because each of the three variable values involved hang directly upon one another, we will not go into lengthy explanations as to the principles involved in each type of evaluation. We present the complete report, commencing here with the Letter of Transmittal.

MODEL APPRAISAL

December 31, 1971

Mr. Floyd W. Rivers, Controller
Frick International, Ltd.
One NCNB Plaza
Charlotte, N.C. 28280

Re: Appraisal Report
920 S. W. 5th Street
Phoenix, Arizona 85202

Gentlemen:

Pursuant to your request, we submit an appraisal report relative to this property. A personal inspection of the real estate and of local conditions has been made by a member of our staff with analysis of all relevant data being utilized in determining the respective values.

The following report, including exhibits, fully describes the method of approach and contains all pertinent data gathered in our investigation of the subject.

After careful consideration, we have concluded that as of September 10, 1971, the following values are applicable:

(a) Value for Insurance Purposes $543,000
(b) Market Value $640,000
(c) Assessment Estimate $160,000

We certify that we have no present or contemplated financial interest in the subject property and that our employment and compensation are in no way contingent upon that value reported.

Respectfully submitted,

SUMMARY OF FACTS AND CONCLUSIONS

Subject Property:	920 S.W. 5th Street
	Phoenix, Arizona
Date of Appraisal:	September 10, 1971
Site Area:	10.11 Acres
Gross Building Area:	60,451 Square Feet
Potential Net Annual Income:	$ 60,936
Site Value:	$101,000
Value for Insurance Purposes:	$543,000
Market Value:	$640,000
Assessment Estimate:	$160,000

TABLE OF CONTENTS

Page

PURPOSE OF APPRAISAL

The appraisal was made for the purpose of estimating the market value of the subject property, including land and improvements, together with the value for insurance purposes and a review of the realty assessment currently applicable to the property.

MARKET VALUE

For the purpose of this appraisal, market value is defined as the highest price estimated in terms of money which a property will bring if exposed for sale in the open market, allowing a reasonable time to find a purchaser who buys with knowledge of all the uses to which it is adapted, and for which it is capable of being used. Frequently, it is referred to as the price at which a willing seller would sell and a willing buyer would buy, neither being under abnormal pressure. It is the price expectable if a reasonable time is allowed to find a purchaser and if both seller and prospective buyer are fully informed.

PROPERTY RIGHTS APPRAISED

The property rights appraised are all rights existing in fee simple as of the appraisal date. These rights are the legal and economic properties of the owner that may rightfully be exchanged for money or equivalent goods. Property rights inherent in the ownership of tangible personal property, and intangible benefits of the property itself, are not the subject of this report.

LIMITING CONDITIONS

Areas and dimensions of the property were not physically measured but were taken from plat plans furnished by the principal. No survey has been made of the property by this appraiser, and he assumes no responsibility for the dimensions or areas determined thereby or for any matters legal in nature.

The resultant estimate of market value is predicated on the financial structure currently prevailing.

It is assumed that there is a good and marketable title and that there are no restrictions as to use except those imposed by public ordinance.

Verification of factual matters contained in this report has been made to the extent deemed practicable.

Market data has been taken from sources deemed to be reliable but which could not be verified in all cases.

The apportionment between the land and buildings in the report applies only under the existing program of utilization. the separate valuations for land and building may not be used in conjunction with any other appraisal and are invalid if so used.

REAL ESTATE TAX DATA

The property is subject to the assessments and taxes as promulgated by the county of Maricopa. The real estate assessments and taxes levied on the property are as follows:

County of Maricopa (25% Ratio)
Land	$16,430.00
Improvements	82,405.00
Total	$98,835.00
1971 Tax Rate/Hundred	x 14.84
Taxes	$14,667.11

ZONING

Under the zoning ordinance for the city of Phoenix, the property is zoned A2.

LEGAL DESCRIPTION

The property is found on the county records as:

19 1N 5G
BEG 980.08' N FR E 4 COR SD SEC TH W 1359.82' TO POB TH S 80' W
926.01' TH N 422' TH CONT N 263' TH S 24 DEGREES 01' E 285.92'
TH E 848.27' TH S 342.02' TH W 36.27' TO POB AND ALSO THAT PT OF
ABANDONED JEFFERSON ST PER D/P 9363-604.
10.11 AC

AREA DATA

Population of metropolitan Phoenix, 1970, was approximately 900,000.
The city of Phoenix is known as the financial and industrial center of
Arizona. The tax rate of the city has remained the same for the past 13 years.
Manufacturers, wholesalers, and retailers are not required to pay any tax on
inventories, which makes Phoenix a fast-growing city.

Transportation

Phoenix is served by ten airlines, two transcontinental railroads, ten
transcontinental truck lines, four transcontinental heavy equipment haulers,
three transcontinental automobile transporters, and thirty-nine interstate
truck lines.

Air transportation is available at Sky Harbor Airport providing international and regional services.

Rail

The Atchison, Topeka & Sante Fe, and Southern Pacific Company
provide transportation service from Phoenix to all of the United States,
Mexico, and Canada.

Roads

There are excellent state and federal freeways and highways servicing
the Phoenix area.

Utilities

Metropolitan Phoenix is served by two major energy suppliers—Arizona
Public Service and The Salt River Project provide a heavy supply of power.

The subject site is centrally located with easy access to all main arteries. The Sky Harbor Air Terminal is located about a mile from the subject
property.

THE APPRAISAL PROCESS

In accordance with our instructions, we shall consider within the
framework of this report:
A. The Appraisal for Insurance Purposes

B. The Appraisal of Current Market Value

In the formulation of this study, we shall utilize two accepted methods of valuation:

1. The Cost Analysis, which will be developed from the preceding insurance value, modified by depreciation from all sources, to which will be added the current value of the land.
2. The Investment Analysis. Under this method of valuation, we have projected the current market rental indicated by an analysis of comparable properties and capitalized the resultant in accordance with market behavior in the sale of such investment properties.

C. Appraisal for Assessment Purposes

We developed from the market value analysis an indication of an assessment value which we would deem equitable and report to you thereunder as to our recommendations in respect of the advisability of appeal.

SITE DATA

The subject site is an irregularly shaped plot. The total land area consists of 10.11 acres. The site is improved with a warehouse, rail, and paved parking areas. The subject site has frontage on 5th Street.

The property has 3.11 acres of excess land reserved for expansion. The primary 7.0 acres is utilized for the existing improvements.

SITE VALUE

In Addendum A, we have analyzed a number of land sales of comparable properties to that of the subject and have concluded that a land value of $10,000 per acre was evidenced for both the primary lands and excess land.

Plant Use	7.0 Acres @ $10,000 =	$ 70,000
Excess Land	3.11 Acres @ $10,000 =	31,100
	Total Site Value:	$101,100
	Rounded to:	$101,000

IMPROVEMENT DATA

The subject property consists of a single-story warehouse building with loading dock. Building, which was built in 1970, comprises an area of 38,199 square feet, and loading dock comprises 22,252 square feet. Construction is of pre-cast concrete. Warehouse area consists of 27,480 square feet with an office area of 10,719 square feet. The ceiling heights are 20 feet in the warehouse and 14 feet in the office area. The building is sprinklered.

The interior finish of the office area has vinyl tile floor covering, frame partitions, fluorescent lighting, and acoustical tile ceilings.

The warehouse area has a concrete floor covered with resilient tile. The roof is flat with wood joists. The frame is of reinforced concrete with timber beam supports.

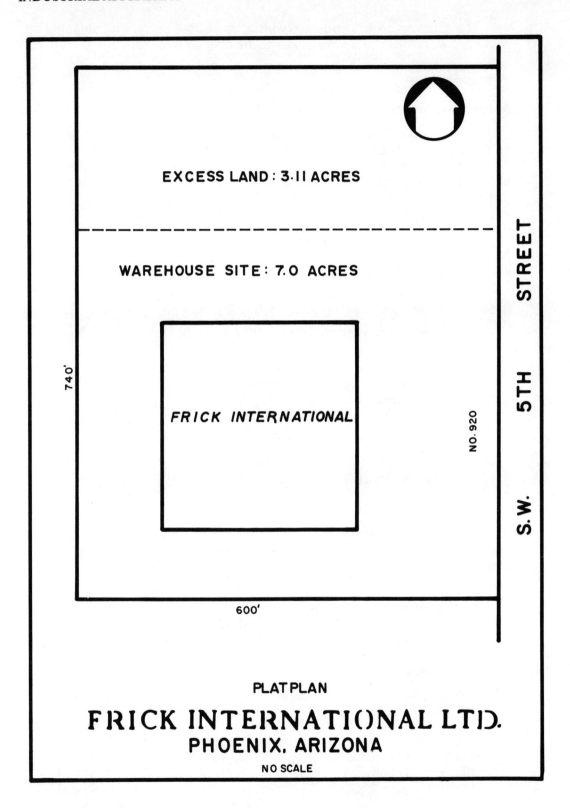

EXCESS LAND : 3.11 ACRES

WAREHOUSE SITE : 7.0 ACRES

FRICK INTERNATIONAL

740'

NO. 920

600'

S.W. 5TH STREET

PLAT PLAN

FRICK INTERNATIONAL LTD.
PHOENIX, ARIZONA
NO SCALE

The shipping dock is concrete with a frame roof cover. The shipping docks and warehouse both have access to the railroad track spur.

THE APPRAISAL

A. Appraisal for Insurance Purposes

In developing unit costs, we referenced a number of accepted publications and adjusted our findings as to local cost indices.

Our instructions, obtained from Clifton & Company Insurance Brokers of Rochester, New York, are that insurable value shall be replacement cost less depreciation and less specific exclusions.

Our worksheets, which follow, indicate an insurable value of:

	$542,720
Rounded to:	$543,000
Value for Insurance Purposes:	$543,000

B. Market Value

We will employ the cost and investment approaches to value.

Cost Approach

Total Replacement Cost	$599,811
Less Depreciation	14,995
Depreciated Cost	$584,816
Add Land Value	100,000
Indicated Value	$684,816
Rounded to:	$685,000
Value by the Cost Approach:	$685,000

Investment Analysis

By an analysis of comparable rentals found in individual sites and industrial complexes, we concluded that the net annual rental value of the premises was as follows:

Office Area	10,719 SF x $1.90/SF	$20,366
Warehouse Areas	27,480 SF x $ .95/SF	26,106
Covered Dock	22,252 SF x $ .65/SF	14,464
Net Annual Income		$60,936

Capitalization Rate

60% Mortgage 9%/25 Yrs. (10.08)		6.05%
40% Equity 10%		4.00
		10.05%
	Rounded to:	10.0%
$60,936 Capitalized at 10.0%		$609,360
Plus Excess Land		30,000
Indicated Value		$639,360
	Rounded to:	$640,000

SUMMARY BUILDING APPRAISAL FORM

OWNER _____

Name of Bldg. __FRICK INTERNATIONAL, LTD.__
Located at __920 S.W. 5th Street__
OCCUPANCY (Present use): __Warehouse/Office__
QUALITY OF CONSTRUCTION: __Good__ GENERAL CONDITION: __Good__
OVERALL DIMENSIONS:
Width: __Irreg.__ Length: __Irreg.__ Height: Office __14'__ Warehouse __20'__
Total Floor Area Above Basement: __38,199__ Sq. Ft.
Total Floor Area of Basement: __N/A__ Sq. Ft.
KIND OF BLDG: Class __C-2__ NO. OF STORIES: __1__

	HIGH	WALL (LENGTH)
U	14'	(
V	20'	(
W		(
X		(
Y		(
Z		(

	AREA
Office	U
	V
Whse.	W
	X
	Y
	Z

TYPE	AREA	FLOOR AREA
		A (X) (X)
		B (X) (X)
		C (X) (X)
		D (X) (X)
		E (X) (X)
		F (X) (X)

BULK EXCAVATION: Width _____ Length _____ Depth _____
Excavation __120,902 Cu. Ft. x .10 = 12,090__
Site Preparation __174,240 Cu. Ft. x .06 = 10,454__

FOUNDATION: Including excavation for concrete footings under exterior
walls, interior partitions and columns. __Concrete Walls__

BASEMENT EXTERIOR WALLS: __N/A__

FRAME: __Wood Joist, Wood, Pre-cast Concrete__

	Replacement Cost			
LETTER DESIG.	UNIT COST	AREA	DEP	Sound Val. or Present Val.
*Bulk Exc.	$	22,544		$
C-2	.38	60,451		
*Foundation	$ 22,971			$
Bmnt. Ext.	$			$
C-2	1.63	60,451		
Frame	$ 98,535			$

329

FLOORS: Concrete on ground. Wood joists, subfloor and hardwood.
Concrete on Ground

	Code	Rate	Quantity	Total
	C-2	.78	60,451	
Floors				$47,152

FLOOR COVERING:
Resilient Tile in Offices
Hardener and Sealer

	Code	Rate	Quantity	Total
	C-3	.48	10,719	
	C-3	.17	27,480	
Floor Cov.				$ 9,817

CEILING:
Acoustical Tile on Suspended Ceiling in Offices

	Code	Rate	Quantity	Total
	C-3	1.05	10,719	
Ceiling				$11,255

INTERIOR CONSTRUCTION: Wood-framed partitions, plaster covered, dividing building into 2 rooms.
Base Warehouse
Office Area Sheet Rock

	Code	Rate	Quantity	Total
	C-2	.17	27,480	
	C-1	2.86	10,719	
Int. Const.				$35,328

ROOF STRUCTURE: (Flat) (Arched) (Gable) type; wood trussed ___ ft. span; wood rafters; purlins and sheathing.
Wood Joists and Deck
Wood Canopy

	Code	Rate	Quantity	Total
	C-2	1.24	60,451	
	C-1	1.00	16,192	
Roof Struct.				$91,151

ROOF COVER: Composition ready rolled, asphalt base. Base.
Canopy

	Code	Rate	Quantity	Total
	C-2	.19	60,451	
	C-1	.17	16,192	
Roof Cover				$14,239

EXTERIOR WALLS: (Wood frame), (Brick), exterior covered with stucco, inside covered with plaster _____

| | Replacement Cost | | | |
LETTER DESIG.	UNIT COST	AREA	DEP	Sound Val. or Present Val.
C-2	2.93	9,080		
C-2	2.66	3,930		
Ext. Walls	$37,058			$
Store Front	$			$
C-2	.53	27,480		
C-2	2.51	10,719		
Lighting	$41,469			$
				(% of the rep. cost or exc.) $
C-2	.27	38,199		
**Plumbing	$10,314			$
C-2	2.66	38,199		
Heating	$101,609			$
Ventilating	$			$

Warehouse, Tilt-up
Office, Block-mud brick

STORE FRONT: ___ lin. ft. plate glass ___ ft. high, metal casing, block tile trim.
N/A

LIGHTING: (fluorescent) (incandescent) fixtures; wiring in conduit.
Base Warehouse
Fluorescent Fixtures in Offices

MAIN AND DISTRIBUTION PANELS INCLUDE:

PLUMBING: 7 toilets, 6 lavatories, ___ sinks, 4 urinals, ___ bathtubs, 1 showerheads, ___ floor drains, ___ water softeners, ___ water heaters, 2 drinking fountains.
Base Warehouse

Price includes supply and vent piping.

HEATING: and Air Conditioning
Hot and Chill Water System

VENTILATING:

AIR CONDITIONING:
    Included in Heating Costs

FIRE PROTECTION: Automatic sprinklers including pipe, valves, fittings and heads.
    Wet System

ELEVATORS:
    N/A

ATTACHED EXTERIOR CONSTRUCTION: Fire escapes, canopies, porches, outside steps.

COMMENTS:

Air Cond.	$	
C-2	.46	60,451
Fire Prot.	$27,807	
Elevators	$	
Att. Ext. Const.	$	

Total Labor, Materials, Incidentals and Profit.	$571,249	XXX	$
Architects' Fees, Plans and Spec. %		XXX	
Architects' Fees, Supervision %		XXX	
Architects' Fees 5%	28,562	XXX	
TOTAL REPLACEMENT COST	$599,811	XXX	
Depreciation ($ 14,995) 2.5%		XXX	
TOTAL (PRESENT) (SOUND) VALUE		XXX	$584,816
LESS: (See Page)			
Rep. Cost of Exclusions	$ 49,957	XXX	
Sound Value of Exclusions		XXX	$ 48,709
REPLACEMENT INSURABLE VALUE	$549,854	XXX	
Deprec. on Ins. Value ($)		XXX	
SOUND INSURABLE VALUE		XXX	$536,107
Actual Sq. Ft. Cost			
OKed By			

ESTIMATED DATE OF CONSTRUCTION:

EXCLUSIONS

	Rep. Cost	Sound Value
*Totally Excluded Excav. Found	$45,515	$44,377
**Partially Excluded		
Underground Piping		
20% of Plumbing	2,063	2,012
Architects' Fees	2,379	2,320
TOTAL EXCLUSIONS	$49,957	$48,709

Appraiser	Estimated Sq. Ft. Cost
Date	Area Divided By

STORAGE TANKS
(UNDERGROUND PIPING EXCLUDED)

Two 6,000 Gallon Tanks	$3,890	x 2	$ 7,780		$

COMMENTS:

ESTIMATED DATE OF CONSTRUCTION: _____
EXCLUSIONS

	Rep. Cost	Sound Value
*Totally Excluded	$	$
**Partially Excluded		
Underground Piping		

Total Labor, Materials, Incidentals and Profit.	$ 7,780		$
Architects' Fees, Plans and Spec. %		XXX	XXX
Architects' Fees, Supervision %		XXX	XXX
		XXX	XXX
TOTAL REPLACEMENT COST	$ 7,780	XXX	$ 6,613
Depreciation ($1,167) 15%		XXX	XXX
TOTAL (PRESENT) (SOUND) VALUE			
LESS: (See Page)	$	XXX	
Rep. Cost of Exclusions		XXX	
Sound Value of Exclusions		XXX	
REPLACEMENT INSURABLE VALUE	$	XXX	$
Deprec. on Ins. Value ($)		XXX	
SOUND INSURABLE VALUE			$ 6,613
Actual Sq. Ft. Cost			
OKed By			

TOTAL EXCLUSIONS	$	$
Appraiser	Estimated Sq. Ft. Cost	
Date	Area Divided By	

333

Conclusion as to Market Value

We are of the opinion that the investment analysis is a more accurate interpretation of market value and consider $640,000 the market value at the present date.

<u>$640,000</u>

C. Appraisal for Assessment Purposes

In the preceding, we concluded that market value was defined at $640,000. Since the taxing authority indicated a market value/assessment ratio of 25 percent, the equitable level of assessment is indicated at $160,000.

Assessment Value $160,000

SUMMATION

In the foregoing analysis, we thoroughly investigated all the factors influencing value for each of the specific purposes required.

In conclusion, it is our opinion that as of September 10, 1971, the following values are applicable:

A. Value for Insurance Purposes $543,000
B. Market Value $640,000
C. Value for Assessment Purposes
   We concluded that $640,000 was representative of market value as of September 10, 1971. This value modified by the assessment ratio declared by the county of Maricopa would indicate an assessment of $160,000.

   A comparison of this figure in relation to the assessed value now prevailing indicates that the assessment is favorable at the present time, and an appeal to the assessing authority is not warranted.

TABLE OF COMPARABLE LAND VALUES

Description	Parties	Date	Zoning	Area	Price	Per Acre
N/S University and W/S 24th	Cabot & Cabot/J.C. Penney	3/31/69	I	19.36 Acres	$781,725	$40,378
N/S Broadway at 43rd Place	Cabot & Cabot/Nauman	3/31/69	I	2.29 Acres	$ 50,000	$21,834
S/S Elwood and Maricopa East of 40th Interchange	Cabot & Cabot/Pepsi Cola	5/ 1/69	I	24.28 Acres	$340,000	$14,003
N/W Raymond and 42nd Street	Cabot & Cabot/Ray Ind.	7/27/70	I	8.00 Acres	$129,329	$16,666
S/E 23rd Street/Sherman	Transamerica/Schellemberger	7/24/69	I	2.12 Acres	$ 90,000	$42,452
E/S 23rd 620's S. Buckeye	Smith/Rumsey	9/16/68	I	2.22 Acres	$ 59,657	$26,872

*Every professional appraiser, whether he is writing a
condemnation report or evaluating for mortgage financing,
for insurable values, or any other purpose, will have his
appraisal reviewed and critiqued by a senior specialist in the
institution, law or accounting firm to whom the report is
submitted. It's important, therefore, that the appraiser
himself know just what the reviewer will be looking for—
why and how his appraisal will be examined.*

21

The Appraiser's Appraiser:
What Appraisal Reviewers Look For

VITAL CONSIDERATIONS IN THE REVIEWER'S APPROACHES

The increased use of professional reviewers by government agencies, lending institutions, and individual attorneys and accountants has placed heavy demands on
independent field appraisers. This screening has developed over the years because of the
following.

Approach 1

Continuous Concentration to Develop Improved Appraisal Techniques. In reading
various professional appraisal publications, one is impressed by the flood of new ideas
and methods in the profession. The efforts of professional organizations to keep their
members abreast of this flood of information, through journals, research grants, appraisal courses, and scholarships, are well known. The professional reviewer absorbs
these activities and uses them daily in his screening process.

Approach 2

The development of new methods and procedures to protect the public and the
provisions for the use of professional reviewers to make broad surveys of the money and
land markets grew out of bank failures, fraudulent insurance claims, unfair prices paid
in eminent domain condemnation procedures, and sloppy, irrelevant work on the part of
the independent field appraiser.

337

Approach 3

Two examples of a reviewer's standards are:

(a) The field appraiser must have senior membership in a recognized national appraisal society.

(b) The reviewer will look to the professional appraisal organizations for continued careful self-policing of their members' ethics and competence. In this connection, the reviewer will refer cases where he finds substantial variations between values assigned by professional appraisers to the national organizations of which they are members. The various professional appraisal organizations have agreed to review such cases and take any appropriate corrective or disciplinary action.

Approach 4

The reviewer will further demand that the report he is reading is coherent and articulated as follows:

(a) Presentation—The report as a whole
(b) Continuity and Articulation
(c) Conviction and Accurate Calculations
(d) Value Conclusion

PRESENTATION

The report cover should be attractive and appealing to the reviewer and the nature of his profession. The paper should be of the highest grade obtainable, and the typewriter used must also be the best available. In addition, the initial appearance of the report should be pleasing, with regular and logical use of main headings, subheadings, and tabulated statements fully documented.

CONTINUITY AND ARTICULATION

In sum, two people are concerned with the report: the writer and the reviewer. They share equally in the worth of the report and must move together in a logical manner through the various findings and conclusions presented. Therefore, the report must certainly be prepared in realistic order. The typical report (for either counselling or valuation reporting services) is divided into sections by four printed pages titled:

Introduction—Letter of Transmittal, Table of Contents, Summary, main photograph, etc.

Report Data—Information regarding method of presentation, definitions, Purpose of the Report, notation as to items omitted from the report, Underlying Assumptions, and generally all other information concerned with the presentation.

Analysis and Conclusions—Containing the main body of data, interpretation, and conclusion.

Addenda—Photographs, maps, charts, involved legal descriptions, and all other matter that might tend to interrupt the reading continuity.

However, at various pertinent points through the counselling study or appraisal report, maps, charts, and diagrams are included. These diagrams, prepared with a view to artistic presentation more than minute detail, show all essential information and are frequently multicolored.

Only area, regional, community, and neighborhood data specifically pertinent to the study in question are included in the report. No extraneous matter clutters the pages, and every word, prepared in draft form, undergoes meticulous editing and proofreading.

A presentation of data is followed by a conclusion pertinent to the study at hand. In this manner, the sense and necessity of the written message is conveyed to the reviewer.

Every step in the narrative must be necessary. Every written word must be pertinent. Every conclusion must be supported by documentation and source. Thus, by a process of flowing continuity, the reviewer is led to the final decision already prepared by the writer of the report.

CONVICTION AND ACCURATE CALCULATIONS

The reviewer must feel that the appraiser has the strength of his convictions and fully believes in the truth of his own report. Therefore, any inadequacies in physical inspection, proposals for utilization, assessment of value, or final conclusion will lead to nothing but failure on the part of the writer and screaming frustration on the part of the reviewer.

Accurate calculations throughout the report are of major importance, of course, because sloppy figures distort the value conclusion, thus making the whole report meaningless.

VALUE CONCLUSION

The reviewer is going to scrutinize the methods used to reach value conclusion, which is the only reason for the existence of the report. The intellectual and physical effort, the data, the presentation, the experience and background are all part and parcel of the conclusion.

If the threads of the report do not lead inevitably to the final value conclusion, the report is useless. If the final conclusion leaves doubt or confusion in the mind of the reviewer, the report is useless. If the report contains errors or omissions in process, the reviewer must spotlight the gap and make a critique of his own, bridging the abyss.

Here I will present an example of such a critique in terms of calculations. Notice that the reviewer puts emphasis on the cash flow multiplier in establishing his overall capitalization rate. Further, in agreeing with the appraisal under review on a 20-year remaining economic life, he carries out that assumption arithmetically to set up straight-line depreciation and its equivalent loss in property over the period of the proposed mortgage loan, as follows:

Assuming a 20-year remaining economic life for the building and building value representing approximately 40% of total property value, then building depreciation equals 5% per year; property depreciation equals 0.05 x 0.40, or 2% per year, and in 10 years equals a 20% loss in property value.

Note: While the appraisal under review had estimated a 20-year remaining economic life, it did not carry out calculations to show a consequent loss in property value. Although the long-term effect against value of subject property was relatively small (the proposed mortgage loan was granted), the example shows how meticulous a lender's conscientious reviewer can be.

The comprehensive range of the reviewer's calculations embraces a highly sophisticated development of the basic exercise shown on page 59, chapter 3 of this book, under the heading "Typical Example of a Mortgage-Equity Overall Rate." It might be called the "proof of the pudding," as it is set forth in the model presented here:

A LENDING INSTITUTION REVIEWER'S MODEL APPRAISAL OF AN APPRAISAL

(Rate Structure by the Market Method) —The Reviewer's Essential Critique—

The mortgage-equity concept is the basis for this method with cash flow plus reversion characteristics.

MORTGAGE	RATE (times)	COVERAGE (equals)	AVERAGE
*(1) Interest	9.00%		
*(2) Amortization (10 years)	6.58		
Debt Service	15.58%	80%	12.46%
EQUITY *(3)	12.00%	20%	2.40
CASH FLOW WEIGHTED AVERAGE			14.86%
Cash Flow Multiplier = 1 ÷ 0.1486 =			6.73

REVERSION (10 years @ 9% int., 20% dep.)

*(4) (1 ÷ 0.0983) x 0.4224 x 0.80		3.44
OVERALL MULTIPLIER		10.17

OVERALL CAPITALIZATION RATE = 1 ÷ 10.17 = 0.0983 or 9.83%

*(1) Prevailing rate for first mortgage financing.

*(2) Level annuity rate at 9% interest, compounded annually or the sinking fund factor or the annuity which at compound interest will accumulate to 1 in ultimate years or 1 divided by 1 per annum accumulated at compound interest.

*(3) Consensus of opinion of knowledgeable investors (a judgment factor).

*(4) Present value of 1, receivable at a future date, end of ultimate year, or 1 divided by 1 at compound interest for ultimate years.

Age/Life: Assuming a 20-year remaining economic life for the building and building value representing approximately 40% of total property value, then building depreciation equals 5% per year; property depreciation equals 0.05 x 0.40, or 2% per year, and in 10 years equals a 20% loss in property value.

At the end of the written narrative and calculations, the value conclusion should be an obvious figure based on every single word that has gone before. The value conclusion, without a convincing report, is useless.

The written word and calculations in the form of a report is symbolic of the structure built by the tools of the real estate appraiser. The reviewer is going to examine every line in the report. To be a truly professional reviewer, he must be convinced. The study and analysis of real property is not a subject to be undertaken lightly. The transference of supported opinion to paper is subject to hazard. However, by intelligent reviewing, the truly professional practitioner can become convinced of the report's stability, rationale and truth in the marketplace.

The appraiser who keeps these points in mind as he writes his report will have no conflict with his reviewer, whoever the reviewer may be working for, the government, lending institutions, or other.

Appendix

Interest Tables and How to Use Them

Because investment value depends upon anticipated future income, or other benefits, the Income Approach calls for the calculation of the *present worth* of such estimated future benefits. In appraisal technique this is termed the "annuity process," and its applications are set forth here as described in *McMichael's Appraising Manual*, 4th Edition, pages 78-113 (Prentice-Hall, Inc., copyright 1951, Englewood Cliffs, N.J.):

An annuity represents a stream of payments, made usually at annual or semiannual periods, of amounts usually, although not necessarily, equal. It is necessary for the appraiser to translate such payments into value by computing their *present worth*. The sum of $1, in hand today, is worth exactly that sum. As the time until collection increases, the *present-day value* of the amount to be collected diminishes. This discount in value is due to the loss of interest in the interim.

For illustration, assume that you hold a well-secured note for $4,000, payable $1,000 at the end of each year, *without interest*. Would anyone be justified in paying $4,000 for that note *today?* Certainly not! How, then, is its *present* value to be computed? This is done by means of tables to be found later in this chapter. When so calculated, it will be found that the present-day value of the stated $4,000 note is just $3,312.12. It is in this manner that future rentals of properties under appraisement are processed.

In any system of appraising in which value is based upon the expected future earnings of property, it becomes necessary to use compound interest tables, or to be able to compute the proper percentages of present values. There are a number of tables used for this purpose that meet most requirements. They are:

Table I: Present value of $1 per annum used in computing the present worth of the rentals to a lessor and the present value of a lessee's profit in a lease, if any.

Table II: Present value of a single payment, used in computing present worth of a reversion.

Table III: For computing sinking funds or amortization requirements.

Table IV: The future value of $1, at compound interest, at the end of a given time.

Table V: The future value of $1 per annum, at compound interest at the end of a given time.

Table VIA: The present value of an annuity of 1, Hoskold premises, with sinking fund interest at 3 percent.

Table VIB: Same as Table VIA, except that sinking fund interest rate is 4 percent.

Table VIC: Same as VIA and VIB, except that the interest rate is 5 percent.

Table VIIA: Present value of increasing and decreasing annuities, compound interest valuation premise, 6 percent interest rate.

Tables VIIB, VIIC, and VIID: Also increasing and decreasing annuities, with interest rates at 7 percent, 8 percent, and 10 percent, respectively.

TABLE I PRESENT VALUE OF $1 PER ANNUM

(For Computing Lessor's Interest in Rentals or Lessee's Profit in a Lease)

This table will be found invaluable in determining today's worth of any saving or increase of income which extends through future years. It shows the present worth of an annually recurring saving or rental or income of $1 per year for any number of years at a given rate of interest. For example, what is the value of an annuity in the form of a leasehold estate to lessor calling for $6,000 annually for 25 years, money being worth 6%? See factor 25 periods, 6%, equals $12.783, which equals the value of $1, multiplied by $6,000 equals $76,698.00. If the rental is payable semiannually, multiply the periods, viz., 25, by 2 and divide the rate by 2, making 50 periods at 3%, which factor is 25.730 multiplied by $3,000 equals $77,190.00. If the rental is payable quarterly, multiply the periods, viz., 25, by 4 and divide the rate by 4, making 100 periods at 1 1/2%, which factor is 51.6247 multiplied by the quarterly payment of $1,500 equals $77,437.05. It will be observed that the difference between a semiannual and an annual calculation is approximately $492 or 2/3 of 1% in the aggregate amount, while the difference between a quarterly and an annual calculation is about $740, or about 5/6 of 1%. Note that these calculations are for full years commencing on the first day of the year. The present worth of such worth as of a particular day should be taken, plus the intervening interest and payment.

Yrs.	1 1/4%	1 1/2%	1 3/4%	2%	2 1/4%	2 1/2%	2 3/4%	3%	3 1/2%	4%	4 1/2%	5%	5 1/2%	6%	7%	8%	Yrs.
1	.988	.986	.983	.980	.978	.976	.973	.971	.966	.962	.957	.952	.948	.943	.935	.926	1
2	1.963	1.956	1.949	1.942	1.934	1.927	1.920	1.913	1.900	1.886	1.873	1.859	1.846	1.833	1.808	1.783	2
3	2.927	2.912	2.898	2.884	2.870	2.856	2.842	2.829	2.802	2.775	2.749	2.723	2.698	2.673	2.624	2.577	3
4	3.878	3.854	3.831	3.808	3.785	3.762	3.739	3.717	3.673	3.630	3.588	3.546	3.505	3.465	3.387	3.312	4
5	4.818	4.783	4.748	4.713	4.679	4.646	4.613	4.580	4.515	4.452	4.390	4.329	4.270	4.212	4.100	3.993	5
6	5.746	5.697	5.649	5.601	5.554	5.508	5.462	5.417	5.329	5.242	5.158	5.076	4.996	4.917	4.767	4.623	6
7	6.663	6.598	6.535	6.472	6.410	6.349	6.289	6.230	6.115	6.002	5.893	5.786	5.683	5.582	5.389	5.206	7
8	7.568	7.486	7.405	7.325	7.247	7.170	7.094	7.020	6.874	6.733	6.596	6.463	6.335	6.210	5.971	5.747	8
9	8.462	8.360	8.260	8.162	8.066	7.971	7.878	7.786	7.608	7.435	7.269	7.108	6.952	6.802	6.515	6.247	9
10	9.346	9.222	9.101	8.983	8.866	8.752	8.640	8.530	8.317	8.111	7.913	7.722	7.538	7.360	7.024	6.710	10
11	10.218	10.071	9.927	9.787	9.649	9.514	9.382	9.253	9.002	8.760	8.529	8.306	8.093	7.887	7.499	7.139	11
12	11.079	10.907	10.740	10.578	10.415	10.258	10.104	9.954	9.663	9.385	9.119	8.863	8.619	8.384	7.943	7.536	12
13	11.930	11.731	11.538	11.348	11.164	10.983	10.807	10.635	10.303	9.986	9.683	9.394	9.117	8.853	8.358	7.904	13
14	12.771	12.543	12.322	12.106	11.896	11.691	11.491	11.296	10.921	10.563	10.223	9.899	9.590	9.295	8.745	8.244	14
15	13.601	13.343	13.093	12.849	12.612	12.381	12.157	11.938	11.517	11.118	10.740	10.380	10.038	9.712	9.108	8.559	15
16	14.420	14.131	13.850	13.578	13.313	13.055	12.805	12.561	12.094	11.652	11.234	10.838	10.462	10.106	9.447	8.851	16
17	15.230	14.908	14.596	14.292	13.998	13.712	13.436	13.166	12.651	12.166	11.707	11.274	10.865	10.477	9.763	9.122	17
18	16.030	15.673	15.327	14.992	14.668	14.353	14.049	13.754	13.190	12.659	12.160	11.690	11.246	10.828	10.059	9.372	18
19	16.819	16.426	16.046	15.678	15.323	14.979	14.646	14.324	13.710	13.134	12.593	12.085	11.608	11.158	10.336	9.604	19
20	17.599	17.169	16.753	16.351	15.964	15.589	15.227	14.877	14.212	13.590	13.008	12.462	11.950	11.470	10.594	9.818	20
21	18.370	17.900	17.448	17.011	16.590	16.185	15.793	15.415	14.698	14.029	13.405	12.821	12.275	11.764	10.836	10.017	21
22	19.131	18.621	18.130	17.658	17.203	16.765	16.343	15.937	15.167	14.451	13.784	13.163	12.583	12.042	11.061	10.201	22
23	19.882	19.331	18.801	18.292	17.803	17.332	16.879	16.444	15.620	14.857	14.148	13.489	12.875	12.303	11.272	10.371	23
24	20.624	20.030	19.461	18.914	18.399	17.885	17.401	16.936	16.058	15.247	14.495	13.799	13.152	12.550	11.469	10.529	24
25	21.357	20.720	20.109	19.523	18.962	18.424	17.908	17.413	16.482	15.622	14.828	14.094	13.414	12.783	11.654	10.675	25
26	22.081	21.399	20.746	20.121	19.523	18.951	18.402	17.877	16.890	15.983	15.147	14.375	13.663	13.003	11.826	10.810	26
27	22.796	22.068	21.372	20.707	20.071	19.464	18.883	18.327	17.285	16.330	15.451	14.643	13.898	13.211	11.987	10.935	27
28	23.502	22.727	21.987	21.281	20.608	19.965	19.351	18.764	17.667	16.663	15.743	14.898	14.121	13.406	12.137	11.051	28
29	24.200	23.376	22.592	21.844	21.132	20.454	19.806	19.188	18.036	16.984	16.022	15.141	14.333	13.591	12.278	11.158	29
30	24.889	24.016	23.186	22.396	21.645	20.930	20.249	19.600	18.392	17.292	16.289	15.372	14.534	13.765	12.409	11.258	30
31	25.569	24.646	23.770	22.938	22.147	21.395	20.681	20.000	18.736	17.588	16.544	15.593	14.724	13.929	12.532	11.350	31
32	26.241	25.267	24.344	23.468	22.638	21.849	21.100	20.389	19.069	17.874	16.789	15.803	14.904	14.084	12.647	11.435	32
33	26.905	25.879	24.908	23.989	23.117	22.292	21.509	20.766	19.390	18.148	17.023	16.003	15.075	14.230	12.754	11.514	33
34	27.560	26.482	25.462	24.499	23.587	22.724	21.906	21.132	19.701	18.411	17.247	16.193	15.237	14.368	12.854	11.587	34
35	28.208	27.076	26.007	24.999	24.046	23.145	22.293	21.487	20.001	18.665	17.461	16.374	15.391	14.498	12.948	11.655	35
36	28.847	27.661	26.543	25.489	24.495	23.556	22.670	21.832	20.290	18.908	17.666	16.547	15.536	14.621	13.035	11.717	36
37	29.479	28.237	27.069	25.969	24.934	23.957	23.036	22.167	20.571	19.143	17.862	16.711	15.674	14.737	13.117	11.775	37
38	30.102	28.805	27.586	26.441	25.363	24.349	23.393	22.492	20.841	19.368	18.050	16.868	15.805	14.846	13.193	11.829	38
39	30.718	29.365	28.095	26.903	25.783	24.730	23.740	22.808	21.103	19.584	18.230	17.017	15.929	14.949	13.265	11.879	39
40	31.327	29.916	28.594	27.355	26.193	25.103	24.078	23.115	21.355	19.793	18.402	17.159	16.046	15.046	13.332	11.925	40
41	31.928	30.459	29.085	27.799	26.595	25.466	24.407	23.412	21.599	19.993	18.566	17.294	16.157	15.138	13.394	11.967	41
42	32.521	30.994	29.568	28.235	26.988	25.821	24.727	23.701	21.835	20.186	18.724	17.423	16.263	15.225	13.452	12.007	42
43	33.107	31.521	30.042	28.662	27.372	26.168	25.038	23.982	22.063	20.371	18.874	17.546	16.363	15.306	13.507	12.043	43
44	33.686	32.041	30.508	29.080	27.748	26.504	25.341	24.254	22.283	20.549	19.018	17.663	16.458	15.383	13.558	12.077	44
45	34.258	32.552	30.966	29.490	28.115	26.833	25.636	24.519	22.495	20.720	19.156	17.774	16.548	15.456	13.606	12.108	45
46	34.823	33.056	31.416	29.892	28.474	27.154	25.924	24.775	22.701	20.885	19.288	17.880	16.633	15.524	13.650	12.137	46
47	35.381	33.553	31.859	30.287	28.822	27.467	26.203	25.025	22.899	21.043	19.415	17.981	16.714	15.589	13.692	12.164	47
48	35.931	34.043	32.294	30.673	29.170	27.773	26.475	25.267	23.091	21.195	19.536	18.077	16.790	15.650	13.730	12.189	48
49	36.475	34.525	32.721	31.052	29.506	28.071	26.740	25.502	23.277	21.341	19.651	18.169	16.863	15.708	13.767	12.212	49
50	37.013	35.000	33.141	31.424	29.834	28.362	26.998	25.730	23.456	21.482	19.762	18.256	16.932	15.762	13.801	12.233	50

TABLE I (Continued)

Yrs.	1 1/4%	1 1/2%	1 3/4%	2%	2 1/4%	2 1/2%	2 3/4%	3%	3 1/2%	4%	4 1/2%	5%	5 1/2%	6%	7%	8%	Yrs.
51	37.544	35.468	33.554	31.788	30.156	28.646	27.248	25.951	23.629	21.617	19.868	18.339	16.997	15.813	13.832	12.253	51
52	38.068	35.929	33.960	32.145	30.470	28.923	27.492	26.166	23.796	21.748	19.969	18.418	17.058	15.861	13.862	12.272	52
53	38.585	36.383	34.358	32.495	30.778	29.193	27.729	26.375	23.957	21.873	20.066	18.493	17.117	15.907	13.890	12.288	53
54	39.097	36.830	34.750	32.838	31.078	29.457	27.960	26.578	24.113	21.993	20.159	18.565	17.173	15.950	13.916	12.304	54
55	39.602	37.271	35.135	33.175	31.373	29.714	28.185	26.774	24.264	22.109	20.248	18.633	17.225	15.991	13.940	12.319	55
56	40.100	37.706	35.514	33.505	31.660	29.965	28.404	26.965	24.410	22.220	20.333	18.699	17.275	16.029	13.963	12.332	56
57	40.593	38.134	35.886	33.828	31.942	30.210	28.617	27.151	24.550	22.327	20.414	18.761	17.332	16.065	13.984	12.344	57
58	41.079	38.555	36.252	34.145	32.217	30.448	28.824	27.331	24.686	22.430	20.492	18.820	17.367	16.099	14.003	12.356	58
59	41.560	38.971	36.611	34.456	32.486	30.681	29.026	27.506	24.818	22.528	20.567	18.876	17.410	16.131	14.022	12.367	59
60	42.035	39.380	36.964	34.761	32.749	30.909	29.223	27.676	24.945	22.623	20.638	18.929	17.450	16.161	14.039	12.377	60
61	42.503	39.783	37.311	35.060	33.006	31.130	29.414	27.840	25.067	22.715	20.706	18.980	17.488	16.190	14.055	12.386	61
62	42.966	40.181	37.652	35.353	33.258	31.347	29.600	28.000	25.186	22.803	20.772	19.029	17.524	16.217	14.070	12.394	62
63	43.423	40.572	37.987	35.640	33.504	31.558	29.781	28.156	25.300	22.887	20.834	19.075	17.558	16.242	14.084	12.402	63
64	43.875	40.958	38.317	35.921	33.745	31.764	29.957	28.306	25.411	22.969	20.894	19.119	17.591	16.266	14.098	12.409	64
65	44.321	41.338	38.641	36.197	33.980	31.965	30.128	28.453	25.518	23.047	20.951	19.161	17.622	16.289	14.110	12.416	65
66	44.761	41.712	38.959	36.468	34.211	32.161	30.295	28.595	25.621	23.122	21.006	19.201	17.651	16.310	14.121	12.422	66
67	45.196	42.081	39.272	36.733	34.436	32.352	30.458	28.733	25.721	23.194	21.058	19.239	17.679	16.331	14.132	12.428	67
68	45.626	42.444	39.579	36.994	34.658	32.538	30.616	28.867	25.817	23.264	21.108	19.275	17.705	16.350	14.142	12.433	68
69	46.051	42.802	39.881	37.249	34.871	32.720	30.770	28.997	25.910	23.330	21.156	19.310	17.730	16.368	14.152	12.438	69
70	46.470	43.155	40.178	37.499	35.082	32.898	30.919	29.123	26.000	23.395	21.202	19.343	17.753	16.385	14.160	12.443	70
71	46.884	43.502	40.470	37.744	35.288	33.071	31.065	29.246	26.087	23.456	21.246	19.374	17.776	16.401	14.169	12.447	71
72	47.292	43.845	40.756	37.984	35.490	33.240	31.207	29.365	26.171	23.516	21.288	19.404	17.797	16.416	14.176	12.451	72
73	47.696	44.182	41.038	38.220	35.687	33.405	31.345	29.481	26.253	23.573	21.328	19.432	17.817	16.430	14.183	12.455	73
74	48.095	44.514	41.315	38.451	35.879	33.566	31.479	29.592	26.331	23.628	21.367	19.459	17.836	16.443	14.190	12.458	74
75	48.489	44.842	41.587	38.677	36.068	33.723	31.610	29.702	26.407	23.680	21.404	19.485	17.854	16.456	14.196	12.461	75
76	48.878	45.164	41.855	38.899	36.252	33.876	31.737	29.807	26.480	23.731	21.439	19.509	17.871	16.468	14.202	12.464	76
77	49.262	45.482	42.118	39.117	36.432	34.025	31.861	29.910	26.551	23.780	21.473	19.533	17.887	16.479	14.208	12.467	77
78	49.642	45.795	42.376	39.330	36.609	34.171	31.981	30.010	26.619	23.827	21.505	19.555	17.903	16.490	14.213	12.469	78
79	50.016	46.103	42.630	39.539	36.781	34.313	32.099	30.107	26.685	23.872	21.536	19.576	17.917	16.500	14.218	12.471	79
80	50.387	46.407	42.880	39.744	36.950	34.452	32.213	30.201	26.749	23.915	21.565	19.596	17.931	16.509	14.222	12.474	80
81	50.752	46.707	43.125	39.946	37.115	34.587	32.324	30.292	26.810	23.957	21.593	19.615	17.944	16.518	14.224	12.476	81
82	51.113	47.002	43.366	40.143	37.276	34.719	32.432	30.381	26.870	23.997	21.620	19.634	17.956	16.526	14.228	12.477	82
83	51.470	47.292	43.603	40.336	37.434	34.848	32.537	30.466	26.927	24.035	21.646	19.651	17.968	16.534	14.232	12.478	83
84	51.822	47.579	43.836	40.525	37.588	34.974	32.640	30.550	26.983	24.072	21.671	19.667	17.979	16.542	14.235	12.480	84
85	52.170	47.861	44.065	40.711	37.739	35.096	32.740	30.631	27.037	24.109	21.695	19.684	17.990	16.549	14.238	12.482	85
86	52.514	48.139	44.290	40.893	37.886	35.216	32.836	30.710	27.089	24.142	21.717	19.698	18.001	16.555	14.241	12.483	86
87	52.853	48.412	44.511	41.072	38.031	35.332	32.931	30.786	27.139	24.175	21.739	19.713	18.010	16.562	14.244	12.484	87
88	53.188	48.682	44.728	41.247	38.172	35.446	33.023	30.861	27.187	24.207	21.760	19.726	18.019	16.586	14.247	12.485	88
89	53.519	48.948	44.942	41.419	38.310	35.557	33.112	30.933	27.234	24.237	21.780	19.739	18.027	16.573	14.250	12.486	89
90	53.846	49.210	45.152	41.587	38.445	35.666	33.199	31.002	27.279	24.267	21.799	19.752	18.035	16.579	14.253	12.488	90
91	54.169	49.468	45.358	41.752	38.577	35.771	33.284	31.070	27.323	24.295	21.817	19.764	18.043	16.584	14.255	12.488	91
92	54.488	49.722	45.560	41.914	38.706	35.875	33.366	31.136	27.365	24.322	21.834	19.775	18.051	16.588	14.257	12.489	92
93	54.803	49.972	45.760	42.072	38.832	35.975	33.345	31.200	27.406	24.348	21.852	19.786	18.058	16.593	14.259	12.490	93
94	55.114	50.219	45.955	42.228	38.956	36.073	33.525	31.263	27.445	24.373	21.867	19.796	18.064	16.597	14.261	12.491	94
95	55.421	50.462	46.148	42.380	39.077	36.169	33.601	31.323	27.484	24.398	21.883	19.806	18.069	16.601	14.263	12.492	95
96	55.725	50.702	46.337	42.529	39.195	36.263	33.674	31.381	27.520	24.420	21.897	19.815	18.075	16.605	14.264	12.492	96
97	56.024	50.938	46.523	42.676	39.310	36.354	33.756	31.438	27.556	24.443	21.911	19.823	18.081	16.608	14.265	12.493	97
98	56.320	51.170	46.705	42.819	39.423	36.443	33.816	31.494	27.590	24.464	21.924	19.832	18.086	16.611	14.266	12.493	98
99	56.613	51.399	46.885	42.960	39.534	36.529	33.885	31.547	27.623	24.485	21.937	19.840	18.091	16.614	14.267	12.493	99
100	56.901	51.625	47.061	43.098	39.642	36.614	33.951	31.599	27.655	24.505	21.950	19.848	18.096	16.618	14.269	12.494	100

TABLE II. PRESENT VALUE OF A SINGLE PAYMENT OF $1 AT A FUTURE DATE

(For Computing the Present Value of a Reversion)

This compound interest table showing the present worth of a dollar payable hereafter will be found useful in determining the worth of annuities or interests arising under long-term leases. For example, what is the value of $5,000 rent payable ten years hereafter, money being worth 6% payable annually? The factor at 6% for 10 years of 1 dollar is $0.558395, which, multiplied by $5,000, equals $2,791.97. This table may also be used when interest is compounded semiannually by doubling the period and dividing the rate by two. Thus, to find the factor for 20 years at 6% compounded semiannually, use factor $0.306557 (factor for 40 years at 3%).

PRESENT WORTH OF $1 FOR ANY TIME FROM 1 TO 100 YEARS AT

Yrs.	1%	1 1/4%	1 1/2%	2%	2 1/2%	3%	Yrs.	1%	1 1/4%	1 1/2%	2%	2 1/2%	3%
1	.990099	.987654	.985222	.980392	.975610	.970874	51	.602019	.530705	.467985	.364243	.283846	.221463
2	.980296	.975461	.970662	.961169	.951814	.942596	52	.596058	.524153	.461069	.357101	.276923	.215013
3	.970590	.963418	.956317	.942322	.928599	.915142	53	.590156	.517682	.454255	.350099	.270169	.208750
4	.960980	.951524	.942184	.923845	.905951	.888487	54	.584313	.511291	.447542	.343234	.263579	.202670
5	.951466	.939777	.928260	.905731	.883854	.862609	55	.578528	.504979	.440928	.336504	.257151	.196767
6	.942045	.928175	.914542	.887971	.862297	.837484	56	.572800	.498745	.434412	.329906	.250879	.191036
7	.932718	.916716	.901027	.870560	.841265	.813092	57	.567189	.492587	.427992	.323437	.244760	.185472
8	.923483	.905398	.887711	.853490	.820747	.789409	58	.561514	.486506	.421667	.317095	.238790	.180069
9	.914340	.894221	.874592	.836755	.800728	.766417	59	.555954	.480500	.415435	.310878	.232966	.174825
10	.905287	.883181	.861667	.820348	.781198	.744094	60	.550450	.474568	.409296	.304782	.227284	.169733
11	.896324	.872277	.848933	.804263	.762145	.722421	61	.545000	.468709	.403247	.298806	.221740	.164789
12	.887449	.861509	.836387	.788493	.743556	.701380	62	.539604	.462922	.397288	.292947	.216332	.159990
13	.878663	.850873	.824027	.773033	.725420	.680951	63	.534261	.457207	.391417	.287203	.211055	.153330
14	.869963	.840368	.811849	.757875	.707727	.661118	64	.528971	.451563	.385632	.281572	.205908	.150806
15	.861349	.829993	.799852	.743015	.690466	.641862	65	.523734	.445988	.379933	.276051	.200886	.146413
16	.852821	.819746	.788031	.728446	.673625	.623167	66	.518548	.440482	.374318	.270638	.195986	.142149
17	.844377	.809626	.776385	.714163	.657195	.605016	67	.513414	.435044	.368787	.265331	.191206	.138009
18	.836017	.799631	.764912	.700159	.641166	.587395	68	.508331	.429673	.363337	.260129	.186542	.133989
19	.827740	.789759	.753607	.686431	.625528	.570286	69	.503298	.424368	.357967	.255028	.181992	.130086
20	.819544	.780009	.742470	.672971	.610271	.537549	70	.498315	.419129	.352677	.250028	.177554	.126290
21	.811430	.770379	.731498	.659776	.595386	.533676	71	.493381	.413955	.347465	.245125	.173223	.122619
22	.803396	.760868	.720688	.646839	.580865	.521893	72	.488496	.408844	.342330	.240319	.168998	.119047
23	.795442	.751475	.710037	.644156	.566697	.506692	73	.483659	.403797	.337271	.235607	.164876	.115580
24	.787566	.742197	.699544	.621721	.552875	.491934	74	.478871	.398811	.332287	.230987	.160855	.112214
25	.779768	.733034	.689206	.609531	.539391	.477606	75	.474129	.393888	.327376	.226458	.156931	.108945
26	.772048	.723984	.679021	.597579	.526235	.463695	76	.469435	.389025	.322538	.222017	.153104	.105772
27	.764404	.715046	.668986	.585862	.513400	.450189	77	.464787	.384222	.317771	.217664	.149370	.102691
28	.756836	.706219	.659099	.574375	.500878	.437077	78	.460185	.379479	.313075	.213396	.145726	.099700
29	.749342	.697500	.649359	.563112	.488661	.424346	79	.455629	.374794	.308449	.209212	.142172	.096796
30	.741923	.688889	.639762	.552071	.476743	.411987	80	.451118	.370167	.303890	.205110	.138705	.093977
31	.734577	.680384	.630308	.541246	.465115	.399987	81	.446651	.365597	.299399	.201088	.135322	.091240
32	.727304	.671984	.620993	.530633	.453771	.388337	82	.442229	.361083	.294975	.197145	.132021	.088582
33	.720103	.663688	.611816	.520229	.442703	.377026	83	.437851	.356625	.290615	.193879	.128801	.086002
34	.712973	.665494	.602774	.510028	.431905	.366045	84	.433515	.352223	.286321	.189490	.125659	.083497
35	.705914	.647402	.593866	.500028	.421371	.355383	85	.429223	.347874	.282089	.185774	.122595	.081065
36	.698925	.639409	.585090	.490223	.411094	.345032	86	.424974	.343580	.277920	.182132	.119605	.078704
37	.692005	.631515	.576443	.480611	.401067	.334983	87	.420766	.339338	.273813	.178560	.116687	.076412
38	.685153	.623719	.567924	.471187	.391285	.325226	88	.416600	.335148	.269767	.175059	.113841	.074186
39	.678370	.616019	.559531	.461948	.381741	.315754	89	.412475	.331011	.265780	.171627	.111065	.072026
40	.671653	.608413	.551262	.452890	.372431	.306557	90	.408391	.326924	.261852	.168261	.108356	.069928
41	.665003	.600902	.543116	.444010	.363347	.297628	91	.404348	.322888	.257982	.164962	.105713	.067891
42	.658419	.593484	.535089	.435304	.354485	.288959	92	.400344	.318902	.254170	.161728	.103135	.065914
43	.651900	.586157	.527182	.426769	.345839	.280543	93	.396380	.314965	.250414	.158556	.100619	.063994
44	.645445	.578920	.519391	.418401	.337404	.272372	94	.392456	.311076	.246713	.155448	.098165	.062130
45	.639055	.571773	.511715	.410197	.329174	.264439	95	.388570	.307236	.243067	.152400	.095771	.060320
46	.632728	.564714	.504153	.402154	.321146	.256737	96	.384723	.303443	.239475	.149411	.093435	.058563
47	.626463	.557742	.496702	.394268	.313313	.249259	97	.381914	.299697	.235936	.146482	.091156	.056858
48	.620260	.550856	.489362	.386538	.305671	.241999	98	.377142	.295997	.232449	.143609	.088933	.055202
49	.614119	.544056	.482130	.378958	.298216	.234950	99	.373408	.292342	.229014	.140794	.086764	.053594
50	.608039	.537339	.475005	.371518	.290942	.228107	100	.369711	.288733	.225629	.138033	.084647	.052033

TABLE II (Continued)

Yrs.	4%	5%	6%	7%	8%	Yrs.	4%	5%	6%	7%	8%
1	.961538	.952381	.943396	.934579	.925925	51	.135301	.083051	.051215	.031726	.019741
2	.924556	.907029	.889996	.873438	.857338	52	.130097	.079096	.048316	.029651	.018279
3	.888996	.863838	.839619	.816297	.793832	53	.125093	.075330	.045581	.027711	.016925
4	.854804	.822702	.792094	.762895	.735029	54	.120282	.071743	.043001	.025898	.015671
5	.821927	.783526	.747258	.712986	.680582	55	.115656	.068326	.040567	.024204	.014510
6	.790315	.746215	.704961	.666342	.630169	56	.111207	.065073	.038270	.022620	.013435
7	.759918	.710681	.665057	.622749	.583490	57	.106930	.061974	.036104	.021140	.012440
8	.730690	.676839	.627412	.582008	.540268	58	.102817	.059023	.034061	.019757	.011519
9	.702587	.644609	.591898	.543933	.500248	59	.098863	.056212	.032133	.018465	.010665
10	.675564	.613913	.558395	.508349	.463193	60	.095060	.053536	.030314	.017257	.009875
11	.649581	.584679	.526788	.475092	.428882	61	.091414	.050986	.028598	.016128	.009144
12	.624597	.556837	.496969	.444011	.397113	62	.087889	.048558	.026979	.015073	.008466
13	.600574	.530321	.468839	.414964	.367697	63	.084508	.046246	.025452	.014087	.007839
14	.577475	.505068	.442301	.387817	.340460	64	.081258	.044044	.024011	.013165	.007259
15	.555265	.481017	.417265	.362445	.315241	65	.078133	.041946	.022652	.012304	.006721
16	.533908	.458112	.393646	.338734	.291890	66	.075128	.039949	.021370	.011499	.006223
17	.513373	.436297	.371364	.316574	.270268	67	.072238	.038047	.020160	.010746	.005762
18	.493628	.415521	.350344	.295863	.250248	68	.069460	.036225	.019019	.010043	.005335
19	.474642	.395734	.330513	.276508	.231711	69	.066788	.034509	.017942	.009386	.004940
20	.456387	.376889	.311805	.258418	.214547	70	.064219	.032866	.016927	.008772	.004574
21	.438834	.358942	.294155	.241512	.198655	71	.061749	.031301	.015969	.008198	.004235
22	.421955	.341850	.277505	.225712	.183940	72	.059374	.029811	.015065	.007662	.003921
23	.405726	.325571	.261797	.210946	.170314	73	.057091	.028391	.014212	.007161	.003631
24	.390121	.310068	.246979	.197146	.157699	74	.054895	.027039	.013407	.006692	.003362
25	.375117	.295303	.232999	.184249	.146017	75	.052784	.025752	.012649	.006254	.003113
26	.360689	.281241	.219810	.172195	.135201	76	.050754	.024225	.011933	.005845	.002882
27	.346817	.267848	.207368	.160930	.125186	77	.048801	.023357	.011257	.005463	.002669
28	.333477	.255094	.195630	.150402	.115913	78	.046924	.022245	.010620	.005105	.002471
29	.320651	.242946	.184557	.140562	.107327	79	.045120	.021186	.010019	.004771	.002288
30	.308319	.231377	.174110	.131366	.099377	80	.043384	.020177	.009452	.004459	.002118
31	.296460	.220360	.164255	.122772	.092015	81	.041716	.019216	.008917	.004167	.001961
32	.285058	.209866	.154957	.114740	.085199	82	.040111	.018301	.008412	.003895	.001816
33	.274094	.199873	.146186	.107234	.078888	83	.038569	.017430	.007936	.003640	.001681
34	.263552	.190355	.137912	.100219	.073045	84	.037085	.016600	.007486	.003402	.001557
35	.253615	.181290	.130105	.093662	.067634	85	.035659	.015809	.007063	.003179	.001442
36	.243669	.172657	.122741	.087535	.062624	86	.034287	.015056	.006663	.002971	.001335
37	.234297	.164436	.115793	.081808	.057985	87	.032969	.014339	.006286	.002777	.001236
38	.225235	.156605	.109239	.076456	.053690	88	.031701	.013657	.005930	.002595	.001144
39	.216621	.149148	.103056	.071454	.049713	89	.030481	.013006	.005594	.002425	.001059
40	.208289	.142046	.097222	.066780	.046030	90	.029309	.012387	.005277	.002267	.000981
41	.200278	.135282	.091719	.062411	.042621	91	.028102	.011797	.004979	.002118	.000908
42	.192575	.128840	.086527	.058328	.039463	92	.027098	.011235	.004697	.001980	.000841
43	.185168	.122704	.081630	.054512	.036540	93	.026056	.010700	.004431	.001850	.000779
44	.178046	.116861	.077009	.050946	.033833	94	.025053	.010190	.004180	.001729	.000721
45	.171198	.111297	.072650	.047613	.031327	95	.024090	.009705	.003944	.001616	.000667
46	.164614	.105997	.068538	.044498	.029007	96	.023163	.009243	.003720	.001510	.000618
47	.158283	.100949	.064658	.041587	.026858	97	.022272	.008803	.003510	.001411	.000572
48	.152195	.096942	.060998	.038866	.024868	98	.021416	.008384	.003311	.001319	.000530
49	.146341	.091564	.057546	.036324	.023026	99	.020592	.007985	.003124	.001233	.000490
50	.140713	.087204	.054288	.033947	.021321	100	.019800	.007604	.002947	.001152	.000454

TABLE III. FOR COMPUTING SINKING FUNDS OR AMORTIZATION REQUIREMENTS

The annual amount which, deposited at the end of each year, with interest will amount to 1 at the end of a given time.

Yrs.	1 1/2%	1 3/4%	2%	2 1/2%	3%	3 1/2%	4%	4 1/2%	5%	5 1/2%	6%	7%	Yrs.
1	1.00000	1.00000	1.00000	1.00000	1.00000	1.00000	1.00000	1.00000	1.00000	1.00000	1.00000	1.00000	1
2	.49628	.49566	.49505	.49383	.49261	.49140	.49020	.48900	.48780	.48662	.48544	.48309	2
3	.32838	.32757	.32675	.32514	.32353	.32193	.32035	.31877	.31721	.31565	.31411	.31105	3
4	.24444	.24353	.24262	.24082	.23903	.23725	.23549	.23374	.23201	.23029	.22859	.22523	4
5	.19409	.19312	.19216	.19025	.18835	.18648	.18463	.18279	.18097	.17918	.17740	.17389	5
6	.16053	.15952	.15853	.15655	.15460	.15267	.15076	.14888	.14702	.14518	.14336	.13980	6
7	.13656	.13553	.13451	.13250	.13051	.12854	.12661	.12470	.12282	.12096	.11913	.11555	7
8	.11858	.11754	.11651	.11447	.11246	.11048	.10853	.10661	.10472	.10286	.10104	.09747	8
9	.10461	.10356	.10252	.10046	.09843	.09645	.09449	.09257	.09069	.08884	.08702	.08349	9
10	.09343	.09238	.09133	.08926	.08723	.08524	.08329	.08138	.07950	.07767	.07587	.07238	10
11	.08429	.08323	.08218	.08011	.07808	.07609	.07415	.07225	.07039	.06857	.06679	.06336	11
12	.07668	.07561	.07456	.07249	.07046	.06848	.06655	.06467	.06283	.06103	.05928	.05590	12
13	.07024	.06917	.06812	.06605	.06403	.06206	.06014	.05828	.05646	.05468	.05296	.04965	13
14	.06472	.06366	.06260	.06054	.05853	.05657	.05467	.05282	.05102	.04928	.04758	.04434	14
15	.05994	.05888	.05783	.05577	.05377	.05183	.04994	.04811	.04634	.04463	.04296	.03979	15
16	.05577	.05470	.05365	.05160	.04961	.04768	.04582	.04402	.04227	.04058	.03895	.03586	16
17	.05208	.05102	.04997	.04793	.04595	.04404	.04220	.04042	.03870	.03704	.03544	.03243	17
18	.04881	.04774	.04670	.04467	.04271	.04082	.03899	.03724	.03555	.03392	.03236	.02941	18
19	.04588	.04482	.04378	.04176	.03981	.03794	.03614	.03441	.03275	.03115	.02962	.02675	19
20	.04325	.04219	.04116	.03915	.03722	.03536	.03358	.03188	.03024	.02868	.02718	.02439	20
21	.04087	.03981	.03878	.03679	.03487	.03304	.03128	.02960	.02800	.02646	.02500	.02229	21
22	.03870	.03766	.03663	.03465	.03275	.03093	.02920	.02755	.02597	.02447	.02305	.02041	22
23	.03673	.03569	.03467	.03270	.03081	.02902	.02731	.02568	.02414	.02267	.02128	.01871	23
24	.03492	.03389	.03287	.03091	.02905	.02727	.02559	.02399	.02247	.02104	.01968	.01719	24
25	.03326	.03223	.03122	.02928	.02743	.02567	.02401	.02244	.02095	.01955	.01823	.01581	25
26	.03173	.03070	.02970	.02777	.02594	.02421	.02257	.02102	.01956	.01819	.01690	.01456	26
27	.03032	.02929	.02829	.02638	.02456	.02285	.02124	.01972	.01829	.01695	.01570	.01343	27
28	.02900	.02798	.02699	.02509	.02329	.02160	.02001	.01852	.01712	.01581	.01459	.01239	28
29	.02778	.02676	.02578	.02389	.02211	.02045	.01888	.01741	.01605	.01477	.01358	.01145	29
30	.02664	.02563	.02465	.02278	.02102	.01937	.01783	.01639	.01505	.01381	.01265	.01059	30
31	.02557	.02457	.02360	.02174	.02000	.01837	.01686	.01544	.01413	.01292	.01179	.00980	31
32	.02458	.02358	.02261	.02077	.01905	.01744	.01595	.01456	.01328	.01210	.01100	.00907	32
33	.02364	.02265	.02169	.01986	.01816	.01657	.01510	.01374	.01249	.01133	.01027	.00841	33
34	.02276	.02177	.02082	.01901	.01732	.01576	.01431	.01298	.01176	.01063	.00960	.00789	34
35	.02193	.02095	.02000	.01821	.01654	.01500	.01358	.01227	.01107	.00997	.00897	.00723	35
36	.02115	.02017	.01923	.01745	.01580	.01428	.01289	.01161	.01043	.00937	.00839	.00672	36
37	.02041	.01944	.01851	.01674	.01511	.01361	.01224	.01098	.00984	.00880	.00786	.00624	37
38	.01972	.01875	.01782	.01607	.01446	.01298	.01163	.01040	.00928	.00827	.00736	.00580	38
39	.01905	.01809	.01717	.01544	.01384	.01239	.01106	.00986	.00876	.00778	.00689	.00539	39
40	.01843	.01747	.01656	.01484	.01326	.01183	.01052	.00934	.00828	.00732	.00646	.00501	40
41	.01783	.01688	.01597	.01427	.01271	.01130	.01002	.00886	.00782	.00689	.00606	.00466	41
42	.01726	.01632	.01542	.01373	.01219	.01080	.00954	.00841	.00739	.00649	.00568	.00434	42
43	.01672	.01579	.01489	.01322	.01170	.01033	.00909	.00798	.00699	.00611	.00533	.00404	43
44	.01621	.01528	.01439	.01273	.01123	.00988	.00866	.00758	.00662	.00576	.00501	.00376	44
45	.01572	.01479	.01391	.01227	.01079	.00945	.00826	.00720	.00626	.00543	.00470	.00350	45
46	.01525	.01433	.01345	.01183	.01036	.00905	.00788	.00684	.00593	.00512	.00441	.00326	46
47	.01480	.01389	.01302	.01141	.00996	.00867	.00752	.00651	.00561	.00483	.00415	.00304	47
48	.01437	.01347	.01260	.01101	.00958	.00831	.00718	.00619	.00532	.00456	.00390	.00283	48
49	.01396	.01306	.01220	.01062	.00921	.00796	.00686	.00589	.00504	.00430	.00366	.00264	49
50	.01357	.01267	.01182	.01026	.00887	.00763	.00655	.00560	.00478	.00406	.00344	.00246	50
55	.01183	.01096	.01014	.00865	.00735	.00621	.00523	.00439	.00367	.00305	.00254	.00174	55
60	.01039	.00955	.00877	.00735	.00613	.00509	.00420	.00345	.00283	.00231	.00188	.00123	60
65	.00919	.00838	.00763	.00628	.00515	.00419	.00339	.00273	.00219	.00175	.00139	.00087	65
70	.00817	.00739	.00667	.00540	.00434	.00346	.00275	.00217	.00179	.00133	.00103	.00062	70
75	.00730	.00655	.00586	.00465	.00367	.00287	.00223	.00172	.00132	.00101	.00077	.00044	75
80	.00655	.00582	.00516	.00403	.00311	.00238	.00181	.00137	.00103	.00077	.00057	.00031	80
85	.00589	.00519	.00456	.00349	.00265	.00199	.00148	.00109	.00080	.00059	.00043	.00022	85
90	.00532	.00465	.00405	.00304	.00226	.00166	.00121	.00087	.00063	.00045	.00032	.00016	90
95	.00482	.00417	.00360	.00265	.00193	.00139	.00099	.00070	.00049	.00034	.00024	.00011	95
99	.00446	.00383	.00328	.00238	.00170	.00120	.00084	.00058	.00040	.00028	.00019	.00009	99
100	.00437	.00375	.00320	.00231	.00165	.00116	.00081	.00056	.00038	.00026	.00018	.00008	100

TABLE IV. FUTURE VALUE OF ONE DOLLAR
At Compound Interest
The Amount of 1, with Interest, at the End of a Given Time

Yrs.	2 1/2%	3%	3 1/2%	4%	4 1/2%	5%	6%
1	1.0250	1.0300	1.0350	1.0400	1.0450	1.0500	1.0600
2	1.0506	1.0609	1.0712	1.0816	1.0920	1.1025	1.1236
3	1.0769	1.0927	1.1087	1.1249	1.1412	1.1576	1.1910
4	1.1038	1.1255	1.1475	1.1699	1.1925	1.2155	1.2625
5	1.1314	1.1593	1.1877	1.2167	1.2462	1.2763	1.3382
6	1.1597	1.1941	1.2293	1.2653	1.3023	1.3401	1.4185
7	1.1887	1.2299	1.2723	1.3159	1.3609	1.4071	1.5036
8	1.2184	1.2668	1.3168	1.3686	1.4221	1.4775	1.5938
9	1.2489	1.3048	1.3629	1.4233	1.4861	1.5513	1.6895
10	1.2801	1.3439	1.4106	1.4802	1.5530	1.6289	1.7908
11	1.3121	1.3842	1.4600	1.5395	1.6229	1.7103	1.8983
12	1.3449	1.4258	1.5111	1.6010	1.6959	1.7959	2.0122
13	1.3785	1.4685	1.5640	1.6651	1.7722	1.8856	2.1329
14	1.4130	1.5126	1.6187	1.7317	1.8519	1.9799	2.2609
15	1.4483	1.5580	1.6753	1.8009	1.9353	2.0789	2.3966
16	1.4845	1.6047	1.7340	1.8730	2.0224	2.1829	2.5404
17	1.5216	1.6528	1.7947	1.9479	2.1134	2.2920	2.6928
18	1.5597	1.7024	1.8575	2.0258	2.2085	2.4066	2.8543
19	1.5986	1.7535	1.9225	2.1068	2.3079	2.5269	3.0256
20	1.6386	1.8061	1.9898	2.1911	2.4117	2.6533	3.2071
21	1.6796	1.8603	2.0594	2.2788	2.5202	2.7860	3.3996
22	1.7216	1.9161	2.1315	2.3699	2.6337	2.9253	3.6035
23	1.7646	1.9736	2.2061	2.4647	2.7522	3.0715	3.8197
24	1.8087	2.0328	2.2833	2.5633	2.8760	3.2251	4.0489
25	1.8539	2.0938	2.3632	2.6658	3.0054	3.3864	4.2919
26	1.9003	2.1566	2.4460	2.7725	3.1407	3.5557	4.4594
27	1.9478	2.2213	2.5316	2.8834	3.2820	3.7335	4.8223
28	1.9965	2.2879	2.6202	2.9987	3.4297	3.9201	5.1117
29	2.0464	2.3566	2.7119	3.1187	3.5840	4.1161	5.4184
30	2.0976	2.4273	2.8068	3.2434	3.7453	4.3219	5.7435
31	2.1500	2.5001	2.9050	3.3731	3.9139	4.5380	6.0881
32	2.2038	2.5751	3.0067	3.5081	4.0900	4.7649	6.4534
33	2.2589	2.6523	3.1119	3.6484	4.2740	5.0032	6.8406
34	2.3153	2.7319	3.2209	3.7943	4.4664	5.2533	7.2510
35	2.3732	2.8139	3.3336	3.9461	4.6673	5.5160	7.6861
36	2.4325	2.8983	3.4503	4.1039	4.8774	5.7918	8.1473
37	2.4933	2.9852	3.5710	4.2681	5.0969	6.0814	8.6361
38	2.5557	3.0748	3.6960	4.4388	5.3262	6.3855	9.1543
39	2.6196	3.1670	3.8254	4.6164	5.5659	6.7048	9.7035
40	2.6851	3.2620	3.9593	4.8010	5.8164	7.0400	10.2857
41	2.7522	3.3599	4.0978	4.9931	6.0781	7.3920	10.9029
42	2.8210	3.4607	4.2413	5.1928	6.3516	7.7616	11.5570
43	2.8915	3.5645	4.3897	5.4005	6.6374	8.1497	12.2505
44	2.9638	3.6715	4.5433	5.6165	6.9361	8.5571	12.9855
45	3.0379	3.7816	4.7024	5.8412	7.2482	8.9850	13.7646
46	3.1139	3.8950	4.8669	6.0748	7.5744	9.4343	14.5905
47	3.1917	4.0119	5.0373	6.3178	7.9153	9.9060	15.4659
48	3.2715	4.1323	5.2136	6.5705	8.2715	10.4013	16.3775
49	3.3533	4.2562	5.3961	6.8333	8.6437	10.9213	17.3775
50	3.4371	4.3839	5.5849	7.1067	9.0326	11.4674	18.4202

TABLE V. FUTURE VALUE OF ONE DOLLAR PER ANNUM
At Compound Interest
The Amount of 1 Per Annum, with Interest, at the End of a Given Time

2 1/2%	3%	3 1/2%	4%	4 1/2%	6%	Yrs.
1.0250	1.0300	1.0350	1.0400	1.0450	1.0600	1
2.0756	2.0909	2.1062	2.1216	2.1370	2.1836	2.
3.1525	3.1836	3.2149	3.2465	3.2782	3.3746	3
4.2563	4.3091	4.3625	4.4163	4.4707	4.6371	4
5.3877	5.4684	5.5502	5.6330	5.7169	5.9753	5
6.5474	6.6625	6.7794	6.8983	7.0192	7.3938	6
7.7361	7.8923	8.0517	8.2142	8.3800	8.8975	7
8.9545	9.1591	9.3685	9.5828	9.8021	10.4913	8
10.2034	10.4639	10.7314	11.0061	11.2882	12.1808	9
11.4835	11.8078	12.1420	12.4864	12.8412	13.9716	10
12.7956	13.1920	13.6020	14.0258	14.4640	15.8699	11
14.1404	14.6178	15.1130	15.6268	16.1599	17.8821	12
15.5190	16.0863	16.6770	17.2919	17.9321	20.0151	13
16.9319	17.5989	18.2957	19.0236	19.7841	22.2760	14
18.3802	19.1569	19.9710	20.8245	21.7193	24.6725	15
19.8647	20.7616	21.7050	22.6975	23.7417	27.2129	16
21.3863	22.4144	23.4997	24.6454	25.8551	29.9057	17
22.9460	24.1169	25.3572	26.6712	28.0636	32.7600	18
24.5446	25.8704	27.2797	28.7781	30.3714	35.7856	19
26.1833	27.6765	29.2695	30.9692	32.7831	38.9927	20
27.8629	29.5368	31.3289	33.2480	35.3034	42.3923	21
29.5844	31.4529	33.4604	35.6179	37.9370	45.9958	22
31.3490	33.4265	35.6665	38.0826	40.6892	49.8156	23
33.1578	35.4593	37.9499	40.6459	43.5652	53.8645	24
35.0117	37.5530	40.3131	43.3117	46.5706	58.1564	25
36.9120	39.7096	42.7591	46.0842	49.7113	62.7058	26
38.8598	41.9309	45.2906	48.9676	52.9933	67.5281	27
40.8563	44.2189	47.9108	51.9663	56.4230	72.6398	28
42.9027	46.5754	50.6227	55.0849	60.0071	78.0582	29
45.0003	49.0027	53.4295	58.3283	63.7524	83.8017	30
47.1503	51.5028	56.3345	61.7015	67.6662	89.8898	31
49.3540	54.0778	59.3412	65.2095	71.7562	96.3432	32
51.6129	56.7302	62.4531	68.8579	76.0303	103.1838	33
53.9282	59.4621	65.6740	72.6522	80.4966	110.4348	34
56.3014	62.2759	69.0076	76.5983	85.1640	118.1209	35
58.7339	65.1742	72.4579	80.7022	90.0413	126.2681	36
61.2273	68.1594	76.0289	84.9703	95.1382	134.9042	37
63.7830	71.2342	79.7249	89.4091	100.4644	144.0585	38
66.4026	74.4013	83.5503	94.0255	106.0303	153.7620	39
69.0876	77.6633	87.5095	98.8265	111.8467	164.0477	40
71.8398	81.0232	91.6074	103.8196	117.9248	174.9505	41
74.6608	84.4839	95.8486	109.0124	124.2764	186.5076	42
77.5523	88.0484	100.2383	114.4129	130.9138	198.7580	43
80.5161	91.7199	104.7817	120.0294	137.8500	211.7435	44
83.5540	95.5015	109.4840	125.8706	145.0982	225.5081	45
86.6679	99.3965	114.3510	131.9454	152.6726	240.0986	46
89.8596	103.4084	119.3882	138.2632	160.5879	255.5645	47
93.1311	107.5406	124.6018	144.8337	168.8594	271.9584	48
96.4843	111.7969	129.9979	151.6671	177.5030	289.3359	49
99.9215	116.1808	135.5828	158.7738	186.5357	307.7561	50

Factors shown are for deposits made at beginning of year; interest compounded annually. The factor for twice any period is the square of the factor for that period.

Factors shown are for deposits made at beginning of year; interest compounded annually. If deposits are made at end of year, add 1 to factor for previous year.

TABLE VIA. PRESENT WORTH OF AN ANNUITY OF 1

Hoskold Valuation Premises

Sinking Fund Interest Rate 3% Speculative Interest Rate as Shown

Yrs.	5%	6%	7%	8%	9%	10%	12%	15%	Yrs
1	.9524	.9434	.9346	.9259	.9174	.9091	.8929	.8696	
2	1.8429	1.8096	1.7774	1.7464	1.7164	1.6874	1.6324	1.5562	
3	2.6772	2.6074	2.5411	2.4781	2.4182	2.3611	2.2546	2.1118	
4	3.4599	3.3442	3.2360	3.1345	3.0393	2.9496	2.7853	2.5705	
5	4.1954	4.0265	3.8706	3.7264	3.5925	3.4680	3.2430	2.9555	5
6	4.8876	4.6599	4.4524	4.2626	4.0883	3.9278	3.6417	3.2830	
7	5.5400	5.2492	4.9874	4.7504	4.5350	4.3383	3.9919	3.5650	
8	6.1555	5.7986	5.4808	5.1960	4.9393	4.7068	4.3019	3.8102	
9	6.7370	6.3118	5.9370	5.6043	5.3069	5.0395	4.5780	4.0252	
10	7.2870	6.7921	6.3601	5.9798	5.6424	5.3410	4.8255	4.2153	10
11	7.8078	7.2123	6.7532	6.3260	5.9496	5.6155	5.0485	4.3845	
12	8.3014	7.6651	7.1194	6.6462	6.2320	5.8664	5.2504	4.5359	
13	8.7697	8.0626	7.4610	6.9430	6.4923	6.0965	5.4339	4.6723	
14	9.2144	8.4369	7.7805	7.2188	6.7328	6.3081	5.6014	4.7956	
15	9.6370	8.7899	8.0797	7.4757	6.9557	6.5034	5.7548	4.9076	15
16	10.0391	9.1232	8.3604	7.7154	7.1628	6.6840	5.8958	5.0097	
17	10.4218	9.4382	8.6242	7.9395	7.3555	6.8515	6.0258	5.1033	
18	10.7865	9.7363	8.8724	8.1494	7.5353	7.0073	6.1460	5.1892	
19	11.1341	10.0186	9.1063	8.3463	7.7033	7.1524	6.2573	5.2683	
20	11.4658	10.2864	9.3270	8.5313	7.8607	7.2878	6.3607	5.3414	20
21	11.7825	10.5405	9.5355	8.7054	8.0082	7.4144	6.4570	5.4092	
22	12.0850	10.7820	9.7326	8.8694	8.1468	7.5331	6.5468	5.4720	
23	12.3741	11.0115	9.9193	9.0241	8.2772	7.6444	6.6307	5.5305	
24	12.6506	11.2300	10.0962	9.1703	8.4000	7.7491	6.7093	5.5851	
25	12.9152	11.4380	10.2640	9.3086	8.5159	7.8476	6.7830	5.6361	25
26	13.1686	11.6363	10.4234	9.4395	8.6253	7.9404	6.8522	5.6838	
27	13.4113	11.8253	10.5748	9.5635	8.7287	8.0280	6.9173	5.7286	
28	13.6438	12.0058	10.7189	9.6812	8.8267	8.1107	6.9787	5.7706	
29	13.8668	12.1781	10.8560	9.7929	8.9194	8.1890	7.0366	5.8101	
30	14.0807	12.3427	10.9867	9.8991	9.0074	8.2631	7.0912	5.8473	30
31	14.2859	12.5002	11.1112	10.0001	9.0910	8.3334	7.1429	5.8824	
32	14.4830	12.6508	11.2301	10.0963	9.1704	8.4001	7.1918	5.9155	
33	14.6722	12.7949	11.3435	10.1879	9.2459	8.4634	7.2382	5.9469	
34	14.8540	12.9329	11.4519	10.2752	9.3178	8.5236	7.2822	5.9765	
35	15.0287	13.0652	11.5554	10.3585	9.3862	8.5808	7.3239	6.0046	35
36	15.1967	13.1920	11.6545	10.4380	9.4515	8.6353	7.3636	6.0312	
37	15.3582	13.3135	11.7493	10.5140	9.5137	8.6872	7.4013	6.0565	
38	15.5137	13.4301	11.8400	10.5866	9.5731	8.7367	7.4372	6.0805	
39	15.6632	13.5421	11.9269	10.6560	9.6298	8.7840	7.4714	6.1034	
40	15.8072	13.6496	12.0102	10.7224	9.6841	8.8291	7.5040	6.1251	40
41	15.9458	13.7528	12.0901	10.7860	9.7359	8.8721	7.5351	6.1458	
42	16.0793	13.8520	12.1667	10.8470	9.7855	8.9133	7.5648	6.1655	
43	16.2080	13.9474	12.2402	10.9053	9.8330	8.9527	7.5931	6.1844	
44	16.3319	14.0391	12.3107	10.9613	9.8785	8.9904	7.6202	6.2023	
45	16.4514	14.1273	12.3785	11.0150	9.9221	9.0265	7.6461	6.2195	45
46	16.5666	14.2121	12.4436	11.0665	9.9639	9.0610	7.6709	6.2359	
47	16.6776	14.2938	12.5062	11.1160	10.0040	9.0942	7.6946	6.2515	
48	16.7848	14.3724	12.5663	11.1635	10.0424	9.1259	7.7174	6.2665	
49	16.8881	14.4481	12.6242	11.2091	10.0793	9.1584	7.7392	6.2809	
50	16.9879	14.5211	12.6798	11.2530	10.1148	9.1856	7.7600	6.2946	50

TABLE VIB. PRESENT WORTH OF AN ANNUITY OF 1

Hoskold Valuation Premises

Sinking Fund Interest Rate 4% ; Speculative Interest Rate as Shown

Yrs	5%	6%	7%	8%	9%	10%	12%	15%	Yrs.
1	.952	.943	.935	.926	.917	.909	.893	.870	
2	1.851	1.818	1.786	1.754	1.724	1.694	1.639	1.562	
3	2.700	2.629	2.562	2.498	2.437	2.379	2.271	2.126	
4	3.503	3.384	3.273	3.170	3.072	2.981	2.813	2.594	
5	4.262	4.088	3.927	3.779	3.641	3.513	3.283	2.989	5
6	4.981	4.745	4.530	4.333	4.153	3.988	3.693	3.325	
7	5.662	5.359	5.086	4.840	4.617	4.413	4.055	3.615	
8	6.308	5.934	5.601	5.304	5.037	4.796	4.376	3.868	
9	6.921	6.473	6.079	5.731	5.420	5.142	4.662	4.090	
10	7.502	6.979	6.524	6.124	5.771	5.456	4.919	4.286	10
11	8.055	7.454	6.938	6.487	6.092	5.742	5.151	4.461	
12	8.580	7.902	7.323	6.823	6.387	6.004	5.360	4.618	
13	9.079	8.323	7.684	7.136	6.660	6.244	5.551	4.759	
14	9.554	8.721	8.021	7.426	6.912	6.465	5.725	4.886	
15	10.006	9.096	8.337	7.696	7.146	6.669	5.884	5.001	15
16	10.436	9.450	8.634	7.948	7.363	6.858	6.031	5.107	
17	10.846	9.785	8.913	8.183	7.564	7.032	6.165	5.203	
18	11.237	10.102	9.175	8.404	7.752	7.195	6.290	5.291	
19	11.609	10.402	9.422	8.610	7.928	7.345	6.405	5.372	
20	11.964	10.686	9.654	8.804	8.092	7.486	6.511	5.447	20
21	12.303	10.955	9.874	8.986	8.245	7.617	6.610	5.516	
22	12.626	11.211	10.081	9.158	8.389	7.740	6.702	5.580	
23	12.935	11.454	10.277	9.319	8.524	7.855	6.788	5.640	
24	13.230	11.684	10.462	9.471	8.651	7.963	6.869	5.695	
25	13.511	11.903	10.637	9.614	8.771	8.064	6.944	5.747	25
26	13.780	12.111	10.803	9.750	8.884	8.159	7.014	5.795	
27	14.037	12.309	10.960	9.878	8.990	8.248	7.080	5.840	
28	14.283	12.498	11.109	9.999	9.090	8.332	7.142	5.882	
29	14.518	12.677	11.251	10.113	9.184	8.412	7.200	5.921	
30	14.743	12.848	11.386	10.222	9.274	8.487	7.255	5.958	30
31	14.958	13.011	11.513	10.325	9.358	8.558	7.307	5.993	
32	15.163	13.167	11.635	10.422	9.439	8.625	7.356	6.026	
33	15.360	13.315	11.750	10.515	9.514	8.688	7.402	6.057	
34	15.549	13.456	11.860	10.603	9.586	8.748	7.445	6.086	
35	15.729	13.591	11.965	10.686	9.655	8.805	7.486	6.113	35
36	15.902	13.720	12.065	10.766	9.719	8.858	7.525	6.139	
37	16.067	13.843	12.160	10.841	9.781	8.910	7.562	6.164	
38	16.225	13.960	12.250	10.913	9.839	8.958	7.587	6.187	
39	16.377	14.072	12.336	10.982	9.895	9.004	7.630	6.209	
40	16.523	14.180	12.419	11.047	9.948	9.049	7.661	6.230	40
41	16.662	14.282	12.497	11.109	9.998	9.089	7.691	6.249	
42	16.795	14.380	12.572	11.168	10.046	9.129	7.720	6.268	
43	16.923	14.474	12.644	11.225	10.092	9.167	7.747	6.286	
44	17.046	14.564	12.712	11.278	10.135	9.203	7.772	6.303	
45	17.164	14.649	12.778	11.330	10.177	9.237	7.797	6.319	45
46	17.276	14.731	12.840	11.379	10.216	9.269	7.820	6.334	
47	17.385	14.810	12.900	11.426	10.254	9.300	7.842	6.348	
48	17.488	14.885	12.957	11.470	10.288	9.330	7.863	6.362	
49	17.588	14.957	13.001	11.513	10.324	9.358	7.883	6.375	
50	17.683	15.026	13.063	11.554	10.357	9.385	7.902	6.388	50

TABLE VIC. PRESENT WORTH OF AN ANNUITY OF 1
Hoskold Valuation Premises
Sinking Fund Interest Rate 5% ; Speculative Interest Rate as Shown

Yrs.	5%	6%	7%	8%	9%	10%	12%	15%	Yrs.
1	.952	.943	.935	.925	.917	.909	.893	.870	
2	1.859	1.825	1.793	1.761	1.731	1.701	1.645	1.568	
3	2.723	2.651	2.583	2.518	2.456	2.397	2.287	2.140	
4	3.546	3.424	3.311	3.205	3.105	3.012	2.841	2.618	
5	4.330	4.150	3.984	3.832	3.690	3.559	3.323	3.021	5
6	5.076	4.830	4.608	4.405	4.219	4.048	3.745	3.367	
7	5.786	5.470	5.186	4.930	4.699	4.488	4.118	3.665	
8	6.463	6.071	5.723	5.414	5.136	4.885	4.450	3.926	
9	7.108	6.636	6.223	5.859	5.534	5.244	4.746	4.155	
10	7.722	7.168	6.689	6.269	5.900	5.571	5.012	4.357	10
11	8.306	7.669	7.123	6.649	6.235	5.869	5.252	4.537	
12	8.863	8.142	7.529	7.002	6.543	6.142	5.470	4.699	
13	9.394	8.587	7.908	7.328	6.828	6.392	5.667	4.844	
14	9.899	9.007	8.263	7.632	7.091	6.621	5.847	4.974	
15	10.380	9.404	8.595	7.915	7.335	6.833	6.012	5.093	15
16	10.838	9.778	8.907	8.179	7.560	7.029	6.163	5.201	
17	11.274	10.132	9.200	8.425	7.770	7.210	6.301	5.299	
18	11.690	10.466	9.474	8.655	7.965	7.377	6.429	5.389	
19	12.085	10.782	9.733	8.870	8.147	7.533	6.547	5.472	
20	12.462	11.081	9.976	9.071	8.316	7.678	6.656	5.548	20
21	12.821	11.364	10.204	9.260	8.475	7.813	6.757	5.618	
22	13.163	11.632	10.420	9.436	8.623	7.938	6.851	5.683	
23	13.489	11.885	10.623	9.603	8.761	8.056	6.938	5.742	
24	13.799	12.126	10.814	9.759	8.891	8.165	7.019	5.798	
25	14.094	12.353	10.995	9.906	9.013	8.268	7.095	5.850	25
26	14.375	12.568	11.165	10.044	9.127	8.364	7.165	5.897	
27	14.643	12.773	11.326	10.174	9.234	8.454	7.231	5.942	
28	14.898	12.966	11.478	10.296	9.335	8.538	7.293	5.984	
29	15.141	13.150	11.622	10.412	9.430	8.617	7.350	6.022	
30	15.373	13.324	11.757	10.520	9.519	8.692	7.405	6.059	30
31	15.593	13.489	11.886	10.623	9.603	8.762	7.455	6.093	
32	15.803	13.646	12.007	10.720	9.682	8.828	7.503	6.124	
33	16.003	13.795	12.123	10.812	9.757	8.890	7.548	6.154	
34	16.193	13.936	12.232	10.898	9.827	8.948	7.590	6.182	
35	16.374	14.070	12.335	10.980	9.894	9.003	7.629	6.208	35
36	16.547	14.198	12.432	11.057	9.957	9.055	7.667	6.233	
37	16.711	14.319	12.525	11.131	10.016	9.104	7.702	6.256	
38	16.868	14.433	12.613	11.200	10.072	9.150	7.735	6.278	
39	17.017	14.542	12.696	11.266	10.125	9.194	7.766	6.299	
40	17.159	14.646	12.775	11.328	10.175	9.236	7.796	6.318	40
41	17.294	14.744	12.850	11.387	10.223	9.275	7.823	6.336	
42	17.423	14.838	12.921	11.442	10.267	9.311	7.850	6.353	
43	17.546	14.927	12.988	11.495	10.310	9.346	7.875	6.370	
44	17.663	15.011	13.052	11.545	10.350	9.379	7.898	6.385	
45	17.774	15.092	13.113	11.592	10.388	9.411	7.920	6.399	45
46	17.880	15.168	13.170	11.638	10.425	9.441	7.941	6.413	
47	17.981	15.241	13.225	11.680	10.459	9.469	7.961	6.426	
48	18.077	15.310	13.277	11.721	10.491	9.495	7.980	6.438	
49	18.169	15.375	13.326	11.759	10.522	9.520	7.997	6.450	
50	18.256	15.438	13.373	11.796	10.551	9.544	8.015	6.461	50

TABLE VII A. PRESENT WORTH OF INCREASING & DECREASING ANNUITIES 6%
Straight Line % Changes—Inwood Premise

Yrs.	Income Annually DECREASING at Rate Shown									Yrs.
	−2%	−3%	−4%	−5%	−7%	−10%	−12%	−14%	−20%	
1	0.94	0.94	0.94	0.94	0.94	0.94	0.94	0.94	0.94	1
2	1.81	1.81	1.80	1.79	1.77	1.74	1.73	1.71	1.66	2
3	2.62	2.60	2.57	2.54	2.49	2.42	2.36	2.31	2.16	3
4	3.37	3.32	3.27	3.22	3.12	2.97	2.87	2.77	2.48	4
5	4.05	3.97	3.89	3.82	3.66	3.42	3.26	3.10	2.63	5
6	4.69	4.57	4.46	4.34	4.11	3.77	3.54	3.31		6
7	5.27	5.12	4.96	4.81	4.50	4.04	3.73	3.42		7
8	5.81	5.61	5.42	5.22	4.82	4.23	3.83	3.43		8
9	6.31	6.06	5.82	5.57	5.08	4.34	3.85			9
10	6.77	6.47	6.18	5.88	5.29	4.40				10
11	7.19	6.84	6.49	6.14	5.45					11
12	7.58	7.17	6.77	6.37	5.56					12
13	7.93	7.47	7.01	6.55	5.63					13
14	8.26	7.74	7.23	6.71	5.67					14
15	8.56	7.99	7.41	6.83	5.68					15
16	8.84	8.20	7.57	6.93						16
17	9.09	8.39	7.70	7.01						17
18	9.32	8.57	7.81	7.06						18
19	9.53	8.72	7.91	7.09						19
20	9.72	8.85	7.96	7.10						20

Yrs.	Income Annually INCREASING at Rate Shown									Yrs.
	+2%	+3%	+4%	+5%	+7%	+10%	+12%	+14%	+20%	
1	0.94	0.94	0.94	0.94	0.94	0.94	0.94	0.94	0.94	1
2	1.85	1.86	1.87	1.88	1.90	1.92	1.94	1.96	2.01	2
3	2.72	2.75	2.78	2.80	2.85	2.93	2.98	3.03	3.19	3
4	3.56	3.61	3.66	3.71	3.81	3.96	4.06	4.16	4.45	4
5	4.37	4.45	4.53	4.61	4.77	5.01	5.16	5.32	5.80	5
6	5.15	5.26	5.38	5.49	5.72	6.06	6.29	6.52	7.21	6
7	5.89	6.05	6.20	6.35	6.66	7.13	7.44	7.74	8.67	7
8	6.61	6.80	7.00	7.20	7.60	8.19	8.59	8.99	10.18	8
9	7.29	7.54	7.78	8.03	8.52	9.26	9.75	10.24	11.72	9
10	7.95	8.25	8.54	8.84	9.43	10.32	10.91	11.50	13.28	10
11	8.58	8.93	9.28	9.63	10.33	11.37	12.07	12.77	14.86	11
12	9.19	9.59	10.00	10.40	11.21	12.42	13.22	14.03	16.45	12
13	9.77	10.23	10.69	11.15	12.07	13.45	14.37	15.29	18.04	13
14	10.33	10.85	11.36	11.88	12.91	14.46	15.50	16.53	19.64	14
15	10.86	11.44	12.01	12.59	13.74	15.47	16.62	17.77	21.22	15
16	11.37	12.01	12.64	13.28	14.55	16.45	17.72	18.99	22.80	16
17	11.86	12.56	13.25	13.95	15.33	17.42	18.80	20.19	24.35	17
18	12.33	13.09	13.84	14.59	16.10	18.36	19.87	21.37	25.89	18
19	12.78	13.60	14.41	15.22	16.85	19.29	20.91	22.54	27.42	19
20	13.21	14.09	14.96	15.83	17.58	20.19	21.94	23.68	28.91	20

TABLE VIIB. PRESENT WORTH OF INCREASING & DECREASING ANNUITIES 7%
Straight Line % Changes—Inwood Premise

Yrs.	Income Annually DECREASING at Rate Shown									Yrs.
	−2%	−3%	−4%	−5%	−7%	−10%	−12%	−14%	−20%	
1	0.93	0.93	0.93	0.93	0.93	0.93	0.93	0.93	0.93	1
2	1.79	1.78	1.77	1.76	1.75	1.72	1.70	1.69	1.63	2
3	2.57	2.55	2.52	2.50	2.45	2.37	2.32	2.27	2.12	3
4	3.29	3.24	3.20	3.15	3.05	2.91	2.81	2.72	2.43	4
5	3.95	3.87	3.79	3.72	3.56	3.34	3.18	3.03	2.57	5
6	4.55	4.44	4.33	4.22	4.00	3.67	3.45	3.23		6
7	5.09	4.95	4.80	4.65	4.36	3.92	3.62	3.33		7
8	5.60	5.41	5.22	5.03	4.66	4.09	3.72	3.34		8
9	6.05	5.82	5.59	5.36	4.90	4.20	3.74			9
10	6.47	6.19	5.91	5.64	5.08	4.25				10
11	6.85	6.52	6.20	5.87	5.23					11
12	7.20	6.82	6.45	6.07	5.33					12
13	7.51	7.09	6.66	6.24	5.39					13
14	7.80	7.32	6.85	6.38	5.43					14
15	8.06	7.53	7.01	6.49	5.44					15
16	8.30	7.72	7.14	6.57						16
17	8.51	7.88	7.26	6.63						17
18	8.71	8.03	7.35	6.68						18
19	8.88	8.16	7.43	6.71						19
20	9.04	8.27	7.49	6.72						20

Yrs.	Income Annually INCREASING at Rate Shown									Yrs.
	+2%	+3%	+4%	+5%	+7%	+10%	+12%	+14%	+20%	
1	0.93	0.93	0.93	0.93	0.93	0.93	0.93	0.93	0.93	1
2	1.83	1.83	1.84	1.85	1.87	1.90	1.91	1.93	1.98	2
3	2.67	2.70	2.72	2.75	2.80	2.87	2.92	2.97	3.12	3
4	3.48	3.53	3.58	3.63	3.72	3.87	3.96	4.06	4.35	4
5	4.25	4.33	4.41	4.48	4.64	4.86	5.02	5.17	5.63	5
6	4.99	5.10	5.21	5.31	5.53	5.86	6.08	6.30	6.96	6
7	5.68	5.83	5.98	6.12	6.42	6.86	7.15	7.45	8.33	7
8	6.35	6.53	6.72	6.91	7.29	7.85	8.23	8.60	9.73	8
9	6.98	7.21	7.44	7.67	8.13	8.83	9.29	9.75	11.14	9
10	7.58	7.85	8.13	8.41	8.96	9.79	10.35	10.90	12.57	10
11	8.15	8.47	8.80	9.12	9.77	10.74	11.39	12.04	13.99	11
12	8.69	9.06	9.44	9.81	10.56	11.68	12.42	13.17	15.41	12
13	9.20	9.63	10.05	10.47	11.32	12.59	13.44	14.28	16.82	13
14	9.69	10.17	10.64	11.11	12.06	13.48	14.43	15.38	18.22	14
15	10.16	10.68	11.20	11.73	12.78	14.35	15.40	16.45	19.59	15
16	10.60	11.17	11.75	12.32	13.47	15.20	16.35	17.50	20.95	16
17	11.01	11.64	12.27	12.89	14.14	16.02	17.27	18.53	22.28	17
18	11.41	12.09	12.76	13.44	14.79	16.82	18.17	19.53	23.58	18
19	11.79	12.51	13.24	13.97	15.42	17.60	19.05	20.50	24.86	19
20	12.14	12.92	13.69	14.47	16.02	18.35	19.90	21.45	26.10	20

Illustration: An annuity for 5 years commencing with an initial payment of $1 and decreasing 7 cents each year, discounted at 7%, is today worth $3.56.

TABLE VIIC. PRESENT WORTH OF INCREASING & DECREASING ANNUITIES 8%

Straight Line % Changes—Inwood Premise

Yrs.	Income Annually DECREASING at Rate Shown									Yrs.
	—2%	—3%	—4%	—5%	—7%	—10%	—12%	—14%	—20%	
1	0.93	0.93	0.93	0.93	0.93	0.93	0.93	0.93	0.93	1
2	1.77	1.76	1.75	1.74	1.72	1.70	1.68	1.66	1.61	2
3	2.53	2.50	2.48	2.45	2.41	2.33	2.28	2.24	2.09	3
4	3.22	3.17	3.13	3.08	2.99	2.85	2.75	2.66	2.38	4
5	3.84	3.77	3.70	3.62	3.48	3.26	3.11	2.96	2.52	5
6	4.41	4.31	4.20	4.10	3.89	3.57	3.36	3.15		6
7	4.92	4.78	4.65	4.51	4.22	3.80	3.52	3.24		7
8	5.39	5.21	5.04	4.86	4.50	3.97	3.61	3.25		8
9	5.81	5.59	5.38	5.16	4.72	4.07	3.63			9
10	6.19	5.93	5.67	5.41	4.89	4.11				10
11	6.53	6.23	5.93	5.63	5.02					11
12	6.84	6.50	6.15	5.80	5.11					12
13	7.12	6.73	6.34	5.95	5.17					13
14	7.37	6.94	6.51	6.07	5.20					14
15	7.60	7.12	6.64	6.16	5.21					15
16	7.80	7.28	6.76	6.24						16
17	7.99	7.42	6.86	6.29						17
18	8.15	7.54	6.94	6.33						18
19	8.32	7.65	7.00	6.35						19
20	8.45	7.74	7.06	6.36						20

Yrs.	Income Annually INCREASING at Rate Shown									Yrs.
	+2%	+3%	+4%	+5%	+7%	+10%	+12%	+14%	+20%	
1	0.93	0.93	0.93	0.93	0.93	0.93	0.93	0.93	0.93	1
2	1.80	1.81	1.82	1.83	1.84	1.87	1.89	1.90	1.95	2
3	2.62	2.65	2.68	2.70	2.75	2.82	2.87	2.92	3.07	3
4	3.40	3.45	3.50	3.55	3.64	3.78	3.87	3.96	4.24	4
5	4.14	4.21	4.29	4.36	4.51	4.73	4.88	5.03	5.47	5
6	4.83	4.94	5.04	5.15	5.36	5.68	5.89	6.10	6.73	6
7	5.53	5.63	5.77	5.91	6.19	6.61	6.89	7.17	8.01	7
8	6.18	6.28	6.46	6.64	6.99	7.53	7.88	8.24	9.31	8
9	6.76	6.90	7.12	7.34	7.77	8.43	8.86	9.30	10.61	9
10	7.30	7.49	7.75	8.01	8.53	9.31	9.83	10.35	11.90	10
11	7.82	8.05	8.35	8.65	9.26	10.16	10.77	11.38	13.19	11
12	8.30	8.57	8.92	9.27	9.96	11.00	11.69	12.38	14.46	12
13	8.79	9.07	9.47	9.86	10.64	11.81	12.59	13.37	15.71	13
14	9.24	9.55	9.98	10.42	11.29	12.59	13.46	14.33	16.94	14
15	9.65	9.99	10.47	10.95	11.91	13.35	14.30	15.26	18.14	15
16	10.03	10.42	10.94	11.46	12.51	14.08	15.12	16.17	19.30	16
17	10.38	10.82	11.39	11.95	13.08	14.78	15.91	17.05	20.44	17
18	10.72	11.19	11.81	12.41	13.63	15.46	16.67	17.89	21.54	18
19	11.03	11.55	12.20	12.86	14.16	16.11	17.41	18.71	22.61	19
20	11.33	11.89	12.58	13.28	14.66	16.73	18.11	19.49	23.64	20

Illustration: An annuity for 5 years commencing with an initial payment of $1 and decreasing 7 cents each year, discounted at 8% , is today worth $3.48.

TABLE VIID. PRESENT WORTH OF INCREASING & DECREASING ANNUITIES 10%

Straight Line % Changes—Inwood Premise

Yrs.	Income Annually DECREASING at Rate Shown									Yrs.
	—2%	—3%	—4%	—5%	—7%	—10%	—12%	—14%	—20%	
1	0.91	0.91	0.91	0.91	0.91	0.91	0.91	0.91	0.91	1
2	1.72	1.71	1.70	1.69	1.67	1.65	1.64	1.62	1.57	2
3	2.44	2.42	2.39	2.37	2.32	2.25	2.21	2.16	2.02	3
4	3.08	3.04	3.00	2.95	2.86	2.73	2.64	2.56	2.29	4
5	3.65	3.59	3.52	3.45	3.31	3.10	2.97	2.83	2.42	5
6	4.15	4.07	3.97	3.87	3.68	3.39	3.19	3.00		6
7	4.60	4.49	4.36	4.23	3.98	3.59	3.34	3.08		7
8	5.00	4.85	4.69	4.53	4.21	3.73	3.41	3.09		8
9	5.35	5.18	4.98	4.79	4.40	3.82	3.43			9
10	5.67	5.46	5.23	5.00	4.54	3.86				10
11	5.95	5.70	5.44	5.18	4.65					11
12	6.20	5.92	5.62	5.32	4.72					12
13	6.42	6.10	5.77	5.44	4.77					13
14	6.61	6.26	5.90	5.53	4.79					14
15	6.79	6.40	6.00	5.60	4.80					15
16	6.94	6.52	6.09	5.65						16
17	7.07	6.62	6.16	5.69						17
18	7.19	6.71	6.22	5.72						18
19	7.30	6.79	6.26	5.74						19
20	7.39	6.85	6.30	5.74						20

Yrs.	Income Annually INCREASING at Rate Shown									Yrs.
	+2%	+3%	+4%	+5 %	+7%	+10%	+12%	+14%	+20%	
1	0.91	0.91	0.91	0.91	0.91	0.91	0.91	0.91	0.91	1
2	1.75	1.76	1.77	1.78	1.79	1.82	1.83	1.85	1.90	2
3	2.53	2.56	2.58	2.60	2.65	2.72	2.77	2.81	2.95	3
4	3.26	3.30	3.34	3.39	3.48	3.61	3.70	3.78	4.05	4
5	3.93	4.00	4.07	4.13	4.27	4.48	4.61	4.75	5.16	5
6	4.55	4.65	4.74	4.84	5.03	5.32	5.52	5.71	6.29	6
7	5.12	5.25	5.38	5.51	5.76	6.14	6.40	6.66	7.42	7
8	5.66	5.82	5.98	6.14	6.46	6.94	7.26	7.58	8.54	8
9	6.15	6.34	6.54	6.73	7.12	7.70	8.09	8.48	9.64	9
10	6.60	6.83	7.06	7.29	7.75	8.43	8.89	9.35	10.72	10
11	7.02	7.29	7.55	7.81	8.34	9.13	9.66	10.19	11.77	11
12	7.41	7.71	8.01	8.31	8.91	9.80	10.40	11.00	12.80	12
13	7.77	8.11	8.44	8.78	9.44	10.44	11.11	11.78	13.79	13
14	8.10	8.47	8.84	9.21	9.94	11.05	11.78	12.52	14.73	14
15	8.41	8.81	9.21	9.62	10.42	11.62	12.43	13.23	15.64	15
16	8.69	9.13	9.56	10.00	10.87	12.17	13.04	13.91	16.51	16
17	8.95	9.42	9.89	10.36	11.29	12.68	13.62	14.55	17.34	17
18	9.19	9.69	10.19	10.69	11.68	13.17	14.17	15.16	18.14	18
19	9.42	9.94	10.47	11.00	12.04	13.63	14.68	15.73	18.88	19
20	9.62	10.18	10.73	11.29	12.40	14.06	15.17	16.27	19.60	20

Illustration: An annuity for 5 years commencing with an initial payment of $1 and decreasing 7 cents each year, discounted at 10% , is today worth $3.31.

PRESENT VALUE OF DECLINING ANNUITIES

Years	PERCENT														
	5	5 1/4	5 1/2	5 3/4	6	6 1/4	6 1/2	6 3/4	7	7 1/2	8	8 1/2	9	9 1/2	10
15	7.29	7.20	7.10	7.01	6.92	6.83	6.75	6.66	6.58	6.42	6.27	6.12	5.98	5.84	5.71
16	7.70	7.60	7.49	7.39	7.29	7.20	7.10	7.01	6.91	6.74	6.57	6.40	6.25	6.10	5.95
17	8.11	7.99	7.88	7.76	7.65	7.55	7.44	7.34	7.24	7.04	6.86	6.68	6.51	6.34	6.19
18	8.51	8.38	8.25	8.13	8.01	7.89	7.77	7.66	7.55	7.34	7.14	6.94	6.76	6.58	6.41
19	8.90	8.75	8.61	8.48	8.35	8.22	8.09	7.97	7.85	7.62	7.40	7.20	7.00	6.81	6.62
20	9.28	9.12	8.97	8.82	8.68	8.54	8.41	8.27	8.15	7.90	7.66	7.44	7.22	7.02	6.83
21	9.65	9.48	9.32	9.16	9.01	8.86	8.71	8.57	8.43	8.16	7.91	7.67	7.44	7.22	7.02
22	10.01	9.83	9.66	9.49	9.32	9.16	9.00	8.85	8.70	8.42	8.15	7.89	7.65	7.42	7.20
23	10.37	10.17	9.99	9.80	9.63	9.45	9.29	9.12	8.96	8.66	8.37	8.10	7.85	7.60	7.37
24	10.72	10.51	10.31	10.11	9.92	9.74	9.56	9.39	9.22	8.90	8.59	8.31	8.03	7.78	7.53
25	11.05	10.83	10.62	10.41	10.21	10.01	9.82	9.64	9.46	9.12	8.80	8.50	8.21	7.94	7.69
26	11.38	11.15	10.92	10.70	10.49	10.28	10.08	9.88	9.70	9.34	9.00	8.68	8.38	8.10	7.84
27	11.70	11.45	11.21	10.98	10.75	10.54	10.32	10.12	9.92	9.55	9.19	8.86	8.55	8.25	7.97
28	12.02	11.75	11.50	11.25	11.01	10.78	10.56	10.35	10.14	9.74	9.37	9.03	8.70	8.39	8.10
29	12.32	12.04	11.77	11.51	11.26	11.02	10.79	10.56	10.35	9.93	9.55	9.18	8.84	8.53	8.23
30	12.61	12.32	12.04	11.77	11.50	11.25	11.01	10.77	10.54	10.11	9.71	9.33	8.98	8.65	8.34
31	12.90	12.59	12.30	12.01	11.74	11.47	11.22	10.97	10.74	10.29	9.87	9.48	9.11	8.77	8.45
32	13.18	12.85	12.54	12.25	11.96	11.69	11.42	11.16	10.92	10.45	10.02	9.61	9.24	8.88	8.55
33	13.45	13.11	12.79	12.47	12.18	11.89	11.61	11.35	11.09	10.61	10.16	9.74	9.35	8.99	8.65
34	13.71	13.35	13.02	12.69	12.38	12.09	11.80	11.52	11.26	10.76	10.29	9.86	9.46	9.09	8.74
35	13.96	13.59	13.24	12.91	12.58	12.27	11.98	11.69	11.42	10.90	10.42	9.98	9.57	9.18	8.83
36	14.20	13.82	13.46	13.11	12.77	12.45	12.15	11.85	11.57	11.04	10.54	10.09	9.67	9.27	8.91
37	14.44	14.04	13.66	13.30	12.96	12.63	12.31	12.01	11.71	11.17	10.66	10.19	9.76	9.36	8.98
38	14.66	14.25	13.86	13.49	13.13	12.79	12.47	12.15	11.85	11.29	10.77	10.29	9.84	9.43	9.05
39	14.88	14.46	14.06	13.67	13.30	12.95	12.62	12.29	11.98	11.41	10.87	10.38	9.93	9.51	9.12
40	15.09	14.66	14.24	13.84	13.47	13.10	12.76	12.43	12.11	11.52	10.97	10.47	10.00	9.58	9.18
41	15.30	14.85	14.42	14.01	13.62	13.25	12.89	12.55	12.23	11.62	11.06	10.55	10.08	9.64	9.24
42	15.49	15.03	14.59	14.17	13.77	13.39	13.02	12.67	12.34	11.72	11.15	10.63	10.15	9.70	9.29
43	15.68	15.21	14.75	14.32	13.91	13.52	13.15	12.79	12.45	11.81	11.23	10.70	10.21	9.76	9.34
44	15.87	15.38	14.91	14.47	14.05	13.65	13.26	12.90	12.55	11.90	11.31	10.77	10.27	9.81	9.39
45	16.04	15.54	15.06	14.61	14.18	13.77	13.38	13.00	12.65	11.99	11.38	10.83	10.33	9.86	9.43
46	16.21	15.70	15.21	14.74	14.30	13.88	13.48	13.10	12.74	12.07	11.45	10.89	10.38	9.91	9.47
47	16.37	15.85	15.35	14.87	14.42	13.99	13.58	13.20	12.83	12.14	11.52	10.95	10.43	9.95	9.51
48	16.53	15.99	15.48	14.99	14.53	14.10	13.68	13.29	12.91	12.21	11.58	11.00	10.47	9.99	9.55
49	16.68	16.13	15.61	15.11	14.64	14.20	13.77	13.37	12.99	12.28	11.64	11.05	10.52	10.03	9.58
50	16.83	16.26	15.73	15.22	14.74	14.29	13.86	13.45	13.06	12.35	11.69	11.10	10.56	10.06	9.61

Index